Transition from
Communism in
CHINA

Transition from Communism in CHINA

Institutional and Comparative Analyses

edited by

Edwin A. Winckler

LYNNE
RIENNER
PUBLISHERS

BOULDER
LONDON

Published in the United States of America in 1999 by
Lynne Rienner Publishers, Inc.
1800 30th Street, Boulder, Colorado 80301

and in the United Kingdom by
Lynne Rienner Publishers, Inc.
3 Henrietta Street, Covent Garden, London WC2E 8LU

Library of Congress Cataloging-in-Publication Data
Transition from communism in China   :   institutional and comparative
    analyses   /   edited by Edwin A. Winckler.
    Includes bibliographical references and index.
    ISBN   1-55587-808-3 (hardcover   :   alk. paper)
    1. Post-communism—China.   2. China—Politics and
government—1976–   3. China—Economic policy—1976–   4. China—
Social policy.   I. Winckler, Edwin A.
HX418.5.T735   1999
338.951—dc21   98-34315
                                                                                      CIP

British Cataloguing in Publication Data
A Cataloguing in Publication record for this book
is available from the British Library.

Printed and bound in the United States of America

The paper used in this publication meets the requirements
∞ of the American National Standard for Permanence of
Paper for Printed Library Materials Z39.48-1984.

5 4 3 2 1

Contents

PART 4
SOCIOCULTURAL TRANSITION

PART 5
CONCLUSION

Preface

This volume has three aims: to place China's transition in the comparative perspective of other transitions from communism, to go beyond comparisons of whole countries to comparisons of institutional sectors, and to compare differing theoretical approaches to regime type and regime change.

I thank everyone who participated in the project that led to this volume. I particularly thank those whose fine papers did not make it through the review process into the final volume. Much to my regret, I had to replace some of those papers with my own versions.

All contributors thank Lynne Rienner for her vision and judgment, executive editor Dan Eades for his advice and support, production director Steve Barr for his infallibility and unflappability, and outside reviewer David Bachman for his helpful suggestions.

Edwin A. Winckler
Dwaarkill, New York
Spring 1998

PART 1

Introduction

1

Describing Leninist Transitions

Edwin A. Winckler

By the late 1990s, there has been much comparison of Southern European and Latin American transitions from authoritarianism, and some comparison of these with Eastern European transitions from communism (e.g., O'Donnell, Schmitter, and Whitehead 1986, Linz and Stepan 1996). There has been surprisingly little comparison of European and Asian postcommunist transitions (though see Nee and Stark 1989, Rozman 1992b, and Walder 1995c). More surprising, there has been even less comparison between the Asian postcommunist cases themselves (though see Scalapino 1992, Kim and Sigur 1992). As for China, sinologists have achieved much penetration of this opaque system, at high standards of scholarship (well surveyed in Lieberthal 1995). Nevertheless, there remains much need for theorizing the Chinese case and comparing it to the other Asian cases, in order to bring them into the comparative mainstream. This volume addresses that need.

As David Stark early observed of Eastern Europe, transitions are plural in a dual sense: Different countries follow different paths, and within each country there are many transitions occurring in different domains, often out of synchrony and in conflict with each other (1992). This volume pursues that insight. On the one hand, two cross-national chapters compare China to other Asian post-Leninist transitions, in order to identify what is distinctive about China. On the other hand, six China-sectoral chapters analyze transitions in different institutional arenas, identifying differences between sectors. The editor's Introduction and Conclusion discuss several dimensions that inform the transition literature and help relate China to it. (For a guide to volume discussion of transition-in-general, please see the Index headings beginning with *Transition, systemic*. For comparison of cases see headings beginning with *Transitions, systemic*. For treatment of sectors, see headings beginning with *Transitions, sectoral*. For discussion of dimensions, see headings beginning with *Dimensions,* and cross-references from there.)

When initiating this project, I asked the other contributors—each of them a respected expert on his topic—to provide a historically grounded analytical model of the transition process in his sector or countries. Most of the chapters establish a late-1970s baseline, then sketch the process of change in the 1980s and 1990s. The China-sectoral chapters model particularly the process by which, since the 1989 Tiananmen incident, China has settled into what appears to be its final and distinctive transition path. The cross-national chapters emphasize the different external circumstances that, during the same period, helped differentiate the Asian transitions from each other. In modeling these processes, the participants attempt to draw on and contribute to institutional analysis. This involves three related but different objectives.

The first is to identify *institutional logics that are generic to Leninism and transition,* including differences between sectors that are similar across systems. Clearly there *are* such logics common to all Leninist and even post-Leninist systems, which is what makes them a meaningful category. This approach was the core of comparative communism and correctly diagnosed communism's impending failure (e.g., Brzezinski 1988 on the dysfunctions of ideology and coercion). It remains central to comparing post-communist transitions, as in any discussion of the changing relationship between "plan and market." However, a fully institutional approach goes beyond these bare-bones mechanisms to flesh them out with the organizational ligaments and political muscles necessary for them to function (Linz and Stepan 1996, 11–13). For example, Asian economists McMillan and Naughton have recently defined postcommunist economic transition as the process of building market institutions and used that definition to integrate interpretations of the European and Asian economic transitions (1996). Analogously, Asian political scientist Friedman regards the general logic of democratization as the institutionalization of fair rules of political competition and uses that formulation to stress similarities between Asian and other political transitions (1994, Introduction).

A second objective is to identify *institutional differences between different Leninisms and their different transitions,* including differences between the same sectors in different systems. Clearly this is essential for an institutional approach, which can hardly ignore institutional variation between cases. It is a main thrust of comparative postcommunism in the 1990s (e.g., Huang 1994, Solnick 1996, Pei 1996). Institutional differences between Leninisms were quite large and can explain much of the difference in transition dynamics and outcomes. However, demonstrating this requires both a general framework for comparing institutions and detailed information on specific institutions across the full range of cases (Huskey 1995). It is only such an approach that can identify the distinctive institutional features of China's distinctive transition path (Goldstein 1995).

A third objective is to distinguish between *different kinds of institution-*

al analysis, as applied to Leninisms and their transitions (Hall and Taylor 1994). How do different forms of institutionalism—for example, macro versus micro, economic versus cultural, contemporary versus historical— relate to each other? In particular, what are the strengths and limits of the microeconomic neo-institutionalism that is currently sweeping the social sciences? At what point, if any, must it yield to more macrostructural or more sociocultural approaches to institutions? What problems arise in transferring institutional theories across systems (from capitalism to post-communism) and regions (from the West to Asia)? At what point must *any* form of institutionalism yield to other approaches? This volume does not fully answer all of these questions, but it does identify some places where they arise in the analysis of Leninism and transition, particularly in China.

Though far-ranging, these comparative and theoretical questions connect directly with practical questions about politics and policy in the world's largest country. It is exactly a "shift in mechanisms" that the successor Chinese leadership is attempting, from direct intervention through bureaucracy and campaigns to indirect control through legislation and enforcement. However, so far, the intended shift appears instrumental not constitutional—the party reserves the right to intervene at its own discretion (Dickson this volume). Military leadership is passing to younger more professional officers, but civilian control still relies significantly on party channels and personal connections. The regime is refining its definitions of political crimes but making penalties even harsher. The regime is creating the legal framework for a market economy, but contracts remain conditional and corruption remains rife. The regime is laying the legal foundations for social and cultural control but continues to rely on periodic campaigns as an interim measure. In the short run, this shift from revolutionization to institutionalization is the main process *retarding* democratization. In the middle run, the legalization of Leninism may buy the regime a surprising amount of time. In the long run, however, institutionalization may become the main process *promoting* democratization, as legalism gradually constrains and undermines Leninism. Indeed, reportedly by the late 1990s national leader Jiang Zemin already was commissioning studies on how democratic systems work, for long-term planning (*FEER* 23 July 1998).

This editor's Introduction begins with a short statement of the descriptive and analytical concerns of the chapters and editorial materials. It continues by defining three main descriptive dimensions of regimes and transitions, noting some major contributions and controversies along each dimension. It concludes by summarizing each of the chapters in more detail and by further situating the volume amid the recent literature comparing transitions. The editor's Conclusion resumes the discussion, treating some more theoretical issues in explaining Leninist transitions.

Introduction

Description

An introductory comparative chapter by Bruce Dickson (Chapter 2) contrasts the initiation and course of transition in China and Taiwan. In China, because the original revolutionary leadership perceived both the international and domestic environments as threatening, it allowed only limited political change. On Taiwan, generational succession within the leadership allowed gradual political liberalization, while changes in the international and domestic environments first inhibited, then encouraged, full democratization.

The China-sectoral chapters describe gradual transition from communism within three functional sectors in China: external and internal security, economic development, and social and cultural policies.

The first pair of China-sectoral chapters highlight the center's struggle to maintain control of the main *security* agencies—the military and the police. Here, despite much modernization of organization and technology, transition from Leninism remains least advanced. In Chapter 3, Edwin Winckler summarizes sinologists' views of "the transition in the military" in order to address the further issue of the role of "the military in the transition." In the 1990s, generational succession has shifted national military politics from personal relationships within a fused party-army to a more distant institutional relationship between party and army. Military professionals have probably gained increased say over defense and foreign policies, while the participation of the Chinese military in nonmilitary affairs remains large relative to that in most countries. Nevertheless, the party center maintains tight control over military assets, and the party has reinstilled military loyalty to party rule. In Chapter 4, Murray Scot Tanner reports debates within the public security system in the late 1980s and early 1990s over how to define the mission of the police during economic reform. Should economic crime be regarded as concerted political opposition and combated with Maoist physical violence? Or should it be regarded as individual social deviance and treated by delivering corrective social services? So far China's police have continued to steer a middle Leninist course between these extremes—actively promoting economic growth but rigorously containing any social and political consequences the leadership considers adverse.

The second pair of China-sectoral chapters describe the politics of maintaining central *economic* control, despite administrative decentralization and marketizing reform. In Chapter 5, James Tong traces the tortuous evolution of central-provincial fiscal relations, starting from the centralized pre–Cultural Revolution fiscal regime and its deterioration during the Cultural Revolution. The post-Mao center relied on the provinces to collect its revenues, while searching for a form of central-provincial revenue contract that maximized provincial collection efforts and minimized provincial expenditure. However, in 1994 the center recentralized tax collection, dividing revenue sources between center and provinces and creating a central agency to collect central revenues. In Chapter 6, Dali Yang analyzes the center's difficulty in controlling local rates of investment and inflation and describes a crucial episode in China's economic transition from communism. Among the causes of macroeconomic instability were not only decentralization of the economy and under-institutionalization of financial controls, but also centrally engineered competition between localities and disagreement at the center over the optimal rate of growth. Yang shows how Deng Xiaoping's 1992 call for faster growth destabilized the economy and how his younger successors then gradually succeeded in restabilizing and recentralizing it.

The third pair of China-sectoral chapters describe the center's increasingly selective intervention in *sociocultural* policy in the 1990s. Transition from communism is quite advanced in some domains, such as population migration and scientific research, but less advanced in other domains, such as limiting population and refunding the arts. In Chapter 7, Winckler describes the leadership's renewed determination and success in the 1990s at controlling the number of births in Chinese families. Within the state, the center defined clear goals and held subnational administrators accountable for achieving them; toward society, the center deployed inexpensive contraceptive technology and reinforced institutions for securing mass compliance. In Chapter 8, Richard Kraus and Richard Suttmeier argue that change has gone faster and further in the sciences than in the arts, but with mixed effect on both. Despite commercialization and internationalization, the state continues to exert substantial control over the production of culture, inhibiting democratization.

A concluding comparative chapter by Winckler (Chapter 9) surveys the origins and outcomes of the six Asian transitions from communism, emphasizing the diversity among them. The outcomes range from rapid democratization and marketization in Mongolia, through gradual economic reform in China, Vietnam, and Laos, to reversal of reform in Cambodia and refusal of reform in North Korea. The extent of external shock produced by the collapse of Soviet support largely determined the rapidity of system change. Nevertheless, elite response remains crucial, as illustrated by Mongolia's alacrity, North Korea's stubbornness, and the tortuous evolution of reform in China and Southeast Asia.

Analysis

Analytically, the volume as a whole adopts an institutional approach that starts from classic organization theory (particularly of power and compli-

ance) and ends in recent neo-institutional analysis (particularly of delegation and agency). Institutions are central to political transition, and institutionalism is central to political analysis. Transitions involve changing solutions to practical problems of governance, whose differences across sectors
can be illuminated by both classical organization theory and recent institutional analysis. The volume demonstrates that classical organization theory
and recent institutional analysis supplement each other. Both illuminate
China, and the Chinese case helps elaborate these Western-based theories.
(For a guide to the volume chapters viewed through classical organization
theory, see the Index headings that begin with *Environment, Organization,*
and *Performance;* for recent institutionalisms see Institutional analysis
under *Analysis, approaches; Agency and Delegation,* and cross-references
from there; and *Ideology.*)

Some chapters draw on Amitai Etzioni's classic 1961 analysis of the
different organizational requirements of order, economic, and ideological
goals (Tong on fiscal delegation, Winckler on birth planning and Asian transitions). Several authors draw on "hard" neo-institutionalism, particularly
delegation theory, analyzing the contractual relationship between principals
and their agents (Tong, Yang, and Winckler on birth planning). Others contribute to "soft" new institutionalism, elucidating the role in regime change
of rival interpretations of organizational environment (Dickson), rival interpretations of organizational history (Tanner), and crises in the "constitu-
tions" governing whole functional sectors (Kraus and Suttmeier). Several of
the chapters show how in China soft new-institutional facts such as weak
economic and political institutions affect the operation of hard neo-institutional processes such as delegation and agency (e.g., Winckler on military,
Tong on fiscal contracting, Yang on macroeconomic control).

Analytically, Dickson's introductory comparative chapter establishes
the vertical-structural dimension of transition—national organization facing
supranational and subnational environments. Dickson analyzes the decision
about whether or not to initiate reform as a constrained choice resulting
from the interplay between these levels. The outcome depends on elite preferences, on how the elite perceives the pattern of challenges and supports in
its subnational and supranational environments, and on the feedback mechanisms through which the elite interprets its environment.

The two chapters on China's *security sector* also both involve both
institutions and their environments. Winckler sketches the many long
chains of delegation and control in Chinese military administration, then
places them in the context of the substantive issues involved. Common
sense and classical organizational analysis show that the military has
played a large role in post-1949 Chinese politics, but neo-institutional delegation theory and new-institutional historical-cultural analysis make that
role look even larger. Tanner describes police debates over how to adjust
the relationship between police and society. The alternatives parallel those
in other sectors—Maoist normative-coercive on the left, Leninist remunera-

tive-coercive in the center, and reformist professional-service on the right. These alternatives also imply different relations between political leaders and the police bureaucracy, including prohibitive transaction costs if leaders and police disagree.

The two chapters on China's *development sector* analyze the institutional setting of delegation in China. Tong uses Etzioni's compliance theory to characterize the change in power mix from the Maoist to Dengist periods; he uses principal-agent theory to explain changes in central-local fiscal relations during the Dengist period. In doing so, he shows how institutional context affects the operation of agency relations. Yang argues that what impairs the center's macroeconomic control is a particular "iterated game" between center and localities that generates boom-and-bust cycles. The problem is not just the transfer of economic resources from center to locality or the weakness of central financial control over the economy. The center itself induces economic competition between localities, and political competition at the center sometimes prevents the center from making a credible commitment to macroeconomic discipline.

The chapters on Chinese *social and cultural policy* too involve both classical and recent institutional analysis. Winckler traces the changing mix of normative, coercive, and remunerative power applied in state birth planning, and he reports the attempt to shift these forms of power from less to more institutionalized forms. He characterizes Leninist systems as a chain of delegation relationships and derives the dynamics of birth planning both from these enduring systemic characteristics and from the center's changing capacity to monitor and sanction compliance. Kraus and Suttmeier, who analyzed earlier organizational alternatives in the Chinese humanities and sciences, show how the alternatives have broadened in the post-Mao period, gradually defining a new "constitution" governing the production of culture. They delineate the institutional channels through which domestic change has invited international influence, and through which international influence has in turn promoted more domestic change.

The concluding comparative chapter returns to more macrohistorical analysis of transition. Winckler distinguishes three degrees of "reform" within Asian Leninist regimes: rationalization of a previously personalistic regime; liberalization within the military-political, political-economic, and sociocultural sectors; and all-out democratization, marketization, and pluralization within these three sectors, respectively. He shows how the interaction of three sectors and three levels produces different transition dynamics in the different Asian post-Leninist cases. What distinguishes each case is the particular conjunction of crises within the resulting nine domains.

Editorial

Collating the findings of the individual chapters, the editor's Introduction and Conclusion discuss descriptive and explanatory issues, respectively.

(No single chapter addresses all of these issues—the editorial dimensions were induced after the fact as the research program implied by the chapters as a whole, not prescribed in advance as a research program that each chapter should implement.) The Introduction argues that regime transition always involves three underlying descriptive dimensions: functional sectors, structural levels, and temporal dynamics. Sectors and levels identify what is changing, dynamics analyzes transition as a process of change over time. The functional or *sectoral* dimension concerns different kinds of governance problems—order, economic, or ideological goals—and the institutional requirements for achieving them. Disaggregating "the state" into functional sectors is a logical next step in analyzing transitions. The structural or *levels* dimension concerns the fact that all of these processes can arise from three different directions—from within national state organization itself, or from its subnational or supranational environments. The temporal or *dynamics* dimension concerns the fact that transition is a process that occurs over time. Transition involves path-dependent relationships, not only between late-communist baseline, transition, and postcommunist outcomes, but also between longer historical processes of communist regime change, societal modernization, and national history. Transitions differ because each is a unique conjunction of universal processes at these three levels.

Sorting cases and theories along these descriptive dimensions is useful for several reasons. It helps identify the similarities and differences between cases—noncommunist and communist, European and Asian, and variations within both regions. It makes explicit the issue of what constitutes a balanced historical or theoretical account, revealing where coverage is incomplete. It helps identify similarities and differences between interpretations—which authors are addressing which issues for which countries, and where they agree or disagree. It prepares the ground for further research by identifying the range of processes that must be addressed and the dimensions for comparing them. For example, in the course of this Introduction, these three dimensions help define post-Mao China's regime type—"decentralized post-totalitarianism" (terms indicating structural level, temporal dynamics, and sectoral scope, respectively). (For a guide see the Index under *Dimensions, descriptive; Dynamics, descriptive; Levels, descriptive; Sectors, descriptive;* and cross-references from there.)

However, filling out such a descriptive grid does not in itself constitute theoretical explanation (Walder 1994). Consequently the editor's Conclusion discusses explanatory issues along more analytical analogues of the temporal, sectoral, and levels dimensions. The Conclusion argues that the recent development of *both* the rational choice and the historical-institutional literatures conclude that *both* are necessary for a theoretically adequate account. In particular, game theory demonstrates the need to model strategic interaction and provides new precision for doing so.

Nevertheless, macrohistory remains necessary to define the concatenation of games in play and to specific preferences and perceptions of the actors playing them. A basic issue for both hard and soft approaches is how to relate stability and change—in macrohistorical accounts as institutions versus crises, in microanalytical models as statics versus dynamics. For example, in China communist institutions themselves produced crises that eventually induced economic transition from communism (Yang 1996). Microeconomic reforms then gradually destabilized increasingly wider relationships, leading to macroeconomic and noneconomic transformations. (For a guide to explanatory hypotheses throughout the volume, see the Index under *Hypotheses*.)

The Conclusion begins by introducing a main idea underlying the volume, that analysis of delegation between principals and agents particularly illuminates Leninist transitions. It then turns to *analytical levels,* discussing the relationship between macrohistorical, mesoinstitutional, and microindividual analysis. All three can be either hard (rationalist, political-economic) or soft (interpretivist, sociocultural). All three analytical levels are needed for explaining Leninist transitions, but institutional analysis is particularly pivotal. The Conclusion turns next to *sectoral analysis,* arguing that state strength and transition dynamics are specific to particular governance problems and governance institutions. This section discusses some likely determinants of the degree of delegation in different sectors and some possible consequences for Leninisms and their transitions. Finally the Conclusion considers *temporal analysis,* proceeding from less to more explicitly temporal approaches. Hard microanalytic approaches identify parameters that affect stability and change but do not explain changes in those parameters. Path dependence helps formalize cross-temporal constraints on choice but does not explain selection between alternatives within those constraints. Historical institutionalism emphasizes the dissonances and disynchronies that produce change. (For a guide see the Index under *Dimensions, analytical; Dynamics, analytical; Levels, analytical; Sectors, analytical;* and any cross-references from there.)

Sectors: Political, Economic, and Sociocultural Affairs

The dimension of communism and transition that this volume particularly stresses is horizontal or *functional.* Most generally, this dimension identifies the *scope* of the matters that the antecedent regime attempted to control, and the process of narrowing that scope and reconstructing their governance during transition from communism. More specifically, this dimension distinguishes the different problems and institutions of governance that arise in particular *sectors* of public policy. Different transitions involve different mixes or sequences of functional problems—from hard or troubled transitions to soft or easy ones. Different analysts assign different weights to these processes and adopt different styles of analysis—most broadly, hard political-economic versus soft sociocultural. Here we begin with general issues of sheer scope, then proceed to differentiation between sectors, then to individual sectors themselves.

Functional Scope

As a dimension of the *communism* from which transition starts, sheer scope is important. Evidently *the broader the scope the less likely a transition,* at least from internal causes. For example, in the late 1980s reformers debated whether China could initiate a transition to democracy directly from totalitarianism, or whether it was necessary first to shrink the economic, social, and cultural roles of the state, leaving a merely political "neo-authoritarianism." The ensuing Chinese experience supports both the reformers' assumption that the system remained at best post-totalitarian and the argument for a gradual transition. Because most sectors remained under active party-state control, the revolutionary elders were able to repress the premature 1989 attempt at a direct transition to democracy, and the direct path appears closed for the foreseeable future.

In less total cases, sectors help identify the particular pattern of party-state control from which transition begins (Hankiss 1990, Linz and Stepan 1996). Some sectors were never completely totalitarianized and have always remained somewhat autonomous (e.g., agriculture and religion in Poland). Some sectors were fully totalitarianized but later developed "second" alternatives (e.g., the economy in Hungary, culture in Czechoslovakia). Arguably, *the less controlled sectors are more likely to initiate transition.* Thus in Europe, societal opposition was most broad-based in never fully totalitarianized Poland; it was the "second economy" that drove the post-totalitarianization of both state and society to full maturity in Hungary; and it was the "parallel culture" that undermined the otherwise "frozen" totalitarianism in Czechoslovakia (Linz and Stepan 1996). In largely rural Asia, the earlier cases fully socialized agriculture and developed more state industry, inhibiting economic transition (North Korea, North Vietnam, China). The late cases never fully socialized agriculture and did not develop much state industry, facilitating economic transition (South Vietnam, Laos, Cambodia). Social and cultural control was less stringent where socialization had never been complete or was later relaxed.

As a dimension of the process of *transition* itself, sectors concern the scope of the ends and means involved—the extent to which transition involves not only political but also economic or sociocultural change, and the extent to which the transition is costly, conflictual, and even violent (hard) or comfortable, consensual, and negotiated (soft). Evidently, overall, *the broader the scope across sectors, the harder the transition.*

Noncommunist transitions are usually only political transitions, while communist transitions are at least "dual"—political and economic—and often "triple"—for example, also ethnonationalist (Haggard and Kaufman 1992, Pei 1994, Offe 1991). Eastern Europe has faced virtually all types of problems, often with little existing institutional basis for managing them (Bunce 1994). So far, most Asian transition has been primarily economic; moreover, in China and Vietnam transition involved not hardship but prosperity. Cambodia may face continuing gradual "state failure," but only North Korea faces the serious possibility of abrupt violent breakdown.

Similarly, *the broader the scope within a sector, the more difficult the transition* within that sector. Minxin Pei has made this argument for economic transition (1996). The more complete European communisms encountered more interlocking institutional obstacles to gradual economic reform and suffered recession-driven transformation with high economic and social costs. These costs produced postcommunist political change from initial liberal governments back toward the more social-democratic center-left. The less complete Asian communisms had more flexible institutions that responded better to initial economic reform, creating growth-driven transformation with low economic costs. This allowed Leninist regimes to remain in power and is producing a center-right coalition of technocrats, indigenous capitalists, and foreign investors.

This brings us to the *postcommunist* outcome of transition. As regards ends, overall, the scope of the state narrows and the state reconstructs the functions it retains. Nevertheless, the state not only loses some functions but gains others—for example, promoting market-oriented development through state entrepreneurship and infrastructure provision, regulating newly liberalized economic and other activities. In Europe, the abrupt collapse of communism meant that institutions had to be constructed from scratch for many functions at once. In Asia, by the time political transition occurs, a panoply of late-Leninist institutions may have enabled the state to manage society with increasing sophistication.

As regards means, Karl and Schmitter argue that *the more violent a transition,* the less likely it is to produce democracy and the more likely is any resulting democracy to be individualistic (1991). Conversely, *the more negotiated a transition,* the more likely it is to produce democracy and the more likely is the resulting democracy to be group-based (i.e., corporatist or consociational). This relationship seems basically true for the Leninist transitions. At one extreme, the violent revolution in Romania and violent repression in China have produced the least democratic outcomes, at least so far. At the other extreme, Taiwan and Czechoslovakia had the most peaceful transitions and have the most democratic outcomes. Underlying this proposition is a more political version of scope—the breadth of the coalition opposing or promoting transition discussed above. Evidently *the narrower the transition coalition the greater the transition violence.*

Differentiation Between Sectors

Differences between policy areas are staples of both comparative political science and the literature on China (e.g., Lampton 1987, Lieberthal and Lampton 1992). Policy areas may differ in technical content and political implications, and in the technical and political context (e.g., Grindle 1980). In China, important distinctions include the resources that agencies command and the information available to leaders for oversight (Lieberthal and Oksenberg 1988, Naughton 1992a). In this volume, most chapters treat particular policy areas, while the editorial materials compare broad sectors. These sectors reflect both theoretical requirements for achieving order, economic, and ideological goals and how, in practice, China's leaders have grouped policies for oversight (Etzioni 1961; Lieberthal 1992, 1995).

Most states display these same three sectors, manifested in the grouping of institutions for policy coordination and in the flow of personnel along career paths. Supraministerial coordination is usually strongest for security concerns, intermediate for economic affairs, and weakest for sociocultural goals (Blondel 1982). Leninist party-states, like most authoritarian regimes, center on three main institutions—army, government, and party (Winckler 1984). The army is the core of a security sector for order goals, which also includes police, law, and courts. The government is the core of a development sector for economic goals, which includes planners, ministries, and state firms. The party is the core of a legitimation sector for ideological goals, which also includes sociocultural institutions such as the educational system and mass media.

Etzioni argues that order goals require coercion, economic goals require remuneration, and ideological goals require normative power (1961). However, as he explains, organizations are complex, pursuing multiple goals and using several types of power. Thus the correspondence between actual sectors and analytical sectors is imperfect. In particular, a Leninist party, because of its ruling role and broad scope, involves all three main kinds of goals and power (Lieberthal 1995, 207). Moreover, policymakers have some latitude about how to define the purpose of particular policies and about what mix of power to use for particular purposes. Finally, policymakers adjust power mixes over time, partly as a result of elite competition and experiment, partly in response to mass reactions to current policies (Skinner and Winckler 1969, Baum 1994).

The three broad sectors are loose groupings of more specific policy domains. China has had six or seven major policy "systems," each containing numerous ministries (Hamrin 1992). These functional specifics too differentiate communisms and their transitions. For example, the relationship between military and police may differ, or the proportions between agriculture and industry may vary. How state organizers assign specific functions to particular systems will also reflect the organizers' political purposes and policy theories. For example, a Western capitalist democracy might regard health and education as professional social-service issues, whereas in pre-communist China social policy served order goals, administered by the police using coercion (Wakeman 1995). Communist China placed health and education under the propaganda system, which hindered their modernization (Lieberthal 1995, 197–199). Similarly, a Western country might define agricultural policy as primarily an economic matter, but the Chinese communists also considered it a political relationship with its original rural political base. Consequently the party directly supervised agricultural policy, which may have eventually contributed to the party's awareness of the need for agricultural reform.

Overall, the China literature has emphasized the need for sectoral qualifications to any generalizations about Leninism or transition in China. For example, the mainstream model of Dengist China has been "fragmented authoritarianism"—a system in which coordination through coercion and ideology have declined while economic decentralization has increased, increasing resort to bargaining (Lampton 1992). However, the model's proponents themselves stressed that it was based on studies of economic policymaking, mostly investment decisions. Later studies of other sectors found different patterns (Lieberthal 1992, details below). Here we begin with politically central military-political affairs, then proceed to political-economic and sociocultural affairs.

Military-Political Affairs

Military organization was central to *communism,* not only to achieve order goals, but also as a model for organizing economic and ideological affairs as well. The Soviet model of party-led army and leader-supervised secret police was replicated in most subsequent Leninisms. Comparative analysis of mature communism assumed basic military support for party rule, but the collapse of communism revealed less military support for the party than most had assumed. Comparative communism also assumed basic party control over military policy, but recent retrospective analysis reveals significant past discrepancy between the Soviet party's foreign policy and the Soviet military's strategic doctrine (Kaufman 1994, Barany 1995). The role of the military has differed across Leninisms and their transitions, mostly because of their different prior histories. The military was particularly central in China, where the party and army long overlapped in leadership personnel, institutional interests, and political role (e.g., Shambaugh 1996c). Under Deng, the military remained one policy domain (along with personnel policy) in which the center still largely commanded not bargained (Lieberthal and Lampton 1992, Pollack and Manion therein).

The police were the internal pillar of Leninism, monitoring and sanctioning both state and society. Within the security sector, differing relations between military and police are important differences between Leninisms and their transitions. On the one hand, the military wants a strong police in order to avoid military involvement in quelling internal unrest, particularly if the police remain under ultimate military control (e.g., China, as discussed by Cheung 1996b and by Winckler in Chapter 3 this volume). If the police cannot maintain order, the military may prefer regime change to doing domestic repression itself (e.g., the Soviet Union). On the other hand, the military may resent a strong police, particularly if used by the leader to control the military itself (e.g., Romania). The military aside, the police are themselves central to analyzing communism and transition (e.g., on China see Dutton 1992a, 1992b). Communism usually had multiple police institutions, and "policing" included not only monitoring from above but also surveillance from within the community. Verdery has emphasized the resulting dispersal not concentration of coercive power (1991, citing Gross). This was a problem in Maoist China—for example, the "mass factionalism" unleashed by the Cultural Revolution.

During *transition,* a main institutional challenge in the security sector is transferring civilian oversight of military and police from party to government. In Eastern Europe, this appears most difficult in Russia itself— after the dismantling of communism, the military establishment lost budgets and capabilities but has retained much internal political influence. The postcommunist Russian police too show remarkable continuity of functions and powers with their communist predecessors (Waller 1994, Knight 1996). In the still-embattled late Leninisms of Asia too, the security sector has remained strong. In China the budgets of both military and police have increased significantly, in part to prevent political transition. Institutionally, the postcommunist role of the military is reflected in whether it is civilians or officers who serve as intermediaries between the national executive and military establishment. An institutional breakthrough necessary for completing transition is an independent judiciary that professionally administers a codified legal system (*CQ*141).

In reform China a main question in the security sector is how much divergence between party and army will be produced by generational succession and institutional professionalization, and how that divergence will play out in high politics (*CQ*146). As recently as the 1989 Tiananmen incident, the People's Liberation Army (PLA) still displayed low professional institutionalization but high personal political loyalty (Pollack 1992). However, the passing of the revolutionary elders leaves civil-military relations less personal and more institutional. The military's role in guaranteeing succession and stability has become more obvious, increasing the military's leverage over the policies that most concern it (e.g., Taiwan).

In reform China the police too have become an institutional hybrid. They continue to use Maoist methods such as mass campaigns that even the Soviets rejected, while allowing commercialization of the police that even the West rejects. Meanwhile China still maintains such mainstream Stalinist institutions as labor camps, and even adapts them to produce exports that both support economic reform and profit the police. At the same time, Chinese police are groping toward more modern forms of police work based on legal institutions and professional training (Dutton 1992, Wong 1994). The police are becoming more central to China's political stability. On the one hand, the leadership counts on armed police to prevent mass revolt (Cheung 1996b). On the other hand, more fundamentally, the leadership counts on institutionalizing coercive controls in the form of a legal system, ultimately enforced by the police (Potter 1994, *CQ*141) In this volume, Tanner reports competing analyses within China's post-Mao public security system over how to define and combat order problems during economic reform.

Political-Economic Affairs

Political administration of the economy was of course also central to *communism*. Economic activity was driven by political goals such as national defense and internal control, not economic efficiency or welfare (Rutland 1985, Verdery 1991). The pivotal institution was central economic planning, an application of political means to economic ends that originated in war. Planning entailed large numbers of economic ministries that attempted to perform complex material tasks. Arguably this is the origin of the fragmented, bureaucratic, and technical nature of economic policymaking still observed in China during transition (Lieberthal 1992, Zhao 1995).

Overall, European communisms began more developed, experienced socialism longer, and achieved a higher level of communist "misdevelopment"—uncompetitive state industry and unsustainable welfare benefits. Institutionally, most Asian communisms adopted the earlier, more mobilizational form of Soviet communism, via "Maoism." There were also country-specific institutional differences, such as the Soviet Union's vertical and unitary organization versus China's more "horizontal" and multitier state (Qian and Xu 1993, Goldstein 1995). Similarly, the high central planning capacity and macroeconomic stability in the former Soviet Union contrast with the weak central capacity and low macroeconomic stability in China (Huang 1994, Naughton 1995).

Economic *transition* is a process of building the institutions of a market economy (McMillan and Naughton 1996, *CQ*144). The state's main challenge is to shift from direct operation to indirect regulation. This involves not just reducing the comprehensive economic role of the state, but also constructing new state capacities for more selective regulation of market processes. The main institutional breakthrough necessary to complete economic transition is achieving an independent central bank that professionally manages the economy for economic not political objectives

(Haggard, Lee, and Maxfield 1993; Yang this volume). Some European cases have achieved such institutional development, particularly those with prior experience of market economies (e.g., the Czech Republic). Other European cases have suffered institutional decay, causing uncertainty that inhibits development (e.g., the Balkans). Overall, in the Asian communist transitions, as in Asian capitalist development, political stability has been a main foundation of economic growth. Even in China, however, economic reform has required some political reform, such as replacing ideologues with technocrats (Lee 1991, Goldstein 1995).

Nevertheless, even largely economic analysis should not focus exclusively on state policy and state autonomy. One should not treat the state as an exogenous umpire, but rather endogenize it into the transition process (Fforde and de Vylder 1996). In Asia economic transition starts largely from mass initiative not elite policy (discussed below under "Levels"). Economic change gradually changes the incentives faced by state institutions (Walder 1995). Moreover, the most successful capitalist "developmental states" display not extreme autonomy but "embedded autonomy"— enough independence from particular interests to make policy, but enough connection to economic actors for that policy to remain realistic (Evans 1995). Accordingly, it matters who staffs the development sector—post-communist industrial technocrats, marketizing economic reformers, or, less frequently, new capitalist businesspeople.

Thus political-economic analysis must address the fact that economic transition changes not only the economy but also politics, and the relationship between the two. In Europe, the dominance of state industry impeded early economic reform. Eventually, when political collapse appeared likely, European communist elites exited the party-state, stealing its economic assets. This accelerated political collapse and left a legacy of politically derived personal networks that still largely run the economy (Meaney 1995, Solnick 1998). In Asia, agriculture was still dominant and led a breakthrough toward markets (except in Mongolia and North Korea). Then a rapidly expanding private sector enabled China and Vietnam, at least, gradually to outgrow the plan (Naughton 1995). In China some party-state cadres have seized some state assets, but most have increased their "collective consumption" through state expenditures, renewing their stake in the existing system. Moreover, after Tiananmen, the party elders made the privileged entry of party elites into public and private business a deliberate strategy for subordinating business to their revolutionary successors (Lam 1995).

In this volume, several chapters treat interactions of political and economic goals. Some of these occur *between* the security and economic sectors—for example, Dickson regards elite perception of political crisis as the main cause of economic reform. Other interactions between order and economic goals occur *within* the development sector itself. Tong traces the center's efforts to combine ex ante economic incentives for local revenue collection with ex post fairness to all provinces. Yang unravels the interplay of politics and economics in central macroeconomic policy.

Sociocultural Affairs

Party-state administration of society and culture was also institutionally central to *communism*. Economic planning provided the model for pursuing social and cultural goals (Winckler on birth planning, this volume). To establish their legitimacy—or at least to preempt alternative legitimacies—Leninist regimes substituted communism for nationalism and ideology for culture. They also trained a corps of professionals to design and provide social and cultural services to both regime and society. Inadvertently, communism spawned informal social networks whose cooperation sometimes bolstered performance but whose corruption eroded legitimacy (Holmes 1993). Similarly, communism could not entirely displace popular culture and itself provoked a counterculture, even if sometimes only "internal migration" into inward alienation (Goldfarb 1989).

Variation in these sociocultural processes has been another source of variation between Leninisms and their transitions. In Europe communism usually conflicted with nationalism, while in Asia communism usually coincided with nationalism. Historically, continental European intelligentsias had depended on the state more than their Anglo-American counterparts but less than their Asian equivalents. Chinese intellectuals have had a particularly close association with the state, which was why the 1989 demonstrations were more remonstrance than rebellion (Hamrin and Cheek 1986, Perry 1991). The People's Republic of China (PRC) achieved quite strict control of society and culture, and the little private activity that persisted did not threaten the regime (e.g., Link, Madsen, and Pickowitz 1989). Urban populations were more incorporated into the state, receiving extensive social welfare and more complete immersion in communist education and media. Rural areas were less incorporated—the state provided little rural social welfare and, when state cultural control relaxed, the countryside resumed many traditional practices (Pei 1994). Minority areas were least incorporated—the state defined minority nationalities but thereby legitimized them, and when state control relaxed, ethnic identities revived (Gladney 1994, on China).

Social and cultural professionals were particularly pivotal, first to stabilizing communism, then to destabilizing it. Their communist training gave these professionals the ideological and technical credentials both for serving and for critiquing the regime (Verdery 1991). Gradual accumulation of practical frustration and moral outrage within the professional elite provided an important precondition for transition (Ding 1994). Lyman Miller has elaborated the point for science in China, arguing that the pursuit of science eventually leads to a demand for democracy, at least philosophically (1996). Nevertheless, ultimate control of culture has remained relatively concentrated and personalistic (Zhao 1995, Kraus and Suttmeier this volume). (On the political role of intellectuals in China, see also Hamrin and Cheek 1986; Goldman with Cheek and Hamrin 1987; Simon and Goldman 1989; Fewsmith 1994; Goldman 1994, 1996.)

Most observers believe that a decline in legitimacy was central to initiating *transition* in Europe and presages the fall of communism in Asia (Holmes 1993, Ding 1994). This position gains some support from the fact that political leaders themselves believe legitimacy important and that most have shifted from communism toward nationalism. Overall, postwar China displays a progressive decline from an initial high commitment to communism, through alienation at the coerciveness of the Great Leap Forward and Cultural Revolution, to political acquiescence based on rising prosperity. Jiwei Ci has explicated the philosophical content of this sequence, from utopianism through nihilism to hedonism (1994). Leslie Holmes sees a further movement forward from hedonism toward rational-legalism (1993). More empirically, recent survey research has identified a conservative-liberal cleavage in Dengist China likely to inform transition outcomes (Nathan and Shi 1993, 1996). The main dimensions concern the ideological correctness of current reform, the practical consequences of reform, and intellectuals' calls for democratization. On these issues, conservatives tend to be rural, female, and older, with less education and lower income, and without party membership and working in nonstate units. Conversely, liberals tend to be urban, male, and young, with more education and higher income, and with party membership and state employment.

Other observers, skeptical about ideologically based legitimacy, regard the processes involved as poorly specified and perhaps even illusory (e.g., Levi 1990, Walder 1994). This position gains some support from the fact that communisms have survived long after their populations ceased to believe in their ideologies. One of the skeptics, Margaret Levi, provides an alternative formulation of the role of normative principles in institutional change, arguing that compliance is contingent on a norm of fairness (1990). If citizens view regime leaders or other citizens as acting too opportunistically, they will withdraw their quasi-voluntary compliance, raising the costs of maintaining the regime, perhaps prohibitively. Levi's analysis helps explain why even communist rulers must make and keep a bargain with their societies, an exchange of material security for political conformity. For China, Levi's analysis may also illuminate such intrastate topics as central-provincial fiscal relations, in which a norm of fairness may play a role (Tong this volume). Nevertheless, Levi's skepticism about purely normative power should not cause one to underestimate the effectiveness of mixed "coercive persuasion" in Leninist systems, particularly in China. Melanie Manion has provided rationalist analysis and empirical demonstration of the central role that constructing new social norms has played in Chinese communist methods of political leadership and policy implementation, albeit reinforced by public coercion and private interests (1993).

The main practical challenge in the legitimation sector during transition is maintaining social and cultural programs despite increasing budget stringency (e.g., on China, Krieg and Schadler 1994). In China the state still devotes relatively few resources to education and other sociocultural policies—the center sets standards but leaves localities to "coping by groping" on their own. As a result, educational policy, for example, constitutes an exception to the "fragmented authoritarian" model of intense bargaining over resources between bureaucracies. (Paine in Lieberthal and Lampton 1992) During transition, commercialization defunds some cultural activities but funds others, eroding state cultural hegemony but also depoliticizing culture (e.g., on China, Zha 1995, Kraus and Suttmeier this volume). The main breakthrough necessary to complete sociocultural transition is stabilizing a variety of institutions under a variety of ownerships and serving a variety of objectives, including public interest objectives involving both professional autonomy and democratic accountability (e.g., on media, *Transitions* 1995 and Zhao 1998). However, such public-interest objectives usually require government support, inviting continued politicization. Again, it matters who staffs the sector—political administrators, sociocultural professionals, or commercial interests.

Social and cultural policies naturally invite soft social and cultural analysis, which also apply to political and economic transitions as well (e.g., Shih 1995 on China, or the journal *Positions* on East Asia in general). A main recent contribution is analysis of public discourse in communist systems, not simply as elite attempts to motivate masses through propaganda, but as genuine elite debate and even mass resistance, through which social categories and evaluations are socially constructed. For example, Yan Sun summarizes debates within China reassessing socialist economics and politics that provide the intellectual foundation for initiating and directing transition (1995). The party leadership's use of language has been fundamental to its control over both cadres and masses (e.g., Schoenhals 1992, Kluver 1996). Even mass participation in culture is an active process of interpretation and resistance, as for example in struggles over the implementation of population policy in China (e.g., Weller 1994, Greenhalgh 1993). Nevertheless, postmodernist theories may need some respecification for postcommunist systems. Theories of domination and resistance derive largely from post-colonial situations involving a clash between alien official discourse and the "hidden transcripts" of indigenous subalterns. In contrast, most postcommunist situations are not post-colonial but post-totalitarian, involving struggle over overt public discourse itself (Humphrey 1994). Not only elites but also masses have been accomplices in constructing the language of post-revolutionary institutions (Siu 1987).

This volume approaches these sociocultural questions by examining concrete policy issues and institutional arrangements. In Chapter 7, Winckler discusses China's most vigorous social policy, state birth planning, arguing that it is so forceful because it is part of a strategy for shifting the long-run legitimacy of the regime from ideological appeals to economic prosperity. Kraus and Suttmeier argue that, despite growing marketization, the Chinese regime maintains basic control of the production of culture in both the sciences and the humanities.

Levels: National, Subnational, and Supranational

A second dimension of communism and transition is vertical or *structural*. Most generally, this dimension queries the "fit" between the state and its domestic and foreign environments—what Linz and Stepan call the "stateness" variable. Do the state's geographic boundaries coincide with a viable combination of defensible borders, economic activities, and ethnic nationalities? More specifically, for communism this vertical dimension measures the degree of centralization within the party-state itself, the depth to which it has penetrated society, and the extent to which state and society become involved in supranational transactions. For transition, this dimension distinguishes initiatives from within the state, challenges from domestic society below, and influences from the foreign environment above. As theoretical approaches, state-centric, sociocentric, and globalist perspectives are all well-recognized alternatives within social science, and periodic shifts between them suggest that all three are indispensable.

Stateness

For *communism,* levels query the relative strengths of party-state, domestic society, and international environment and the nature of the linkages between them. Communist party-states not only extended deep into their societies, they were also deeply embedded in the institutions of the socialist bloc and eventually also in transactions with capitalism beyond. These ties were closest between the Soviet Union and its component republics and next most close between the Soviet Union and its nominally independent Eastern European satellites. In contrast, postwar Asian communist regimes soon achieved much independence, not only from the Soviet Union, but also from each other. Consequently, in transition path, they differ from Europe and from each other. Moreover, most Asian regimes are relatively high in domestic stateness—most center on distinct and historic ethnic nationalities. Among the Asian regimes, China was the most geopolitically independent and socioculturally coherent, enabling it first to resist reform, then to embrace it, selectively.

For the communist cases, the most elegant integration of internal and external processes is that of Bunce, who posits what she calls the "two tiers" of the Stalinist model. Stalin applied the same principles of monopoly of functions and merger of sectors to the supranational Soviet bloc that he applied within subnational Soviet society (Bunce 1992; see also Jowitt 1992, 284–305). Both externally and internally, these assets gradually became liabilities; mixing politics and economics eventually proved counterproductive, as keeping satellites came to cost the Soviets more than they were worth (Bunce 1985). This is a remarkable analysis, not only because it explained the Soviet withdrawal from Eastern Europe even before it occurred, but also because it was written at about the same time that reportedly the Soviet politburo came to the same conclusion, deciding never again to intervene to keep their European satellites (Remnick 1993, 234). However, even Bunce's sophisticated analysis would be slightly improved by explicitly recognizing sectors and levels. As regards sectors, a salient consideration in the Soviet decision was military-political, to avoid "another Afghanistan." Bunce also omits supranational sociocultural flows. As for levels, her analysis is implicitly three-tier, as she implicitly recognizes by identifying the national party as the "dual monopoly" where her two tiers overlap.

For *transition,* levels raise the "stateness" question of the viability of existing boundaries. In communist Eastern Europe, the typical problems were economic underbounding and sociocultural overbounding—not enough economic variety but too much ethnic diversity. Most Eastern European cases have moved toward a new equilibrium by reorienting their trade from East to West (Koves 1992) and by splitting countries that were not ethnically stable (Czechoslovakia, Yugoslavia, the Soviet Union). Most Asian Leninisms have strong ethnic cores and could have viable economies, but still face some stateness questions. In China, always politically a unitary state, some form of federalism may prove necessary to accommodate subnational identities such as Tibet and Taiwan (discussed below). The "stateness" issue has bedeviled Taiwan's own transition— China will not tolerate independence for Taiwan, and Taiwan's own inhabitants disagree about whether Taiwan is part of China. The stateness variable particularly threatens North Korea—as with East Germany, a noncommunist North Korea would have little rationale for an existence separate from South Korea. Vietnam is sufficiently large, strong, and ethnically Vietnamese to remain stable, but Laos and Cambodia are smaller, weaker, and more diverse (Winckler Chapter 9 this volume).

For *postcommunism,* levels help query the genuineness of any democracy that results from political transition. Among several criteria for *democracy,* Robert Dahl (1971) stipulated that elected officials must actually rule, not social elites from behind the scenes. For the process of *democratization,* Karl and Schmitter have added stipulations against undue influence by unelected officials or external actors, declaring these two kinds of interference to be the two main inhibitors of consolidation (1991). In statist East Asia, the most likely source of interference in postcommunist democracy is unelected officials—the military, powerful civilian bureaucracies, or left-over party-state elites. Interference might also come from society—for example large business groups on post-transition Taiwan, or crippling penetration by social networks in China. Interference seems least likely from external actors, since both noncommunist states and transnational firms now mostly promote democratization

Party-State

Not surprisingly, most analysis of Leninist transitions has focused on the Leninist party-state itself. Here levels distinguish the successive layers between leader, colleagues, bureaucracies, and localities. These vertical relationships are important even in small countries (among Asian communisms, Mongolia has only 2 million, Laos 4 million, and Cambodia 8 million). However, in China, where the party-state itself numbers some 40 million, much of the dynamic of Leninism and transition lies in vertical relationships between the elements of the party-state itself. Overall, analysts find greater personalism and greater concentration of power at the very top of the system within the top political leadership, and at the very bottom of the system within small-scale communities (Zhao 1995, Walder 1992). The bureaucracies in between are more institutionalized and more fragmented (Lieberthal 1992, Zhao 1995).

A first vertical relationship is that between *the leader and his colleagues.* Such relations among senior revolutionaries were long central to Leninism, and their passing is central to transition. Roeder (1993) has analyzed the evolution of Soviet leader-colleague relations as growing institutionalization—from personal domination by Stalin to a more collegial "communist constitutionalism." Most Leninisms display a similar tendency, though with much variation according to the founding ruler's dominance and longevity and the political capital and skill of successors. In China, Deng was more collegial than Mao, but ultimate power remained concentrated in personal relationships between revolutionary elders. Institutionalization was interrupted by Tiananmen but may resume under Jiang Zemin. (A recent major discussion of such "informal politics" in China is *China Journal* 1995.)

As for transition, it is usually the death of the founder that creates the opportunity for economic and political reform. No communist system has liberalized much politically under its original leaders, though some senior Asian revolutionaries proved pragmatic about economic reform (China, Laos). Even in the late 1990s, the least-changed Leninisms are those that remain under their original leaders, or under a successor closely identified with them (Cuba, North Korea). However, Taiwan shows that a dynastic founder can choose economic liberalization, and a dynastic successor can choose political liberalization, if the circumstances require. Similar propositions may apply to separate state sectors, with transition proceeding more slowly in those sectors whose founding organizers survive the longest.

A second vertical intrastate relationship is that between *the leadership and the bureaucracies,* and between successive levels within ministries. Under communism, the main trend was again institutionalization. However, much depended on the leader's idiosyncracies—for example, Stalin's state building versus Mao's state wrecking. During transition, a conservative leadership could frustrate progressive administrators (e.g., the revolutionary elders in China), or a conservative bureaucracy could frustrate a progressive leader (e.g., Gorbachev, Zhao Ziyang). In China it is the middle levels within and between ministries that are most institutionalized and that most display "fragmented authoritarianism," at least in economic policy (Lieberthal 1992, Zhao 1995). In this volume, it is the security-sector papers that most treat leadership-bureaucracy relations. Winckler examines the shifting balance between continuingly strong institutional controls over the Chinese military and the military's possibly rising influence over substantive policy. Tanner wonders how in China a more progressive leadership could control China's still-Leninist security apparatus.

A third vertical intrastate relationship is that between *center and localities.* Here decentralization has been a hallmark of Chinese communism and transition. This huge topic requires disaggregation by sector.

Economically, decentralization and recentralization was a frequent axis of communist reorganization, particularly in large countries. In China decentralization of economic functions from central to local government began in the late 1950s and remained a main feature of post-Mao economic reform, at least until the mid-1990s (e.g., Jia and Lin 1994, Goodman and Segal 1994). Studies of subnational levels in the post-Mao period tend to confirm the "fragmented authoritarianism" model (e.g., Schrodeder 1992, Walder 1992, Zweig 1992a). However, economic decentralization has produced quite different kinds of local state in different parts of China (e.g., Blecher 1991 on "entrepreneurial" versus "developmental" localities). Moreover, many differences between localities in economic performance have resulted largely from their different treatment by central economic policies, which remain strongly influential (Solinger 1996). In this volume, it is the economic chapters that most treat central-local relations—Tong on revenue sharing and Yang on macroeconomic control.

Politically, all Leninisms have been highly centralized. For China, studies suggest that at least some politically sensitive sectors remain highly centralized. For example, in the military, a combination of leadership concern about loyalty and modernization of technology may actually have increased centralization (e.g., Pollack 1992, Yang et al. 1994, Winckler Chapter 3 this volume). In civilian central-local relations, most China-watchers have argued that economic decentralization was diffusing political power (e.g., Jia and Linn 1994). However, Huang has recently argued that the center's increased control of personnel appointments and increased monitoring of administrative performance have more than maintained its authority (1996).

Socioculturally, Lenin accepted federalism to placate non-Russian nationalities, a compromise that eventually undermined the union itself (Roeder 1991). In contrast, the PRC has remained a unitary nation-state and conceded at most token cultural recognition to minority nationalities (Dreyer 1976, Heberer 1989). Under both Mao and Deng, the center set standards for social and cultural functions but decentralized responsibility for funding and implementing them to local levels, now particularly the county (Paine 1992, Zweig 1992, Shue 1995).

Huang argues that China's present combination of political centraliza-tion and economic decentralization is optimal for an authoritarian regime—vertical division of functions between levels provides some of the advan-tages of a horizontal division of powers between institutions (1996). Huang does not address the possible need to accommodate subnational sociocul-tural identities. China's leading reformist political scientist recommends federalism for all sectors (Yan 1992). Andrew Nathan, stressing the likely conservatism of China's institutional evolution, doubts that China's Leninist elites will allow either horizontal separation of powers or formal vertical federalism (1996).

A brief discussion of the "decentralized" nature of Chinese commu-nism and transition will provide a bridge to discussing state-society rela-tions. Maoist totalitarianism combined decentralization of the administra-tion of government from center to localities, with decentralization of the administration of daily life from localities to work units. These included urban bureaus, state firms, and rural communes, each usually a spatially concentrated small-scale community. Thus did the Maoist state penetrate to the very bottom of society, embedding all individuals in multifunctional organizations on which they depended for economic employment, daily necessities, and sociocultural services. In the transition from Maoist "decentralized totalitarianism" to Dengist "decentralized post-totalitarian-ism," decentralization from center to locality has strengthened, but decen-tralization from locality to work unit has weakened, particularly in the countryside. When rural communes disbanded, township governments assumed only part of their functions and powers, leaving rural individuals more self-reliant than before. In urban areas, privatizing the functions of state-sponsored work units has been more gradual. Overall, the boundary between state and society remains somewhat blurred.

State-Society Interaction

In the comparison of Leninist transitions, the most concerted argument about levels concerns *state versus society*—to the extent that Leninism has fallen, did it jump or was it pushed?

The *society-centered* position is largely European in origin, based on the gradual historical emergence of "civil society" during Europe's capitalist development and involving the late-postwar reemergence of civil society as a challenge to communism. This approach applies best to Eastern European societies with long precommunist histories of civil society and communist histories that include an anticommunist uprising (Czechoslovakia, Poland, and Hungary). This approach has been applied to the Soviet Union and China—for example, Pei (1992) argues that both reveal "societal takeover" of state powers. Most Asianists doubt that "civil society" was strong in Asian societies, partly because Asian precommunist history was largely precapitalist, partly because communist states arose indigenously and have remained strong. (For debate about historical China see Huang 1993; for a contemporary report see White, Howell, and Shang 1996.)

Most Asianists take a more *state-centered* position, arguing that in Leninist systems it is largely decline in state control that permits societal advance (e.g., Walder 1994). In late-communist systems, the boundary between state and society is not usually a sharp line of demarcation and confrontation, but rather a broad zone of interpenetration and collaboration (Deng 1994, Solinger 1993). Moreover, postcommunism continues to carry the impress of previous totalitarianism, such as a "flat" civil society and social networks derived from previous state connections (Linz and Stepan 1996, Solinger 1989). This approach applies best to cases with the least precommunist history of civil society and with communist histories that do not include major anticommunist uprisings—particularly China, but also the Soviet Union, and even some of the less developed Balkan countries. In these terms, most of the chapters in this volume are basically statist.

In fact the China case involves a combination of sociocentric and statecentric processes, a combination that differs between rural and urban. Several authors have argued persuasively that in the post-Mao era "farmers changed China," not by collective political action through civil society against the state, but by individual economic initiative that the party later endorsed (Kelliher 1992, Zhou 1996, Yang 1996). However, even these accounts involve strong statist elements—it was extreme state regimentation that reduced individuals to identical straits and that produced uncoordinated but similar reactions whenever state pressure relaxed. Moreover, local officials informally protected these initiatives and later parlayed their success into formal party policy. Urban areas remained under much tighter organization and control—more so for potentially powerful groups such as workers and students, less so for private social and cultural activities (Davis et al. 1995). Thus a more nuanced account relates state and society by examining the institutions mediating between them.

Which level initiates transition has implications for transition outcomes. Karl and Schmitter (1991) argue that the more elite-driven a transition, the more likely it is to produce democracy but the more state-dominated the resulting democracy. Conversely, the more mass-driven a transition, the less likely it is to produce democracy but the more society-dominated any resulting democracy. Again the Leninist cases provide some confirmation. Overall, European political democratization was more mass-driven and more democratic in outcome, Asian political liberalization more elite-managed and still quite limited. Variation within Europe provides further confirmation—political transitions in Russia (and the Balkans) were elite-initiated and remain relatively authoritarian. There is less variation within Asia, since there has been little mass success. Nevertheless, the Taiwan transition, though basically initiated and still dominated by elites, contained enough mass demand to help consolidate a genuine democracy.

In this volume, it is the sociocultural chapters that most treat the *interaction between state and society.* Winckler stresses the effectiveness of the Chinese party-state at birth planning. Kraus and Suttmeier find that the Chinese state continues to fund and control such areas of culture as are really important to it.

Supranational Environment

In the transition literature, arguments concerning the role of the *supranational* level have not been joined so elaborately as those concerning state-society relations. The early transition literature downplayed supranational processes, partly because southern Latin America is relatively remote from the Cold War, and partly in reaction to dependency theory (O'Donnell and Schmitter 1986, Whitehead 1986). International influences became more conspicuous in later transitions, so later formulations acknowledge them (e.g., Schmitter 1993, Bunce 1994, Linz and Stepan 1996). Analysis of supranational influences on democratizing transitions would benefit from more explicitness about levels, sectors, and dynamics. Such influences arise at several supranational levels (contiguous, regional, global) and differ in their regional density and spatial reach. Each sector contains many functional types, whose relative weights may differ by country and period. Many processes simultaneously both promote and retard democratization, in proportions that can differ by country and period.

Thus the greater salience of supranational processes in the postcommunist transitions arises partly from the fact that many are close to major geopolitical powers (e.g., Eastern Europe to the Soviet Union) or to major political-economic models and sociocultural influences (Eastern Europe to

Western Europe and communist eastern Asia to noncommunist eastern Asia). (In this volume, to encompass the scope of the comparisons and transformations involved, "eastern Asia" refers not just to "East Asia" but also to Siberia, Mongolia, and Southeast Asia.) During the last twenty years of democratization, global integration has increased dramatically in all sectors (e.g., for Leninist transitions, Baum 1991, Bunce 1994). Moreover, the decline of the Cold War gradually reversed the direction of many influences, as foreign states and firms increasingly sought stability from democracy not authoritarianism. In particular, the domestic requirements of "deep" integration into world trade has exerted increasingly powerful transformative effects, not only on small European trading countries, but even on large and formerly autarkic China.

Supranational context helps differentiate the European and Asian cases, both regionally and nationally. In the postwar period, both regions were buffer zones between the superpowers, which affected the pace of transition—in Eastern Europe, long Soviet constraint followed by relatively abrupt release; in eastern Asia, a more gradual shift of alignment from Soviet toward U.S. involvement. A main difference is that, historically, Europe was divided into many comparable powers, whereas Asia was dominated by China. Not only did this make China nearly as independent as the Soviet Union, it also differentiated the Asian cases by their relationship to China. Eastern Europe was a periphery of European civilization that could be "rescued" by democratizing influences from its Western European core. In eastern Asia, China itself has been the geopolitical and sociocultural core. It was only in the economy that, in the postwar period, the rest of eastern Asia temporarily achieved superiority, which contributed to China's starting its transition in the economy (McCormick and Unger 1996). In this volume, Winckler emphasizes supranational differentiation of the Asian communist transitions from each other.

Transition theory needs still more explicit and systematic formulations of differences in supranational influence. Ideally, accounts of transition would always *situate* a country in all three sectors, distinguish different supranational sublevels (e.g., bilateral, regional, and global), and indicate the main dynamic in each of these domains (e.g., geopolitical bipolarity to multipolarity, developmental boom-to-bust, or rising sociocultural interaction and conflict). For example, Crawford and Lijphart propose two supplements to the "legacies" and "liberalization" models of Eastern European transitions—"international processes" and "hegemonic norms" (1995). "International processes" is obviously supranational and turns out to be mostly political-economic. However, "hegemonic norms" are also supranational, but sociocultural—they may reside in the heads of domestic actors, but they originate in the West and arise from the desire of many in Eastern Europe to renounce "Asian" influences and to rejoin their "European" home. Crawford and Lijphart neglect supranational military-political processes, which may still prove as crucial in the future as they have in the past (e.g., NATO expansion).

Ideally too one should recognize the reciprocal impact of national transitions on supranational processes, including *interaction* between transitions themselves. For example, in the late 1980s, the Chinese democracy movement helped inspire Eastern European mass demonstrations; in turn global revulsion at the PRC repression of its democracy movement inhibited most European communist regimes from repressing them. In the early 1990s, the political chaos accompanying transition in parts of Europe helped cool Chinese enthusiasm for abrupt democratization, while the continuing prosperity of China's gradual economic transition strengthened European doubts about abrupt marketization.

Ideally, transition theory would also address the *institutional* dimension of supranational interactions. The effect of supranational processes on national decisions is mediated by institutions—not only the national institutions that perceive and respond to supranational processes, but also institutions such as international regimes linking the national and supranational domains (Ilkenberry, Lake, and Mastanduno 1988). "Institutional mediation" should be particularly important for the Leninist cases, which were not only heavily statist but also strongly integrated into the communist bloc. Some have explained the Fall of the Soviet Union by rising geopolitical pressure from the United States (Nee and Lian 1994), others by economic pressure from rising debt and falling competitiveness (Verdery 1995), and still others by sociocultural penetration from rising travel and telecommunications flows (Friedman and Baum in Baum 1991b). Institutionalist critics have retorted that many of these trends were long-standing, and what really needs explaining is particular responses at particular times, probably as a result of generational change and other processes within the party (Walder 1994). In this volume, Kraus and Suttmeier go furthest in specifying the institutional channels through which interaction between the national and supranational levels occurs, comparing the mix of channels through which China is acquiring foreign humanities and sciences.

Thus an institutional approach helps identify differences between sectors in supranational connections, particularly the different international interests of the different arms of different party-states. In communist systems, the military and police are likely to be keenly aware of supranational developments and may even contribute to launching reforms. In the Soviet Union and China, party-state economic managers long remained insulated from the supranational economy and therefore contributed little to pressure for transition (Evangelista 1996, Shirk 1996). However, in China, managers of industries that benefited from international "opening" supported transition once it began (Shirk 1996). Social and cultural professionals are particularly likely to be oriented toward supranational professional institutions, which helps impel transition (Kraus and Suttmeier this volume). In Leninist systems, political leaders themselves are particularly important as mediators of supranational influences (Dickson this volume).

Let us conclude our discussion of levels by acknowledging the *limits* of institutional analysis, using an example from the China literature. Susan Shirk has used her institutional model of "reciprocal accountability" between national and subnational leaders to explain how China "opened its door" to the global economy (1994). The center "played to the provinces" in order to maintain political support for economic opening, resulting in a process that, like domestic reform measures, was gradual, decentralized, and particularistic. Harry Harding, in accompanying comments, concedes that institutional characteristics played a role, but emphasizes not the institutionalization and decentralization through which Shirk explains how the policy was implemented, but the personalism and centralization that enabled the national leadership to pursue economic opening at all. More fundamentally, Harding argues that institutional analysis alone cannot identify the main dynamics behind economic opening. Instead he finds the real reasons at our three main levels: commitment of central leaders, support of Chinese society, and accommodation by the international community (1994).

Dynamics: Baselines, Processes, and Outcomes

As a process of change, transition from communism involves a longitudinal dimension of temporal dynamics. Here one question concerns the *tempo* of transition—gradual versus abrupt pace, and linear, cyclical, or discontinuous patterns. A second question is the relationship between *stages*—pretransition baseline, transition processes, and post-transition outcomes.

Tempo

In the early 1990s, the European and Asian transitions were taken to exemplify abruptness versus gradualism, as regards both precipitating events and responding policies. Europe stood for simultaneous reform of both economics and politics and the simultaneous adoption of multiple economic reforms. Asia stood for economic reform before political reform and the gradual evolution of economic reform. (Actually, the main contrast was between selected aspects of selected exemplars—principally the "big bang" in early 1990s Poland versus the economic gradualism in 1980s China.) To the neoclassical economists advising the European economies, a big bang was necessary because all aspects of an economy are interrelated, and the Asian economies appeared stuck in halfway reform. To the more institutional economists observing the prosperity accompanying the gradual Asian economic transitions, the European approach imposed excessive economic transition costs too early in the process, undermining political support for continuing reform (e.g., Amsden, Kochanowcz, and Taylor 1994).

By the late 1990s, many observers are downplaying the regional contrast in tempos. Some of the European transitions have proved slower, and some of the Asian transitions faster, than at first appeared. Poland has survived "shock therapy" to become the fastest-growing economy in Europe; China has advanced beyond halfway reform through rapid growth toward full marketization. The contrast in transition costs between Europe and Asia results more from differences in levels of "misdevelopment" than from differences in the speed of reform. (Europe had more useless industry and more extravagant welfare programs, requiring a more painful adjustment.) Nevertheless, neoclassical economists continue to argue that the more quickly the state reforms its own macroeconomic institutions, the better (e.g., World Bank 1996). In their view, when things went right in Asia it was because reforms did occur quickly (e.g., Vietnam and Laos). In contrast, some Asian institutionalists now argue that all transitions are inherently gradual. No country can reform everything simultaneously, so some sequencing is inevitable. In any case, building new institutions takes time (McMillan and Naughton 1996).

Both these positions contain much insight, but both overgeneralize. After all, there *were* contrasts in pace between most of Europe and most of Asia. In this volume, Winckler argues that these derived largely from different relationships to the Soviet Union. In Europe, both Soviet political intervention and East bloc economic integration were higher, tying the pace of change in Europe more closely to that in the Soviet Union. European reform was first delayed until Soviet reform, then accelerated by Soviet promotion, withdrawal, and collapse. In Asia, both Soviet political intervention and East bloc economic integration were much lower, leaving most Asian communisms freer to try reforms early (China) or to resist reform late (North Korea). In most Asian communisms eventual Soviet withdrawal and collapse produced much less disruption than in Europe, allowing gradual partial economic reform and little political reform. Having restored this overall contrast, we now consider some suggestive qualifications to it.

First, as regards change of formal political regime, there were significant differences in tempo within both regions. In Europe, the early northern postcommunist political transitions were famously less rapid than the later southern ones. These differences in tempo reflected differences in substance—unavoidable real change versus preemptive cosmetic change. Most Asian communisms rejected change in formal political regime. It was accepted only by Mongolia, which was the least independent, and by Cambodia, which was the most foreign-penetrated (see Winckler Chapter 9 this volume).

Second, one should distinguish between formal political transition and informal change in political and other matters. In most European cases, a formal change of political regime came relatively early in the process and in some cases was a necessary precondition to major economic and other reform. In most Asian cases, more change is occurring within the old regime before formal political transition, which most Asian cases have indefinitely postponed. This points to a fundamental difference of political purpose between European and Asian economic and other reforms—in postcommunist Europe they are part of a deliberate effort to destroy political Leninism, while in transitional Asia they are an attempt to preserve it (Walder 1995b). It also points to a fundamental theoretical difference between the European and Asian transitions—in Europe "constitutional" change accompanied "institutional" change, while in Asia "institutional" change has proceeded without "constitutional" change (Fforde 1994, after Ostrom).

Third, even as regards informal nonpolitical change, there is much variation within each region. East Germany and North Korea showed the least change under the old regime—both of them as the socialist parts of divided countries bracing themselves against their capitalist counterparts. Among the communist cases, Hungary and China showed the most change under the old regime—both embarked on early economic reforms that produced much economic viability and institutional variety (Nee and Stark 1989, Hankiss 1990, Naughton 1995, Walder 1995c). Taiwan shows the most change, starting from a near-totalitarian early postwar state, then accepting first early economic reform and then late political reform, as part of its external struggle with China and involvement with the United States.

Considered as a whole, each economic transition may be gradual. Nevertheless, significant difference remains between "big bang" state policy packages and incremental, society-initiated change. The main candidate as a temporal model for transition processes is the now popular "punctuated equilibrium"—long linear internal drift culminating in abrupt externally generated crisis (Somit and Peterson 1992). Differentiating transitions requires concepts for relating slow and rapid phases in processes of change that are less or more deliberate. In Europe the earlier northern Leninist transitions do resemble punctuated equilibria, particularly if one recalls the gradual changes occurring long before 1989 (e.g., in Hungary and Poland). However, the later southern transitions have involved both less linear drift and less abrupt transformation; incumbent elites remained in power by changing leaders and labels (e.g., in Romania and Bulgaria). Moreover, several of the Asian transitions display not drift but dynamism and originated from earlier internal crises, not recent external ones (e.g., in China and Vietnam).

Policy cycles supplement linear trends and crisis discontinuities as patterns of change. Eastern Europe had tried drastic "rightist" reform in the 1950s and 1960s, with calamitous results in Hungary and Czechoslovakia.

This made later rightist reform cycles in Hungary and Poland more mild and less conclusive (Ekiert 1996). By contrast, in Asia the drastic and calamitous policy experiments in the 1950s and 1960s had been "leftist," allowing later rightist reform cycles to be more significant and more successful (Hamrin 1990, Baum 1994, Dittmer and Wu 1995). In China, politically, economic booms strengthened reformers while economic busts helped conservatives (Dittmer 1992). *Both* liberalization and consolidation phases of the economic cycle furthered economic transformation (Naughton 1995).

Stages

The possible relationships between gross stages help define many of the basic arguments about transitions. Which has more impact on outcomes: the baseline from which transition starts, the process of transition itself, or some future goals toward which transition is striving? Crawford and Lijphart provide a good discussion of this question for postcommunist Eastern Europe, contrasting a past-oriented "legacies of Leninism" approach with an "imperatives of liberalization" approach, which is future-oriented in the sense of stressing progress toward a particular type of society (1995). Their own approach is present-oriented, emphasizing that the immediate situational context and immediate political interests determine what part of past legacies and future projects becomes politically relevant.

The chapters in this volume characterize baseline, process, or outcome mostly in terms of the type of governance problem at stake, and assess the relationship between stages as continuity or change in the performance of those functions. Both the precondition and process approaches recognized these substantive problems—the modernization literature in its functional crises and the transition literature in its functional "moments" (Binder 1971, O'Donnell and Schmitter 1986). However, these substantive problems have not been much elaborated, perhaps because they were not at issue between these two approaches.

So far, the most persuasive general approach to relating the stages of transition is *path dependence* (North 1990, Arthur 1994). The outcome of change is crucially affected by initial conditions and by the constraints that accumulate with each subsequent choice. Similar processes operating on different initial conditions are likely to produce different outcomes. Change has no predetermined end state, either communist utopia or capitalist democracy. In Leninist transitions, postcommunist outcomes are constrained by the transition process, which in turn is constrained by the immediate pretransition baseline. Moreover, as Yu-shan Wu has argued, the sequence in which governance problems arise during transition can crucially affect the outcome (1993).

China illustrates. For example, within China's still largely economic transition, the fact that administrative decentralization to local governments occurred before marketizing decentralization to firms created China's distinctive pattern of "local state corporatism" (Oi 1992, Ho 1994). The fact that administrative decentralization originated from local experiments enabled local officials to influence central policy. The fact that the private sector grew before the growth of formal institutions to govern it left businesspeople vulnerable to local officials and dependent on personal networks (Young 1995). The same initial ingredients, combined in a different order, would have produced a different result. According to Yu-shan Wu, in the long run it bodes well for both economic and political transition in China that economic transition is occurring before political or ethnonational transition (1993). The post-totalitarian state can maintain the political stability necessary for economic development, but economic development will gradually transform the post-totalitarian state.

Of course, causal chains can be traced back beyond the sequence of events within transition, to the national and international trajectory of *communism* during the twentieth century, to the longer-run course of *modernization* within countries and regions, and to the historical *formation* of states and nations. For example, within the communist timescale, Dali Yang has recently extended the origins of the post-Mao decollectivization of Chinese agriculture back from the immediate circumstances of the post-Mao period, or even the institutional weakening produced by the Cultural Revolution, to the calamity following the Great Leap Forward. It was localities that experienced the worst famine in the late 1950s that took the initiative in decollectivizing agriculture in the late 1970s (Yang 1996). At a longer national-modernization timescale, the prospects for democratization in China look quite different, depending on whether one regards modern Chinese history as an interaction between continental Eastern despotism and maritime Western democracy (e.g., Su and Wang 1991, Fu 1993), or as an accelerating process of indigenous modernization (Rowe 1985, 1990; Miller 1996). At a still longer global-historical timescale, the significance of China's post-Mao takeoff looks different when viewed as China's finally gaining equality with the West, or as regaining China's previous global dominance (Frank and Gills 1993). (On situating China's post-Mao reform in longer time periods, see Lieberthal et al. 1991, and Womack 1991.)

Path dependence implies equal attention to both the accumulation of constraints and the process of choice. For example, Karl and Schmitter's "structured contingency" contains the historical-structural constraints, while their "contingent choice" highlights actor strategies (1991). Thus path dependence has the advantage of being neither deterministic nor teleological. It is not deterministic because, although previous choices strongly affect the probabilities of possible later developments, they do not completely determine them. Not only do there remain many later choices to make, but also earlier choices can be partially reversed by later events. Path dependence is not teleological because it does not assume any particular outcome. This is a caution appropriate to transitions from systems that one dislikes, since one is inclined to hope that they will evolve toward systems that one prefers (Stark 1992, Bruckner 1995). Nevertheless, path dependence does not preclude all sense of direction—global trends can be built into the constraints, and actor aspirations can be built into the choices, particularly the aspirations of those actors with the greatest power.

Communist Baseline

Early discussions of transitions from authoritarianism emphasized the constraints that *baseline* places on outcomes. The earliest accounts focused on society—socioeconomic development, class structure, and political culture (Lipset 1960, Moore 1966, Almond and Verba 1965). Societal characteristics remain important (e.g., Lipset 1993, Bartlett and Hunter 1993, Huntington 1984). Here the question about China is whether its socioeconomic modernization and political culture make it "ready for democracy." Many Chinese intellectuals would respond "no" (Goldman 1994), but most Western China political scientists would respond "yes" (e.g., Nathan 1985, 1990).

Most later discussions of transition baseline shifted to regime-type and state institutions, which create different political dynamics and mediate responses to policy crises differently (Stepan 1986, Linz and Stepan 1996, Haggard and Kaufman 1995). Thus it matters how one characterizes China's regime. Moreover, any characterization should have a strong temporal dimension, because China has changed continuously, creating different baselines for different aspects of transition. Most China scholars agree that at the height of Maoism the intended reach of the state was extremely broad, though some reject the term "totalitarian" in order to emphasize the elite conflict, bureaucratic infighting, or mass resistance that this attempted domination provoked (e.g., Nathan 1992 versus Shue 1988). Similarly, most China scholars agree that under Deng the functional scope and vertical penetration of the state greatly declined, though some emphasize that the state has thereby increased its effectiveness (again Nathan 1992 versus Shue 1988). To reflect this change, most China scholars labeled the Dengist period "authoritarian." Strictly speaking, however, Dengist China was "post-totalitarian"—that is, still bearing many legacies of totalitarianism, such as a relatively monistic party-state and "flattened" civil society (Linz and Stepan 1996). Moreover, the temporal dimension identifies differences within post-totalitarianism—for example, early versus late and changing versus "frozen" (Linz and Stepan 1996). In these terms, Deng advanced China into early and middle post-totalitarianism, then attempted to continue economic change while "freezing" the system politically and ideologically.

Thus China illustrates that transitions from communism involve multiple baselines: on the one hand, the greatest extent of totalitarianism; on the other, the extent of detotalitarianization at the time of particular later changes. Accordingly, this volume focuses on the party-state and its reach but stresses that the baseline for transition is irregular—not a straight line of ideal-typical Leninist institutions and communist practices lined up in full array awaiting their simultaneous Fall, but a jagged line of different sectors at different stages of preliminary transition away from communism (Stark 1992, footnote 4). This unevenness itself contributes to the possibility and dynamic of change. Moreover, the baseline results from a composite of processes with varying timescales, whose effects therefore continue for different lengths of time after transition. Though path dependence makes jumping-off points crucial, long-term historical processes also have continuing effects.

The chapters in this volume that most emphasize baseline focus on its institutional makeup. For example, Winckler's chapter on the military stresses how basic it has been historically to constructing institutions in other sectors. Winckler's chapter on Chinese population policy derives much of its dynamic from the intrinsic properties of a Leninist party-state. Kraus and Suttmeier find the origins of the marketization of culture in prior Cultural Revolution decentralization.

Transition Process

Later discussion of transitions from authoritarianism argued that the *process* of political transition itself is the main influence on outcomes (O'Donnell and Schmitter 1986). A helpful early typology distinguished both the rate and nature of change (Share 1987). The classic image of revolution is of mass revolt overthrowing a regime "from below." However, most of the Eastern European communist cases are variants of relatively sudden "transition through collapse," a more "top-down" process in which a still highly centralized Establishment self-destructs even in the absence of much organized Opposition (Share 1987). This leaves the direction of change unclear and actors' strategies highly uncertain. Most of the Asian Leninist cases are likely to be closer to a gradual "transition through transaction" between a still robust but decentralizing Establishment and an only gradually rising Opposition. Here the direction of change is more deliberately constrained and the uncertainty of actors and strategies much lower.

However, in communist countries, transition through transaction presupposes a long prior period of gradual devolution, in which the economy expands beyond state control and the state reduces its intervention in society and culture (e.g., Poland or Hungary). Until then, in China, "transaction" is likely to be quite unequal, given the party-state monopoly of political resources and the underdevelopment of political opposition (Nathan

1993). Indeed, the communist cases are so state-centric as to suggest a new transition path, "from within." This is a slow form of top-down collapse in which the regime's capacity for monitoring and sanctions gradually withers, particularly as the regime abandons central economic planning (Walder 1995c, on Hungary and China). Transition "from within" may produce political decay and economic corruption. However it could also involve political reconstruction—for example, reducing party control and transferring policy oversight to the national legislature (Nathan 1996).

In O'Donnell and Schmitter's formulation of the transition process, the key to success was elite coalitions between centrists against extremists (1986). Such negotiated or "pacted" transitions result in limited but stable democracies. Friedman argues that such centrist consensus has underlain democratization in noncommunist Asia as elsewhere, and hopes for the same process in communist Asia (Friedman 1994, Introduction). More recently Linz and Stepan have observed that such moderate coalitions are unlikely in transitions from totalitarianism, which lack not only organized public oppositions but also strong reformers within the party-state (1996, 65). Even under early post-totalitarianism, the likely scenario remains either successful repression or state collapse (still true even in 1989 China). Such coalitions become possible only in late post-totalitarianism (true for China by the early twenty-first century?). (For applications of transition theory to the Leninist cases, see Bova 1991, and Linz and Stepan 1996; for critiques, see Ekiert 1991; Janos 1991; Terry 1993; and Bunce 1994, 1995.)

Overall, the chapters in this volume describe a transition process that in 1990s China is still strongly guided—and restrained—"from above." The security apparatus remains robust, the economy remains dynamic, and sociocultural liberalization remains limited. For the foreseeable future, the Chinese party-state does not appear likely either to collapse, to wither away, or to negotiate itself out of power. What the chapters show instead is a deliberate, selective, and strategic retreat—from trying to control everything to better controlling a few things, through more sophisticated forms of control.

Postcommunist Outcome

Some analysts treat transition as at least somewhat teleologically oriented toward a partially *predetermined outcome*. Contemporary transitions may be at least partially pulled along by a global trend toward marketization and democratization, and at least partially pushed by latecomers purposively attempting to join that trend. Several of the approaches to transition that Crawford and Lijphart identify are similarly goal-oriented, including "imperatives of liberalization," "hegemonic norms" of capitalism and democracy, and the "international influences" promoting them (1995). Moreover, if the goal is marketization or democratization, there may be optimal sequences for pursuing it (e.g., McKinnon 1993). The objection to this as "designer capitalism" or "designer democracy" underlines its future orientation (Offe 1991). Obviously a transition away from a nonmarket or nondemocratic system is not necessarily a transition to capitalism and democracy, particularly when incumbent elites deliberately pursue a nonmarket or nondemocratic outcome. Transition from communism may develop into some form of authoritarianism, as already in much of postcommunist southern Europe and perhaps eventually in much of postcommunist eastern Asia. For example, China remains formally committed to an ultimate outcome that is communist and Chinese, and meanwhile promotes socialist economic marketization and Singaporean political authoritarianism. Alternatively, transition from communism may decay into a "failed state," as already in some of postcommunist Europe (e.g., the former Yugoslavia) and perhaps eventually in some of postcommunist Asia (e.g., Cambodia, North Korea).

A second question concerns the problematic relationship between *intentions and outcomes.* In transitions, actors can produce change as much by combating it as by promoting it. For example, communist leaderships originally intended marketization only to supplement planning, not to supplant it. In Asia agricultural reform was intended to save collectivization not abolish it. Similarly, in politics, the purpose of early political reform is usually to forestall democratization, not to promote it. When democratization occurs anyway, the objective shifts to maintaining the dominance of a ruling party by making it electorally competitive. This in turn requires transforming the ruling party itself, the opposite of the original intention (e.g., as on Taiwan).

Finally, we should note a third, less discussed question along the temporal dimension—the *role of time* itself in transition. Ideologically, communism was relentlessly future-oriented—ambitious visions of national construction demanded much present sacrifice to achieve them. Institutionally, however, communism was quite present-oriented—to maintain their own power and discretion, leaders would not allow institutions to make future commitments of resources or rules. Transition requires setting up institutions that not only can plan ahead, but also can stick to those plans. For example, in China, social policy promised state workers pensions, but enterprises had no long-term pension funds. Instead, all expenses were paid out of current revenues, with little cost accounting. Now social transition requires a longer time horizon and institutions for pooling resources and exercising fiduciary responsibility over time (Krieg and Schadler 1994). Cultural transition too requires temporal restructuring—public struggles over the interpretation of history, private struggles over the meaning of experience, and the readaptation of precommunist and communist cultural forms for postcommunist domination and resistance (Unger 1993, Lee and Syrokomla-Steganowska 1993, Watson 1994).

The chapters in this volume do not predict the eventual outcome of transition from communism in China. Nevertheless, their modeling of the 1990s suggests likely features of that outcome. The Chinese leadership has decided largely to swim with global waves of marketization and even democratization, but at its own pace and on its own terms, along a transition path that preserves essential party-state interests even while transforming the party-state's functions. Unlike Eastern Europe, but like Taiwan, the future is likely to be a substantial but gradual transformation of the past.

Chapters

Aside from the editor's Introduction and Conclusion, the volume begins with a comparison of the initiation and extent of transition in China and Taiwan and concludes with a comparative survey of the origins and outcomes of the Asian postcommunist transitions. In between, the China-sectoral chapters probe the transition process within particular sectors.

Transition Process

The introductory comparative chapter (Chapter 2) treats the initiation and course of reform.

Bruce Dickson compares the adaptability of two regimes—the quasi-Leninist but anticommunist Nationalist Party on Taiwan (KMT) and the fully Leninist and Communist Party in China (CCP). He establishes a macroframework (the interaction of the national, supranational, and subnational levels) and elaborates it with mesoanalysis (the interaction of organization and environment). For Dickson, in Leninist systems it is the national party, not the subnational society, that is the most likely source of change. Adaptation is least likely if, as in China, the party elite perceives both the domestic and international environments as threatening but containable. Adaptation is most likely if, as eventually on Taiwan, the party elite perceives the domestic environment as demanding change and the international environment as supporting it. These elite perceptions are strongly informed by the party's stage of development—particularly succession of leadership, goals, and personnel. Typically what induces the party to undertake adaptive change is the perception, usually by a new leadership, that a crisis threatens core party institutions and values.

The KMT on Taiwan provides a rare example of a Leninist party that, through incremental adaptation, initiated and survived both economic and political reform. Can the CCP do the same? Dickson thinks not. The CCP can last somewhat longer without adapting politically so is unlikely to do much political reform. Moreover, the CCP is less likely to succeed if it tries. Reconciling Marxism-Leninism with democratization will be hard, and the CCP may now be so unpopular that attempting political reform might speed not slow its demise.

Military-Political Affairs

The first pair of China-sectoral papers establish the power parameters of Chinese policy, analyzing control processes within China's military and police.

Edwin Winckler argues that while the nature of the transition in China's military has been well analyzed, the role of the military in China's transition from communism has not been much addressed. Winckler begins by summarizing some main themes in the latest literature on Chinese military politics—much consensus about the effects of generational succession, some disagreement about the tightness or looseness of civilian control. The field's main analytical tool remains the lessening conflict between politics and professionalism, which may understate the centrality of political commitment to professional identity. Winckler then outlines Chinese institutions for controlling military assets, stressing the number and length of the chains of delegation involved. Careful selection of commanders remains the first line of control, supplemented by political work systems that have positive functions as well as control. National command briefly suffered from potential multiple principals, but the leadership recognized and solved the problem. Many analysts have discussed the possibility of military regionalism, but few believe it likely.

Winckler then places such formal-institutional controls in the context of substantive issues. Recent transition literature argues that a well-institutionalized civil-military relationship is fostered by a clear external mission, which the Chinese military has. Institutionalization is undermined by large military involvement in combating a strong internal threat, which the Chinese leadership is trying to avoid. Institutionalization is also eroded by large military roles in nonmilitary affairs, which in China continue. Finally, Winckler more directly addresses the role of the military in transition. China challenges the comparative tenet that in totalitarian systems controlling the military is not a problem, suggesting the relevance of authoritarian cases. Regionally, many other Asian regimes have been similarly militarized, Eastern Europe shows the centrality of nationalism during transition, and Latin America illustrates recurrent reliance on the military as ultimate guarantor of national stability. Finally, until the end of the 1990s, the Chinese military remained active in all three kinds of compliance—not only defending the party with force, but also setting ideological standards and even promoting commercialization.

Murray Scot Tanner explores the range of views among Chinese policy planners and policymakers about how to adapt the internal security system to reform. In communist parlance the question was whether social deviance should be analyzed in class terms and, if so, who the class enemy is during reform. Tanner identifies a spectrum of positions within this debate and considers the implications of ideological disagreement for the political leadership's control of the security police. On the eve of the 1989 Tiananmen incident, legalist *reformers* within the public security system regarded Mao-era campaigns as involving excesses that actually undermined security work. They regarded reform-era deviance as reflecting not class struggle but social transition. The *Leninist* mainstream defended earlier attacks on landlords and capitalists. They viewed the corruption and violence that emerged under reform as defining a new category of class enemies who should be combated with equal force. Third, after Tiananmen, a few *neo-Maoist* voices denied any validity to protesters' critiques, which they insinuated were part of a broad class conspiracy extending even into the party leadership.

Tanner then documents that, at the beginning of the 1990s, tension existed within the Leninist mainstream between some of China's most important internal security policymakers—for example, the distinctly conservative founding organizer of the security sector, Peng Zhen, and the distinctly liberal recent security czar, Qiao Shi. By 1992 both the security debate and political leadership had shifted back toward the center. However, the question remains of how a future democratizing leadership could secure the compliance of a still mostly Leninist security apparatus. Tanner draws on Douglass North to argue that ideological congruence is a necessary precondition for legal-organizational oversight. Again, weak institutionalization undermines effective delegation.

Political-Economic Affairs

Economic decentralization has been the lead process in Chinese devolution, during both the Maoist and Dengist periods. The second pair of China-sectoral papers refines existing analysis of this important process.

James Tong explores the evolution of fiscal relations in both Maoist and Dengist China—as he puts it, from "strong arm" to "hidden hand." The pre–Cultural Revolution fiscal regime was highly centralized, successfully using a combination of normative commitment and coercive discipline to induce provincial leaders to comply with central demands for fiscal effort and expenditure control. The Cultural Revolution damaged the central leadership's personal legitimacy and paralyzed its coercive capacity. Consequently in the post-Mao era the center relied increasingly on material incentives—as in other policy areas, the refinement of remunerative "contracts" for achieving compliance. Here, as Tong says, principal-agent theory takes up where Etzioni left off, further specifying the different incentive effects of different kinds of remunerative contracts—wages, rent, and revenue-sharing.

Post-Mao fiscal experimentation provides Tong with a laboratory for testing these ideas, both across provinces and over time. Provinces differed both in the form of remunerative contract and, for the majority of provinces with revenue-sharing, in the size of the central and provincial shares. Moreover, these arrangements changed over time, from more heterogeneous in the early 1980s to more homogeneous by the mid-1980s. Using provincial budget data, Tong finds that most of the expectations of principal-agent theory are realized. Long-term revenue-sharing induces more effort at revenue collection than annually adjusted revenue-sharing, and higher rates of revenue-sharing induce more effort at revenue collection than lower ones.

However, Tong also finds an exception that highlights the characteristic discrepancy in China between nominal and actual arrangements. Nominally, the center favored coastal development targets Guangdong and Fujian by allowing them to keep all but a fixed amount of revenue. Actually, when these provinces ran large surpluses, the center confiscated them in the form of compulsory loans from province to center that the center never paid back. Consequently these provinces displayed only middling collection effort and expenditure control. Like Tong's analysis of the long-run shift from normative to remunerative compliance, this underlines the impact of institutional context on principal-agent relations.

Dali Yang shows that the cause of boom-and-bust cycles in China's economy was not just weak institutions and fiscal decentralization, but also central demands for rapid growth that drove localities into competition for early development. Macroeconomic instability has been "the unintended result of an iterated game between center and localities." Yang argues that previous studies have been too casual in assuming that devolution of property rights by itself explains local developmentalism, and too casual in implying that local autonomy by itself explains national overexpansion. Yang argues that both points require further specification of institutional context.

First, strong central political encouragement and economic incentives penalized late-liberalizing localities and encouraged local developmentalism. Second, weak central macroeconomic control allowed localities to overinvest, forcing the center to resort to political discipline to restore economic stability and leaving the center great latitude about what measures it would employ. Third, weak central political institutions allowed leader initiatives and succession politics to complicate central economic policies. In 1992 Deng Xiaoping ended a period of economic retrenchment by signaling local leaders to ignore central restraints and resume economic expansion. Since then his technocratic successors have labored with much success both to contain the inflation his initiative unleashed and to institutionalize less personal mechanisms for conducting policy. This episode may prove to have been the critical one in China's economic transition toward more institutionalized regulation of a market economy.

Sociocultural Affairs

The last pair of China-sectoral papers treat social and cultural policies.

Edwin Winckler examines China's most important social policy, state birth planning, arguing that it remains surprisingly robust, despite economic liberalization. Around 1990, in conjunction with drafting a new ten-year development plan, population control was reintensified in the short run through crash campaigns and reinstitutionalized for the long run by beginning a shift toward more legalistic sanctions and more economic incentives. The vigor of this policy results from the political leadership's determination to raise per capita incomes to achieve popular support. Its effectiveness results partly from the political leadership's willingness to invoke party discipline over subnational leaders to ensure their compliance, and partly from the technical feasibility of cost-effective contraception and surveillance.

Winckler analyzes this success in terms shared by classic organization theory and neo-institutional analysis—institutions, incentives, and information. Policy outcomes are affected by general institutional characteristics of a dual party-state regime, here summarized as *multiple delegation* from party to government and center to locality, *mixed implementation* through both routine government administration and party-led crash campaigns, and *sequential attention* to competing policy goals that varies intensity of implementation. Policy outcomes are also affected by the logic of incentives. Controlling fertility is an order goal for which coercion is effective, though policymakers rely on persuasion and rewards as much as possible and try to adapt both goals and power to each locality's level of development. Characteristics of information also affect policy outcomes. Population is more measurable than most policy outcomes, and reformist China has greatly improved the collection and analysis of demographic data.

Richard Kraus and *Richard Suttmeier* analyze the changing organizational models the state has applied to the production of culture, comparing the humanities with the sciences. Under Mao, cultural policy had shifted between various combinations of bureaucratic, professional, and revolutionary models. Under Deng, culture first moved back from revolutionary mobilization toward bureaucratic professionalism, then forward toward a combination of bureaucratic control and marketizing reform. With technology-intensive economic development, the sciences became more important. In contrast, as the state reduced its reliance on propaganda, the humanities became more diverse but less important. Kraus and Suttmeier then consider the interplay of marketization, internationalization, and democratization in cultural transition.

In both the sciences and the humanities, the main change has been the reduction of state subsidies and the *marketization* of cultural activities. In the sciences, contract research and technological entrepreneurship have helped replace state funding and helped reorient research toward production. In the humanities, state retreat has allowed the flourishing of commercial popular culture but has left all but the most elite humanities largely unfunded. Updating Chinese culture has also required *internationalization*. In the sciences this has clarified the appropriate technical standards and social organization for scientific research, but in the humanities it has complicated the question of what is politically correct and aesthetically Chinese. However, cultural reform has not produced much *democratization*. The state continues to impose its aims on areas it can still fund or regulate, and state cultural policymaking remains personalized and centralized. The sciences provide some precedent for state-initiated liberalization of a cultural domain, but state-funded humanities remain a propaganda tool for reform policies.

Transition Outcomes

The concluding comparative chapter treats the origins and outcomes of transition in all of the Asian communist cases.

Edwin Winckler surveys the six cases of Asian communism, emphasizing the differences between them and the processes that differentiate them. He argues that the single most basic difference between communist countries was their degree of geopolitical centrality to Russian security, and that the single largest impetus to systemic change was the extent of external shock produced by the collapse of Soviet support. Among Asian communisms, China was the most independent and least Soviet-oriented. Responding early to largely internal problems, it pioneered the transition path of gradual economic reform based on continued political control. In contrast, Mongolia was the most Soviet-oriented Asian communism, and its reform path was closest to that of the Eastern European Soviet satellites. Late and abrupt withdrawal of Soviet support precipitated abrupt and drastic political and economic reform.

Other Asian cases range between these two extremes. In northeastern Asia, North Korea achieved substantial independence from both the Soviet Union and China and pursued its own idiosyncratic path. Its personalistic leadership has eschewed both economic and political reform. In southeast Asia, Laos and Cambodia belong to a subsystem centered on a largely independent Vietnam. Here postcommunist transitions have diverged somewhat in form but remained similar in substance, mostly marketization not democratization. Economically, Vietnam and Laos continue to espouse an eventual communism, and politically they remain determinedly Leninist. In Cambodia, the international community brokered a political transition from Vietnamese-backed communist rule to a domestically elected coalition government. Nevertheless, the former communist party-state apparatus has remained politically dominant, as formalized by the 1997 coup.

Conclusion

Descriptively, the upshot of this Introduction is a 3 x 3 x 3 cube for relating sectors, levels, and dynamics. Those are the dimensions that I found in these chapters as I assembled them, and in the transition literatures as I collated them. These dimensions are merely commonsensical and descriptive, but they inform important understandings and disagreements. No single analysis can pursue all of them simultaneously, but together they help anticipate what a complete account involves. Let us briefly consider three final examples.

First, the essays and authors in this volume illustrate the tendency of scholarly discourse gradually to fill out the grid of dynamics, sectors, and levels. For example, Dickson's interplay of structural levels calls for differentiating treatment of different functional sectors. Conversely, the China-sectoral essays all require some attention to all levels—not only state-society relations, but also their interaction with global processes.

Second, the succession of approaches to comparative (post)communism too raises the question of a balanced account. For example, the totalitarian approach, starting from the party-state, emphasized ideology and politics. It was therefore a logical antithesis for the modernization approach to start from society and to emphasize economy and society. It was logical then to synthesize the two approaches, as has happened through increasingly sophisticated formulations of the interaction between state and society (e.g., Migdal, Kohli, and Shue 1994, including Shue and Perry on China). Along the levels dimension, another logical sequel would be to integrate the supranational level (again, for China, Yang 1991, Zweig 1992a, Howell 1993, the commentary at the end of Chung 1995, and Shirk 1996).

On other dimensions, another logical sequel is integrating political and economic with sociocultural processes. In the China field, sociocultural analysis of subnational regionalism has suddenly blossomed (e.g., Dittmer and Kim 1993, Friedman 1995) but so far has not been much integrated with political-economic analysis (though see Hoston 1994). Finally of course there is integrating the present with the past (always the China field's strong point—see, for example, Lieberthal et al. 1991 and, again, Perry's 1994 commentary). What is *not* a logical sequel, however, is to junk the insights of previous approaches. Nor is "institutionalism" a logical sequel along any of these dimensions—it is an analytical approach to all of the above.

Third, the comparative transition literature reveals the same tendency gradually to fill out the grid of descriptive discourse. It too has progressed from an exclusive preoccupation with state-society relations to their supranational context (e.g., Schmitter 1993), from interactions between politics and economics to their sociocultural counterparts (e.g., Horowitz 1993), and from the immediate process of transition to the longer-run processes in which transition is embedded (e.g., Chirot 1995). However, recent debate between noncommunist and communist comparativists shows the process still under way (e.g., Schmitter and Karl 1993 versus Bunce 1994, 1995).

Compared to noncommunist transitions, Schmitter and Karl regard the following as distinctive to communist transitions (in approximate order of importance): the simultaneity of crises in multiple sectors, the strong role of supranational processes, the suddenness and completeness of the collapse of the old regime, and "flat" socioeconomic stratification that inclines postcommunist systems away from class issues toward ethnic issues. Schmitter and Karl consider these differences profound but argue that authoritarian and communist transitions are nevertheless still comparable. This is particularly so because most Leninist systems deteriorated toward something approximating authoritarianism before they collapsed.

Bunce's reply likewise emphasizes the broad range of the issues simultaneously in play and the role of international processes. However, she stresses the large role of mass mobilization and the profundity of the historical problems involved, particularly the questionable viability of some communist states, given their geographic mismatch with ethnic nationalism. Bunce concludes that the two types of transition are too different to be fruitfully compared and recommends comparing communist transitions themselves.

Thus the two sides largely agree on the facts but disagree on the methodological implications. Neither has a scheme for articulating the continuum between "minimal" and "maximal" transitions or for discussing the impact of incremental differences of scope on the incremental comparability of cases. Neither has a scheme for suggesting, in different transitions, what depth of historical problems are likely to be involved, what range of problems is likely to arise, or when what levels are likely to intervene. Neither resorts to political science to provide substantive grounds for clarification or reconciliation: Schmitter and Karl appeal tongue-in-cheek to the Machiavellian "new sciences" of "transitology" and "consolidology," Bunce to the methodological common sense of comparative communism (Bunce 1994).

One suspects the need for some shift in the center of gravity, not only of transition theory, but also of comparative politics as a whole, toward a more robust paradigm for relating timescales, sectors, and levels. Evidently the approaches reigning in political science in the 1980s and 1990s provided inadequate guidance, not just to the Fall but to the whole trajectory of communism and postcommunism, and even to its retrospective reexamination. Some may prefer an unbalanced approach, in which disciplines alternately emphasize one perspective or another and alternately bring each "back in." Others may prefer a balanced approach in which, heuristically, all are given equal weight from the outset, until their empirical weights in each situation are determined. Either way, the long-run development of the literature, like the long-run development of history itself, will involve them all.

The rest of this volume prompted, illustrates, and elaborates these themes.

2

Leninist Adaptability in China and Taiwan

Bruce J. Dickson

Why have ruling Leninist parties had such difficulty adapting to changes in their environment? Under what circumstances are they most likely to adapt? Does adaptation strengthen or weaken their status as ruling parties? This chapter explores these questions by comparing the evolution of two Leninist Chinese ruling parties: the Chinese Nationalist Party (KMT) on Taiwan and the Chinese Communist Party (CCP). In particular, I concentrate on the periods when the issue of adapting arose—when the KMT was led by Chiang Ching-kuo and the CCP by Deng Xiaoping. The KMT provides a case of a Leninist party that liberalized its authoritarian rule and ultimately presided over the democratization of its political system. In contrast, the CCP provides a more familiar case of a Leninist party that abandoned its totalitarian aspirations for the sake of economic modernization but maintained its authoritarian controls over the political system and repressed political demands emanating from society. Comparing these two parties is particularly meaningful because not only did both start as Leninist parties, but also they shared the same domestic governmental traditions and political culture and were situated in the same geopolitical region.[1]

The chapter focuses on the Leninist party because in Leninist systems the party, not the society, is the most likely source of change. I examine why parties respond the way they do, not what causes the environment to change. I argue that whether adaptation occurs is largely determined by how the party elite chooses to interpret its domestic and international environments. These environments may be so threatening or so benign that their interpretation is obvious, but usually there is much room for interpretation. The ruling elite brings to these interpretations its own gradually changing composition and goals. Its interpretations and reactions are affected by its strategies for monitoring the environment and for coping with change. Adaptation is least likely if the party elite perceives both the domestic and international environments as threatening. Adaptation is most likely if elites perceive the domestic environment as demanding change and the international environment as supporting it. Reform is triggered by the perception, usually by a new leadership, of a crisis that threatens cherished traditions and core institutions.

The first section of this chapter will discusses the factors that facilitate or obstruct adaptation. Case material drawn from the experiences of the KMT and the CCP will then be presented to illustrate a proposed model of adaptation. It will be shown that although the basic characteristics of Leninist parties have inhibited their adaptation, they have not prevented it. Rather, the adaptability of these parties has been determined by elite choice under environmental constraints.

Environmental Change and Organizational Adaptation

I begin by outlining some alternative organizational reactions to environmental change, some stages in the development of Leninist parties, and some prerequisites for adaptation in Leninist systems.

Organizational Reactions to Environmental Change

All complex organizations resist reform. Stinchcombe (1965) has noted three factors creating organizational inertia: The original structure may be the most efficient for the task involved; traditional ideology and vested interests support that structure; and the organization may not have to do better than competing organizations in order to survive. Leninist parties forbid competition, they have particularly strong ideologies and particularly sweeping interests, and they have been slow to realize that a structure that is efficient for making political revolution and transforming society is, after a certain stage, no longer efficient for developing the economy or culture.

More politically, the benefits of reform are usually long-term and uncertain while the costs are immediate and clear. Research on decision-making shows that people give greater weight to potential losses than to potential gains and discount future gains when faced with immediate costs (Kahneman, Slovik, and Tversky 1982, Axelrod 1984). Consequently opponents of reform can argue that the riskiness of change outweighs the potential gains. This is particularly true in nondemocratic regimes, whose rulers enjoy the perquisites of unchallenged rule and face the risk of post-authoritarian reprisals. As O'Donnell and Schmitter have argued, the resulting delay in adaptation reduces the likelihood that a ruling party will survive transition (1986).

When confronted with a change in its environment, an organization may attempt to do one of three things: ignore the change, alter the environment, or adapt to the changed environment (Pfeffer and Salancik 1978). Of these the easiest and most likely response is to attempt to *ignore* the change. This response is most likely for organizations that lack a feedback mechanism, which in a Leninist organization is often weak. For example, during the Chinese civil war, the KMT made little effort to investigate the deterioration of social conditions and the infiltration of communists into its own organization, contributing to its defeat. In the 1990s, the CCP is content to ignore the part of its environment that Tang Tsou calls the "zone of indifference," but nevertheless allows it to exist (1983).

A second and more energetic organizational response is to attempt to *alter* the environment instead of itself. This is a particular temptation for Leninist parties, which typically believe their mission is to transform their environment and typically have created much organizational capacity to do so. A ruling party may preempt demands by good performance, satisfying demands before they are articulated. The ruling party may limit access to communication channels—for example, by controlling the media. It could mobilize supporters to drown out demands. The party may define the demand in such a way that it can declare it has already been met (the symbolic presence of other parties demonstrates the commitment to democracy). The party may conduct propaganda to criticize those making demands or deny that problems exist. It may imprison its opponents, send them into exile, subdue them with fear, or even kill them to silence them. Alternatively, the ruling party may coopt those making demands, removing them from the environment and absorbing them into the organization. Cooptation, however, may introduce pressure for change into the organization instead of silencing advocates of change, as was the case for the KMT. Therefore, cooptive parties are more likely to adapt than those with restrictive recruitment policies. As shown below, the CCP excluded the individuals and groups most likely to press for change.

The third and most difficult organizational response is to attempt to *adapt* to the changed environment. In this chapter, adaptation entails a movement along a spectrum away from totalitarianism toward democracy.[2] Movement in the opposite direction, away from democracy, is defined as reactionary change. Adaptation may occur in gradations, beginning with less use of coercion and political terror, at one extreme, up to and including full democratization at the other extreme. For analytical purposes, it is best to distinguish two kinds of adaptation. The first kind leads to greater *efficiency*. Organizational reforms are undertaken to better correspond with the changed goals of the party. This is often the initial step: Party goals change, new policies are adopted, and organizational and personnel reforms are attempted to facilitate their implementation. The key point here is that efficient adaptation is the result of changes in elite goals and policies, not their cause. The second kind of adaptation leads to greater *responsiveness* of the party to external pressures, whether domestic or foreign. This is a more advanced form of adaptation and indicates that the party is no longer able to change its environment but is now being changed by it. Efficient and responsive adaptations may be intertwined in practice, but it is best to distinguish them analytically because they result from different causal sequences, provide different scenarios of future trends, and are not interchangeable, as shown below.

Stages in the Development of Leninist Parties

The interaction of organization and environment occurs under specific historical circumstances. For analyzing the adaptability of Leninist parties, an important circumstance is the stage of development of the Leninist party itself.

As many scholars have recognized, in Leninist systems, leadership succession is both a crisis and an opportunity. It is a crisis because Leninist parties do not have regular procedures for replacing their leaders and instead wait until the death or purge of the incumbent leader to choose a successor. It is a rare opportunity for policy innovation because new leaders overturn policies with which their predecessors were identified in order to consolidate their own authority. Many of the most dramatic reforms in China and the Soviet Union immediately followed a change of leaders (Bunce 1981, Esherick and Perry 1983, Harding 1987b).

As in all organizations, goal succession is also a fundamental turning point for Leninist parties. In particular, when the revolution is won, political opponents defeated, and "class enemies" eliminated, communist parties search for new goals, in particular economic development (Lowenthal 1983, 1970). This new goal requires a new relationship between state and society—a decline in the use of coercion and political controls over social life. It also requires leaders with different skills.

Thus another important form of personnel change in Leninist systems is the transition from revolutionaries to technocrats. As new leaders emerge within the party, they introduce new skills and new agendas. Typically the new generation has more education and more exposure to foreign countries and different social backgrounds and career lines. The older generation attempts to resocialize new members into the organizational culture of the party, but this secondary socialization is only partially successful (Berger and Luckman 1966). Younger leaders tend to be less ideological—less eager to change the environment and more willing to adapt to it.

The next stage is the transition from technocrats to representatives. Increasing reliance on popular elections shifts support from the party organization toward society. Representatives pressure party leaders to adopt policies that are more responsive to public opinion, even if they conflict with party traditions. For instance, conservatives in the KMT, mostly of mainland origins, are increasingly concerned that the party is losing its commitment to reunification with the mainland as more and more Taiwanese are elected to the legislature and appointed to government posts. Reunification is more important for the KMT's traditional supporters than the electorate at large, who prefer retaining the status quo indefinitely. However, the transition between revolutionaries and technocrats is still under way in the CCP, and the emergence of representatives is but a remote possibility.

Prerequisites for Adaptation in Leninist Systems

The adaptability of Leninist parties depends on three variables: elite preferences, the environmental context, and feedback mechanisms with which the elites interpret their environment. This section briefly explains each of the variables and shows their interaction; more detailed case material follows.

Elite preferences. The first prerequisite for adaptation is that *party elites, and the preeminent leader in particular, must be willing to undertake adaptive change.* This may seem like a truism, but it alludes to the fact that Leninist parties are not unitary actors but coalitions of individuals with distinct points of view. When these parties are confronted with pressures for change, their response is influenced by, among other things, the party's ideology, its history, and the specific preferences of specific leaders. Adaptation may not occur even if it is in the best interests of the party. This was first observed by Robert Michels (1962): The individual goals of party leaders supplant the collective goals for which the party was originally formed. For instance, the CCP refused to compromise with demands for political change in 1987 and 1989, even though many of the demands were consistent with the party's own policies and might have enhanced its popularity. Leninist parties in a democratic environment may refuse to adapt even at the expense of becoming irrelevant. The French Communist Party retained its traditional policy positions and style of campaigning despite sharp declines in its share of the vote and strong internal pressures to adapt to new environmental conditions (Ross 1992). In other words, whether or not a party adapts to its environment is not an automatic response determined by organizational routines but a deliberative choice often accompanied by acute elite conflict. The crackdowns in China in 1987 and 1989 were accompanied by the demotions of party leaders who favored a more conciliatory response to pressures for political change.

Environmental context. Elite support is necessary, but not sufficient, for adaptation to ensue. In addition, *a conducive environment* must exist in which adaptation may occur. Ruling parties face separate domestic and foreign environments, and pressures from each environment may be either benign (the party is offered rewards for greater responsiveness) or hostile (the party is threatened with social turmoil or military invasion if it does not comply). (See Table 2.1.) Domestic and foreign environments are generally independent of one another, meaning that a change in one environment need not lead to a change in the other. But the interplay of benign and hostile forces is likely to have distinctive results (see Table 2.2). Above all, it is predicted that adaptability is inhibited by a hostile foreign environment; the inverse of this proposition is that adaptive change is likely to occur only when party leaders believe they face a benign foreign environment.[3] A party or its leaders may try to change the environment in order to create a less threatening atmosphere for domestic reforms. For instance, Gorbachev tried to reduce tensions with the United States in order to create a less hostile international environment in which *perestroika* and *glasnost* could unfold. In other situations, a party may take advantage of changes in its environment over which it had no control to push ahead with preferred policies. As shown below, this is what happened for the KMT: The perception of a reduced threat from China was a necessary precondition for the democratizing reforms begun in the mid-1980s. Whether adaptation takes the form of partial adaptation or full democratization depends on whether the domestic environment is benign or hostile, respectively. In other words, a ruling party is unlikely to offer democracy as a gift from above; rather, it must be demanded from below.

Table 2.1   Sources of Pressure for Change on Leninist Parties

	Benign	Hostile
Outside country (international environment)	Demands for political or economic changes in exchange for greater political, economic, or diplomatic support	Threats to existing political-economic-social system and survival of ruling party
Within society (domestic environment)	Economic or social demands that do not threaten privileged position of ruling party (demands for liberalization)	Political demands that threaten the privileged position of ruling party (demands for democratization)

Elite perceptions. Leaders may disagree on how to interpret the environment. In some cases, the environment is clearly benign or clearly hostile, but most of the time the environment is more ambiguous: Some forces benefit certain leaders but hurt others. In other words, objective measures of the environment matter less than the elite's reading of it (Oksenberg and Dickson 1991). For instance, China's leaders have been divided for nearly a century between modernizers, who see the solutions to China's problems in greater openness to the outside world; and nativists, who feel that this

Table 2.2 A Model of Adaptation: The Response of Leninist Parties to Environmental Pressures for Change

		FOREIGN PRESSURES	
		Benign	Hostile
	Benign	Partial Adaptation Respond to demands for greater liberalization, but not democratization	Minimal Adaptation Ease repression but no fundamental change in political system
DOMESTIC PRESSURES	Hostile	Full Adaptation Democratization, allow organized opposition	No Adaptation Repress domestic critics

openness has caused or exacerbated China's problems (Lieberthal 1984). Different interpretations of the environment and how best to respond to it make the decision to adapt so difficult and hotly debated. The debate over whether or not to adapt is hampered not only by the ambiguity of the environment, but also by the uncertainty of the results, as noted above. Will reform lead to the rejuvenation of the party or hasten its demise? Uncertainty and ambiguity prevent a ready answer to this question.

One means of reducing uncertainty about the domestic environment is to employ a well-functioning *feedback mechanism*. This requires not simply surveillance by the security apparatus or other internal reporting methods, which are used to control and repress society, but meaningful opportunities to engage in exit and voice—above all, having a choice in elections or the chance to publicly criticize party policies (Hirschman 1970). Leaders of Leninist parties are ambivalent about feedback: On the one hand, they recognize the need to develop links with society to ensure a popular base of support; on the other hand, they believe they know the interests of society better than society does itself. Moreover, there is a long-standing belief, at least in China, that a harmony of interests exists between leaders and led, making feedback unnecessary. Therefore, whether the party is willing to provide opportunities for exit and voice and, more important, use that feedback to change its goals and policies, or whether it rejects critical feedback and instead demands loyalty from party members and the country's citizens, is a good indicator of its potential for adaptation.

The remainder of this chapter evaluates the utility of this model of adaptation. The case material concentrates on the periods when the KMT was led by Chiang Ching-kuo and the CCP by Deng Xiaoping; it was under their respective tenures that the issue of adaptation arose. The case material highlights how the interplay of elite perspectives and environmental conditions has a decisive impact on the adaptability of Leninist parties.

Successful Adaptation by the KMT Under Chiang Ching-kuo

The KMT's evolution away from its Leninist origins began in the early 1970s with the succession of Chiang Ching-kuo to the leading posts held by his father, Chiang Kai-shek. Its evolution included the abandonment of its original mission to retake the mainland in favor of the social and economic development of Taiwan to reinforce the legitimacy of its rule. This entailed the recruitment of younger elites into all levels of the party and the gradual and fitful expansion of political participation outside the party. The democratization of the mid-1980s was not the inevitable culmination of the Taiwanization of the party over the previous decade. The two processes were categorically different and, while not mutually exclusive, were independent of one another. Democratization was contingent upon changes within the party elite and in the domestic and international environments over which party leaders had little control.

Initial Adaptation: Liberalization in the 1970s

Environmental conditions. The beginning of the Chiang Ching-kuo era coincided with sudden changes in the KMT's domestic and international environments. First of all, the international environment turned more hostile. During the early 1970s, Taiwan lost its diplomatic ties with Canada, Japan, and other Western countries that normalized relations with China (neither Taiwan nor China accept dual recognition), lost its seat in the United Nations, and watched relations between the United States and China improve, symbolized by President Richard Nixon's trip to China in 1972. With the United States simultaneously withdrawing from Vietnam, KMT leaders were less confident of U.S. protection from an attack by the PRC. This loss of international support led the KMT to place less importance on its traditional goal of retaking the mainland. The KMT transferred resources away from its military aspirations and toward the development of Taiwan's economy and society.

As Taiwan's international position deteriorated, university professors and students raised nationalistic appeals for political reform (Huang 1976). Four demands were prominent: Replace the aging representatives elected on the mainland in 1947 who still dominated the National Assembly, the Legislative Yuan, and the Control Yuan; replace veteran bureaucrats with younger, better educated, and especially Taiwanese officials; guarantee civil rights and the rule of law, including academic freedom, a free press, and the end of arbitrary arrests and imprisonment; and open the decision-making process by including experts into the deliberations. Given the special status of intellectuals in the Chinese political culture, these demands for reform meant that a crucial sector of society had given its support for the kinds of changes later carried out by the KMT. This reduced the uncertainty of how the domestic environment would react to the initial adaptation by the KMT.

These demands for political rejuvenation were not only benign, in that they did not threaten the party's power, but they were also partially orchestrated by the KMT's new generation of leaders, especially Chiang Ching-kuo and Li Huan, head of party organization and youth work in the early 1970s. These leaders used the support of intellectuals to pressure the older revolutionaries into loosening some of the party's authoritarian controls and thereby improve its image (Huang 1976, H. Peng 1990b). Support for democracy, however, was a potentially hostile threat because it required accountability of incumbent leaders and the possible decline of the party's near monopoly on political power. Calls for Taiwan's independence, which challenged the KMT's claim to be the ruling party of all China and not just an island off its coast, were present at this time, but not part of the mainstream. This was a more radical demand guaranteed to elicit quick and harsh action by the government. Most demands were for greater liberalization and to a lesser extent democracy, but not revolutionary change.

As indicated by the adaptation model, the combination of a generally benign domestic environment and a hostile foreign environment led to an easing of repression, but the status quo was essentially maintained. The most significant changes at this time occurred within the party (see below), not the political system itself. Although supplementary elections for the central legislative organs were held in 1972, only the seats vacated by death or resignation were open for reelection; incumbents, who held the vast majority of seats, did not have to run for reelection. Despite some relaxation of the KMT's authoritarian controls over society, martial law remained in force and the opposition was not allowed to organize its activities.

Elite preferences and responsiveness. The leadership succession that brought Chiang Ching-kuo to power was an intergenerational transition. This is a more significant test of a party's adaptability than an intragenerational transition because it brings new experiences and preferences into the elite (Huntington 1968, 14–15). The new generation of leaders believed that more rapid political reform was necessary for the party to survive. Chiang's influence had spread from the political warfare system, the security apparatus, and the Youth Corps during the 1950s into the government beginning in the mid-1960s, but by the early 1970s he still did not have much support within the party. He was confronted with party leaders who were more senior than himself and who had enjoyed long tenure in their posts. One means of building support for himself with the party bureaucracy was the "Taiwanization" (*bentuhua*, literally indigenization) of the party. This strategy had two components: On the one hand, Taiwanese KMT members replaced mainlanders in local party offices; on the other hand, central party and government posts were filled by young political elites who had been raised on Taiwan but most of whom had been born on the mainland or were the children of mainlanders.

The Taiwanization strategy had elements of both the efficient and responsive forms of adaptation. It was an efficient adaptation because it replaced the older generation of revolutionaries with a younger, better educated, and more technologically sophisticated generation of leaders. This facilitated Chiang Ching-kuo's succession strategy by giving him a network of supporters at all levels of the party bureaucracy. It also facilitated the shift in the party's work from reunification with the mainland to issues of local development by bringing the necessary skills into the appropriate positions. Taiwanization was also a responsive adaptation. By replacing mainlanders with Taiwanese in local posts where the people had direct contact with the party, the party gained the image of being more responsive to local issues. By expanding opportunities for political participation within the party, it preempted them from joining the "brain drain" abroad or the opposition at home. But coopting these potential threats into the party also brought supporters of more extensive political reforms into the party. These advocates for change had a major impact on the KMT's support for democratization in the mid-1980s.

For more than a decade, proponents and opponents of political reform competed at the central level for key personnel appointments, the support of Chiang Ching-kuo, and consequently the ability to decide how the party would respond to its environment. The main conflict was between the Youth Corps, headed by Li Huan, which preferred to adapt to the environment, and the political warfare system, headed by Wang Sheng, which was in charge of security and favored a more reactionary response (Shen 1986). Chiang's ties to both men went back to the 1930s and 1940s (Winckler 1988, 156); during the KMT's state-building efforts of the 1950s, he put Li in charge of youth work and Wang in charge of security and political-military affairs. During the early 1970s, Li Huan was simultaneously the director of the central organization commission, which was in charge of personnel assignments and the party's election strategy; the Anti-Communist Youth Corps, from which many of the new party leaders were drawn; and the Revolutionary Practice Institute, the main cadre training school. These concurrent posts facilitated the implementation of the Taiwanization policy but eventually caused resentment by those who believed they were not benefiting from the changes he was bringing about. Even some of its beneficiaries grew impatient with the slow pace of political reform and their failure to receive party nominations for elected posts. They left the party and joined the opposition: The most obvious example is Hsu Hsin-liang, who later became chairman of the leading opposition party, the Democratic Progressive Party (DPP). The weak showing by the KMT in 1977 elections and antigovernment demonstrations against alleged election tampering by the KMT forced Li's resignation. The conflict between the Youth Corps and the political warfare system did not end with Li's resignation, but rather contributed to the political stalemate of the 1980s (see below).

The KMT also responded to changes in its domestic environment by invigorating the election process as a feedback mechanism on party performance. Rather than simply nominate candidates with the political and financial support of local factions, as had been done in the past, the KMT began to nominate candidates who were also more popular, more competent, and more attractive (Chen Yangde 1987; Chen Yitian 1984). At the same time, the party continued to limit the political participation of non-KMT candidates. While it tolerated the more moderate opposition candidates, it also tried to alter its environment by denying some petitions for candidacy, imprisoning some opponents, and coopting others. It did not allow opposition politicians to organize themselves, campaign together, offer a common platform, or have access to the media. It provided only a narrow window for campaigning and canceled some election results. In short, the KMT expanded opportunities for participation by the politically ambitious within the party, but continued to restrict participation outside the party.

Although elections remained far from fair and open, the change in the KMT's election strategy and the greater tolerance for independent candidates had several unintended consequences for the KMT and its transition from Leninism. First, the election of candidates chosen for their own popularity and not simply their party loyalty meant that they became increasingly autonomous. Their ability to win elections without the KMT's formal nomination limited the party's authority over them. In time, local government leaders became more powerful than their party counterparts, a reversal of the traditional arrangement. Second, the opposition used election campaigns both to criticize the KMT and to educate voters on how democracy is supposed to work (Peng 1990b, 11; interview data). The KMT's own propaganda, including its public education policy, also emphasized the superiority of democracy over other forms of government. Over time, voters became more convinced of the merits of this argument and more frustrated at the absence of representative democracy under the KMT's rule.

Environmental change. In the late 1970s, the KMT's domestic and inter-national environments both grew increasingly hostile, leading to reac-tionary changes in party policy. First, the United States announced in December 1978 that it would establish diplomatic relations with China and cancel its mutual defense treaty with Taiwan. The KMT's immediate response was to cancel scheduled elections. This step was taken without prior consultation with the opposition or an announcement of a new date for elections, suggesting that the KMT was retreating from its commitment to democratization. Second, the increasing assertiveness of the opposition led to anti-KMT demonstrations in Chungli in 1977 and Kaohsiung in December 1979. After the 1979 demonstrations, most prominent opposition politicians were arrested, suggesting again that the KMT would not tolerate an organized opposition. Informal negotiations with the opposition were suspended, increasing the uncertainty and tension between the two sides. Finally, China stepped up its campaign to reunify Taiwan with the main-land. While offering various inducements, it also pointedly reminded Taiwan's leaders that it reserved the right to use military force to achieve reunification and would not remain patient indefinitely. The KMT used this threat as a rationale to repress political protest. These hostile trends benefit-ed hard-liners in the party. Wang Sheng was added to the Central Standing Committee (CSC, the equivalent of the Politburo in other Leninist parties) and Liang Hsiao-huang, a member of the political warfare system, became director of the organization commission, which was responsible for person-nel appointments and election strategy.

Summary. At the beginning of the Chiang Ching-kuo era, the interplay of environmental conditions led to a change in the priorities of the KMT's goals and the limited liberalization of its control over society, but stopped far short of a transition from authoritarian rule. The KMT's power was not weakened as a result of these changes; indeed, some have argued that the better-educated younger elites made the authoritarian rule of the party more efficient and sophisticated (Li and White 1990, Peng 1990a). The Taiwanization program temporarily reduced pressures for greater political participation by channeling participation into the KMT without changing the political system itself. Any challenges to the KMT's privileged position were strongly and immediately repressed. However, hostile demands were increasingly raised as the opposition and even KMT members who had been passed over for official nomination sought to be elected. Moreover, the loss of formal ties with the United States increased Taiwan's vulnerabil-ity and made the KMT less tolerant of political instability. As central party leaders debated the appropriate response to environmental pressures for change, Taiwan's political system alternated between periods of "hard" and "soft" authoritarianism (Winckler 1984).

Full Adaptation: The Beginning of Democratization in the 1980s

Party elites. Party leadership factions stalemated in the early 1980s as Chiang Ching-kuo's health deteriorated and no successor was apparent. This conflict was resolved by 1985, not as a result of elite consensus but by a series of personnel transfers and scandals implicating the hard-liners in the party.

First, reactionary leader Wang Sheng was exiled from Taiwan. Chiang was bothered by Wang's growing political ambitions, symbolized by the creation of the "Liu Shao-kang" office, an informal but powerful body. During Chiang's prolonged illness, this office usurped decisionmaking authority from the formal party organs. In May 1983, Chiang ordered the disbanding of the office, fired Wang as director of the General Political Warfare Department, and in November named him ambassador to Paraguay. Because he was posted outside Taiwan, Wang was forced to resign from the Central Standing Committee. Wang's exile eliminated the main spokesman for reactionary policies within the KMT elite. Second, the KMT's security sector was involved in the murder of a biographer of Chiang outside his California home in October 1984. The murders demonstrated the lengths to which some in the party were willing to go to repress its critics, including assassination in a foreign country. In 1985, military intelligence chief Wang Hsi-ling and two Bamboo Gang leaders were tried and convicted in Taiwan's courts for the murder. Third, a financial scandal involving the suspected bribery and improper investments of several high-ranking KMT officials forced the resignations of two government ministers and the KMT's secretary-general. Others implicated in the scandal received lesser or no punishments (Hsiung 1986). These scandals further damaged the party's reputation and led not only to increased public criticism of the government but also to a reevaluation of the condition of the party by its own leaders. As hard-liners were replaced by more moderate leaders, many of whom were beneficiaries of the Taiwanization program, the party softened its stance toward its critics. In 1983, informal negotiations with the opposition resumed, and the following year Li Huan was appointed minister of education, further indicating the shift toward more responsive policies.

Environmental conditions. The domestic environment grew more hostile in the early 1980s, partially in response to the KMT's reactionary policies. Demands for democracy grew in intensity. Confidence in the KMT's responsiveness was falling: The revelations of recent scandals increased the belief that the KMT would not be responsive to public demands without the inclusion of alternative politicians within Taiwan's political system. Beginning in 1981, opposition politicians organized mutual assistance offices to pool resources for elections and political rallies and grew closer to becoming a formal political party. This finally happened in the summer of 1986, when opposition leaders formed the DPP, the first and still the largest opposition party. Indirect communication between the KMT and the opposition reduced the uncertainty about the ultimate goals of the DPP and the likelihood of instability, facilitating the KMT's willingness to adapt to this major change in its domestic environment and accept for the first time an organized opposition.

Changes in the KMT's international environment also facilitated its adaptation. The KMT experienced sharper foreign pressure to democratize its political system by lifting martial law and the emergency regulations that had been in force since its arrival in Taiwan in the late 1940s. Congressional hearings following the murder of Chiang's biographer in 1985 brought unwanted publicity to the authoritarian nature of Taiwan's politics and threatened to further reduce U.S. support for the KMT regime. The KMT was vulnerable to shifts in U.S. support because, as Tun-jen Cheng put it, Taiwan was a security consumer and the United States was its supplier (1989, 487–488). Once Chiang decided to lift martial law, he made the initial announcement to Katherine Graham, publisher of the *Washington Post*, because the intended audience was the KMT's supporters and critics abroad, especially in Washington, D.C., not in Taiwan (interview data).

The most significant change in the KMT's international environment was the perception by KMT leaders of a reduced threat from China. During the early 1980s, economic reform became the main focus of the CCP and the Chinese government. One result was that defense spending declined and the armed forces were reduced by over a million troops. While the Taiwan issue remained an extremely sensitive area of concern in the PRC's diplomatic relations, China allowed increased economic, social, and scientific exchanges between Taiwan and other countries with whom China had diplomatic ties. China's leaders maintained the right to use force against Taiwan if necessary to achieve reunification, but offered opportunities for Taiwanese to invest and travel in China. Taiwan investors pressured the KMT to loosen its strict policy of prohibiting all contacts, exchanges, and negotiations with the mainland in order to tap into the cheap labor and natural resources available in China. Moreover, with younger and more moderate leaders replacing older revolutionaries in the CCP, KMT leaders felt China was less likely to attempt a risky effort to reunify Taiwan by force. The most hostile element in the KMT's international environment was now more benign.

Interviews with several KMT officials support a key proposition of the adaptation model: The moderation of the Chinese threat was a necessary precondition for the KMT's decision to enact widespread political reforms beginning in 1986–1987. China has always reserved the right to use force if Taiwan declared independence, repeatedly refused to negotiate reunification, acquired nuclear weapons, or became politically unstable. In the past, this latter threat had been the KMT's rationale for delaying political reform. But the situation had now changed. On the basis of informal communications with the DPP, KMT leaders calculated that instability rising from democratization would be limited and manageable. They also believed that China would not divert resources away from the economy toward the symbolic goal of reunification and that China's reliance on foreign capital and export markets would prevent it from risking a diplomatic uproar by taking military action against Taiwan.

Elite responsiveness. When martial law was lifted and democratization began in 1986–1987, the necessary conditions for adaptation had been met: Party leaders, and Chiang in particular, supported the creation of a more democratic system; changes in the domestic and international environments created a context most likely to result in full adaptation; and party elites agreed on how to interpret the environment. Opponents of political reform within the party were marginalized after the earlier scandals. Chiang recognized that his life would soon be over and that the democratization of his party and his country would give him a favorable historical legacy. His closest advisers, the product of the Taiwanization program of the past decade, were strongly supportive of the relaxation of authoritarian controls. While few of them could be mistaken for Jeffersonian democrats, their exposure to Western democracies, the democratic values taught in Taiwan's schools, and the ineffectiveness of the existing political system convinced many of them that democratization managed by the KMT was the best means to maintain their hold on power, increase support for the KMT at home, and improve the KMT's reputation abroad. With an organized opposition ready to challenge its status as a ruling party, KMT leaders decided that refusing to adapt to the changed environment was a greater threat than setting and enforcing the terms and pace of political change.[4]

The KMT's willingness to adapt to its environment continued after Chiang's death in 1988. Lee Teng-hui, who succeeded Chiang as head of the party and state, has extended the commitment to democratization charted by Chiang. Beginning with a limited power base, Lee deepened the democratization of Taiwan's political system (Ling and Myers 1992). During his tenure, the period of national emergency (i.e., the communist threat) was declared over, allowing for the election of new national representative bodies. Elections have been held for previously appointed positions: mayors of Taipei and Kaohsiung, governor, and president. Moreover, Lee has been active in promoting an independent identity for Taiwan in the international sphere, in particular seeking observer status in the United Nations and GATT and establishing quasi-official bilateral links with China. Despite low diplomatic standing, Taiwan's record of socioeconomic progress and successful democratization has led to improved economic and political ties with many countries. It has been helped in this regard by the inevitable comparison with China, which resisted the wave of democracy that swept over much of the rest of the world during the 1980s.

But these efforts have so far not benefited the KMT at the ballot box. The KMT has continued to lose public support despite its efforts to be more responsive and despite the continued trend of having more Taiwanese in top party, government, and military positions. Although Lee Teng-hui won the 1996 presidential election with a clear majority, his party has suffered declines in all other elections. The KMT received only 46.9 percent of the vote in the 1995 Legislative Yuan elections (down from 60.5 percent in 1992) and 49.7 percent of the vote in the 1996 National Assembly elections (down from over 70 percent in 1991). In the 1997 county and municipal elections, the KMT for the first time came in second, receiving 42.1 percent of the vote compared to the DPP's 43.5 percent. As a result, the KMT won only eight of the twenty-three county and municipal races, the DPP won twelve, and independents won the remaining three. Despite its recent efforts to adapt to Taiwan's changing society, the KMT suffers from its reputation for corruption and inability to uphold law and order (ironically, given its authoritarian past).

As a result of these trends, splits have emerged within the party that may lessen its ability to remain in power. During Lee Teng-hui's tenure as president and party chairman, the party divided between his supporters (the mainstream faction) and his opponents (the nonmainstream faction). Well-publicized battles between the party mainstream and some of the KMT's most popular politicians, such as then governor James Soong and former minister of justice Ma Ying-jeou, further damaged its reputation. In 1993, a group of KMT legislators identified with the New KMT Alliance split off to form the Chinese New Party to protest the influence of moneyed interests in elections, Lee's growing power (particularly his success at replacing the older generation of mainlanders with his supporters in the government and party bureaucracy), and the relaxed commitment to reunification with China, a long-cherished party goal. Similarly, as the DPP softened its stand on Taiwan independence to gain more votes, its radical faction split off to form its own party. With no party in a dominant position, negotiations and coalition building are replacing ideological conflicts in the legislative process. This has helped consolidate Taiwan's democratization (Tien and Chu 1996), but the blurring of party lines has cost the KMT at the polls.

Democratization also changed the KMT's Leninist nature. The KMT no longer has a monopoly on political organization, traditional party ideology is less relevant as a guide to policy, party cells in the government and military have been deactivated, and the party no longer controls the groups it used to mobilize society on behalf of regime goals. As the influence of elected representatives rose in the party relative to first-generation revolutionaries and second-generation technocrats, both of whom relied on the authoritarian controls of the state to achieve their goals, the advantages of a

Leninist party were abandoned for the sake of electoral competition. Once the KMT began to adapt to popular pressures from Taiwan's society and stopped trying to transform it, the Leninist model was no longer relevant for the KMT, either as an organizing principle or as an analytical tool.

Summary. Actions taken by the KMT in response to environmental conditions conform to the predictions made by the adaptation model. Its adaptation was facilitated by changes in the party elite, resulting from both the generational succession begun in the early 1970s and the intra-elite strife of the 1980s. These changes brought into positions of influence younger leaders who supported adapting to changes in Taiwan's society rather than trying to alter that environment with propaganda and persecution, as in the past. This change within the party elite coincided with rising demands for greater democracy from the domestic environment and greater incentives for granting those demands. In particular, the perception by KMT leaders that China was markedly less hostile toward Taiwan provided a necessary precondition for democratizing reforms. Although the KMT made the transition from Leninism and authoritarian rule look relatively easy, a different set of circumstances (e.g., the continued presence of hard-liners among the inner core of leaders, or a less benign perception of China's intentions) might have resulted in a different outcome, or at least a less smooth transition. The KMT continues to face the challenge of adapting to ongoing changes in Taiwan's society in order to remain in power without totally abandoning party traditions and alienating its core supporters.

Limited Adaptation by the CCP Under Deng Xiaoping

The initial conditions of the post-Mao period were highly conducive to adaptation by the CCP. Beginning in 1977, leaders committed to economic and political change returned to top posts. The party abandoned the utopian policies of Mao Zedong and his radical supporters and deemphasized ideology and politics for the sake of economic development based on market-oriented principles. The domestic and foreign environments facilitated these changes. Weary of Maoist campaigns, Chinese society welcomed the opportunity to focus on material well-being over political correctness. The "crisis of confidence" evident at Mao's death was ameliorated by the economic and political policies associated with Deng Xiaoping. Although China faced a military threat from the Soviet Union along its northern border and fought a brief war with Vietnam in 1979, improving ties with the United States balanced this threat. Closer ties with the West also provided China with new sources of capital, technology, and markets, necessary ingredients for its modernization drive.

The CCP adapted to environmental conditions as they existed at the time of Mao's death in 1976 but subsequently tried to alter the environment rather than be further changed by it. Whereas the KMT undertook political reform for political goals (i.e., popular support and political stability), the CCP used political reform primarily as a means to economic ends. Consequently, the reforms of the post-Mao era have been generally limited to the efficient form of adaptation. In contrast, the CCP responded to recurring episodes of spontaneous popular demands for more democracy by altering the environment with propaganda and repression rather than adapting. But this consistent response was not predetermined. Each episode occasioned intense debate over how to interpret and respond to environmental conditions and about the implications of adaptation for the party's survival.

Elite preferences.   One of the unexpected consequences of the Cultural Revolution was that many of China's leaders personally experienced the poverty and arbitrariness of the political system they helped create. During the early 1970s, many future reformers were punished for their supposed crimes by being sent to the countryside, where they saw for themselves how little the communist revolution had improved the lives of most Chinese. Thus, they acquired first-hand feedback on the performance of the party, the declining popular confidence in the party's ability to rule, and the desire for better standards of living.

After Mao died and his Gang of Four followers were arrested in 1976, most remaining party leaders were aware of the pressing need for economic modernization and a respite from the political turmoil of the late Maoist period. At the momentous Third Plenum of December 1978, the party called an end to the period of class struggle and declared that economic modernization would become the primary task of the party. This shift in the party's work has been repeatedly reaffirmed. Even in 1987 and 1989, when the CCP cracked down on student demonstrations advocating democratic reforms, party leaders were quick to declare their continued commitment to economic reform despite the political repression.

This shift toward economic work was accompanied by the decline of ideology as a rationale, much less a guide, to policy. Hu Qiaomu, a leading party theorist, set the tone for this shift in a June 1978 speech advocating the use of economic principles to guide the economy. The controversial nature of this proposal is suggested by the long gap between the delivery of the speech in June and its release in the press in October. The amount of time devoted to political study was reduced to allow more time for professional work and, by extension, economic productivity. The growing irrelevance of ideology as a guide to policy was epitomized in a December 1984 *People's Daily* article that concluded that Marx and Lenin had written in times and places different from China's present and therefore could not solve China's problems; this conclusion was later amended to read *all* of China's problems, but the point was clear (*RMRB* 1984).

The shift in the party's work toward economics was accompanied by changes in the policy process. During the late Maoist era, the policy process was characterized by factional competition, "empirical" evidence drawn from model units, and attempts to gain the support of Mao, the ultimate arbiter of policy. In the post-Mao period, the policy process became more institutionalized. In their study of policymaking in post-Mao China, Lieberthal and Oksenberg note the goal of China's leaders has been to "forge nationally accepted, more rigorous methods of analyzing policy choices and for decentralizing the decision-making process" (1988, 158). In particular, professionalism has replaced ideological slogans, the quality of data on which decisions are made has improved, reliance on feasibility studies has encouraged closer consultation during the planning stage, and economic signals are gradually replacing the personal connections and bureaucratic deals that characterized the Chinese economy and policy process in the past. Central ministries and local governments with an interest in a given issue negotiate over the final outcome in a depoliticized atmosphere. Regularly scheduled meetings bring together central and local officials to review and discuss major policies. Between meetings, the circulation of documents facilitates horizontal and vertical communication throughout the bureaucracy.

In support of the new goal of economic modernization, a series of political reforms were attempted. The party and state bureaucracies were reorganized to make them more efficient for economic work and to undo the damage of the Cultural Revolution. Party and government personnel from the central to the local level who were unsympathetic to or unqualified for the reform initiatives were replaced, and a new generation of better-educated and more highly skilled cadres was recruited (Ch'i 1991, Lee 1991). The separation of the party from administrative matters (*dangzheng fenkai*) was envisioned to reduce the meddling of party cadres in daily operations. A three-year rectification campaign tried to educate veteran cadres about the new party line, but it was hampered by unclear signals from central leaders on the specific goals of the campaign (Dickson 1990). All these efforts were designed to make the party's work support economic development; in other words, the party engaged in efficient adaptation.

As indicated above, efficient adaptation is triggered by a change of leaders, as occurred in the succession to Mao. It is not designed to make the party more responsive to domestic pressures for change. Even Deng Xiaoping, who spearheaded the attack on the party and state bureaucracies and cadres who were unenthusiastic about economic modernization, put strict limits around possible political reforms. The Four Cardinal Principles announced in 1979 allowed no challenge to the privileged position of the party or its basic ideological line: The purpose of reform was to improve the party, not challenge or dismantle it (Deng 1979). Throughout the 1980s, the party was deeply divided between those who believed political reform was necessary for further economic development and those who felt that previous economic reforms had already created excessive instability and that the proposed political reforms would further weaken the party's leadership. This lack of consensus effectively killed the most ambitious proposals. Even Zhao Ziyang's proposed civil service system, the centerpiece of his speech to the Thirteenth Party Congress in 1987, was quickly shelved and not revived until 1993 (Burns 1989; Zhao 1987). His proposal to use objective criteria for personnel hiring would have undermined the political patronage that largely determined such decisions. The absence of elite consensus has prevented political reform in China from venturing beyond bureaucratic changes, that is, efficient adaptation.

The domestic environment and elite responsiveness. The domestic environment initially facilitated the party's reform efforts. After the unrelenting mass campaigns of the late Maoist period, most Chinese resisted mobilization efforts on behalf of radical policies. Under Deng's leadership, the CCP rehabilitated thousands of victims of previous campaigns and restored their political rights, granted greater artistic and academic freedoms, allowed goods and services to be bought and sold on the market outside state control, and abandoned political campaigns. These new policies depoliticized much of everyday life for most Chinese and resulted in significant, if limited, liberalization (Harding 1986). Although the reforms proved popular, they are best understood as a "revolution from above." Society was not involved directly in the decisionmaking process and had little recourse if they were harmed by the reforms and few options if the party chose to retract them (for opposing views on the role of society in the initiation of reforms, see Hartford 1985, Kelliher 1992). While individual complaints could be articulated (in letters to the editor, visits to the local government and party offices, etc.), there were no legitimate means of offering feedback or promoting organized political interests, such as lobbying or forming a political party. Despite the institutionalization and decentralization of the policy process outlined above, interest groups and concerned citizens still did not have ready access to the arenas in which policies were made.

Post-Mao reforms brought relief not only from the economic destitution of Maoist policies, but also from the overt pressures for political conformity. State-society relations have been altered from the totalitarian impulses of the Cultural Revolution to more complicated patterns of behavior. Individuals were encouraged to distrust authority and to think for themselves instead of relying on the official interpretation of the "correct line." Personal trauma suffered during the Cultural Revolution further undermined the legitimacy of the party and political system. These developments planted the seeds for a civil society that emerged in the post-Mao period (Whyte 1992). On the one hand, the "zone of indifference" widened to allow a greater scope of traditional folk practices, artistic expression, and recreational activities (Tsou 1983). This zone of indifference was ill-defined and subject to expansion and contraction over time, but it made possible some kinds of behavior that were unthinkable during the Cultural Revolution, when a person's fashion sense and taste in art acquired political meaning. On the other hand, a more orderly civil society gradually took shape, a public sphere between state and society. Individuals were increasingly able to organize to pursue their collective interests, particularly if those interests were economic or cultural in nature. These groups included local chambers of commerce, study groups, religious associations, and hobby clubs (White 1993, Solinger 1992). Autonomous labor unions and groups with overtly political goals emerged only briefly in the course of the 1989 demonstrations; their leaders and members were harshly dealt with after the crackdown, indicating the limits of permissible action within the new civil society as well as the CCP's unwillingness to engage in responsive adaptation.

China has experienced several episodes of political protest during the post-Mao era. The party viewed these unmobilized demands as challenging its authority and threatening its rule. The CCP reacted as it has consistently throughout the history of the CCP: by persecuting the protestors, rejecting both the form and content of their demands, and when necessary retreating from the policies that made the protests possible. The Democracy Wall movement of 1978–1979 had been instrumental to Deng's attack on Hua Guofeng and promotion of economic and political reform. Urban intellectuals and workers who resented the abuse of power and privilege in the Cultural Revolution spoke out in favor of Deng and the loosening of political controls over most aspects of their lives. But once the movement began to question Deng's own abuse of power and the legitimacy of the CCP, it was quickly repressed and many of its participants were imprisoned (Nathan 1985). In 1980, the CCP also deleted from the constitution the right to display big-character wall posters, the most common medium of political protest in China. An experiment with democratic local elections in 1980–1981 overlapped with the final stages of the Democracy Wall movement (McCormick 1990, especially chapter 4; Womack 1982). Party leaders tried to alter the environment by equating demands for greater democracy with the actions of Red Guards during the Cultural Revolution and suggesting that those who sought democracy would only bring chaos, not positive results (*RMRB* 1981; Deng 1980b, 341, 351; Cheng 1981, 187).

The slow pace of political reforms led to student demonstrations in Shanghai and elsewhere in the winter of 1986–1987. The party reacted by repressing this student-led protest, expelling several of the most prominent critics from the party (Fang Lizhi, Liu Binyan, and Wang Ruowang) and intensifying its propaganda campaign against "spiritual pollution" and "bourgeois liberalization," the supposedly evil foreign influences that gave rise to the protests. General-Secretary Hu Yaobang was accused of failing to prevent the spread of these influences and forced to resign his post in January 1987. His death in April 1989 was the catalyst for the popular democracy movement. The original goals of the movement were consistent with the party's own policies: the control of inflation and crackdowns on corruption and nepotism among party and state cadres. As the movement escalated, the party could not reach a consensus on how to address the demands: Some counseled compromise, others advocated the party's traditional strategy of rejecting the demands and repressing the protestors. With the elite stalemated, the demands of some protestors grew more hostile: the resignation of Deng Xiaoping, Li Peng, and other leaders, and the recognition of autonomous student and labor unions. The latter demand would have created organized political interests outside the party's control and would have marked a fundamental change in this Leninist system. Hard-liners in the party ultimately prevailed and the "counterrevolutionary" movement was violently ended, with many participants imprisoned or executed (Manion 1990).

In each episode of unmobilized political protest, the CCP refused to adapt to these pressures for change and instead attempted to alter its environment with a crackdown on dissent, propaganda to disparage the demands of the protestors, and a retreat from even limited political reforms. But the environment was ambiguous to party elites; the decision to alter the environment came only after sharp conflict with those who advocated adaptation. The CCP also sought to isolate itself from changes in its domestic environment. After the June 1989 crackdown, the CCP banned the recruitment of private entrepreneurs (Lam 1989a, 1989b), although local officials still found ways of getting around this ban. The ban sought to prevent entrepreneurial interests, antithetical to party traditions but of growing importance to the economy and society, from influencing the party from within. Whereas the KMT coopted potential threats, the CCP excluded them. By banning entrepreneurs from the party, it again signaled its reluctance to adapt to the domestic environment it helped create.

Party conservatives used the pro-democracy movement as a rationale to slow economic reforms temporarily, but the reform momentum returned following Deng Xiaoping's favorable comments regarding markets and privatization during his Southern Tour of 1992. However, party leaders were intent on sticking to Deng's formula of economic dynamism and political order. Hard-liners saw evidence of the dangers of adaptation in the experience of other Leninist parties. Poland's Solidarity movement and Gorbachev's *glasnost* indicated that political reforms weakened Leninist regimes by exposing them to increased demands from the domestic environment. The demise of ruling communist parties after 1989 confirmed such fears. Even the KMT, which had previously shown how an authoritarian party could achieve economic and social development, lost its political monopoly following the democratization of its political system. In each case, the reform of Leninist parties led to outcomes that were distasteful to CCP hard-liners. With the cost of adaptation plain to see and the benefits highly uncertain, hard-liners have been able to hold the line against political reform.

Even after Deng's death in 1997, his successors showed no inclination to undertake political reform. Jiang Zemin's report to the Fifteenth Party Congress in September 1997 announced new policies of privatization but made little mention of political reform (Jiang 1997). Central party leaders who were seen as most likely to favor political reform, such as Qiao Shi and Hu Qili, were forced into retirement. Although most of the original generation of revolutionaries are now gone, the second generation of technocrats shows no sign of being willing or able to solve the dilemma of how to open the political system without jeopardizing the CCP's hold on power.

The one exception to this general rule is the spread of village elections. Beginning in 1987, but especially since 1991, elections for various village officials have been held in many areas of China. They are designed to make local governments more accountable to popular concerns—and thereby forestall political instability in the countryside—and also to appease foreign critics calling for democratization (Kelliher 1997). In some areas, elections have improved the quality of local governance by eliminating ineffective or domineering leaders and facilitating the implementation of even unpopular policies, such as family planning and taxation. In other areas, however, party and government officials hand-pick candidates, prevent discussion of issues, and rig the election results to suit their needs (O'Brien 1994). Whether these elections can be the type of feedback mechanism that allowed the KMT to successfully engage in responsive adaptation remains to be seen.

The foreign environment and elite responsiveness. The international environment has been largely benign during the post-Mao period. Foreign countries provided economic, technological, and diplomatic support for China's modernization strategy. Diplomatic relations with the United States were normalized in 1978, coinciding with the CCP's Third Plenum, generally seen as the beginning of the reform era. Tensions with the Soviet Union declined, allowing China to divert resources from the military to the civilian economy. During the early 1980s, China also gained access to most international lending institutions. Through a combination of foreign loans, joint ventures, direct foreign investment, production agreements, and other projects, China's economy became more closely linked with the global market. Participation in international institutions encouraged several market-oriented reforms, including price reform.

Greater involvement with the international community facilitated economic modernization, but its political and social impact was more ambiguous to party leaders. Proponents of modernization believed China's hopes
for rapid modernization were tied to greater exposure to and involvement in
the international community. They were willing to accept some political
and cultural change as the price of economic modernization, but underesti-
mated the extent of those foreign influences and the implications for the
unquestioned rule of the party. Nativistic leaders saw the increasing foreign
influence as detrimental to the party, Marxist-Leninist orthodoxy, and
Chinese civilization more generally (Lieberthal 1984, Harding 1987b).
They were concerned with rising crime rates, the reemergence of youth
gangs, drug use, prostitution, and other "unhealthy tendencies" they considered to be the direct, if unintended, consequences of reform. Foreign goods,
values, and visitors brought with them an alternative way of life and outlook. The nativists correctly saw that political and economic values could
not be separated, and consequently preferred to limit foreign economic
relations in order to preserve the political system upon which their power
rested. The proponents of political reform ran up against the kinds of
appeals to tradition and ideology that often create obstacles to adaptation
(Hannan and Freeman 1989): the party's avowed adherence to Marxism-
Leninism, the traditional ban on organized interests outside the party's control, widespread concerns about the uncertain future of the party if it undertook fundamental reform, and the self-interest of lower- and middle-level
cadres, whose powers and privileges would be sharply reduced if the party
reduced its leadership role.

In the latter part of the 1980s, party leaders were more willing to
ignore the pressures from the international environment than adapt to or
even alter that environment. Although China is dependent on foreign countries for key resources, party leaders were not too concerned with how
domestic policies would affect access to those resources. Following the student demonstration of 1986–1987, Deng Xiaoping dismissed the danger of
foreign reaction to a crackdown on dissidents; in his view, China had not
suffered for imprisoning prominent dissident Wei Jingsheng in 1979 and
was unlikely to be punished if the party repressed its critics again (Deng
1987, 19). Foreign criticisms of China's human rights record, population
planning program, policy toward Tibet, export of arms, and unfair trading
practices were denounced as meddling in its internal affairs. Hard-liners
among the CCP elite portray the foreign environment as hostile and a challenge to the party's authority and the sovereignty of the country.

Following the Tiananmen crackdown and the collapse of communism
in Eastern Europe and the Soviet Union, China was no longer seen as a
pacesetter but as the last major holdout of a failed political and economic
experiment. In the wake of 1989's repression, China's media protested
"peaceful evolution," an alleged plot by Western countries to gradually

change China's political system through economic and other contacts. These allegations were largely true. The United States, in particular, has used a variety of bilateral and multilateral channels to try to change China's policies on trade, human rights, and Taiwan. U.S.-China negotiations over China's entry into the World Trade Organization dragged on for years without resolution. At the beginning of the Clinton administration, the United States also tried to link improvements in China's human rights record to renewal of its most-favored-nation trade status. The lack of cooperation from China and support from Congress and U.S. business forced President Bill Clinton to delink the issues (Lampton 1994), but the United States continued to pressure China on human rights issues in bilateral discussions and by annually supporting proposed resolutions to criticize China in the United Nations Commission on Human Rights (which China was able to defeat). China did release some prominent dissidents into exile (most notably Wei Jingsheng and Wang Juntao), but there has been no general amnesty for China's political prisoners and no tolerance for political dissent. Although the intensity of criticism from foreign governments diminished during the 1990s, nongovernmental human rights groups, many led by Chinese émigrés, continued their efforts to promote political freedom in China.

The Taiwan issue remained the focal point of U.S.-China tensions. Although the United States repeatedly pledged to abide by the "one China" policy, China vehemently protested what it perceived as tacit support for Taiwan's bid for international recognition. When the United States issued a visa to Lee Teng-hui to visit Cornell University in 1995 and sent two aircraft carrier fleets toward Taiwan during the missile crisis of 1996, China saw a threat to the integrity of the Chinese nation-state. Intense diplomacy eventually improved the atmosphere of U.S.-China relations, culminating in the Clinton-Jiang summit of October 1997, but the Taiwan issue— together with trade and human rights issues—renewed fears of foreign meddling in China's internal affairs, creating a hostile foreign environment that would inhibit the prospects for political liberalization at home.

Summary. The CCP's adaptability has been inhibited by several factors. The transition from revolutionaries to technocrats is not yet complete; consequently, the conflict between nativist and reformist sentiments remains unresolved. Because elections are so insignificant in China's political system, there is no institutionalized feedback mechanism on the party's performance. For the same reason, the party lacks "representatives" who derive their power from social support. As a result, party elites have little incentive to adapt to societal interests that conflict with the party's institutional interests or the elites' individual interests. Whereas general agreement exists on the need for economic reform and limited liberalization to facilitate it, a lasting consensus on the desirability of political reform has been elusive. Because of the ambiguity of the environment and the uncertain outcomes of political reform, the CCP has limited itself to efficient adaptations and forgone more responsive adaptations to its rapidly changing domestic environment.

Conclusion

This analysis of the evolution of the KMT and the CCP shows how the adaptability of Leninist parties is influenced by the three independent variables identified at the beginning of this chapter. First, leadership transition facilitated adaptation by changing the preferences of party leaders. The succession from Chiang Kai-shek to Chiang Ching-kuo initiated an intergenerational transition that brought younger leaders with new values and new goals into the top ranks of the party. This led to changes in party policy in the 1970s (notably the Taiwanization program) and eventually the democratization of Taiwan's political system after 1986. The CCP's role changed dramatically after Mao's death in 1976: After the victims of the Cultural Revolution returned to their former posts, they shifted the party's work from class struggle to economic modernization. In addition, tensions between revolutionaries and experts have been a part of the evolution of both parties. The KMT began choosing experts to fill most influential government posts beginning in the early 1960s, and a similar transition occurred in the party organization beginning in the 1970s. The influence of "reds" and experts in the CCP has waxed and waned without a definitive resolution, and similar sets of issues and concerns have repeatedly entered the debate regarding the costs and benefits of modernization. While the CCP has waffled between these two poles, a third group has emerged in the KMT as a result of the emphasis on elections in the party's work: representatives. This has put greater pressure on the KMT to further adapt to societal pressures for the sake of electoral success. This kind of transition is still unimaginable for the CCP.

Second, the nature of the foreign environment influenced how the parties reacted to pressures from their domestic environments. Neither party has undertaken adaptation when it faced a hostile foreign environment. Only when the foreign environment became benign did either party move in that direction. Sometimes the environment had actually changed; in other cases, only the elite's characterization of it had changed. Either way, a hostile foreign environment has been accompanied by the preservation of the status quo and when necessary the repression of critics of the regime.

Third, the adaptability of these parties has at times been hampered by the ambiguity of the environment and the uncertain outcome of political change. The KMT was deadlocked in the early 1980s between those who believed a hard-line approach was necessary and those who believed more conciliatory policies were appropriate. This stalemate was resolved after political scandals discredited the hard-liners. The CCP has not resolved the decades-old debate about whether the ways of the Western world are the cause of or the solution to China's problems, and therefore cannot agree on whether adaptation would strengthen or undermine the regime.

As a result of the above factors, the two parties have differed in their adaptability. The KMT has been willing at certain times to adapt to changes in its environments. It has responded affirmatively to some opportunities and threats and repressed others. Changes within the party coincided with changes in the domestic and foreign environments in a manner that the adaptation model indicates is most conducive for democratization. In contrast, the CCP has consistently rejected domestic and foreign pressures for change. The CCP has taken advantage of changes in its environment to pursue preferred policies (especially at the beginning of the reform era), but it has not adapted its policies to fit its environment. Liberalization has been a voluntary undertaking for the CCP, not induced by social demands. To a far greater extent than the KMT, the CCP has tried to alter or ignore its environment rather than adapt to it. In part, this reflects disagreement within the party elite about how to correctly interpret and respond to the ambiguous environment. Much effort has been spent on defining the environment in terms that fit the policy preferences of individuals and groups within the party and little on adapting policies to fit the environment.

What are the implications for the future adaptability of these parties? The KMT has already completed the transition from Leninism. Faced with electoral competition from other parties, its future evolution is likely to be shaped by mass preferences more than party traditions and elite preferences. Its success will be determined by how well it can respond to the changing wants and needs of society with popular and effective policies. Whereas the threat from China had previously forestalled political change, it now reinforces the commitment to democratization among both elites and the masses. On the eve of Taiwan's first presidential election, China launched live missiles off the northern and southern tips of the island. The missiles failed to intimidate the voters or the presidential candidates; if anything, they bolstered support for Lee Teng-hui and his pragmatic diplomacy and also brought more international support for Taiwan. The challenge for Taiwan and the other political parties on Taiwan is to adopt a foreign policy that satisfies domestic desires for increased international stature but also is acceptable to the foreign countries—especially China and the United States—that determine its national security environment.

The CCP's domestic and foreign environments remain so ambiguous that elite preferences and perceptions will remain the primary variable affecting the party's future adaptability. At home, much of society has been distracted by the pursuit of business opportunities and has remained politically quiescent; at the same time, intellectual elites repeatedly make public demands for democratization. Some leaders see opportunities for greater foreign economic and security cooperation, while others see an international environment more intent on containing China than cooperating with it. The current generation of party leaders comes from a technocratic background and has not shown much enthusiasm for political reform. Their foreign experience has primarily been working or studying in the formerly communist countries of Eastern Europe and the Soviet Union, and they have little understanding of the workings or benefits of democratic institutions. The adaptability of the KMT increased as new leaders emerged with extensive experience in Western countries where they were exposed to new political ideas and institutions. If more CCP leaders gain this type of experience, the support for adaptation may rise. In the meantime, CCP leaders appear unwilling to sacrifice social stability and the party's authority to the uncertain benefits of political reform.

The CCP has many advantages that allow it to survive without adapting. It has a monopoly on legitimate violence, it is able to prohibit the formation of organizations that pose a threat to it, and the stakes for engaging in political protests have risen dramatically in light of the 1989 crackdown. But we would be too hasty if we entirely dismissed the potential for a return to political reform in China. After all, the KMT's evolution also ran into opposition from hard-liners in the late 1970s and early 1980s before resuming. Without trivializing the significance of political reform in Taiwan, however, the KMT's lifting of martial law and the ban on new parties was still a *policy* change that did not require revising or reinterpreting the guiding ideology. The CCP will have a more difficult time reconciling democracy with its Marxist-Leninist traditions. Opponents of change will see democratic proposals as the abandonment of the party's basic ideology and most cherished traditions and even a threat to the party's survival and privileges. These objections provide a more legitimate defense than pure self-interest and have been successful in the past.

But the survival of the CCP is not guaranteed, even if it tries to adapt. The collapse of communism elsewhere shows that the survival of ruling communist parties is not inevitable; the Tiananmen massacre shows that the current regime is not willing to accede to even those demands that are consistent with the regime's own propaganda; and Taiwan's democratization shows that democracy is possible in a Chinese society, which many analysts claim lacks the traditions that are most appropriate for democracy. The CCP may now be in a position where it is so discredited, so unpopular, that attempts at adaptation, such as meaningful elections, would hasten its demise rather than strengthen its support. The post-1949 history of the CCP offers little hope for its ability to fully adapt, and the experience of other Leninist parties in Eastern Europe and the Soviet Union indicates it is unlikely to survive if it attempts to do so. If democracy comes to China, it is more likely under a new regime than as the result of continuous political change as occurred in Taiwan.

Notes

This chapter benefited from the comments of several people: Dorothy Solinger, Steven Solnick, and Edwin Winckler offered suggestions on a version presented at the panel "Political Economies of Leninist Transitions: Macro, Meso, and Micro" at the annual meeting of the American Political Science Association in Washington, D.C., September 1993; Jae Ho Chung, Kenneth Lieberthal, Michel Oksenberg, and Martin Whyte made suggestions on the larger project from which this chapter is drawn (Dickson 1997).

1. For lack of space, this chapter takes for granted that both the CCP and KMT were organizationally Leninist. On the CCP, see Schurmann, 1971, especially chapters 1 and 2; on the KMT, see Cheng 1989 and Dickson 1997.

2. As my operational definition of democracy, I use the one offered by Schmitter and Karl (1991, 76): "Modern political democracy is a system of governance in which rulers are held accountable for their actions in the public realm by citizens, acting indirectly through the competition and cooperation of their elected representatives."

3. This proposition is apparently not valid for military governments. When faced with external security threats, military governments may decide to give up their governing role in order to concentrate on their core mission of national defense. According to Stepan (1986, 77–78), this contributed to democratic transitions in Greece, Portugal, and Peru.

4. Although media reports at the time suggested that recent political turmoil in South Korea and the Philippines cautioned the KMT against refusing to adapt, the KMT leaders I interviewed denied that this was a part of their calculus. Instead, they focused on the diminution of the Chinese threat.

PART 2

Military-Political
Transition

3

Military Dimensions of Regime Transition

Edwin A. Winckler

[The Chinese army] is different from the army of other countries in the world . . . even different from the army in other socialist states, because their armies and ours have different experiences. Our army will in the final analysis be loyal to the Party, loyal to the people, loyal to the state and loyal to socialism.　　　　　　　　　　　*—Deng Xiaoping*

Turmoil in China will be unlike that in Eastern Europe or the Soviet Union. If it happens in China, one faction [of the party] will control part of the army and the other, another part. A civil war could then erupt.
　　　　　　　　　　　　　　　　　　　　　—Deng Xiaoping

In military-political affairs, transition from communism in Eastern Europe and the former Soviet Union characteristically has involved multiple crises. *Politically,* the fall of the Communist Party shattered old institutions of civilian control and required the construction of new ones. *Ideologically,* the demise of international communism shifted the rationale of military doctrine and troop indoctrination from communism to nationalism. *Economically,* shock therapy and shrinking budgets imposed unprecedented austerity on both military procurement and soldiers' welfare. In the less westernized countries, personalistic control by the party leader over the military establishment largely remained in place, inhibiting transition from post-totalitarianism to full democracy. In the more westernized countries, more institutional controls facilitated transition to full democracy (Barany 1991, Danopoulos and Zirker 1996, Szemerkenyi 1996, Gow and Birch 1997).

　　In China, transition in military-political affairs is of course less advanced, but it also has taken a somewhat different form. *Politically,* Leninist institutions for civilian control of the military remain in place. The military remains the party-state's ultimate defense against domestic disorder, including any immediate transition toward democracy. Nevertheless, *ideologically,* in China too the basis for regime legitimacy and soldier loyalty has shifted significantly from communism toward nationalism. Such patriotism rededicates the military to national goals, but strengthens its sense of professional mission and corporate autonomy and its potential for making independent judgments about what the national interest requires. *Economically,* in China too revenue constraints and price inflation have strained military budgets and soldiers' incomes. Unlike in Europe, however, economic boom has provided the military with some alternative earnings and much continuing progress at modernizing military technology and maintaining military welfare (*CQ*146, Lane, Weissenbloom, and Liu 1996).

This chapter relates recent literature on the Chinese military to recent literature on military politics, in order to identify some mutual implications between the two. A *problematique* summarizes some findings and issues in the sinological literature about the Chinese military in the 1990s. It also discusses the main comparative formulation that the sinological literature has employed—the relationship between politicization and professionalization. A second section focuses on China's *institutions* for civilian control of military affairs—delegation and oversight between national political and military leaders, and between them and regional and local forces. A third section places those institutional structures in the context of the *substance* of military participation—in external defense and foreign policies, in domestic power politics and leadership succession, and in internal economic and sociocultural policies. A fourth section then relates China more directly to the comparative literature on the role of the military in regime *transition,* by regime type, world region, and compliance process.

Throughout, the chapter emphasizes the militarized nature of modern Chinese politics and the breadth and depth of the role that the People's Liberation Army (PLA) has played in communist China. As the sinological literature only sometimes stresses, the transitions *to* communism in Russia and China were quite different (Adelman 1980). In Russia, urban-centered transition through abrupt collapse left the Bolsheviks a weak military with low prestige and little connection to party leaders. The Red Army had tsarist officers and few troops, little organization of rural peasants, and little nonmilitary role in society. The party leadership relied more on secret police than military officers, and the military played little role in designing the Soviet political order. Seventy-odd years after 1917, the army tried only halfheartedly to block Russia's equally abrupt transition *from* communism.

By contrast, in China, rural-based transition *to* communism through protracted civil war left the communists a strong military with high prestige, organized by party leaders themselves. The PLA had communist officers and huge manpower, much popular support against both internal and external enemies, and wide roles in economy, society, and culture. The party has constituted the ultimate arena for legitimizing and exercising power, but controlling the military has remained essential to controlling the party. Most party founders played both civilian and military roles, and the military has had strong representation *within* the party. Political cleavages have run not between party and military institutions but between party factions and their military allies. The PLA has repeatedly played a large *explicit* political role, from conquering and garrisoning the country, through orchestrating and controlling the Cultural Revolution, to repressing the 1989 democracy movement. Moreover, the military has continuously played a large *implicit* political role, from ultimate guarantor of national independence and party rule, through ultimate arbitrator of intraparty disputes, to ultimate founder of many civilian institutions—subnational government, economic organization, and revolutionary ideals. Seventy-odd years after the launching of the Chinese communist movement, military transition *from* communism looks likely to remain a protracted process.

Problematique: Military Transition and Regime Transition

A recent special issue of *China Quarterly* titled *China's Military in Transition* provides an authoritative overview of the Chinese military in the 1990s (*CQ*146). The superb introduction by editor David Shambaugh discusses how the China field has characterized military change, thereby helping identify what may still be missing. Shambaugh discusses politics, professionalism, procurement, and power projection.

Sinological Consensus

Politically, the pivotal short-run event affecting state-society relations in the 1990s was of course the revolutionary elders' use of the PLA to repress the 1989 democracy movement, again involving a reluctant PLA in civilian domestic politics. On the one hand, this involvement increased the representation of the PLA in party bodies, increased the role of the PLA in policymaking, and increased the funding for military modernization. On the other hand, along with the fall of European communism and a rise in PLA corruption, the Tiananmen incident also prompted the revolutionary elders to reinforce Leninist institutions for party control of the military (party committees, political commissars, and discipline commissions). The regime also reintensified efforts to create a paramilitary force to control domestic disorder—to relieve the PLA of that unwelcome mission. The main long-run processes changing elite military politics have been generational succession and economic marketization. The passing of the revolutionary elders has reduced the long-standing overlap between civilian and military leadership, and increased the institutional separation between party and army (Joffe 1996a). The lesser stature of "third-generation" civilian leaders has required them to court military support and coopt military agendas. Commercialization has employed PLA assets and earned PLA income but diverted the PLA's attention and undermined its discipline.

Substantively, the PLA has become "the self-appointed guardian of Chinese sovereignty and nationalism," joining with internal security organs and conservative party ideologues to oppose what they view as U.S. efforts to subvert China's communism, contain China's nationalism, and even to split China's unity by abetting Taiwan independence. Under *professionalism*, the main shifts have been a fundamental revision of strategic doctrine—from Mao's passive interior defense by mass mobilization against superpower invaders, through Deng's active border defense by modernized forces, to Jiang's still greater emphasis on high technology. These shifts in doctrine have dictated organizational changes—reducing manpower to create a leaner but meaner PLA, improving the education of officers and the training of troops, and reorganizing forces into combined-service armies under tighter central control. In *procurement* the main trend has been modernizing China's largely obsolete military technology, mostly by upgrading existing equipment. The upshot for *power projection* has been some increase in China's ability to assert itself along its immediate borders, but also some increase in the gap between China and cutting-edge military technology.

This brief summary cannot do justice either to Shambaugh's overview or to the articles he was introducing, let alone to the rest of the sinological literature on the Chinese military. Nevertheless, this summary does indicate some of the strengths of that literature, and perhaps also some of its weaknesses. As Shambaugh points out, relatively few political scientists have analyzed Chinese military politics, and "more attention needs to be paid" to party-army relations "when considering scenarios for China's future" (1996a, 269). Given this, it is striking that in this entire monumental issue of *China Quarterly* there is not a single reference even to the possibility that "China's military transition" might need to be analyzed in the context of the comparative literature on regime transitions. Nor are there many references to the comparative literature on the role of the military in communist and postcommunist regimes, or any comparisons of China with any other communist country. Finally, there are no references to recent progress in analyzing civil-military relations in Western societies or to the microeconomic neo-institutionalism on which they draw (e.g., Avant 1994, Feaver 1996b). The same is true for most of the rest of the sinological literature (though see Shambaugh 1991 and Zhong 1991).

To be sure, on many important topics, research on the Chinese military faces unusual difficulties in obtaining enough facts to support even the most elementary analysis. Moreover, analysts face urgent practical questions about China's internal political stability and external capabilities and intentions. Furthermore, China remains at a relatively early stage of transition from communism, particularly in military-political affairs. Finally, China might be so distinctive that models from elsewhere require much respecification. Existing comparative theorizing may prove little help in solving any of these problems. That may explain why I was unable to find an expert on the Chinese military with the time to pursue such questions. Nevertheless, I could hardly offer the reader an analytical volume on "transition from communism in China" without at least raising these issues. Consequently, I broach them below myself. First, however, let us note some differences of emphasis within the existing sinological treatments.

Sinological Issues

On many issues, the lack of transparency of Chinese military politics leaves researchers uncertain between "tight" and "loose" interpretations of civilian controls and military roles—within the party-army-state itself, in central-local and state-society relations, and in external defense and foreign policy. Both tight and loose interpretations have both positive and negative implications for transition from communism, but along different transition paths with different outcomes. (No single author consistently approximates either extreme, and most authors take judicious intermediate positions.)

Within the *party-army-state* itself, according to a tight version, Leninist institutions for party control of the military have been and remain effective. Moreover, as the founding generation has died off, personal networks have become less important and the PLA itself has become increasingly institutionalized. Occasional civilian interventions to correct potential military problems (such as the 1992 purge of the Yangs) are evidence more of good management than of great difficulty. Such tight post-totalitarian civilian control should facilitate eventual democratic civilian control.

In contrast, according to a loose version, the PLA is a huge and sprawling organization with much de facto autonomy within the party-state, even a "state within a state" (Lieberthal 1995, 204–207). Formal institutions give the PLA great access to party decisionmaking bodies (Cheng Hsiao-shih 1990). Moreover, both civil-military relations and military command-and-control remain weakly institutionalized. As a result, personal networks remain important and crosscut formal lines of authority in ways that potentially undermine command-and-control (Swaine 1992, 174). Such looseness would saddle any successor regime with a military that was not accountable to civilians, a requirement of political stability under both authoritarianism and democracy.

In *state-society* relations, according to a tight version, the Chinese military remains the cornerstone of the regime but, exactly because of that, the civilian leadership has successfully reinforced Leninist controls. Construction of the paramilitary People's Armed Police (PAP) should relieve the PLA of domestic riot control. Any threat that commercialization poses to politicization and professionalism has been addressed, particularly by restricting business activities to the national and regional levels and by forbidding group armies to do business. Such tight civil-military relations would retard political transition from communism so long as civilian superiors oppose transition, but would facilitate political transition once they favor it.

In contrast, according to a loose version, the fact that the military remains the cornerstone of the regime gives officers much leverage over politicians (Shambaugh 1996b). Civilian efforts to intensify political control over the military is evidence of weakness not strength (Shambaugh 1996a). The PAP is unlikely to be able to quell serious insurrection, and PLA units are unlikely to respond uniformly to civil orders to intervene, "with unpredictable consequences" (Shambaugh 1996a). PLA participation in society remains large, and commercialization undermines both politicization and professionalism. Such loose civil-military relations might aid political transition by weakening military support for civilian leaders, but is more likely to allow conservative military actors to obstruct civilian-sponsored political liberalization.

Externally, according to a tight version, civilians dominate military policy, which is basically defensive. China's recent military buildup attempts only to mitigate extreme technological backwardness and has not been very successful even at that (Godwin 1996, Nathan and Ross 1997). Military participation in policymaking is restricted to defense and foreign policy, on which the military's planning and procurement faithfully correspond to the intentions of the civilian leadership. Representation of military interests occurs only through the appropriate formal channels, notionally through the highest-ranking military representative on the party Central Military Commission (CMC). Some officer interviewees affirm that open lobbying would be an unthinkable breach of military discipline (Swaine 1996). Such tight controls foster regional peace, which favors continued political liberalization, not only in China but also in its neighbors (e.g., Taiwan and Vietnam).

In contrast, according to a loose version, the passing of the revolutionary elders has given military professionals greater say over defense policy, and perhaps even latitude to implement their own priorities regardless of civilian policy (e.g., in arms sales). China's military leadership wants to secure regional dominance against present U.S. and future Japanese threat, and China's military modernization already poses a significant threat to neighbors such as Taiwan (e.g., Bernstein and Munro 1997). Military leaders have no difficulty communicating their views to civilian leaders, not only in the party CMC and through the military media, but also formally through military representatives in the National People's Congress (NPC) and informally through personal networks. Hong Kong journalists insist that during the 1990s military leaders have strenuously lobbied civilian leaders on numerous issues, and officer interviewees confirm those stories (Garver 1996, Shambaugh 1996a). Such loose controls threaten regional stability and democratization.

Politicization and Professionalization

The relationship between *politicization and professionalization* has been central to academic formulations of civil-military relations, it has been crucial to most past analysis of the Chinese military, and it will be pivotal to the role of the military in any future political transition from communism in China. Some leading analysts of the Chinese military have gradually switched from their past assessment that in Maoist China politicization and professionalization were inimical, to arguing that in Dengist China they became increasingly compatible (e.g., Godwin 1978, Joffe 1996a). Recent critiques of the classic literature on U.S. civil-military relations argue that it is necessary to distinguish several senses of professionalization (Feaver 1996a). Following this lead, the argument here will be that it is necessary also to distinguish several senses of politicization, and that some components of politicization and professionalization are more compatible than others.

Some delegation is inevitable in any military system, and all political-military systems attempt to minimize any resulting agency costs through some system of internal-motivational and external-institutional controls. Motivationally, the system can pursue commitment to the organization through some combination of selectivity and socialization—recruiting those already presocialized into appropriate values, or socializing new members after recruitment (Etzioni 1961). Institutionally, the system must install systems for monitoring and sanctioning—routine performance reviews and resulting promotions, real-time oversight by political officers or military intelligence. The two approaches interact—for example, external personnel policy and career incentives are essential to establishing internal values and organizational culture (Avant 1994). An adequate theory of civilian control over the military would inventory the elements of both internal and external approaches, and it would propose some deductive model of which are likely to be effective under what circumstances and why (Feaver 1996a).

In particular, an adequate theory of civil-military relations would dissaggregate the concept of professionalism, which has included not only officer schools, structured careers, and corporate identity, but also the internalization of loyalty to any legitimate civilian government (Feaver 1996a on Huntington and Janowitz). Moreover, the dominant theories have made that loyalty virtually the sole explanation for military acceptance of civilian authority. In the United States, the institutionalization of military careers and the indoctrination of military officers have worked, at least in the sense of preventing coups. (As Feaver points out, for such a case—which China somewhat resembles—one should turn to a dependent variable less blunt than coups: the extent and pattern of civilian control, differentiated by the type of military issue at stake.) By contrast, in Latin America, professionalization turned weak militaries into strong ones, loyal to their nation-states but for that very reason willing to overturn particular partisan governments (Rouquie 1982/1987). Essentially that is what happened in Eastern Europe and the Soviet Union, where ostensibly communist militaries allowed the fall of communism, in the name of nationalism. The same could happen in China eventually.

In the Chinese case, one needs to disaggregate not only "professionalization" but also "politicization." Most comparative literature has followed Huntington in expecting the military to be patriotically loyal to its nation-state but equally willing to serve any legitimate partisan government (1957). However, some comparativists have noted that military professionalism is unlikely to be completely neutral politically, since it always involves some sociotechnical tenets that are more compatible with some civilian political platforms than others (Abrahamsson 1972). The sinological literature was long mostly preoccupied with the distinctively Maoist meanings of politicization—Mao's claim that social factors are more important than technical factors for achieving military effectiveness, and Mao's demand that the social organization of the military should be egalitarian and unspecialized. This Maoist meaning of "politicization" was by definition in conflict with most modern versions of military professionalism, which emphasize both technical expertise and professional authority. Equating politicization with "redness" and professionalism with "expertise" remained particularly likely so long as few reds were expert, there were real career conflicts between reds and experts, and there were real practical conflicts between ideological indoctrination and military training (Joffe 1965, Gittings 1967, Godwin 1978, Jencks 1982).

By the 1990s, however, China has increasingly achieved its long-standing objective of making its military not only red but also expert, and has again committed itself to schooling professional officers. Arguments in China over redness and expertise have continued but declined (Lam 1995, 222–225). Claims that redness can substitute for expertise have been largely discredited, particularly by the Gulf War. The post-Deng leadership continues to stress ideological indoctrination, but for political loyalty not military effectiveness. Most fundamental, the military ethos of technical expertise and professional authority has been quite compatible with the post-Mao civilian leadership's program of societal modernization.

The most general possible object of military loyalty would be a *supranational* cause such as international communism, international peacekeeping, or some regional grouping of nation-states. In practice, the most general form of politicization is usually *patriotism*—loyalty to the historically given nation-state. This does appear to be an intrinsic component of military professionalism, at least the kind institutionalized in most national military establishments. A somewhat less general form of politicization is *constitutionalism*—loyalty to a particular form of government and obedience to the constitutionally specified commander-in-chief. This form of politicization appears more problematic—a usual tenet of professionalism, but subject to override on grounds of patriotism or corporate interest.

A more specific form of politicization is *partisanship*—commitment to the incumbency of a particular political party or faction. Democratic regimes proscribe this from professionalism, but single-party regimes prescribe it. Arguably even partisanship is compatible with professionalism so long as most politicians, officers, soldiers, and citizens all share the same partisan commitment, as perhaps in early post-revolutionary China. In these terms, the problem in China since the late 1980s has been that the regime has insisted on a highly partisan form of domestic military involvement, in a situation in which public approval is not just problematic but the very issue at stake. Finally, the most specific form of politicization is *personalism*—loyalty to a particular national or military leader. This form appears least compatible with modern professionalism but remains a factor in China. Even Jiang Zemin has made adherence to Deng's military thought the public cornerstone of Chinese military doctrine and privately cultivated personal loyalty to himself (Shambaugh 1996b).

The distinction between partisanship and patriotism is pivotal to "military transition," at least from communism, which consists precisely in a shift in the content of the military's political commitment from party to nation. A patriotic but not partisan military can and must make its own judgment about the party's claim that its incumbency is best for the nation. Of course, the military may continue to support the party, particularly if the party tries hard to satisfy the military. In the 1990s China's leaders have attempted to do so, granting the military more rapid modernization. However, military modernization carries the risk that, along with upgraded military equipment and defense doctrine, the Chinese military will import a Western nonpartisan definition of military professionalism—as started happening in the 1980s (Lam 1995, 203). The Chinese military are among the most vehement opponents of "peaceful evolution" away from communism by importing Western values, but they themselves may be particularly at risk. (Transfer of military technology was, of course, the opening wedge to westernization of values in the nineteenth century.)

Institutions

This section moves beyond the general issue of politicization and professionalization to address the specific institutional arrangements for military management in China. First we characterize Chinese military-political institutions as a whole, then the relationship between national political and military leaders, then the relationship between them and subnational regions and units. Throughout the main theme is the length and multiplicity of chains of delegation and how that might affect transition.

Chinese Leninist Military-Political Institutions

Looking backward and upward from the paramount leader to the historical and contractual origins of his authority, the argument is that in communist-revolutionary China political legitimacy has been intrinsically military. The revolutionary elders regarded themselves as the legitimate "owners" of power because they had conquered the country (Whitson and Huang 1973). Among themselves, they delegated power to an agent, the "paramount leader," who constructed and managed a governing coalition in which senior military figures were key components. Looking forward and downward from the apex of power toward its actual exercise, the argument is that the elders conducted affairs through whatever institution seemed necessary and appropriate—army, party, or government. During the revolutionary struggle these institutions remained largely undifferentiated; after 1949 differentiation increased but fluctuated—higher in the 1950s and 1980s, lower during the Maoist period. Initiatives in the 1980s toward separating the party from the government and army were reversed in the early 1990s.

Formal civilian hierarchies include the party (with both Central Committee and Central Military Commission) and the state (with both president and premier). Formal military hierarchies include the General Staff Department (GSD) and its commanders, the General Political Department (GPD) and its commissars, and the General Logistics Department (GLD) and its facilities—not to mention the division of the military into army, navy, and air force, and supplementary systems such as military education (Nelsen 1977/1981). In addition there are informal personal networks originating in the histories of military units during the civil war, in the grouping of these units into field armies during conquest and consolidation, and in later career lines in military academies and military units (Whitson and Huang 1973, Swaine 1992, Li and White 1993).

The formal chain of command crosses several institutions and levels—from the party CMC, through the military GSD, to the military regions and group armies. This vertical system maximizes central control during emergencies. Another formal chain of civilian security administration runs vertically level-by-level down through territorial subnational governments, and horizontally at each level to local reserves and militia. This horizontal system maximizes delegation of routine functions to local party and government administration, but functions can be transferred to vertical central control in emergencies. During the post-Mao period the regime has created a third, intermediate system of paramilitary People's Armed Police—

usually under horizontal-territorial civilian control but staffed and trained by military officers who can readily revert to vertical central control in a crisis.

The multiplicity of channels has created the possibility of multiple principals at several levels within the chain of command, making staffing strategic (Swaine 1992, Paltiel 1995). A main way to combat ambiguity is through concurrency—having one person hold all the relevant posts. Thus communism's dual formal institutional design itself requires and reinforces informal personalism. All of these formal chains begin united by personal networks at the apex of the system and end united by personal networks within localities and units at the bottom of the system. In theory they remain formally compartmentalized from each other in between, but probably all of them are crosscut by personal networks at many levels. Such networks have the *potential* to alter the balance between command and delegation, between politics and professionalism, and between vertical and horizontal control (Swaine 1992). Evidently system managers regard these risks as real, since they have repeatedly noted them and taken measures to combat them. For example, Deng stressed that army unity is crucial to national stability and referred openly to the existence of factionalism within the Chinese military—"the five lakes and the four seas" (Lam 1995, 220–222).

However, the seriousness of these risks remains unclear. Outsiders have only the vaguest idea of what the operative factions in Chinese military politics may be. Do the politically most important ones originate within the party not the military? To what extent do cleavages coincide with formal divisions such as service rivalries, and to what extent do they crosscut such formal boundaries, originating instead in personal ties or policy views? To what extent do factions undermine military cohesion, and to what extent might they contribute to it? After all, it is a staple of military sociology that elite schooling produces officer spirit and that personal relations underpin unit cohesion. Moreover, in formal organizations it is often necessary for informal systems to confirm that official persons are who they say they are and that official channels really mean what they say. For example, Swaine notes that in China authentication of commands may involve both oral recognition and written confirmation (1992, 125).

As in Western civil-military systems, so in China too, *commanders* themselves give civilian principals their first line of defense against agency costs. Even in China the party's CMC has regarded the commanders (through the GSD) as the main executives, and the commissars (through the GPD) only as a support. Evidence includes the fact that Mao and Deng devoted more attention to the appointment of commanders than commissars, that the commander not the commissar served as the first secretary of their military unit's party committee, that most marshals and generals were commanders not commissars, and that PLA reforms in the early 1990s abolished some political posts (You 1994, reviewing Swaine 1992). Even in 1989–1990 at the peak of the post-Tiananmen influence of political commissars, the PLA was still dominated by professional commanders, who mostly doubted the wisdom of PLA intervention in internal politics (Lam 1995, 225). The desire of commanders to avoid politics could facilitate eventual political transition.

The party has deployed several *political* systems within the military (Swaine 1992, 134–138). Evidently the redundancy is a deliberate design to prevent any one system from gaining too-exclusive control, but how these systems actually work is affected by the rise and fall of contending factions. Thus the *party committee system* under the civilian party Central Committee institutionalizes both collective governance within military units and party control from above. Shambaugh thinks it the most important system (1991, 548–549). The *commissar system* under the GPD monitors performance, processes promotions, and does propaganda among troops. Swaine thinks it the most important system (1992, 136–137). An *intelligence system,* also under the GPD, can report directly to its central headquarters, also affecting promotions. (In most communist countries such intelligence was gathered by the civilian secret police, reflecting their greater strength relative to the military.) The *discipline inspection system,* newest and reportedly weakest, was revived in 1978 under the party's CMC, but placed under the military's GPD after Tiananmen. These political systems obstruct political transition, which would require abolishing at least some of them, particularly party committees.

National Political and Military Leaders

Management of military affairs at the apex of a political system inevitably involves many people, between whom arrangements can vary. At one extreme, the leader may concentrate nearly all power in his own hands, working through assistants who have little independent authority (e.g., Stalin and Mao). The leader may delegate significant power to one or a few people acting as his policy czars for military affairs (e.g., Deng to Yang Shangkun for political oversight and Liu Huaqing for military modernization). Both Mao and Deng delegated some authority to temporary political czars to purge other opponents, then revoked the delegations when the agents allegedly overreached themselves (Lin Biao in 1971, the Yangs in 1992). Toward the other extreme there may be more delegation of responsibility to military professionals (e.g., under Brezhnev and Jiang). Evidently Jiang Zemin holds unquestioned formal authority in military affairs but manages them in collaboration with military leaders (Lam 1995, 216).

The design of military-political institutions in communist China creates the *potential* for multiple principals even at the level of commander-in-chief. During the Tiananmen crisis in 1989, at least four Chinese leaders could reasonably have claimed authority over PLA forces: (1) the de facto paramount leader and then chairman of the party Central Military Commission Deng Xiaoping, (2) the state president and first vice-chairman of the CMC Yang Shangkun, (3) the then party secretary-general and CMC vice-chairman Zhao Ziyang, (4) the government premier Li Peng (Latham 1991, 112). In practice, if there was a problem with formal arrangements, it was that the party secretary-general was not the CMC chairman (because Deng had retained the chairmanship to placate military leaders who did not trust Zhao). Thus some younger liberal officers—who would have preferred the orders that party secretary-general Zhao Ziyang would have issued—dared to wonder why, since Zhao was a CMC vice-chairman, Deng could issue the order alone (Lam 1995, 203). However, for most officers if there was a procedural issue, evidently it was not institutional but personal—they wanted confirmation that the orders were in fact Deng's, by implication regardless of what formal position he held.

Evidently the Chinese leadership recognized the problem and gradually solved it. The new party secretary-general Jiang Zemin became the CMC chairman in November 1989. Yang Shangkun remained as state president and, with his half-brother Yang Baibing as CMC secretary-general, oversaw the purge of officers who wavered during the Tiananmen incident. However, after they completed that task Deng purged them, Jiang added the state presidency to his portfolio, and the CMC secretary-generalship was abolished. Since then, generational succession, Jiang's political success, and leadership succession have further reduced ambiguity. The revolutionary elders gradually died, removing any possibility of their reintervention. At the Fifteenth Party Congress in September 1997, Jiang Zemin purged both liberals and conservatives, reducing the chance of political polarization. In March 1998, the premiership passed from Jiang rival Li Peng to Jiang ally Zhu Rongji. In summer 1998 the new administration issued a "white paper" on China's military that contained indications of stronger civilian government control of the military establishment (*Washington Post* 29 July 1998).To some extent this new equilibrium should be permanent—there will be no more revolutionary elders, little advocacy of leftist Maoism, and much attention to legality. Nevertheless, to some extent this new equilibrium remains contingent on Jiang's personal political power. The process of succession to a new leader could redivide top posts, and new polarization may emerge (e.g., between today's centrist political authoritarians and tomorrow's rightist liberalizing reformers).

Management of military affairs below the apex of a political system can involve alternative institutional arrangements. Deng took opposite approaches before and after 1989. When initiating military modernization in 1982, he found military organization inadequate. ("The army's present structure and its leadership system and methods are not that good.") Surprisingly, he suggested reducing the authority of the party's military commission by establishing a counterpart within the state and by upgrading the state's Ministry of Defense. His 1984 appointment of his protégé General Qin Jiwei as minister of defense may have been a step toward implementing that plan (Lam 1995, 234). (However, the appointment was also a step backward from the previous appointment of the first civilian as defense minister, Geng Biao.) Reportedly in the late 1980s Deng supported separating the party from the army as well as from the government (Lam 1995, 234–235). Although aborted, these initiatives provide precedent for a future resumption of military transition from communism.

The Chinese democracy movement and the collapse of European communism completely reversed Deng's approach. Not only did he switch back to integrating the party with the government and army, but also he favored doing so through personalistic means. Thus a 1991 General Political Department circular warned against "bourgeois-liberal" thoughts in the ranks of the PLA, targeting three "dangerous" ideas: that the army and party should be separated, that the army should be politically neutral and not interfere in internal politics, and that the army should be brought under state control (Lam 1995, 235). To stabilize the system after the 1992 purge of the Yang brothers, reportedly Deng strove for factional balance—using Third Field Army veterans to balance the Second and Fourth Field Armies (General Zhang Zhen), using the navy to counter the army (Admiral Liu Huaqing), and promoting nonfactional professionals (Fu Quanyou and Zhang Wannian) (Lam 1995, 220–222). Meanwhile Deng restaffed key institutions with reliable personnel, preferably the children of revolutionary elders (e.g., Deng's own daughter and son-in-law), or key personal aides (e.g., Deng's personal secretary Wang Ruilin). In Lam's caustic formulation, Deng's intention was that the PLA should remain a private army, not only of the Communist Party, but also of the Deng faction (Lam 1995, 236). The party center remains reluctant to delegate civilian authority over military affairs to government posts such as the presidency and premiership, much less to China's representative assembly, the National People's Congress. For example, the Defense Law drafted by the NPC later in the 1990s did not give the NPC oversight over the PLA, instead merely systematizing existing PLA regulations (Lam 1995, 235).

Subnational Military Regions and Local Forces

The possibility of military regionalism in China is a perennial topic in foreign discussion of Chinese military affairs and one possible scenario for future military-political transition (e.g., Yang et al. 1994). Historically, China fluctuated between centralization and decentralization, because of the difficulty of integrating a subcontinental area using premodern technology (Elvin 1973). In the first half of the century, the breakdown of the last dynasty devolved power to regional warlords; even the Nationalist government migrated from region to region. In the second half of the century, regional military commanders twice held overt power—during conquest and consolidation, and again while restoring order during and after the Cultural Revolution. A future transition scenario could involve attempts at secession by peripheral nationalities (Tibet, Taiwan) or some form of political federalism to accommodate divergent regional interests.

Nevertheless, most discussions of military regionalism conclude that in fact it is unlikely (even Yang et al. 1994, and certainly Huang 1995). The trend of Chinese history has been toward ever tighter logistic integration underpinning ever more stable unity (Elvin 1973). Even Republican warlords were competing to unify China, not to dismember it (Pillsbury 1980). Post-1949 regional military leaders have been part of a national system of patriotic loyalties and career aspirations (Nelsen 1977/1981). Post-Mao military modernization has still further increased military centralization—toward an elite force that is well trained and well equipped, highly mobile and rapidly mobilizable. Improved logistics allowed larger defense theaters requiring fewer regions, and the switch toward U.S.-style combined service operations has dictated fewer group armies and greater central control (Lam 1995, 218). Reportedly leaders even considered abolishing military regions altogether (Lam 1995, 222).

In subnational Chinese military administration, the center has used both institutional design and management procedures to combat possible separatism (Swaine 1992, 121–151). *Institutionally,* the staff, political, and logistics systems all provide the center with controls. Only Beijing can order significant troop movements, which it carefully monitors. During crises Beijing can reach across levels to command military units and paramilitary forces directly. Political controls operate at all levels of command. The center manages the logistics necessary for troop movement and supply, particularly civilian railroads. The center permits only limited lateral communication and contact between military regions, using this vertical compartmentalization to prevent lateral alliances between subnational units against the center. Other institutional tools include reorganizing military regions and units, and reducing the powers of military regions.

Procedurally, Western democratic systems of civilian control rely on either personnel policy by the executive or budgetary power by the assembly (Avant 1994). Executive exercise of personnel power is more likely under parliamentary systems that unify executive and assembly, while assembly exercise of budget power is more likely under presidential systems that divide them. Thus the unity of Leninist states may help explain why they rely so heavily on personnel policy. Regular officer rotation and ordinary career incentives should suffice to prevent localism and keep units responsive. However, evidently China's use of personnel policy has been highly political. Transfers, retirements, and promotions have come in waves, linked to shifts in political leadership. In the post-Mao period these waves have been rationalized as reducing age and raising educational levels, which were indeed necessary given the extended tenures and antiprofessional philosophy of the Maoist period. Nevertheless, these objective criteria have also provided an excuse for purging opponents and appointing allies. During the 1990s, Jiang's succession has involved repeated waves of retirements and promotions.

During the post-Mao period China's leaders have tried to avoid using military units to suppress internal disturbances. Their main preparation for preventing political transition has been the progressive strengthening of paramilitary forces. In 1982 they formed the People's Armed Police, constituted by units transferred from the PLA, commanded by officers from the PLA, and manned by troops demobilized from the PLA. After the PAP proved unable to cope with the 1989 democracy movement on its own, in the 1990s the leadership has still further strengthened it, again partly through transfers of still more officers and men from the PLA. Normally PAP units are under "horizontal" supervision by local party and government but during emergencies can readily be transferred to vertical central control (Swaine 1992, Cheung 1996b). Evidently the long-run goal is to make the PAP a separate career service with a separate identity. For example, in elections for the 1997 Fifteenth Party Congress, the PAP even constituted an independent constituency for electing representatives, equal in constitutional status to the PLA (*CNA* 1 October 1997, 2).

Also relevant to prospects for political transition are local reserves and militia. There have been several million reserves and over a hundred million militia, but they have been poorly trained, badly equipped, organizationally fragmented, and spatially scattered. In the mid-1980s, to replace the manpower lost by a reduction in main force PLA units, China began modernizing and integrating some of these paramilitary forces for possible emergency work, while relegating the rest to routine tasks. Select elite reserve units provided a framework for integrating select "armed militia." After Tiananmen, China increased the security role of the integrated reserve-militia forces, as a supplement to the PAP, forming still more elite rapid deployment units. Nevertheless, the reliability of these forces for crisis management remains questionable. Since these units are financed by localities and profess loyalty to them, they might participate in any local power struggle that might erupt, or prove too close to the local populations they would have to repress (Lam 1995, 227). These problems may be greater at the provincial and rural-local levels, less between major cities and the forces stationed nearby (Swaine 1992, 148).

Clearly institutions are central to controlling the military and to shaping the role of the military in transition. Nevertheless, analysis of institutional controls is not enough by itself—we must also consider the scope and means of the *substance* of military participation in power and policy (Colton 1978). Systems of political oversight can help prevent erratic behavior by individual officers but seem unlikely to be able to contain the entire military-as-institution, unless it basically accepts the substance of the policies it is implementing.

Substance: Military Participation in Policy and Politics

The 1992 Fourteenth Party Congress affirmed three continuing roles for the PLA: external defense, internal security, and internal construction. This section briefly canvasses military participation in these three substantive areas. In the 1990s that participation has been less broad than under Mao but remains extensive, with mixed implications for the PLA's role in transition. On the one hand, the breadth and depth of the PLA's roles are an obstacle that must gradually be shrunk to minimize its nonmilitary roles, as most transition literature recommends (e.g., Goodman 1996). On the other hand, the breadth of these involvements "endogenizes" the PLA into transition. Unlike a narrower and more isolated military, the PLA cannot stand entirely above the process with the autonomy to block it, but instead is itself to some extent embedded in transition and being transformed by it.

External Defense and Foreign Policy

The recent transition literature argues that a clear mission to defend against a strong external threat may be the most fundamental foundation for well-institutionalized relations between a military establishment and its would-be civilian overseers, a mission that in the post–Cold War world many militaries increasingly lack (Desch 1996). In these terms, turn-of-the-millennium China continues to enjoy fairly favorable preconditions for civilian control. Although in the 1990s actual immediate external threat is relatively low, the Chinese military appears fully preoccupied with achieving regional military dominance against future contingencies. At the same time, transitologists warn that achieving actual civilian control of defense policy and military procurement is more difficult than establishing formal institutions of civilian control (Diamond and Plattner 1996, xxxi–xxxii). In these terms, a key question about 1990s China is the changing relative weight of civilian and military leaders in deciding external policy. Correspondence between civilian defense philosophy and actual military procurement is not guaranteed, even in Leninist systems. For example, in the Soviet Union, Brezhnev's delegation of military matters to military professionals allowed a dangerous gap to emerge between defensive civilian strategy and offensive military procurement (Kaufman 1994).

In China, to date there has been no such gap, but for changing reasons—Mao dominated the military, Deng both reformed and consulted it, while indications are that Jiang has largely accommodated it. Overall, Mao paid low agency costs but got low agency gains. As principal he dominated his military agents but forfeited some of the advantage of professional expertise (what one might call a "dominant equilibrium"). Arguably Deng achieved a better balance than Mao—low agency costs and some agency gains. Deng was able to impose many of his own preferences but was more willing to listen to professionals (what one might call a "consultative equilibrium"). So far, Jiang may have achieved a good balance between agency costs and agency gains on military matters, both in his relations with his civilian colleagues and in their joint relationship with military leaders (what one might call an "accommodative equilibrium"). The main episode has been China's demonstration of force in the Taiwan Strait. Clearly the military lobbied for action, but in the end the entire leadership may well have agreed both that it was necessary to reaffirm the coercive side of China's mixed cooperative-coercive strategy toward Taiwan and that China's demonstration should be only symbolic. (On post-Mao PLA doctrine, see Joffe 1987, Li 1996, Pillsbury 1997.)

Any future political transition from Leninism should not bring nearly so much change in defense policy to China as it did to Eastern Europe (where transition included a reorientation from subordination to independence and from East to West), or even as in Russia (where the end of the Cold War drastically reduced military expenditure, but the breakup of the Soviet Union transformed the regional security environment). If China is seeking military power and regional dominance "commensurate with its economic and political status," that is unlikely to change with political transition from Leninism, or even with democratization. A democratic China might be less concerned about combating "peaceful evolution" from global influences, but would probably remain equally concerned about defending its borders from regional powers and continue to claim territories such as Taiwan and the South China Sea.

Internal Security and Domestic Politics

The recent transition literature argues that extensive involvement in combating a strong internal threat is a fundamental contributor to poorly institutionalized civil-military relations and to military involvement in domestic politics (Desch 1996). In these terms, turn-of-the-millennium China enjoys at best ambiguous preconditions for civilian control. On the one hand, actual unrest is restricted to occasional ethnic outbursts in outlying minority areas and scattered demonstrations by economically disadvantaged workers and peasants. On the other hand, the regime continues to fear potentially wider economic distress and even political defection by workers and farmers. The regime has done what transitologists recommend, withdrawing the military from politics and shifting internal security functions to professionally trained police. Nevertheless, the possibility remains of renewed internal security involvement, and with it the classic question about military participation in domestic politics: Since military agents command force, what restrains them from displacing their erstwhile civilian principals? This question is particularly apt for China, where politics from 1850 to 1950 was highly militarized, and where since 1949 the PLA has continued to command large political resources that have remained central to Chinese politics.

Harry Harding has provided the most pointedly causal and accurately predictive formulation of what has determined the extent of overt military involvement in domestic politics in communist China (1987a). The political resources of the PLA have included high political *legitimacy* among both elites and masses, high formal and personal *access* to decision arenas, great size and power as a military *organization*, and *usefulness* for a wide range of nonmilitary tasks. However, the conversion of these PLA resources into political power has remained incomplete because of two main restraints: institutional and personal divisions within the Chinese military itself, and control from outside through institutional systems and personal loyalties. As Harding astutely anticipated, during the 1990s the passage of time and the succession of generations have deprived the PLA of much of its legitimacy and access, while professionalization has moderated internal cleavages and strengthened consensus on corporate interests. Arguably these changes have been offsetting but transformative—both resources and restraints are weaker, leaving roughly the same level of *potential* military influence, but in a form that is less personally integrated and more institutionally separated (Joffe 1996a).

Within these parameters, the *actual* conversion of PLA resources into political power has fluctuated drastically over time—as a result, Harding argues, of the interaction between three main variables. The first has been the strength of civilian institutions and the *unity* of political leaders. Institutional decay invites military intervention, and conflict between principals invites agency reversal (Huntington 1968). The second variable has been the particular political *role* in which the PLA has been cast—pursuing its interests through ordinary bureaucratic lobbying, enjoying privileged access to the policy process as a coalition partner, balancing organizational interests and personal loyalties when arbitrating intra-elite conflict, or attempting to achieve preeminence by contending for power. The third variable has been the kind of *interest* pursued. The PLA has done best at personal perquisites such as salaries and privileges, and at nonmilitary programmatic objectives such as supporting conservative foreign policies and stable domestic policies. The PLA has done somewhat less well at securing civilian leadership favorable to its interests, and least well at pursuing its own corporate goals such as greater funding for a more modern defense. Since the mid-1980s, drastic fluctuations in the actual levels of military influence have continued, induced by continued variation in unity of lead-

ership and strength of institutions. In the late 1980s, elite disunity aggravated mass challenge, which the elders ordered the PLA to repress. Jiang's
succession has gradually consolidated elite unity and reduced overt PLA
influence over domestic politics.

For explaining variation in military influence, Harding appropriately
focused on positive actions by the military, acting as a principal on its own
behalf, through a variety of kinds of military actor. However, anticipating
the likely role of the military in transition requires attention to progressively less obvious forms of possible influence—overt behavior identifiable by
classical organization theory, covert behavior identified by neo-institutional
delegation theory, and implicit "constitutional" roles identified by historical-cultural "new" institutionalism.

Thus a first category of military influence on domestic politics is
ongoing behavior such as Harding's roles of bureaucratic lobbyist and
coalition partner. The most important summary indicator of the PLA as
overt principal in domestic politics is its official representation on leading
party bodies such as the party Central Committee, Politburo, and Standing
Committee. For example, military membership on the Central Committee
was high at takeover then declined, high again during the Cultural
Revolution and then declined again, and somewhat higher after Tiananmen
but has not yet declined (22 percent at the Fourteenth Party Congress in
1992, still 22 percent at the Fifteenth Party Congress in 1997). Central
Committee membership does seem a good proxy for the changing size of
the military role in Chinese politics. Nevertheless, it is worth noting that
the sinological literature has never fully articulated exactly what these
memberships mean. To what extent do military representatives act as individual principals in their own right, as representatives of their organizations, or as agents of whoever appointed them? To what extent do they
decide policy, coordinate administration, or simply receive these posts as a
reward for service? The answers may differ across time and by individual.

The most important example of the PLA as *overt agent* in domestic
politics is the party-state-as-a-whole using the military-as-institution to
implement political policy, ranging from mere propaganda to mass repression. Whether or not the military actually wanted this role, evidently the
fact of the military's having performed it gives the military more leverage.
(Rises in military representation on the Central Committee have followed
just such services.) It is worth noting that, in performing these tasks, delegation from central principal to military agent has often been problematic.
First, as in any delegation relationship, there have been some agency costs.
For example, when put in charge of subnational governments after the
Cultural Revolution, evidently military actors made some marginal use of
them to advance personal, organizational, or factional interests. Second and
more serious has been ambiguity in the original delegation contract, which
asked local officers to make difficult political choices but did not specify

criteria (Nelsen 1972). As comparative politics suggests, putting an orderly military in charge of messy politics produces not orderly politics but a messy military (Huntington 1968). Third and most serious is that incentive incompatibility between principal and agent undermined the delegation contract. During the Cultural Revolution Mao ordered the army to "support the left," but local commanders detested radical civilians and eventually mutinied, forcing Mao to retreat. Orders to "suppress the right" at Tiananmen nearly produced mutiny and would be even more likely to do so in the future (evidently much of the PLA has sworn "never again").

A second category of military influence on domestic politics is behavior that is observable only when the system is in political crisis and delegational disequilibrium. Neo-institutionalism argues that it is only such episodes that reveal who is principal and who is agent and that test their relative powers. Perhaps the most important example of military actors as *covert principals* in Chinese politics is their role in selecting and vetoing potential successors to the paramount leadership (close to Harding's arbiter-of-conflict and contender-for-power). Founding officers supported Mao, military moderates supported Deng, and evidently modernizing commanders eventually supported Jiang, who courted them assiduously (Shambaugh 1996b). Conversely, military actors helped veto Deng's first two successors when they proved too liberal and allowed disorder (Hu Yaobang in 1987 and Zhao Ziyang in 1989). In 1976 the military even intervened, quitely but directly, to remove the Gang of Four as contenders for succession. (Scobell 1995 argues this was the only PLA intervention that has qualified as a military coup, arguably by the military-as-institution.) Such episodes reveal that formal representation on official civilian bodies has not been where ultimate political power has resided.

Political crises also expose the role of military actors as *covert agents* in domestic politics. For example, as noted above, after the Tiananmen coup and repression, Deng used the Yang brothers to purge any officers who had objected, then purged the Yangs themselves because they showed signs of pursuing their own post-Deng agenda. Deng then elevated two other officers as agents to backstop the succession of Jiang Zemin (Admiral Liu Huaqing and General Zhang Zhen). At the subnational level, a first rule of post-1949 Chinese politics has been to secure military control of the capital region. Mao, Deng, and Jiang have all been careful to appoint military allies as commanders of the Beijing Military Region and Beijing municipal garrison. A second rule is, in a real crisis, to redeploy reliable units from other regions to the capital to backstop those ally-agents. That is what Mao did in 1966 and Deng did in 1989 (Nelsen 1972, Brook 1992). A third rule is, when blocked at the center, retreat to some region controlled by military allies. These covert "rules of the game" become conspicuous only during political showdowns.

A third and still "deeper" category of military influence on domestic politics is institutional residues of past behavior. As historical-cultural "new" institutionalism would expect, the military-as-institution has exercised profound influence on Chinese politics through its role in *constituting* other institutions, either directly by helping establish them, or indirectly by providing a model. Thus, during the civil war in the 1930s and 1940s, the army was the matrix for base area civilian government institutions. During the initial periods of takeover and institutionalization in the 1950s, the military-as-institution not only ran most subnational regions and helped organize their governments, but also schooled the personnel for staffing not only them but virtually all levels of subnational administration. During the Cultural Revolution in the late 1960s, the military again substituted, not only for local government but also for the local party. The following section notes many more ways in which the PLA has played the same constitutional role in the economy, society, and culture. This constitutional role is even more profound than temporary "intervention" by the military in other Third World countries. In any case, with this kind of record, if party and government should falter, one would expect the constitutive role of the military to be renewed.

Internal Economic, Social, and Cultural Construction

The recent transition literature argues that giving the military large and continuous nonmilitary roles degrades civil-military relations by eroding institutional barriers between military and society and by legitimating military involvement in nonmilitary issues (Goodman 1996). In these terms, turn-of-the-millennium China bears a uniquely unfavorable and strongly persistent legacy. Outside of politics too the domestic role of military actors has been much broader in China, not only than in Western democracies, but also than in most developing countries, and even than in most other communist regimes (Shambaugh 1996c). (On the sometimes broad roles of other developing country militaries, see Goodman 1996.)

Under Mao, the PLA played an active role in domestic construction, not only economic but also social and cultural. Economically, the PLA has always grown much of its own food and built much of the country's infrastructure. The PLA provided the militant models of economic regimentation and campaign methods that Maoist radicals imposed from 1958 to 1978. Defense needs have dictated much of economic development strategy, and the PLA has been the final user of much of industrial production. In society, the PLA long provided a major channel for upward mobility and a major model for social mores. In culture too the PLA has been a major sponsor and user of scientific research and technological development, and it has been an active model and critic in literature and the arts. Under Mao, there may have been some conflict in time and resources between military mission and these activities, but there was little conflict in terms of ethos—

the PLA applied the same normative-coercive compliance structure to all endeavors and expected society to do so as well (Etzioni 1961).

Under Deng, rapid economic growth and PLA withdrawal from large-scale construction reduced the PLA proportion of economic activity. Moreover, the PLA lost its role of organizational model, as the civilian leadership turned to market principles. The PLA itself retained much of its old Maoist ideals and developed a new military professionalism, but both became increasingly incongruent with a liberalizing cultural environment. The PLA undertook to protect the society from "peaceful evolution" away from socialist values but itself suffered from spiritual malaise, such as the appeal to the ranks of imported popular culture such as music, novels, and TV (Lam 1995, 202, 206–207). Meanwhile most officers and troops suffered a growing disparity between their incomes and living standards and the prosperity and inflation in their economic environment. This increased the difficulty of recruitment and reduced the PLA's role as a channel for social mobility (Lam 1995, 233).

Under Jiang, in the 1990s the PLA's economic role was first somewhat reenlarged, through the PLA's bigger budget, renewed coordination between military and civilian industry for high-tech development, and the PLA's own plunge into business. The military expanded from its previous specialization in arms trade, diversifying into real estate, manufacturing, retailing, and services (Lam 1995, 227). The PLA participated actively in the boom kicked off by Deng's spring 1992 Southern Tour. As part of its struggle to control that boom, the government tried to limit PLA commercialism by restricting business enterprise to the military region and above, but that is where most such enterprise has been conducted anyway. Meanwhile army clout prevented criticism from the National People's Congress or liberal intellectuals (Lam 1995, 229–231).

Military commercialization earned useful revenues and consolidated PLA support for marketization. However, military commercialism produced both conflict and collusion between military units and local governments, and even outright corruption and smuggling. More important, military commercialism created potential cleavages between officers favoring and opposing it, between military units competing in business activities, and between winners and losers among officers and troops. Still more fundamental, commercialization should undermine both politicization and professionalization, both of which require a normative compliance structure incompatible with calculative opportunism. Not only must military organization combat a commercialized environment, the military itself has become commercialized, marketing many of the very luxuries and vices that it ostensibly condemns (Cheung 1994, 1997; Cheung in Lane, Weissenbloom, and Liu 1996; Ding 1996; Joffe in Segal and Yang 1996).

By the late 1990s evidently these political costs loomed larger, and Jiang Zemin's political position became stronger. After the Fifteenth Party

Congress, the new administration ordered the PLA to get out of money-making entirely and to rely exclusively on its official budget. Moreover, the new administration set about breaking up China's military-industrial complex, taking the production of weapons from the military and placing it under stronger civilian management. To the extent that this effort succeeds, it will improve China's chances for eventual transition to democracy (*New York Times* 28 July 1998, *Washington Post* 29 July 1998).

The 1990s provide a remarkable example of the PLA's role in *formulating policy* on nonmilitary matters, not as a principal but as an agent. Reportedly when Deng wanted to restart economic reform after Tiananmen, the conservative media failed to broadcast his initiative (1991 speeches in Shanghai). So he recruited PLA support for a spring 1992 trip south to Guangdong and allowed chief political commissar Yang Baibing to declare the PLA the "escort" of reform (Lam 1995, 198–199). This is a startling concept if it meant not just assisting implementation or combating side effects, but "escorting" reform through the policy process itself. This episode may prove to have been the last use of the PLA by the paramount leader to force through a policy initiative.

Having recalled the breadth of the PLA's substantive roles, we may now more directly address its likely role in future transition.

Transition: The Role of the Military in Regime Change

This section relates the Chinese case to the comparative literature on military roles in political transition, first by regime type, then by world region, and finally by compliance process.

Comparison by Regime Type

The literatures on the role of the military in each of the three basic types of regime—democratic, authoritarian, and totalitarian—each have something to contribute to analyzing the role of the military in regime change in China. However, there are also problems in relating each of these literatures to China.

The most influential early formulations of civil-military relations concerned *democracies*. As discussed above, the professionalism central to Huntington's 1957 analysis *has* in fact been a central issue in China and remains pivotal to transition. Nevertheless, Huntington's concern was institutional design for an already existing democracy with an established tradition of civilian rule—mostly a question of optimizing the relationship between civilian and military elites. Huntington's 1957 framework was not intended to address nastier and larger problems such as demilitarizing the struggle for political power or democratizing the relationship between state and society.

The comparative literature that does address these larger issues treats mostly developing-capitalist *authoritarian regimes*. For example, Stepan identifies the military as the central institution in most authoritarian situations and therefore the central obstacle to transition from authoritarianism (most succinctly in Stepan 1986). He distinguishes different kinds of military actors—individual officers participating or intervening in politics, a group of officers constituting a government cabinet, or a corporate institution of the entire military establishment. Moreover, he identifies the circumstance under which the military-as-institution might support regime change—usually when it comes to regard the performance of the existing regime as inadequate for its own corporate purposes. These purposes are likely to include a strong concern for internal order and external defense, some calculation of defense budgets and military welfare, and some commitment to a larger cause, usually nationalism. These insights are potentially quite relevant to China's future, but only as China moves further away from its protracted-revolutionary, decentralized-totalitarian past.

Comparative politics argues that *totalitarian systems* are unlikely to be purely praetorian. At least in Leninist totalitarianisms, the party prevails, and that does change the range of transition paths available. (As often observed, a ruling party may accept a transition to democracy if it thinks that it can become electorally competitive, whereas a ruling military probably does not have that alternative.) However, focus on the party in Leninist systems has diverted attention from the military, whose role in both regime and transitions has varied significantly. Even comparative communism largely assumed party dominance. However, during regime crises Leninist institutions did not prevent the military from acting independently of the party (in Eastern Europe usually to allow transition, in the Soviet Union to try only halfheartedly to prevent it). In China, where the role of the military is vastly larger, the military is even more likely to act independently.

In sum, the China case requires a new synthesis of themes from the literatures on all three main regime types, both to define the baseline from which transition begins and to measure change during transition. From the totalitarian literature the China case needs the high coerciveness and broad scope of military involvement. From the authoritarian literature the China case needs the centrality of the military to both regime type and regime change, and institutional specificity about its role. From the democratic literature on civil-military relations, the relationship between politics and professionalism can then be respecified for China's post-totalitarian, coercive-authoritarian context.

Comparison by World Region

As noted above, comparative politics suggests that the main spectrum of possibilities for the role of military actors in transition lies along a continuum from strong civilian institutions and a subordinate military role, through weak civilian institutions replaced by a strong military role, to the decay of both civilian and military institutions (Huntington 1968). Evidently the key to maintaining a regime and avoiding civil war is to resolve issues through civilian processes, in order to maintain at least ostensible civilian unity, as the Chinese communist regime itself insists. So long as the party and government remain viable institutions, the military is likely to remain ostensibly their servant. Given the experience of Tiananmen, both party and army will probably do everything possible to avoid military involvement. However, if the party and government decay too far, the military might have little choice but to intervene to arrest the breakdown of the old regime. Then the military could serve as an interim government leading either to renewed civilian authoritarianism or to limited democracy.

At the beginning of the 1990s, China's conservatives insisted that the military prevent transition. "Officers and soldiers now understand that in economics, China cannot implement privatization; in politics, we cannot have a multi-party system; ideology must never be multidimensional; and the army must not be weaned from the party or become depoliticized" (*People's Daily* late 1991, quoted in Lam 1995, 206). At the end of the 1990s, the PLA remains committed to blocking, if not economic transition from communism, then at least political transition from Leninism. Nevertheless, the comparative literature suggests that the role of the military in China's political transition could be more positive, if the Chinese military thought its corporate interests were best served by a change of regime. Military support for regime change would be most likely if decay of the Communist Party had caused decay in domestic order, and if some alternative, even limited democracy, seemed more likely to preserve stability. Such a judgment might be reinforced by corporate military economic interests, if stability was good for business. One can reverse each of the terms in the conservative exhortation: The PLA itself might well favor some degree of economic privatization, some role for itself as a quasi-political party, some freedom to think in more than unidimensional party-ideological terms, and some degree of depoliticization.

Analogous processes in different world regions shed some light on these alternatives. Twentieth-century eastern Asia provides mostly more examples of the same militarized Asian environment producing similarly strong military establishments that mostly support strong civilian nationalist authoritarianism. Few Asian militaries have formally taken over the government, but few have voluntarily allowed democratization. In most other Asian Leninist cases evidently the militaries have taken their cue from China during the 1990s, supporting economic reform but opposing political reform (Garcia and Gutierrez 1992, Hernandez 1996, Crouch 1997, Winckler this volume).

Other Third World regions mostly raise the issue of under what circumstances military individuals or institutions will intervene to remove incumbent civilians and to replace them as the official government. For example, what is typical of Latin America is an environment of low external threat but high internal local militarization, resulting in a military that acts as the ultimate guarantor of national interests, through repeated cycles of military intervention and withdrawal. China differs from Latin America in the fusion of civilians and military and in the fact that military intervention has occurred at civilian orders not military initiative. Nevertheless, China resembles Latin America in its recurrent reliance on the military as ultimate guarantor of national security and stability, suggesting that, as in Latin America, the cycle may continue for some time (Rouquie 1982/1987, Aguero 1997).

Comparison by Compliance Process

The military plays potential roles in transition through three kinds of compliance processes—coercive, normative, and economic. In each, as an institution with both external and internal roles, the military is affected by a distinctive conjunction of influences from three levels—national, subnational, or supranational. Each kind of compliance involves different temporal patterns, particularly the mix of routine and crisis (editor's Introduction to this volume).

China remains highly *coercive*, both in routine police work to prevent initiation of transition and in the threat to use force against any such initiative (Cheung 1996b, Tanner this volume). A coercive crisis that requires reinvolving the military is most likely if the regime simultaneously confronts both a supranational threat from above and a popular challenge from below (Dickson this volume). Key intervening variables will be the party's and army's perceptions of threat, informed by their philosophy of response. Chinese statecraft has long involved a "strategic realism" that uses force to "teach a lesson" to threatening adversaries, as the revolutionary elders chose to do at Tiananmen (Johnston 1995, 1996). A renewed coercive crisis between state and society would probably again block any political transition from Leninism. However, it could also result in a "hard" transition, involving open and long quasi-military conflict, probably leading to some form of authoritarianism. However, the experience of the Tiananmen crisis makes it less likely that either mass popular initiative or mass military repression will recur.

Much of the *normative* transition from communism has already occurred in China, at least among urbanites. The regime's legitimation formula—stipulating identity of interests among party, army, government, and society—has grown increasingly implausible (Paltiel 1995). At least among urbanites, Tiananmen largely completed the delegitimization of both party and army, diminishing the PLA's former normative role as a model and propagandist for communism. Legitimation crisis has become routine. To achieve a largely normative transition—either the rest of the way "from communism" or the beginning of the way "to democracy"—requires the emergence of a real consensus between regime and society. This in turn requires some ideological accommodation by the regime, probably by giving old formulas new meaning. The most likely ideological common ground for such a "soft" transition is nationalism, of which the military does remain the main institutional exemplar. Moreover, the military's own normative transition to professionalism could contribute.

China's *economic* transition from communism is far advanced, and the Chinese military has become deeply involved in it. The effects of military commercialization on transition could be both positive and negative. Economically, it re-expands the economic scope of the state and complicates institutionalizing a law-governed economy. Commercialization consolidates PLA support for marketization, though whether a "developmental regime" or "crony capitalism" remains to be seen. Either way, military commercialization makes the military in effect a fraction of the conservative-authoritarian bourgeoisie typical of late capitalist development (Meisner 1996). Politically, if commercialization does somewhat undermine central control, that might aid "transition from" the old regime, but might also make transition itself chaotic and complicate "transition to" a new regime. Military commercialization may shift the PLA's interest in political stability from internal security toward the "business environment," making the PLA less inclined to enforce order for a failing Leninism and more inclined to foster some more popular regime. Ideologically, military commercialization could undermine the old regime through public disgust at military venality, but that venality too could complicate constructing a new regime. For the military, marketization means not only diversifying its domestic and foreign business ventures, but also adapting strategically to a supranational environment in which "complex interdependence" requires not only military force but also economic power and international prestige. Economic internationalization may make the PLA more sensitive to the economic and other costs of domestic repression. In any case, the distinctive commercialization of China's military transition will contribute to the distinctiveness of the military's role in China's transition from communism.

Conclusion

This chapter has tried to help build some bridges over the chasm that remains between the sinological and comparative literatures.

To sinologists the chapter has argued the centrality of the military to political transition and the utility of engaging the theoretical and comparative literatures. The Chinese case falls somewhere between purely civilian and purely praetorian but has been more "military" than the Chinese

Communist Party has pretended. Recent advances in institutional analysis of Western civil-military relations can help clarify Chinese military politics. Nevertheless, anticipating the likely future role of the Chinese military in political transition requires directly addressing the comparative literature on transition itself.

To recent institutional analysis of civil-military relations, the chapter has argued that arrangements for delegation and oversight do shape the political behavior of Chinese military actors. However, their effect has been strongly conditioned by institutional history and organizational environment, and by the substance of the matters of policy and power at stake. The chapter illustrates the interaction between microrational neo-institutionalism and macrohistorical new-institutionalism discussed in the Conclusion to this volume.

To the comparative literature on transitions, the chapter has argued that China's trajectory is from totalitarianism to post-totalitarianism, but that the PLA's political role has been larger than the role of the military in other Leninist systems, nearly as large as in military-based authoritarian regimes. Moreover, the breadth of the PLA's other roles has been greater than usual in either authoritarianism or totalitarianism. Compared to more specialized and isolated militaries, these many involvements make the PLA both more central to transition and more subject to transformation.

4

Ideological Struggle over Police Reform, 1988–1993

Murray Scot Tanner

With the exception of the top party leadership, there is probably no sector of the Chinese political system about which we know less than the public security system. Even the uniformed military have proven more amenable to outside research than the civilian coercive apparatus. Yet, if China is to entertain any hope of a successful transition toward democratization and sustained market-oriented economic growth, then a major reform of the civilian coercive system must be a cornerstone of that process. The future character of the public security system will go a long way toward determining, among other things, whether China will enjoy the social stability, legal predictability, political openness, business and property rights protection, and manageably low rates of corruption that are essential to any vision of market and political reforms. In other words, the success or failure of public security reform will help determine whether China's future will more closely resemble (as many Chinese hope) Taiwan, Singapore, and Japan, or (as many Chinese fear) present-day Russia, Mexico, or the Philippines.

Unfortunately, this leaves reformers with a very tall order to fill. For centuries, Chinese public security work has been premised on the assumptions of a largely nonmobile populace—neighborhoods and villages where residents at a minimum knew each other's business (and often were kinsmen), and in which flows of information, goods, and commerce were slight and slow. To this tradition, the Communist Party's security services brought more than twenty years of underground conspiratorial experience born of the bitter legacy of Chiang Kai-shek's nearly fatal 1927 counterrevolutionary attack (Xiao 1992). After 1949, many public security forces received their trial by fire in the movements for land reform, attacks on corrupt businesspeople, and most of all, the suppression of counterrevolutionaries (Schurmann 1971, Leng and Chiu 1985, Teiwes 1987, Lieberthal 1995). For thirty years, from 1949 to 1979, the terms of the ideological debate over security work rarely got past the issue of whether or not the "first principle"—party control over the security system—should even be augmented

111

by codified legal predictability; and only briefly and sporadically did the supporters of "rule by law" hold the edge. Completely beyond the pale were any notions about the depoliticization of the police, or a system of "rule of law" that was binding on the party-state as well as the people.

This chapter examines ideological debates over reform within the public security system between 1988 and mid-1992. It has by now become a commonplace of analysis on China to note the declining importance that *ideology,* in the grander sense of that term, has in politics. But the reform of the *organizational ideology* of the security sector will play a key role in determining whether that sector facilitates or undermines any future political reform or post-Leninist transition. As North has argued, ideology is an indispensable companion of legal-organizational oversight in establishing a successful relationship between the top government leaders and those agencies that carry out their policies (1981, 7–8, 201–205). As the current Chinese leadership well knows, the "transaction costs" (e.g., information, staffing, rewards, and punishments) of constantly and directly monitoring the policy compliance of a bureaucratic sector as vast and secretive as the security system are simply too great. Mao's life was a constant and ultimately futile struggle to find alternative informal information networks to help him monitor the fidelity of his bureaucrats. (For example, he used his personal security guard for information about their home localities.) Premier Li Peng has expressed exasperation at the tenacity with which local officials protected their subordinates from reprisals in the post-Tiananmen purges. More recently, press reports of the widespread complicity of public security and military officials in sheltering truly enormous corruption schemes have been nothing short of astonishing (*FEER* 9 June 1994, 22–30). To succeed, any post-Leninist Chinese government will, to be sure, be forced to develop new organizational-legal systems for efficiently monitoring and enforcing compliance by their public security services, such as legislative oversight, a more aggressive press, public access to some police information, and more independent courts and prosecutors. But even if these new leaders are successful in quickly establishing such organizational-legal devices (a large assumption), any transitional leadership will also have to find new means of ensuring more voluntary, lower-cost compliance within the security sector. Otherwise, as the new governments in Russia, South Africa, Panama, and Haiti are painfully aware, the potential for rogue elements within their security services to undermine the transition through subversion or corruption is enormous. If we assume, as seems reasonable, that any transitional Chinese state will at first have far weaker organizational-legal means of enforcing compliance available to it than its Leninist predecessor, then the need for at least minimal ideological congruence between the top leadership and the public security system becomes even more obvious.

The key questions, then, are how do officials in the Chinese public security system see the political and economic reforms of the last fifteen years, and how do they feel they must adapt their work to them? What, in their view, are the new dangers and challenges reform has brought to China? How serious are these threats? How do the views of public security professionals and scholars compare with those of the top leaders who oversee this sector? Is there, within the public security sector, an indigenous base of ideological support for reform on which reformist leaders could build? Or would any prospective reformist leaders face a security sector that is, as we might assume, overwhelmingly dominated by die-hard Leninist adversaries to reform? These are the questions this chapter addresses.

Until recently, Western sinologists have had very little access to information that would help us analyze the spectrum of views within the public security system. But the relatively new availability of numerous national and local legal and public security newspapers and journals has greatly expanded our access to information. This chapter draws in particular on a unique new source to analyze organizational attitudes and ideology in the public security sector: the articles published between 1988 and 1993 in *Gongan yanjiu* (Public Security Research), the top internal circulation theoretical journal of the Ministry of Public Security (MPS). *Gongan yanjiu's* articles cover the full range of public security issues: from senior leaders' hortatory messages, to general theoretical works and statistical research on criminal trends, to local field reports on methods for improving policy work, to some fascinating research and reminiscences on the history of Chinese security and intelligence work. For Western sinologists interested in the public security system and social order, *Gongan yanjiu* is a potential gold mine. These articles represent our first major opportunity to evaluate the spectrum of opinion among the ranks of the CCP's "enforcers" as expressed at a time when they most likely did not believe "outsiders" (both foreign and domestic) were reading.

During 1988–1993, the most prominent ideological debate within the security sector focused on the issue of class struggle and the nature of the "people's democratic dictatorship" during the "the initial stage of socialism." The debate initially focused on the proper "object" (*duixiang*) or target of the people's democratic dictatorship during this stage. Later security specialists debated the nature and magnitude of class struggle in present-day China, the size and power of the threat faced by the party-state from its various "class enemies," foreign and domestic. Throughout, two other issues formed an undercurrent: how the public security sector should evaluate its own historical background; and how the sector should evaluate the current reformist leadership of the party. The period under review produced a fascinating spectrum of debate, encompassing the relative intellectual liberality of the post–Thirteenth Party Congress period and the 1989 Beijing Spring, plus the post-Tiananmen Leninist counterattack, and finally the first signs of a partial reversal in the immediate wake of Deng Xiaoping's December 1991–January 1992 Southern Tour.

This debate has potentially huge bureaucratic stakes. The power to define the "object" of the people's democratic dictatorship is the power to define the current "enemies of the people," as well as the size, power, ferocity, and immediacy of the threat faced by "the people" and their "guardians" in the MPS. For this reason, debates over the nature of class struggle in the current age—at their highest, most authoritative level—have usually been left to the top party leaders (especially Mao and Deng). But the "ripples" of the more concrete, lower-level debate analyzed here would still radiate widely. The debate helps to frame China's other ongoing discussions about building up its criminal laws and legal procedure, as well as a host of other internal debates about general issues of social control, human rights, international police cooperation, and so forth. In the sixteen years since the Third Plenum refocused the CCP's work away from "class struggle," and Deng Xiaoping ordered most of China's "rightists" released from detention, the MPS has persistently found itself in a situation not unlike that currently faced by the U.S. Department of Defense—it must identify new credible threats and enemies of social order in order to continue to justify its mission, powers, prerogatives, manpower, and budgets. The greater and more persuasive the perceived threat, the greater is the MPS's institutional leverage. The debate over the identity and number of class enemies in society would, in particular, affect the MPS and the Ministry of Justice's future access to the dubious fruits of prison labor, which we now know are an enormously lucrative source of foreign exchange (Wu 1993). As this debate makes clear, at least some MPS officials are heavily involved in "a search for enemies."

A longer version of this essay traces the evolution of the debate from 1988 to the end of 1992 in much finer detail. For brevity's sake, this chapter merely sketches out the three major contending schools of thought and their relationship to the leadership of the security sector at that time. I have chosen to label these three viewpoints the Public Security Reformers, the Leninist Mainstream, and the Neo-Maoists. These distinctions should not be drawn too sharply, however; for example, among the Leninists, we can distinguish those authors and leaders who lean slightly more to the reformist or hard-line edges.

During the entire period covered by this chapter, Politburo Standing Committee member Qiao Shi oversaw the civilian coercive apparatus as secretary of the CCP's Central Political-Legal Group, which oversees China's public security, state security, procuratorate, justice, and court apparatus. Qiao also chaired the party's Central Commission for the Protection of Secrets, which has partial control over the Ministry of State Security. Wang Fang served as minister of public security from early 1987 until December 1990, when he was sacked, reportedly in large measure for failure to foresee and prevent the spring 1989 demonstrations, and for the relative ineffectiveness of the arrest campaign after 4 June when many dissident leaders targeted for arrest escaped to Hong Kong and the West.

Given the terrific shifts in top leadership politics during this period, Qiao and Wang remained remarkably consistent in their stated views of public security work. Using the ideological spectrum described below, the two men's views remained within the "Leninist mainstream," though generally somewhere to the "reformist" edge of that mainstream. But Qiao and Wang did not enforce a consistency of views on their lower-level associates within the security sector. Throughout this period, top scholars, ranking provincial security chiefs, even MPS vice-ministers and bureau chiefs felt free to publicly stake out positions often sharply to the "reformist," "Leninist," and even "neo-Maoist" sides of Qiao's and Wang's views. In the year leading up to Tiananmen, increasingly radical reform voices did battle with the Leninist mainstream. After Tiananmen, Qiao, and especially Wang Fang's policies, suffered savage attacks (though not by name) from more leftist leaders alleging a failure of class vigilance by high-ranking party and state security leaders, which permitted the demonstrations to begin and get out of control. Some of the most severe of these attacks came from a top party security veteran, Peng Zhen, from ranking officials of the Beijing City Public Security Bureau, and even from several of Wang Fang's top aides within the Ministry of Public Security.

Historical Backdrop

As in all such debates, the uses of history were crucial, and hidden within the *Gongan yanjiu* articles is a referendum on party security policy and the MPS's organizational history. Controversy focused on several key periods and events. First, underlying many authors' views on the seriousness of current class threats were starkly different assumptions about the effectiveness of the land reform and "suppression" campaigns of 1948–1953. Many officials confidently saw these as a historic turning point that had secured once and for all the ultimate victory of socialism and the Communist Party in China. Others clearly felt that the revolution could still be lost. The 1957 Anti-Rightist Campaign represented another problematic era. More devout Leninists proudly reaffirmed the necessity of the campaign and its fundamental correctness. All authors conceded the party's current official verdict on the campaign, that although the campaign was necessary, it had been "exaggerated" and had harmed many innocent and patriotic people. But at issue was the relationship between the "exaggerations" of 1957–1958 and the universally condemned chaos of the Cultural Revolution, which had backfired and virtually destroyed the public security sector. Defenders of the Anti-Rightist Campaign treated the two as unrelated. But advocates of a more fundamental reassessment of security policy saw 1957 as the beginning of the "exaggeration of class struggle" that inevitably telescoped into the self-destruction of the Cultural Revolution.

The post-Mao era presented a whole new set of historical controversies. Some reform critics strongly intimated that the twin 1978 decisions to remove the rightist "caps" from the 1957 dissidents and refocus the party's work away from class struggle had resulted in an overrelaxation of vigilance against class enemies. For reformers, on the other hand, these two decisions marked a long-overdue return to the socialist legality advocated in the mid-1950s. The 1983–1986 anticrime campaign (known as the campaign of "stern attack" or "stern blows") was the most recent point of historical controversy. To some, the campaign, which involved thousands of executions, was an effective and valid model of crime suppression. They pointed to official figures that indicated a more than 45 percent drop in overall crime during the first year of the campaign (Leng and Chiu 1985, 136–138; Amnesty International 1984). Critics, citing contradicting figures, characterized the campaign as a spasmodic, outdated, and ultimately ineffectual reaction to the far more complex social order problems of the reform era. They cautioned that the traditional focus on crime as class struggle was not only superficial but dangerous, running the risk of again exaggerating class struggle. As one reformer put it, "The more we struggle, the more there is chaos." To these authors—all of whom were anxious to make public security work support economic and social reform—crime and social protest in the reform era reflected the inevitable and temporary birth pangs of a new and fundamentally more healthy social order. China's police needed to get used to it and learn how to manage it.

Public Security Reformers

Throughout 1988 and 1989, the debate focused principally on the relationship between crime and class struggle in the "initial stage of socialism," in particular, whether or not serious criminals constituted a new form of class enemy or should simply be seen as elements of "the people" who had committed mistakes. The "public security reformers" argued that China's security system needed a far more sophisticated theoretical understanding of the roots of crime—one better suited to a diverse, reforming society.

These authors criticized simplistic explanations of crime that stressed only class struggle, or the remnant influence of the Gang of Four, or the quality of police work, or party economic and social policy since 1978. None of these explanations could account for the fact that crime rates had shot up since the early 1980s, notwithstanding the unprecedented economic success and political stability of that period (Dai 1988). Some reformers, most notably MPS Social Order Bureau deputy director Mou Xinsheng, sought to explain the crime increase as the inevitable result of the "accelerated circulation" of people, property, and commodities caused by reform and opening up. Caught between the old and new systems, and lacking well-developed new laws and regulatory systems, China had many new opportunities for corruption and crime (Mou 1988).

Before Tiananmen, many public security reformers had reaffirmed those periods when the party had emphasized "socialist democracy," a focus on economic development, and a broadly inclusive definition of "the people." The most notable events here were the 1956 Eighth Party Congress, the 1978 Third Plenum, and the 1987 Thirteenth Party Congress. Conversely, they argued that the party and the public security organs had committed their most self-destructive errors beginning in 1957 when they "exaggerated class struggle," and later "took class struggle as the key link," treating ordinary cases of crime and political dissent as life or death class struggles. For these authors, there was a direct, logical link between the chaos of 1966–1976 and the excesses begun in 1957. Turning to recent history, these reformist authors felt similar errors of exaggeration had been made during the 1983–1986 "stern attack" campaign. Reformers also discounted the effectiveness of this campaign—the major event in post-1978 public security history. No less an authority than deputy bureau director Mou Xinsheng charged that the alleged successes of the campaign had been only temporary, partial, and geographically limited (Mou 1988, 8–9). Crime statistician Dai Wendian went further, charging that many of the reported decreases in crime were actually fabricated reports by local officials afraid to disappoint their superiors (Dai 1988, 2–3). In any case, Dai noted, the number of major criminal cases and violent crimes had continued their rise as soon as the campaign was over. Public security officials had to update their thinking and abandon the hope that through campaigns they could ever restore the levels of social order China enjoyed during the mid-1950s, when the country was closed and society immobile. Reformers also attacked related efforts by more Leninist officials to expand the scope of crimes and criminals that would be considered objects of dictatorship (Wu 1988).

Counterattacks by the Leninist Mainstream

Ever since their first articles in early 1988, the public security reformers had faced stiff counterattacks from more mainstream Leninist security professionals. They argued that reform and opening up had produced a new and expanding class of violent and/or corrupt criminals who increasingly were replacing such "traditional" class enemies as landlords, capitalists, KMT spies, and "bad elements" as the principal "object" of the People's Democratic Dictatorship.

For mainstream Leninist authors, a key proposal was the idea that all "serious" criminals (including the new class of criminals) who had been convicted and sentenced to terms of ten years or more should automatically be considered "objects of dictatorship" (Hong 1988, 6–7). As such, these criminals would be deprived of political rights and, after the end of their sentences, should be subjected to especially strict control and surveillance by both police and citizens. Reformers attacked this proposal as a needless expansion of class struggle. The Leninists also vigorously defended the police's various past struggles, especially the 1957 Anti-Rightist Campaign, which they stressed was absolutely necessary, even though it got out of hand. They also upheld the more recent struggles against "counterrevolutionaries," "spiritual pollution," and "bourgeois liberalism" in 1978–1979, 1983, and 1986–1987. The Leninists argued that past exaggerations of class struggle were an aberration limited mostly to the period 1966–1978. With the demise of the party's radical wing, the Leninists felt sure that these were unlikely to be committed again. By contrast, they saw the 1983–1986 "stern attack" campaign as an effective model of crime control and urged it be reused in the future when necessary.

Reform-Tinged Leninism at the Top

Qiao Shi and other top security leaders did not join the reformers' historical attack, but echoed some of their other themes during the annual National Political-Legal Work Meeting. Analyzing the past year's dramatic increases in crime, Qiao stressed the multiplicity of socioeconomic causes as well as mass resentment with inflation and intraparty corruption. He avoided entirely the rhetoric of class struggle and enemy conspiracy that characterized more hard-line Leninists, though he also seems to have resisted Zhao Ziyang's efforts to loosen Communist Party committee control over public security forces (Yun 1990). Qiao focused instead on the need to build or revive a variety of party and government-led local social control mechanisms to deter and restrain crime. Likewise, MPS vice-minister Yu Lei endorsed the "inevitable increase" thesis that China could never go back to the crime-free days of the 1950s and 1960s when it closed its doors and had no market economy. (See _RMRB_ 24 January 1989, 1; Reuters 24 January 1989; UPI 24 January 1989; _Chicago Tribune_ 10 February 1989, 18-C; interview with Yu in _SWB_ 1 February 1989.) Though Yu probably did not intend it as such, his analysis of 1988 crime increases also represented an implicit critique of the long-term effectiveness of the "stern blows" anticrime campaign. Yu also criticized Nanjing police officials for their ham-handed and excessively brutal treatment of student demonstrations there the previous month, and accused them of turning small student protests into large ones through their ineptitude. Coming just two years after major student demonstrations had resulted in the firing of Hu Yaobang and Wang Fang's predecessor (Ruan Chongwu) and a nationwide campaign against bourgeois liberal enemies, the meeting was striking for its relative apoliticism (Qiao 1989a, Tanner 1997).

Beijing Spring 1989

During the spring-summer 1989 "Democracy Movement," a couple of reformist public security scholars opened the debate far wider than any top leader had been willing to go, revisiting the fundamental question of the relationship between "dictatorship" and "democracy" under "the people's" state. Indeed, they directly attacked the question of whether or not there was a continuing need for large-scale "dictatorship" during the reform era. By far the brashest of these reformers was Liu Zaiping, a scholar in the Management Department of the People's Public Security University in Beijing, who argued that under socialism, the police needed to radically scale back their dictatorial activities and depoliticize their functions (Liu Zaiping 1989). Liu boldly based his argument on no less than Marx's theory of the post-revolutionary "withering away of the state" (1989, 8).

Liu Zaiping directly and explicitly took on the Communist Pantheon. Liu criticized, by name, the views of Marx, Engels, Lenin, Stalin, Mao (and, implicitly, Deng) that either people's dictatorship or proletarian dictatorship represented the highest form of democracy, and that "socialist democracy" and this dictatorship were inextricably interdependent (1989, 9). After socialist society had accomplished the destruction of classes, Liu argued, democracy and dictatorship increasingly diverged. Not only could dictatorship never make for "perfect" democracy, but it was now necessary for the dictatorial organs and functions of the state to begin to "wither away" (1989, 9–10). China must make its state organs more democratic, including the public security organs.

Such a thesis would have been radical enough without elaborating its implications in detail. But Liu went on. Democratizing the public security organs, he argued, meant a dramatic depoliticization in some very non-Leninist ways. Because the public security organs are armed and enjoy both the coercive power to arrest and the judicial power to investigate, their democratic role must be completely different from those of other state administrative organs. Most important, their democratic function requires them not to get actively involved in politics. "On the contrary, the public security organs should precisely maintain their relative independence from Party and government organs at every level" (*baochi xiangdui de dulixing*) (1989, 11). The public security organs must be responsible only to the constitution and not to "orders from above" or "local policies." And laws governing their activities must be debated by China's legislature, the National

People's Congress. Finally, just in case anyone missed the point, Liu suggested that the Ministry of Public Security, which borrowed its very emblem from the Soviet KGB, should now start copying yet another foreign model: the U.S. FBI (1989, 11).

Like many other public security reformers, Liu also argued for numerous changes in policing designed to help establish and protect a commodity economy, which he felt was the socioeconomic basis of democracy. These changes involved (1) greater protection for property and commercial flows, (2) an attack on new economic crimes, and (3) new residence, visa, and passport systems designed to ease freedom of mobility at home and abroad (Liu Ziaping 1989, 11–12).

Sadly, Liu Zaiping's article was at once both ahead of its time and behind it, and the reforms he called for, if they were ever to arrive, were still many years off. And as for his advocacy of those ideas, they were the stuff of the spring of 1989, when Liu had actually written his article. Although Liu was permitted to publish, I have discovered no evidence that any political-legal sector official at or above the rank of bureau chief ever came close to embracing Liu's notions of apolitical police professionalism. Rather dramatically, Liu's article was finally published in *Gongan yanjiu* (1989, 3), which came out about a month after the 4 June massacre. That issue was led off by a hastily inserted lead editorial entitled "Thoroughly Root Out the Evil, Leave Behind No Future Trouble. Public Security Organs Must Decisively Pacify the Counter-Revolutionary Riot" (Wang Dingfeng 1989).

Qiao Shi and Wang Fang's very different ideological journey through the spring demonstrations had gradually toughened their stance and placed still greater distance between them and more cutting-edge reformists such as Liu Zaiping. But by the time martial law was declared, these top security leaders were hardly much less out of step with the other more hard-line Leninist and neo-Maoist security leaders. During April and early May, at Qiao Shi and Wang Fang's direction, the public security forces and the paramilitary People's Armed Police (PAP) had largely (though not always) shown considerable restraint in coping with the demonstrators (Baum 1994, Brook 1992). Qiao and Wang apparently sympathized somewhat with student anger over corruption, speculation, and economic mismanagement; but both men were also emphatic in their tactical desire to avoid incidents of bloodshed and "martyrdom" that would make the demonstrations even worse (Baum 1994, Brook 1992, Gao 1996, Qiao 1989b, Tanner 1997, Wang Fang 1989a). By late May, however, both men were deeply conflicted in their thinking, more solidly on the side of the Leninists but still tinged with reformist sympathies. Several days after martial law was declared, both men still vocally opposed a massive violent suppression; and Wang Fang was still voicing sympathy for the motives of the majority of the students. But neither man had any more patience for what they saw as concessions to the demonstrators; and both had a Leninist's conviction that the demonstration leaders were hard-core, implacable, antisocialist conspirators who had to be repressed (Qiao 1989b, Tanner 1997, Wang Fang 1989a).

Hard-line Leninists Counterattack

In the wake of Tiananmen, and for almost two years thereafter, a group of unreconstructed Leninist authors seized back the debate from the reformers, castigating both the party and their public security brethren for having allowed bourgeois liberal thought to lull them into an unconscionable loss of vigilance and focus on their principal responsibility—class struggle (Liu Wenqi 1990, 21–24; Mu 1991; Yang and Wang 1990; Liu Enqi 1989). During this period, a "Leninist mainstream" of views coalesced around the following five main propositions:

1. Unquestioned CCP control of the security forces. "Proper" party leadership must also include a strong revival of ideological-political education and organizational discipline that would simultaneously root out the corruption that had angered so many demonstrators and eliminate the "disloyalty" reflected in so many police who had been too sympathetic to the protesters.

2. A world view that was still strongly conspiratorial. In sharp contrast to the "neo-Maoists," however (see below), the mainstream Leninist view did not portray *all* (or even, necessarily, most) unrest and crime among "the people" as instigated by class enemies (Mu 1991). Their strong assertions of the need to reassert ideological discipline often represented a tacit concession on this point.

3. Nevertheless, a still fairly unsophisticated, class-based view of the nature, origins, and methods of coping with serious crime. In the mainstream of this debate, however, the strong tendency was also toward far more sophisticated views than the neo-Maoists.

4. A general, though not always decisive, acceptance of the proposition that the exaggeration of class struggle represents a somewhat greater threat to China than a relative neglect of class struggle. This acceptance seems to be based largely on bitter memories of the Cultural Revolution's damage to the public security system.

5. A clear belief that in the 1980s, the party and public security organs seriously neglected class enemies, class struggle, and the need for dictatorship (Liu Wenqi 1990, Wang Dingfeng 1989). This failure was a significant cause of the 1989 demonstrations. Most Leninist authors, accordingly, couple this criticism with a strong contempt for the notions of human rights and freedom that many of the demonstrators espoused.

During the fall and winter of 1989–1990, Qiao Shi and Wang Fang chose to reassert their Leninist credentials by emphasizing the need to strengthen party ideological and political discipline among the security forces (point number one above). They particularly stressed the problems of official corruption, and indeed Qiao's public appearances in the fall were far more frequently connected with his work as head of the party's Discipline Inspection Commission than as head of internal security. In addition to stressing ideological discipline, party leadership, and a "clean workstyle," Wang spoke marginally more about the bourgeois liberal threat than he had in the spring (Wang Fang 1989b, 1989c). Wang's actions spoke more loudly for his Leninism, as he led a massive nationwide campaign of arrests of suspected dissidents, replete with classically brutal Stalinist police tactics (Amnesty International 1989, Asia Watch 1990). Nevertheless, Wang reportedly faced considerable criticism as several key dissidents escaped the dragnet.

Several other top party security leaders embraced a far more hard-line Leninist view than Qiao and Wang and often appeared to be criticizing the failures of security work under their watch. The hard-line Leninist counter-attack also seemed to have at least two discernible organizational bases: the Beijing City Party Committee and Public Security Bureau (PSB), and Wang's own Ministry of Public Security.

Peng Zhen, the longtime Beijing party chief and founding father of CCP police work, who had been eased out of power in late 1987, roared back with bitter attacks lambasting the lack of class vigilance by the party leadership in general and the political-legal institutions in particular. His attacks were leavened slightly by his vision of a "legalist" Leninism in which the party would retain unquestioned rule but would exercise that power within the strict confines of a far stronger, better-defined legal system (Peng Zhen 1989, 1990). Peng's concerns about lax vigilance had also been powerfully echoed by then Beijing mayor Chen Xitong (a former Beijing policeman when Peng was mayor), and by Yang Zhaomin and Wang Gongfan of the Beijing PSB Research Office (Chen 1989, Yang and Wang 1990).

Wang Fang also had to endure criticism and attacks from at least one of his own vice-ministers, Gu Linfang, and at least two of his bureau chiefs, Legislation Office director Liu Enqi and First Bureau (political security) chief Tan Songqiu (see below). In a lengthy September internal report on the origins of the demonstrations, Gu meticulously detailed an alleged ten-year "conspiracy" led by the CIA, Taiwan intelligence, and domestic liberals to undermine and overthrow CCP rule. Far outdoing Peng Zhen, Gu repeatedly criticized unnamed leading comrades in the political-legal sector for lax, indecisive handling of these uncompromising enemies of the party (Gu 1989).

"Neo-Maoist" Voices

As the fall-winter 1989–1990 collapse of European Leninism seemed to place Tiananmen within a global anticommunist trend, a third and most ominous set of voices emerged in the debate. These voices are worthy of the title "neo-Maoist." A few authors, using a variety of clever linguistic formulations, attempted indirect ideological "end runs" around two corner-stones of reform-era security ideology: (1) that ever since China's former exploitative classes were destroyed as coherent classes in the early 1950s, class struggle has no longer been the principal contradiction in Chinese society and thus, by implication, (2) "taking class struggle as the key link" constitutes a far more serious error and a greater risk for the party than does underestimating class struggle (Tan 1990, Song 1989, Dai 1990; Vice-Minister Gu Linfang 1989 also sounds like this in many places). All of these authors spun elaborate class conspiracy theories as their dominant (and usually sole) explanation of China's current social order difficulties. They made meticulous use of innuendo or guilt by association to establish connections among an absurdly broad array of domestic dissident voices, the reformist leadership within the party, international class enemies, and the collapse of communism in Europe. In a chilling echo of early pre–Cultural Revolution rhetoric, some even insinuated that the class enemy had in fact found its way into the party leadership. The reformist leadership under Zhao Ziyang was guilty at best of being asleep at the switch, and at worst of consciously suborning CIA infiltration. Most disturbing, these authors reflected a dogged unwillingness to concede any validity to the protest leaders' criticisms of Chinese society. They revealed not the least interest in carrying out a careful self-examination of the role the party's structural and policy failures—such as inflation, intraparty corruption, nepotism, crime, regional and interpersonal inequality, or just general authoritarian rule—may have played. Still less were they willing to concede the prophetic point that several public security reformers had made a year earlier: that increased levels of crime and social disorder were absolutely natural and predictable during an era of rapid reform, economic growth, and increased mobility of people and property. In these authors' worldview, wrong things did not "just happen," they were planned.

One of the boldest voices for expanding class struggle was MPS First Bureau chief Tan Songqiu (1990). Tan began, as did many others of his viewpoint, with a moderate Leninist mainstream tone, appearing to concede that the former enemy classes now lacked the wealth or the coherence needed to form a real threat to socialism and the party-state. But then Tan and his allies quickly turned to chipping away at these assumptions, making charges and arguments from which a reasonable reader could easily conclude that class struggle was in fact the principal contradiction facing

China. The language they used to describe the stakes of China's current class struggle was severe and glaringly incompatible with doctrines downplaying its importance. They evoked the specter of a reactionary victory, characterizing the current class struggle as a "struggle of life or death with the enemy" (Tan 1990, 3; Song 1989, 1), or alternatively "a struggle over whether or not CCP leadership will be abolished" (Tan 1990, 3; Dai 1990, 1; Wei 1991, 6).

The neo-Maoists carefully forged a conspiratorial interpretation of the spring protests and the Tibetan uprisings as an unbroken chain leading back through all of China's post-Mao dissident movements, even into the party center itself (Song 1989, 3–4; Gu 1989). The "backstage bosses" of 1989 were the very same "intellectual elite" that had called for "freedom and human rights" during the 1979 Xidan Democracy Wall movement and had promoted "spiritual pollution" in 1982–1983, as well as "bourgeois liberalism" in 1986–1987 (Tan 1990, 2). This ten-year-long plot was part of the same reactionary scheme that led to the overthrow of communist governments and parties in Eastern Europe, and later to the collapse of the Soviet Union (Tan 1990, 3; Mu 1991, 4).

Tan Songqiu went further than any other toward resurrecting the Cultural Revolution–era charge that the class enemy had found its way into the party leadership. Tan charged that leaders within the party had directed the student uprising from behind the scenes. Indeed "many of them" (*bushao*) "had been trusted by, and entrusted with important responsibilities by, key Party leaders." Other Leninist and neo-Maoist authors had already bitterly criticized Zhao Ziyang for coddling bourgeois liberals, suggesting willful neglect of the class enemy. (For other attacks on Zhao, see Song 1989, 4; Yang and Wang 1990, 9.) But Tan seemed to fix the locus of this class struggle very close to the top of the system, even appearing to suggest that Zhao's party lieutenants (and possibly Zhao himself) were representatives of the enemy class within the party.

> In the past, it was said that there was a bourgeois class within the Party, and contradictions within the Party were all viewed as a reflection of class struggle within the Party. This is incorrect. But, to say that struggle within the Party is not a reflection within the Party of class struggle, would also, in my view, be incorrect. (Tan 1990, 3)

The 1990 Political-Legal Work Conference

Surprisingly, with such heated rhetoric around him, Qiao Shi does not seem to have given in to the pressure to join the hard-liners. Qiao's address to the February-March 1990 Political-Legal Work Conference is a striking piece of moderation when considered in its time context—eight months after Tiananmen, two months after the Berlin Wall came down, and six weeks after Nicolae Ceaucescu's own security failed him and he was executed. Qiao's address also contrasts profoundly with Peng Zhen's speech five days later to the same conference. Qiao spoke first with an almost eerie professionalism, picking right up where he had left off at the January 1989 meeting as though nothing noteworthy—Tibet, Tiananmen, Eastern Europe—had happened in between. Peng, speaking five days later, reflected all the emotion of that year some have now called "the Leninist extinction." Qiao was detached and analytical; Peng was critical and conspiratorial. Peng spoke of nothing but the demonstrations, Eastern Europe, and the CCP's internal and external enemies; and he endorsed the center's "decisive measures" (*guoduan cuoshi*) against the counterrevolutionary riot. Qiao's speech alluded only once, briefly and tangentially, to the recent "turmoil" and apparently did not even use the words "class struggle," "peaceful evolution," "counterrevolution," "Tibet"—or mention the collapse of European Leninism. Instead of talking about the sources of disorder and crime, he again talked about their "complex" social, political, and economic origins. Aside from a brief call for "strengthening socialist spiritual civilization," Qiao gave hard-liners little to sink their teeth into. Only in their mutual insistence on revitalized party controls and ideological education did Qiao and Peng come full-circle to agreement (Peng Zhen 1990, Qiao 1990).

1991-1992 Return to the Center

The pendulum began to swing back to the center only in late 1991 and 1992. This shift slightly preceded Deng Xiaoping's Southern Tour, where he reinvigorated reforms and pronounced "leftism" a greater current threat than rightism. Qiao Shi has been accused of being a "bystander," "fence-straddler," and a "born-again reformer" who came on board late in supporting Deng's new reform drive (Baum 1994, 350–353). But Qiao's activities in the security sector do not seem to confirm this characterization. During his own Southern Tour to inspect provincial security work in October 1991, Qiao forcefully reaffirmed the "reform and opening up" policies to local public security officials, and called on them to create a security system that would both promote reform while managing its unwanted criminal side effects:

> Without reform and opening, today's China would not exist. Our Party's reform and opening policy, originating with the people and practice, has won the support of the broad masses of the people, and has brought tremendous changes to China in the last 12 years. Practise has proven that the basic line and various principles and policies made since the Third Plenum of the 11th Central Committee were totally correct. . . .
> While vigorously promoting economic development, reform and opening has also brought some negative things and the emergence and

spread of certain social ills. It is, therefore, necessary to adapt the management of public order to the new situation of reform and opening and take effective measures to crack down on crimes, protect the people, and maintain social stability . . . [and provide] . . . an important guarantee to smooth reform and opening and healthy economic development. (Qiao 1991)

Even before Deng's Southern Tour made reformism once again politically fashionable, Qiao had reasserted a key public security reformist tenet—that reform and opening up were fundamentally healthy, and the task of public security forces was to cope with the inevitable increases in crime that came along with reform.

About the same time as Qiao's speech, articles began to appear in *Gongan yanjiu* that reminded public security colleagues of the disasters engendered by the party and the state in the past when they had exaggerated class struggle and overestimated how many citizens were actually cooperating with "the enemy" (Wei 1991, Mu 1992). Senior adviser Mu Fengyun strongly argued that the organs of dictatorship must learn to better recognize that some levels of disturbance and dissent were normal "among the people" in a healthy society. Mu also reached back in history to compare current excesses with those of the early 1940s Rectification Movement and the Sino-Japanese war, when vast numbers of innocent persons were imprisoned or executed, often based on forced confessions or false charges. Without naming names, Mu was making a historical allusion no experienced party security official could miss; he was implicitly comparing the current leftist witch-hunters with Mao's most infamous security chief: Kang Sheng.

A brief note about power, personnel, and ideas is in order. A review of the power structure in China's public security system at the end of this period suggests that moderate Leninists and reformers were somewhat more effective at maintaining their positions. None of the neo-Maoists or the most hard-line Leninists discussed here has emerged in a top security position. Peng Zhen's health could not support his ambition, and his March 1990 speech on political-legal work was apparently his last before his death in 1997. Qiao Shi retained his leadership over party security affairs at least until the spring of 1993, when he was named to head the legislature. Supreme Court chief justice Ren Jianxin took over the Central Political Legal Group and Central Commission for the Protection of Secrets until 1997 and continued as a voice for greater rule of law, albeit a less influential one than Qiao. Wang Fang, as noted, was fired as minister at the end of 1990, after overseeing a brief anticrime crackdown and security preparations for the Asia Games. He continued as state councilor in charge of political-legal affairs until spring 1993. His successor, however, was neither Gu Linfang (who was also removed in 1993), nor, as some hard-line leaders had apparently hoped, the ill-fated and corrupt Beijing ex-mayor Chen Xitong. Wang was succeeded by Tao Siju, a career MPS official and one-time aide to Luo Ruiqing, who seems to have scrupulously avoided any personal commentary during the spring and fall of 1989. Neither of the two hard-line MPS bureau chiefs who implicitly attacked Wang Fang—Tan Songqiu and Liu Enqi—was promoted to vice-minister, though Mou Xinsheng, the reformist deputy director of social order, whose criticisms launched the entire debate, was promoted to serve as Tao's vice-minister. Both Tao and Mou retained their positions at least through the end of 1997.

Conclusions and Speculations About a Transition

Although the vast majority of recent scholarship on state and society in China has focused on economic affairs, it never hurts to recall the Weberian first principle that coercion is the sine qua non of state power. The 1988–1992 battles over class struggle and public security provide some tremendous new insights into the minds of the men who wield that power in China. This chapter underscores that there is an enormous range of ideological views among the top leaders, upper-level professionals, and scholars of the public security system. Which of these leaders or schools of thought prevail in the post-Deng era is likely to make an enormous difference for how repressive and intrusive the future Chinese state is likely to be.

As a subtext, there is an important debate in the *Gongan yanjiu* articles about proper control relationship between the party's top leadership and the public security professionals. Public security reformers seek a fundamental change in the relationship between the party leadership and the police. Most of the reformers and Leninists (even, sometimes, a "hard-line" Leninist like Peng Zhen) cannot fully resolve their historic Leninist conflict about whether their first duty is to the current party leadership or to the party-state's laws. The few most vocal reformers, however, make no bones about their desire to build a wall of apolitical professionalism between the two. What necessitates such a wall is precisely the requirements of market-oriented economic reform and more "socialist democratic" legal and political reforms. Hence, they embrace a (rather idealized) model of FBI apoliticism and public security accountability to the legislature, the courts, and enacted law.

The authors I have tagged as mainstream Leninists are most content with the current model of the relationship between the party leadership and the police, based as it is on strict party control over a disciplined security system. This does not prevent them from criticizing current leadership policy when it becomes "too liberal." But their ethic about such policy still seems to be that of the "good soldier." While they oppose apolitical reform, they are still, at least publicly, willing to follow the orders of top-level leaders, even reformers.

This distinction brings us to the neo-Maoists, who clearly see certain of the party's top leaders as so infected with bourgeois liberalism that they are willing—however cautiously—to turn their backs on idealized Leninist organizational discipline and perhaps collaborate in efforts to undermine the authority of such leaders. A "communist" leader taking "the capitalist road" is not a leader worth following.

The wide range of views represented in the public security community leads us to a contradictory set of images when we try to imagine a post-Leninist transition in China. Reformists within the party and society can take some consolation from the fact that there is already an indigenous base of support for reform, however small, within China's security bureaucracy. This support base, moreover, is not limited to academics, but includes at least some high-ranking security professionals such as Vice-Minister Mou Xinsheng. For such a base even to exist within China's most notoriously Leninist bureaucratic sector is something at least. But if the number of articles and persistence of viewpoints mean anything, the Leninists still constitute the overwhelming mainstream at the MPS.

Furthermore, nothing in the new personnel and policy arrangements announced at the October 1997 Fifteenth Party Congress appears to have changed this balance; and Qiao Shi's removal means a moderating force against more hard-line Leninists is now gone. Any transitional government in China will have to cope with the formidable burden of reforming this apparently deeply entrenched organizational ideology. Even a relatively liberal-minded reform leadership will face continued problems of public security officers, still embued with statism and class theories of crime, harassing, or more likely corruptly "shaking down" entrepreneurs and repressing new political activists. To more authoritarian-minded transitional leaders, the powerful residuum of Leninism will likely make the public security forces a tempting tool to use against new political opponents. Boris Yeltsin's continued use of the old KGB for political purposes should remind sinologists of a fundamental paradox of transitions from authoritarianism: that when former regime opponents come to power, they frequently turn to the very organs of coercion they once saw as the quintessence of the former regime's evil (Rahr 1993, Knight 1996). The neo-Maoist elements may present an even thornier dilemma, particularly if their discipline erodes and some of them choose to use their power and access to information to actively undermine the stability of the transition.

PART 3

Political-Economic Transition

5

A Principal-Agent Analysis of Fiscal Decentralization

James Tong

This chapter analyzes post-Mao China's experiments with fiscal contracting and its eventual shift to a tax-based fiscal system. Etzioni's classic analysis of compliance provides the political setting for neo-institutional models of incentive contracts and principal-agent relationships. The first section sketches the main features of the pre–Cultural Revolution fiscal regime, the compliance problems created by the Cultural Revolution, and the resulting need to shift from persuasion and coercion to remuneration in the post-Mao period. The body of the chapter then outlines the center's 1979–1993 attempts to fine-tune the terms of contracts under which provincial governments collected central revenues, showing the effect of these experiments on provincial efforts to collect revenues and control expenditures. The 1979–1993 system of delegation-by-contract increased overall revenues but significantly reduced the center's share of them. The concluding section briefly reports the center's resulting 1994 shift from fiscal contracting to a tax-based system, in which the center directly collects its own revenues.

This chapter analyzes formal institutional arrangements and the systematic budgetary data they produce. The formal system is not the whole story of central-local fiscal relations, which include occasional ad hoc exactions, rising extrabudget funds, and other informal flows that supplement and adjust the outcomes of the formal system. Nevertheless, the formal system establishes the framework within which the informal processes occur, or, in Nathan's imagery, it serves as the trellis upon which the informal institutions grow and take shape (Nathan 1973, 44). The formal system is also the center's *programmatic* efforts to build fiscal institutions, and the only system that produces data comprehensive enough to permit systematic analysis. Similar lack of data precludes investigating the more political aspects of this relationship. (For rare primary documentation, see *CZSL* 221–224, 232–233, 235–236.) Lack of space precludes examining the interactions of reforms in central-provincial fiscal relations with related reforms in planning, material allocation, banking, investment, pricing, commerce, foreign trade, and investment. (Good relevant studies include Lieberthal and Oksenberg 1988, Shirk 1993, and Huang 1996, among others.)

Background

The Pre–Cultural Revolution Fiscal Regime

Before economic reforms were launched in 1979, the Maoist period achieved three decades of extensive economic growth and dramatic advances in social services (Eckstein 1966, Perkins 1980, Prybyla 1981, Jamison et al. 1984, World Bank 1989b, Tong 1990). These achievements in growth and welfare are attributable in significant part to the centralized Maoist fiscal management system, which had the following basic features (Lardy 1978, Donnithorne 1981, Oksenberg and Tong 1991). First, the central government enjoyed virtual monopoly of fiscal policy and budgetary authority. Provincial budgets and final accounts had to be approved by the central government. Their execution was closely monitored by local financial departments and the central People's Bank, and was subject to a uniform set of financial operations, accounting procedures, reporting formats, and schedules set by the central government.

Second, Beijing did not adopt the *income* approach of assigning fixed revenue sources to local governments, which were then free to determine how much to tax and spend. Rather, its *expenditure* approach first assessed local needs for specific services and programs, then allocated just sufficient funds to cover these local needs. If provincial revenue exceeded budgeted expenditure, the province had to remit the excess to the central government. If revenue was insufficient to meet expenditure, the central government would appropriate the additional funds. Through such mechanisms, the central government redistributed funds from the affluent provinces to those it deemed in need. For most years in the Maoist era, Shanghai had to remit around 90 percent of the revenues it collected to the central government, while remote and rural Tibet received close to 100 percent of its expenditure from the central government. (On alternative approaches to fiscal systems see Marshall 1969, Hicks 1977, Matthews 1980, and Davey 1983.)

Two sets of organizational problems arise from the centralized nature of such a fiscal regime. The first concerns how the central government could make the provinces comply with its fiscal directives. Given the fact that most state revenues were collected by local governments, and that rich provinces had to remit revenues in excess of assessed expenditures to the central government, why should they be rigorous in collecting revenue? For provinces both rich and poor, how could the central government make them spend within the expenditure limits? Second, such a centralized system is also predicated on an extensive administrative, monitoring, and coordinating structure at the national level, which has to plan and prescribe revenue and expenditure targets for local governments and coordinate horizontal and vertical fiscal transfers. What are the effects on central-provincial fiscal relations when this administrative structure breaks down? This chapter focuses on these compliance relationships. Where necessary, it also refers to problems in the administrative structure itself.

Compliance Relations in the Maoist Regime

Etzioni suggests that social organizations employ three sets of power instruments to enforce compliance by lower levels (1961, 3–21). To simplify his elaborate discussion, *normative* power rests on ideological appeals and manipulation of symbolic rewards, *remunerative* power is based on the use of material incentives, while *coercive* power relies on the use of threat or sanctions. Compliance relationships are congruent if the power instrument corresponds with the orientation of the participants. The use of normative power requires the participants to be highly and positively committed, as in the case of the party faithful. Remunerative power is congruent if the participants are calculative (e.g., buyers and sellers in trade). Coercive power is appropriate if the organizational members are alienated (e.g., prison inmates). To be effective, the use of power instruments has to be considered legitimate by subordinates, and organizations have to shift from incongruent to congruent compliance relationships.

From the founding of the Communist regime in 1949 through the mid-1960s, the central government appeared to use largely normative instruments rather effectively, supplemented by coercive instruments. The Chinese communist movement had begun as an underground organization that could not rival the ruling Nationalist regime in material resources and coercive capacity and had to rely instead on communist ideology and organization, both stressing the importance of hierarchy to enforce compliance. In later central-provincial relations, provincial party secretaries had to abide by the Leninist principle of democratic centralism, which requires subordinates to submit to superiors. Democratic centralism was a pervasive organizational feature of the new regime, enshrined in the 1954 state constitution, the 1956 party constitution, as well as the 1957 constitution of the Chinese Youth League (*RMRB* 21 September 1954, 2; Tang and Maloney 1967, 156, 192). It was frequently a dominant theme in the rhetoric of top party leaders and was encoded in propaganda phrases such as "the larger perspective should be considered" (*quanju guandian*), and "the part must give way to the whole" (*jubu fucong zhengti*) (Mao 1965; Tang and Maloney 1967, 16–17, 151, 214). The provinces were called upon not only to accept the center's values, but also to internalize them. Taking "the whole nation as a single chess board," there should be unity of goals and wills between the center and the provinces (*RMRB* 21 November 1958, 2). A single player, the party center, alone made the moves. The rules of the game required the provinces to be pawns. Very often, provinces had to be sacrificed for the good of the master game plan.

As heirs of two millennia of statecraft, and as students of the Soviet system, Beijing's leaders knew that ideology alone was insufficient and that they had to rely on controls and sanctions to exact compliance (Tong 1989a). The central government monopolized material and financial resources through central planning and distribution. This made the local government dependent on the center for raw materials for its plants, markets for its goods, and budgets for its programs (Donnithorne 1967). More important, through its *nomenklatura* system, the party's Central Committee controlled the appointment, promotion, transfer, and removal of the top and second-echelon officials in the provincial party and government hierarchy (Manion 1985). The center did exercise its power to remove and transfer the provincial elite (Teiwes 1966, 1970, 1971, 1974). From 1956 to 1966, no fewer than seven provincial first party secretaries were removed (Teiwes 1971, 1974).

In sum, during the 1950s and 1960s, through ideological exhortation and institutional controls, the center was able to exact compliance from the provinces. The provincial first party secretaries could be either faithful or foolhardy lieutenants who embraced party norms and willingly sacrificed local interests for the entire nation. Or they could be calculating realists and careerists who knew that the best interests of both themselves and their provinces lay in conforming to central demands and policy initiatives. Whatever the case, at least in public, provincial party secretaries upheld the primacy of national interests and considered themselves central agents rather than provincial defenders. Beijing was able to enforce compliance and quell localist demands. (Additional sources are Solinger 1977, Vogel 1980, Goodman 1986, and Falkenheim 1972.) Occasionally, some provincial leaders were even more zealous than the center. For instance, Henan's first party secretary, Wu Zhipu, surpassed central targets and mobilized 10 million peasants on water control projects at the height of the Great Leap Forward in late 1957 and early 1958 (Chang 1978, 81–92; Lieberthal and Oksenberg 1988, 344–347).

Incongruence of the Post–Cultural Revolution Fiscal Regime

The Cultural Revolution that broke out in 1966 led to radical changes in compliance relationships. It undercut the efficacy of the normative and coercive instruments and undermined the legitimacy of the central elite and the capacity of the administrative apparatus. Mao unleashed the Red Guards to drag out top party and government leaders and to expose their peccadillos in mock trials. For the first time, the nation learned that behind the austere facade and lofty rhetoric, many top central leaders were hedonists and lechers. Whatever the truth of such reports, they did undermine party appeals for national sacrifice. This normative loss was compounded by remunerative and coercive paralysis. In the state bureaucracy, anarchic infighting and administrative disruption halted central planning and management. The ability of the central government to prescribe targets and monitor local compliance was severely compromised. In the provinces, Mao demolished party committees, replacing them with revolutionary committees made up of warring factions.

When ideology could no longer inspire and organization could no longer enforce, it was the rich provinces that were most dissatisfied with the centralized and redistributive aspects of the fiscal regime. In a later section, I attempt to show how rich provinces underfulfilled and overspent their fiscal targets in the 1980s. Lack of budgetary data precludes similar analysis for the 1970s, but provincial dissatisfaction can be inferred from two developments. To summarize an earlier study (Tong 1989b), in the campaign to repudiate the "vertical dictatorship" (*tiaotiao zhuan zheng*) of central ministries in allocating resources and enterprise management, sixteen articles were published from June to September 1976 in the two national dailies (*RMRB* and *Enlightenment Daily*) and in the party's theoretical monthly (*Red Flag*). All were contributed by rich provinces that remitted 35 percent or more of the locally collected revenues to the central government. Similarly, the greater the share of a province's revenues to be remitted to the central government, the more likely that the province's first party secretary would be purged and replaced by outsiders, often a former central economic official. Taken together, these two patterns suggest that relations between central authorities and remitting provinces were conflictual. In Etzioni's terms, the compliance relationship had become incongruent. Both normative power and coercive instruments had become ineffective at enforcing provincial compliance with centrally prescribed fiscal targets.

Post-Mao Fiscal Regimes, 1979–1993

Principal-Agent Analysis

This chapter examines the more remunerative post-Mao central-provincial compliance relationship through principal-agent analysis. It assumes contractual market relations in which the principal has to devise economic incentives to make the agent act according to the principal's preferences. The common examples are management and labor, landlord and sharecroppers, the government and contractors. In these relations, a basic premise is the existence of a conflict of goals between the principal and the agent. The principal wants the agent to maximize the principal's benefit (e.g., profit, productivity), but the agent wants to maximize his own welfare (e.g., material gain, leisure). The principal's task is to design a compensation scheme to motivate the agent to act in the principal's interest. (For principal-agent theory see Grossman and Hart 1983, Arrow 1985, Fama 1980; on contracts see Hallagan 1978, Hart 1983, Braverman and Stiglitz 1986.)

In designing the scheme, the principal faces three sets of agency problems. The first, known as moral hazard, refers to shirking by agents. The second, known as risk-sharing, refers to the problem of overcoming the agent's aversion to risks. The third, adverse selection, concerns the problem of screening out undesirable agents. In central-provincial fiscal relations, the risk-sharing problem emerges in the goal-setting stage, when the center and the province negotiate to set yearly revenue and expenditure targets. Since there are uncertainties that affect both targets, provinces want the risks in fulfilling them to be shared by both center and province. The moral hazard problem surfaces in the implementation stage, when provinces tend to collect less revenue and spend more than the prescribed targets, motivated both by the desire to shirk and by the fear that a higher level of fiscal effort might lead to higher fiscal targets in the following year. Adverse selection is pertinent in the center's effort to choose the type of local agents. The challenge is for the center to design fiscal contracts that have built-in incentives and disincentives, so that the province will comply with central directives with minimal agency costs.

In considering compensation schemes, the principal can choose from three general types of contractual relations (Hallagan 1978, 344; Hart and Holmstrom 1978). (See Table 5.1.) The first is the salary or *wage contract*, in which the agent is paid a fixed fee for his service. In this type of contract, there is no incentive for agent effort, since remuneration is not tied to performance. The risk of performance failure, whether attributable to the agent or to exogenous factors, is assumed entirely by the principal. To prevent shirking, constant monitoring is required, hence the information cost for the principal is high. The second type of arrangement is the reverse of salary contracts. In a *renting contract,* the agent pays a fixed fee to the principal for proprietary rights to use the asset. This arrangement thus provides incentives for agent effort, since the agent's reward is tied to his performance. As the agent also assumes all the risk of performance failure, information cost to the principal is minimal, since there is little need for the principal to monitor agent performance. Between these two polar types is the *profit-sharing contract,* where the principal and agent share profits and risks. Thus there is incentive for agent effort, although not as substantial as in the renting arrangement. There is also need to monitor agent performance, although not as much as in the salary contracts.

Table 5.1   Types of Contracts

Contract Type	Incentive for Agent Effort	Principal's Information Cost	Risk Burden	Provinces
Wage	None	High	Principal	Metropoles
Revenue-sharing	Provided	Moderate	Shared	Majority and ethnic
Renting	High	Minimum	Agent	Guangdong and Fujian

Post-Mao Reforms in the Fiscal Regime

The post-Mao fiscal regime began in 1976 as local experiments and was implemented nationwide from 1979. It has undergone two decades of reforms in which the central government sought a fiscal regime that would enhance revenue and meet provincial demands for increasing fiscal authority on the one hand, while ensuring central fiscal capacity, maintaining macroeconomic balance, and preserving some measures of interprovincial fiscal equality on the other. The tortuous search throughout the 1970s and 1980s—involving short-lived fiscal regimes, none of which lasted more than three years—never reached equilibrium. But the general direction was clear. First, the provinces gained greater budgetary authority. Instead of central government ministries prescribing targets for local spending, the provinces were empowered to arrange the structure of local spending within an overall ceiling. Second, central-provincial fiscal relations became more predictable. Unlike the pre–Cultural Revolution fiscal regime, under which provincial retention rates were set in annual rituals of central-provincial bargaining, the post-Mao reforms introduced multiyear contractual schemes. Third, provinces received incentives to enhance their fiscal effort. They were allowed to retain all of year-end budgetary surpluses and all or part of above-target revenue and of savings on budgeted expenditure. Fourth, the provinces also gained the power to determine their fiscal relations with subordinate levels. Fifth, some subprovincial cities acquired budgetary independence from their home provinces. In addition to the thirty provinces and municipalities, fourteen other major cities have acquired provincial-level fiscal powers. In the pages to follow, "provinces" includes these fourteen cities (*ZGQ* 1992, 122, 135, 138; *CZ* August 1980, 57; *ZCTN* 1992, 831).

Fiscal Regimes and Contractual Schemes

Like structural reforms in agriculture and industry, fiscal reforms are based on contractual responsibility. As in those sectors, reform involves (1) a fis-

cal contract between the government and subordinate levels that (2) provides material incentives to lower levels for (3) fulfillment and overfulfill-
ment of fiscal targets. The specific fiscal arrangements between the central
and provincial governments closely resemble the three types of principal-
agent contracts described above. (For more detail see Tong 1989b.)

In the most autonomous form, the *lump-sum* arrangement is a fixed-
quota delivery. The locality contracts with the center for a specific amount
to be remitted or received, regardless of its actual revenue. This resembles
the *rental* contract. The two southern coastal provinces had this special
arrangement with Beijing. Guangdong had to remit a lump-sum to Beijing,
while Fujian received a grant from the central government, in amounts that
were fixed for five years. Aside from this fixed amount, the provinces
could retain almost all other locally collected revenue and arrange the
structure of their own spending, provided they balanced their budgets. Thus
the provinces assumed all the risks in implementing the budget but would
also receive all above-target revenue and expenditure savings. On the most
centralized end, metropolitan Beijing, Tianjin, and Shanghai had to negotiate with the central government a revenue-sharing rate that was adjusted
every year. They could not arrange the structure of local spending. Not having their revenue-sharing rates locked in for several years, these metropoles
feared that revenue increases resulting from greater fiscal efforts would
lead to lower shares of revenues in the following year. To the extent that
this arrangement provided little incentive to collect more revenue and save
on spending, it resembles a *wage* contract.

In between the renting and wage contracts, there were a variety of *revenue-sharing* arrangements. The *overall sharing* scheme sets a basic revenue-sharing rate that determines the percentage of budgeted and above-
budget revenue that go to central and provincial government coffers. The
overall sharing with marginal rates arrangement sets a basic provincial
retention rate for budgeted revenue and a different, usually higher, rate for
above-target revenue. Adding an *incremental adjustment* component to
these three basic revenue-sharing arrangements creates three more forms.
After the initial year, it adds an annual increment to the basic sum or sharing rate, to adjust for anticipated inflation or anticipated changes in provincial revenues or expenditures. These revenue-sharing arrangements, in
which both risks and benefits are divided between Beijing and the
provinces, resemble a *profit-sharing contract*. In different years, twenty-
four provinces had various forms of revenue-sharing. They had to negotiate
a five-year fixed rate, sharing both within-budget and above-target revenue
with the central government. They too were given the budgetary authority
to arrange the structure of local expenditures.

These reforms were first introduced in late 1976 on an experimental
basis in selected provinces and were implemented nationwide largely from

1980. Subsequently the State Council promulgated three distinct contracting regimes. Overall, the direction of change was toward higher institutionalization, greater complexity, and broader geographic inclusiveness. Unlike the annual and biennial regimes in the 1970s, the first two fiscal regimes in the 1980s lasted three years, and the 1988–1993 regime lasted six years. Multiple variants elaborated the three basic contractual schemes. Meanwhile, contracting was extended to fourteen major cities that acquired province-level authority at various times after 1983.

In the 1980–1984 fiscal regime, there were five coexisting schemes with the overall-sharing-with-marginal-rates as the modal arrangement (Oksenberg and Tong 1991; *CZSL* 1982, 205–217). The succeeding 1985–1988 fiscal regime was a more homogeneous system, with a bimodal distribution, having an equal number of provinces in the overall sharing scheme and the others in the lump-sum arrangement (Bahl and Wallich 1992; *CZ* May 1985, 10–12). In the 1988–1993 regime, there were six concurrent schemes with the lump-sum as the modal scheme (Agarwala 1992: *ZGQ* 1992, 135–137). In all three of these regimes, there were subsequent adjustments to the initial arrangements, in both the overall scheme and individual provinces. The addition of fourteen major cities that have acquired provincial-level fiscal authority since 1983 has further complicated these regimes. (For more detail see *ZGSZ* 1988, 278–284; and *CZ* May 1985, 10–12; April 1985, 23–25; April 1986, 10–11; and November 1986, 19–21.)

Effects of Fiscal Regimes on Fiscal Effort, 1979–1993

Our remaining task is to examine whether or not these different fiscal arrangements had significant effects on provincial fiscal effort during this period. Three sets of data are analyzed. The first concerns the level of effort with which the three categories of provinces collected and remitted the bonus tax in 1984–1985. Supplementing this, the second reports fulfillment of fiscal targets under different fiscal arrangements in 1982–1983 and 1984–1987. The third analysis, of provincial fiscal effort for the 1988–1993 fiscal regime, cross-tabulates revenue-retention rates with the differential between revenue growth and expenditure growth. Throughout, both the budget and final account refer to those officially adopted by a plenary session of the Provincial People's Congress, rather than to preliminary figures or the readjusted budget. For the 1988–1993 period, all thirty-seven provinces and municipalities with provincial-level fiscal authority are included. In the earlier period, since not all provinces published their annual budgets during the period of study, the analysis is based on provincial budgetary data for about twenty-four provinces from 1985 to 1987, twenty-one provinces in 1983 and 1984, seventeen provinces in 1981 and 1982, ten in 1979, and eleven in 1980. (For convenient data series see *ZCT* 1950–1991, and *ZCN* from 1992.)

Provincial Efforts in Collecting the Bonus Tax, 1984–1985

In June 1984, to induce state-run enterprises to be fiscally responsible in granting bonuses, the State Council levied a new bonus tax. The new levy imposed a progressive tax rate of 30 percent to 300 percent on all bonuses given out by state-run enterprises that exceeded four months of the wage bill. The tax was to be remitted to the local treasury before the bonuses were disbursed, and all the state-run enterprises were required to file the tax reports by 4 February of the following year (*ZGSZ* 1988, 278–284). Tax revenues were to be shared between the central government and the provinces at the revenue-sharing rate (*CZ* April 1985, 25). On 22 April 1985, or more than two months after the filing deadline, the Ministry of Finance made the unusual move of publishing data on the amount of the bonus tax each province had paid by the end of March of that year. An accompanying article by a commentator of the official New China News Agency drew attention to variations in provincial efforts to collect the tax and assailed provinces that had been delinquent in collecting the tax (*FBIS* 25 April 1985, K1–K2). On 8 May, the Finance Ministry made a second announcement publishing new data on the bonus tax collected by the end of April 1985 (*FBIS* 14 May 1985, K1). Taken together, these two reports illustrate that the level of provincial effort in collecting the bonus tax was a contentious issue in central-provincial fiscal relations. They also provide data for analyzing variations in provincial compliance.

To analyze the level of fiscal effort by provinces to collect the bonus tax, I first calculate the difference in tax receipts between the March and April figures. The first figure represents the amount the provinces collected without prodding from Beijing; the second represents results of collection efforts with central government pressure. The difference between the two sets of figures can be regarded as a measure of provincial delinquency in collection efforts. Since the amount of the bonus tax is a direct function of the total wage bill of state-run industrial and commercial enterprises in the province, I standardize the measure by dividing the delinquent amount by the wage bill. The resulting figure is then used to compare the level of provincial effort in collecting the bonus tax. A higher ratio indicates greater delinquency. I use 1985 provincial revenue-sharing rates to classify the twenty-nine provincial units into those that retain (1) 100 percent, (2) 61–99 percent, and (3) 60 percent or less of locally collected revenue (World Bank 1989b, 441). The first group of fifteen provinces could retain all revenues collected. These include the eight ethnic minority provinces, as well as five provinces whose budgeted expenditures exceeded their budgeted revenues (Shaanxi, Gansu, Jilin, Heilongjiang, and Jiangxi). This group also includes Guangdong and Fujian, which could also retain all locally collected revenue, after making or receiving a fixed transfer. A second group of seven provinces had revenue-sharing rates between 61 and 99 percent (Hebei, Shanxi, Anhui, Henan, Hubei, Hunan, and Sichuan). The remaining seven provinces form a third group allowed to retain 60 percent or less of the revenues they collect (Shandong, Zhejiang, Liaoning, Jiangsu, Beijing, Tianjin, and Shanghai). I compute the mean delinquency level of bonus tax receipts within each of the three groups. Just as taxpayers in higher tax brackets are more inclined to evade taxes, provinces with lower revenue-retention rates should be more delinquent in collecting and remitting the bonus tax receipts to the central government.

Table 5.2 presents these figures. Provinces that were allowed to retain more revenue were indeed less delinquent than those with higher revenue-retention rates. Provinces that retained all of local revenue were only 12 yuan delinquent for every 1,000 yuan of the wage bill. The intermediate group that retained 61–99 percent of local revenue showed somewhat greater delinquency (17 yuan), while provinces with the lowest revenue-retention rates had the highest delinquency rate (53 yuan). Both analysis of variance and correlation tests show a significant relationship between retention rate and collection effort. (Analysis of variance produced an R-square of 0.49 at the 0.0002 level of confidence; and the correlation coefficient was a highly negative –.76 at the 0.0001 level of confidence.)

Table 5.2   Mean Bonus Tax Receipts of Provinces by Fiscal Regime, 1984–1985 (in million yuan)

Revenue-Sharing Rates (%)	Receipts by 31 Mar. '85 (A)	Receipts by 30 Apr. '85 (B)	Payment Delinquency (A-B)	(A-B)/ Wage Bill
100	29.54	68.61	39.07	0.012
61–99	61.43	101.55	40.12	0.017
<60	10.25	138.37	128.12	0.053

Fulfillment of Fiscal Targets, 1982–1983

To broaden the analysis of provincial agent behavior, this section examines four basic measures of provincial compliance with central fiscal targets. (For related analysis see Tong 1989b.) Methodological rigor would require us not only to compare different levels of fiscal effort across fiscal arrangements, but also to compare different levels before and after the implementation of the fiscal reforms. Data constraints, however, limit us to a less perfect test. Since provincial budgetary data are not available before 1979, and the data from 1979 to 1981 are insufficient for statistical analysis, we can perform cross-sectional comparisons for most provinces only in 1982 and 1983. The test consists in comparing, for each fiscal arrangement, four measures of fiscal effort. These are the ratios of (1) the final revenue (FR) to the revenue target (RT), (2) the final revenue to that of the previous year, (3) the final expenditure (FE) to the expenditure target (ET), and (4) the final expenditure to that of the previous year. Greater fiscal effort is indicated by a *higher* ratio in the first two measures, which means that the provincial government was able to collect more revenue over the target, or to raise more revenue over the previous year.

Revenue increments alone, however, may reflect only economic growth, not vigorous tax collection efforts. We thus need to examine the third and fourth measures, which indicate the extent to which the province has spent within the expenditure target. Principal-agent analysis suggests that the provinces having the lowest level of fiscal effort should be the three metropoles that fell within the wage arrangement, which provides the least incentive for provinces to fulfill their fiscal targets. Conversely, the best performance should come from the two southern provinces that have the renting arrangement, which should give them maximum incentive to collect more revenue and to save on spending. The remaining provinces, which share their revenue with the central government at a fixed rate, should display an intermediate level of fiscal effort.

As shown in Table 5.3, the wage system of the three metropoles does show the least fiscal effort in 1981 and 1982 (see salary system column). They almost always missed the revenue target (0.96, 0.89), incurred budget overruns (1.17), and increased their spending level over the previous year (1.29, 1.06). In addition, on all four measures, they show significantly lower levels of fiscal effort, not only than the mean, but also than the other fiscal systems. (The only exception is Jiangsu 1982, which spent more than budgeted but exceeded its revenue target.) However, next to the metropoles, Guangdong and Fujian had the worst fiscal performance (see rental system column). Although they were granted the most generous incentive scheme, they collected less than the targeted revenue, below the 1981 level. Also they spent more than the approved budget and more than in the previous year. Where available, data also show lower levels of fiscal effort than the mean on three of the four measures, and the second lowest level in fiscal effort in all four measures (after the metropoles).

A plausible explanation for this deviation from our expectations is that the central government did not meet its contractual obligation and allow the two provinces to retain the favorable year-end budget surpluses that their efforts had produced. In 1979–1981, the state budget had run record deficits of nearly 33 billion yuan, nearly twice those in the disastrous Great Leap era (*ZCTN* 1950–1985, 15–16). Meanwhile, both Guangdong and Fujian had enjoyed substantial budget surpluses (*FJRB* 15 March 1982, 2;

Table 5.3   Level of Fiscal Effort in Three Fiscal Arrangements, 1982–1983

Fiscal Measure	Mean	Salary System	Revenue-Sharing	Rental System
82FR/82RT	1.07	0.96	1.13	0.99
82FR/81FR	1.04	0.96	1.08	0.99
83FR/83RT	1.17	0.89	1.24	—
83FR/82FR	1.10	0.65	1.57	—
82FE/82ET	1.03	1.17	0.93	1.14
82FE/81FE	1.16	1.29	1.14	1.15
83FE/83ET	1.16	0.98	1.20	—
83FE/82FE	1.21	1.06	1.24	—

NFRB 4 March 1982). To balance the central government budget, Beijing forcibly borrowed 1.6 billion yuan from Guangdong and 154 million yuan from Fujian in 1981, in addition to the contracted transfers (*NFRB* 4 March 1982, *FJRB* 8 July 1982). The loans represented 1.6 times the amount that Guangdong had contracted to turn over to the central government and 40 percent of its revenue for the year, and 10.6 percent of Fujian's revenue in 1981. In 1982, the center again skimmed much of these two provinces' favorable balances as loans (*NFRB* 12 April 1982, *FJRB* 22 April 1982). The central government never repaid these loans, which it wrote off in 1983. As in the case of the three metropoles, then, Guangdong and Fujian were major losers in the central government's redistribution policies.

This aberrant outcome illustrates the problems inherent in lump-sum contracts and principal-agent relations. The parties negotiated an arrangement where the agents were committed to remit or receive a fixed amount to the principal, a sum that was considered to be reasonable and fair. However, they did not anticipate that the principal would incur large deficits while the agents reaped substantial surpluses. Elsewhere the principal would have had to honor its obligation. In China, however, other factors intervened. Since the central government is the sovereign actor and is constitutionally empowered to set fiscal policy, it could claim that its fiscal exigency overrode contractual commitments. In addition, the center could claim that such contracts were never sacrosanct, since exogenous shocks to the economy often require the central government to act in the national interest, revising the budget and renegotiating contracts. Whatever the case, the rational reaction to the principal's default would be for the agents to relax their fiscal effort, which Guangdong and Fujian appeared to do in 1982 and 1983.

Analysis of Fiscal Effort, 1984–1987 and 1988–1993

The homogenization of the fiscal regime in 1985 blurred the formal differences in the three types of fiscal arrangements. To analyze the effects of the fiscal contracts, we will divide the twenty-nine provinces into three fiscal

regimes—100 percent, 61–99 percent, and 60 percent or less of locally collected revenue—and compare the four measures of fiscal effort across the
three regimes. As in the previous analysis, we expect provinces with higher
revenue-sharing rates to exercise higher levels of fiscal effort, since their
marginal rates of return were higher than provinces with lower revenue
shares.

As in the previous fiscal regime, provinces with higher revenue-sharing rates generally manifested higher levels of fiscal effort, collecting more
revenue over target and spending largely within budget. (See Table 5.4.)
The results are monotonic except for expenditures in 1984 and 1985, the
transitional years between the two fiscal regimes. (An analysis of variance
test shows that the results are significant at the 0.01 level for the revenue
measures for all years and for the expenditure measures, except for 1984
and 1985.)

Table 5.4   Level of Fiscal Effort by Revenue-Sharing Rates, 1984–1987

Fiscal Effort Measure	100%	61–99%	<60%
84FR/84TR	1.19	1.11	1.05
85FR/85TR	1.48	1.25	1.13
86FR/86TR	1.67	1.11	0.98
87FR/87TR	1.15	1.04	1.01
84FE/84TE	1.10	1.07	1.10
85FE/85TE	1.06	0.93	1.06
86FE/86TE	1.01	1.05	1.13
87FE/87TE	0.98	0.99	1.07

For the 1988–1993 fiscal regime, a gap in the data series precludes a
test based on annual measures. Instead, we conduct the following truncated
analysis. We first compute the percentage change in provincial revenue
from 1988 to 1993 (R), and the corresponding percentage change in provincial expenditure for the same period (E), then subtract (E) from (R) to show
the difference between change in revenue and change in expenditure $(R–E)$.
A positive value suggests a higher level of fiscal effort for the province, a
negative value suggests the reverse. We expect the provinces with higher
retention rates to show higher fiscal effort. (This analysis includes the original twenty-nine provincial units and seven major cities that were given
new provincial-level fiscal powers by 1 January 1988—Chongqing,
Wuhan, Shenyang, Dalian, Harbin, Ningbo, and Qingdao. Xian and
Guangdong had provincial status but did not negotiate a revenue-sharing
rate with the Ministry of Finance. The data gap is that the seven municipalities are missing for 1991–1992.)

Table 5.5 cross-tabulates provincial retention rates with the fiscal effort differential ($R–E$), grouping provinces into those with retention rates of lower than 60 percent, between 61 and 99 percent, and 100 percent. It can be seen from Table 5.5 that a great majority (five out of six) of the provinces that had the lowest retention rates (under 60 percent) had a negative fiscal effort differential—that is, they spent funds faster than they collected revenues. There is a close split among the second group of provinces with retention rates between 61 and 99 percent, with eight having a positive and the other seven having a negative fiscal effort differential. Among those that retain all their revenue, fourteen of the fifteen (except Hubei) have a positive fiscal effort differential. Thus, again, provinces and cities with higher retention rates do display higher fiscal effort.

Table 5.5   Fiscal Effort Differential and Provincial Revenue Retention Rates, 1988–1993

Provincial Revenue Retention Rates	$R\% > E\%$	$R\% < E\%$
Under 60%	Tianjin	Beijing, Shanghai Jiangsu, Liaoning Harbin*
61–99%	Shanxi, Heilongjiang Shandong, Hebei Anhui, Henan, Guangdong, Hunan	Zhejiang, Henan, Chongqing*, Wuhan*, Shenyang*, Dalian*, Ningbo*, Qingdao*
100%	Nei Monggu, Jilin, Fujian, Jiangxi, Guangxi, Sichuan, Guizhou, Yunnan, Xizang, Shaanxi, Gansu, Qinghai, Ningxia, Xinjiang	Hubei

Note: * indicates major cities with provincial fiscal powers

Conclusion

Reprise Through 1993

In terms of Etzioni's framework, compliance relations in China's fiscal regime changed in the post-Mao period. In the 1950s, when ideological commitment was able to override parochial interests in favor of the revolutionary vision of an egalitarian society, the predominant use of normative instruments, backed by coercion, was sufficient to induce provincial compliance. As the incarnation of the will of the people, the central party and state apparatus claimed the right to redistribute financial resources to build

China's industrial base, to provide basic services, and to bridge the gap between the affluent coastal provinces and the impoverished rural hinterland. As most provincial leaders were tested cadres in the revolutionary struggle, who had staked their welfare and cast their lots with the revolutionary cause, either their intense moral commitment or self-selected conformity sustained the unity of goals between center and province. The *nomenklatura* system of personnel appointments and dismissals, as well as the centralized control of material and financial resources, provided the supplementary coercive instruments to ensure adherence to central directives. Thus the normative-coercive compliance structure was congruent with the ethos prevalent among provincial leaders.

The gradual erosion of ideological fervor and the power struggle during the Cultural Revolution demoralized the party faithful and undermined the legitimacy of normative instruments. Ideological appeals for egalitarianism or about the need for democratic centralism had little effect on skeptical and alienated subordinates. Coupled with the administrative breakdown during the Cultural Revolution, when the regulatory and control functions of government agencies ceased to operate, the regime lost its coercive prowess as well. The compliance relationship became incongruent, from one premised on goal-unity to one predicated on goal-conflict. The instrument with which the central government exacted compliance therefore also changed, from one using mainly ideological and coercive instruments to one using remuneration. Forty years after the revolution, and a decade into the Thermidorean Reaction, China rediscovered the effectiveness of incentive schemes to motivate provincial compliance.

By focusing on the incentive mechanisms within contractual arrangements, principal-agent theory takes up where Etzioni leaves off. It suggests which type of contractual schemes would make provinces act in the interests of the central government. It shows which type of arrangement would allocate what share of benefit and burden to the principal and agent. Examining budgetary data in the post-Mao period, the above analyses have shown that the empirical pattern of provincial compliance with central fiscal targets corresponds closely to what the principal-agent framework suggests. Provinces in the equivalent of the revenue-sharing and renting contracts did collect more revenue and practice greater restraint in spending than those in the wage contract. Those with high revenue-sharing rates were less delinquent in remitting the bonus tax as well as more rigorous in the general fiscal effort. Taken together, the above analyses underscore the importance of the use of remunerative instruments to induce compliance from agents whom ideology ceases to persuade and coercion no longer compels. The more the Chinese leadership replaces the strong arm with the invisible hand for pulling economic levers, the more the principal-agent framework will illuminate China's fiscal transition.

The 1994 New Fiscal System

On 1 January 1994, after two years of local experiment, the center introduced a new fiscal system, backed by the promulgation of China's first "Budget Law" (*ZCN* 1995, 499–503). Hailed as historic and unprecedented, the new system marks the departure from the delegative responsibility contracting of 1980–1993, toward a fiscal system where the central and local governments have their own respective tax revenues and expenditure responsibilities. Recognizing that state revenue constituted only about 15 percent of its GNP in recent years, in comparison to the 30 percent range in other capitalist and postcommunist countries, the center resolved to increase that ratio. Concerned that in the early 1990s the central government share of revenue collected was only about 22–28 percent of the state budget revenue, it resolved to double that share to between 50 and 60 percent (Zhang 1997; Bird and Wallich 1993, 22). To accomplish these goals, the central government continued its movement to replace enterprise profits by a new system of personal and corporate income and value-added taxes, and restructured the allocation so that a substantial share of these taxes would go to the state treasury. In addition, for the first time in China's fiscal history, it established field offices of the State Tax Bureau in provincial capitals to collect central government taxes, thus putting an end to central dependence on local collection. While the new fiscal regime has features of a federal fiscal system, where the national and subnational levels of government have their own independent tax administration, separate tax revenues, and distinct expenditure responsibilities, it remains a unitary, albeit decentralized, fiscal system. Unlike other subnational governments in federal systems, local governments in China's new fiscal system cannot introduce new levies, set tax rates and bases, or borrow loans from domestic and international lenders. Their budgets need the approval of the central government.

Principal-agent theory helps explain this historic shift. The basic premise of the framework is the existence of goal conflict between the revenue-maximizing and expenditure-minimizing central principal and the local agent that shirks at attaining fiscal goals. Given the vastness of China, the lack of systematic economic data collection, and constant policy shifts during the reform period, the central principal knows little about current local fiscal conditions. To overcome this problem of information asymmetry and to motivate the local agents to exert their best efforts, the central government experimented with various contractual schemes that delegated budgetary authority to local governments and provided incentives for fiscal target fulfillment. However, from 1979 to 1993, the story of fiscal transition in China was the failure of repeated central attempts to fine-tune fiscal contracts to reduce agency costs. Setting the marginal tax rates of the local governments low or at zero, these fiscal contracts gave most of the increase in revenue collection to the provincial and local governments. While the arrangement did accomplish its fiscal goal of augmenting total state revenue, the central government has not benefited commensurably. By the early 1990s, the results of fiscal reforms in the previous decade clearly benefited the provinces more than the central government. Feeling that its interests had not been served, the central government changed the relationship to accord with its preferences.

Principal-agent theory can also shed light on why China did not adopt a federalist system in 1994. To give provinces complete fiscal autonomy would unleash even more local agents who had pursued economic policies that benefited their own localities at the expense of national economic interests. Throughout the reform period, local agents have erected regional trade barriers, levied illegal taxes and charges, engaged in commodity speculation, invested in sectors with excess capacity, pressed local banks to make risky loans, auctioned state assets at fire-sale prices, and failed to heed State Council injunctions to decelerate investment projects during periods of high inflation (Wedeman 1995; Wong, Heady, and Woo 1995, 127–131). Looking beyond China, they can also see the self-destructive policies of Russia when it adopted fiscal federalism, incurring in the process the highest budget deficit and highest inflation rate among all former communist states in Eastern Europe (Bird and Wallich 1993, 25).

Principal-agent theory also helps explain the selection of agents in both the prereform period and the current fiscal regime. When profits from state-owned enterprises were the main source of state revenue in the prereform era, the central government collected enterprise profits through enterprise managers, who were under direct central ministerial control. China's market reforms reduced the market share and monopoly rents of the state-owned enterprises, diminishing their profits and revenue contribution. When enterprise profits were replaced by tax receipts as the main revenue source, the central government established direct control over the collection of tax receipts. By creating the new infrastructure of field offices of the State Tax Bureau, and by replacing indirect provincial agents with direct central agents, the central government reduces agent shirking and enhances both monitoring and sanctions.

Three years into its implementation of the new fiscal regime, the Ministry of Finance has reported good results. After a hesitant start, directors of the State Tax Bureau in thirty provincial capitals were formally appointed by mid-August 1994 (*ZCN* 1995, 78–79). Tax receipts now constitute the predominant share in the state budget, accounting for 98.3 percent of total state revenue in 1994, 91.4 percent in 1995, and 93.7 percent in 1996, while total state revenue has increased by more than 40 percent in the three years 1994–1997 (*CZ* August 1994, August 1995, April 1996; *ZGCZ* April 1997). At the same time, state revenue as a share of GNP, having dropped steadily from 22–26 percent in the early 1980s to only 14.5

percent in 1991, 13.1 percent in 1992, and 12.6 percent in 1993, stabilized to 11.2 percent in 1994, 10.9 percent in 1995, and 11.0 percent in 1996. Most noteworthy is the share of central government revenue in the state budget, which increased from 28.1 percent in 1992 and 22.0 percent in 1993, to 55.7 percent in 1994, 52.2 percent in 1995, and 49.4 percent in 1996 (*ZTN* 1997, 233, 247). Thus the new fiscal regime appears to have accomplished its goals. (One should be careful in making temporal comparisons. In Chinese fiscal lexicon, central and local government revenues refer to those collected respectively by those two levels of governments, excluding two-way vertical transfers. Starting in 1994, the state budget does not include debt income and debt payments. The foregoing figures have been adjusted for these reporting and accounting changes.)

For much of China's fiscal history then—Maoist, post-Mao contractual responsibility regimes, and the current tax-based fiscal system—several of its important features are consistent with principal-agent theory, namely the relationship between the type of compliance used by the central government, the degree of local compliance, the type of fiscal arrangements, the choice of fiscal systems, and the selection of agents. Principal-agent analysis may well apply to other aspects of the Chinese economy, as well as to the political, legal, and other dimensions of central-local relations in China.

6

Economic Crisis and Market Transition in the 1990s

Dali L. Yang

Faced with deepening legitimacy problems in a world where democratic values are more and more widely accepted, authoritarian regimes have typically depended on performance, particularly economic performance, to enhance their legitimacy (Huntington 1991, 46–58). In the case of China, the credibility gap between the leaders and the led is especially difficult to bridge in light of past traumas perpetrated by the Chinese Communist Party (CCP) (such as the Great Leap Famine and the Cultural Revolution), the successes of China's noncommunist neighbors (Japan and the Asian newly industrializing countries), and the collapse of communist regimes in the former Soviet Union and Eastern Europe. Thus it was not surprising that the Chinese leadership that launched the crackdown of 1989 would seek to shore up its legitimacy through the promotion of stable economic growth (Yang 1989). The communiqué of the Party Central Committee plenum held in June 1989, for example, emphasized the continuity of reformist policies, especially the "one focus and two basic points" ("one focus" referred to economic construction; "two basic points" were adherence to the four cardinal principles and to reform and opening up) set down at the Thirteenth Party Congress in 1987 (*Qiushi* 1989 no. 13, 2–3). Following the death of Deng Xiaoping in 1997, the Communist Party enshrined Deng Theory at the Fifteenth Party Congress and made Deng's "three favorable comments" the fundamental criterion for action, that is, "judge everything by the fundamental criterion whether it is favorable to promoting the growth of the productive forces in a socialist society, increasing the overall strength of the socialist state and raising the people's living standards" (Jiang 1997).

Yet the goal of sustained, stable, and harmonious economic development is more easily proclaimed than accomplished, especially in a country that is undergoing the difficult transition from an administered to a market economy. On the one hand, if the growth rate falls below a certain level, it will adversely affect state revenue, which remains heavily dependent on state enterprises, and cause the unemployment rate to rise. On the other hand, extremely rapid economic growth tends to generate inflationary pressures that may also lead to social instability, as was indeed the case in 1988–1989. Therefore, the state seeks to use various macroeconomic mechanisms (such as monetary policy) as well as extra-economic measures (such as political discipline) to keep the economy from growing either too fast or too slow.[1]

In this chapter, I first provide an outline discussion of those features that tend to undermine macroeconomic stability during the transition to a market economy. I suggest that while inadequate economic institutionalization and fiscal decentralization have contributed to economic overheating, these two factors cannot adequately account for the dynamics of boom-bust cycles in China's economy during the transition. Instead, I propose a simple model of local competition, which, coupled with an iterated game between center and localities, illuminates the mechanisms through which the boom-bust cycles are produced. I then focus on the most recent cycle, arguing that in 1992 the politics of succession upset the balance between center and localities and, as in 1988, unleashed economic turmoil. Faced with crisis, central leaders circled their wagons to present a united front for stabilization. Learning from the lessons of the previous austerity program, they eventually succeeded in reining in the economy without plunging it into recession. Thus the political center demonstrated again that, when it is united, it can still prevail over the local state and the national economy.

The economic crisis and the impending succession to Deng Xiaoping also prompted the central leadership to push through sweeping institutional reforms in the economy. These reforms, in government finance, revenue collection and sharing, banking reform, foreign exchange management, corporate organization, and other spheres of the economy, have woven a web of institutions that promise fundamentally to reshape the way the Chinese central government governs the economy. Thus, the economic crisis that started in 1992 and the stabilization program that ensued should remain a crucial watershed in China's transition from planning to market.

The Context:
Under-institutionalization and Fiscal Decentralization

The transition from planning to market poses special challenges to macroeconomic stability. Most prominent, the shortage of consumer products in a command economy invariably leads to inflation when administrative measures such as rationing are removed. Fortunately, China's gradual reforms started with agriculture and a sharp increase in consumer goods production in the early 1980s. The sequencing of reforms thus served to alleviate the pressures for consumer price inflation in later stages of reform.

Yet, in the Chinese case, three factors made macroeconomic stability particularly difficult to achieve during the transition. First of all, the embryonic nature of economic institutions appropriate to a market economy called for greater political intervention in the economy, and such intervention tended to exacerbate rather than moderate the cycles of economic growth. Second, the acceleration of fiscal decentralization during the reform era gave localities and enterprises strong incentives to pursue their own interests, which also tended to increase the difficulties of macroeconomic coordination and control. Third, reform policies produced competition among localities that made a fundamental contribution to macroeconomic imbalance (discussed in the next section). Below I provide an overview of each of these factors as they existed at the beginning of the 1990s.

Under-institutionalization

Despite the multitude of bureaucracies in China, it is undeniable that the Chinese economy, like its counterparts in other developing countries, is not yet adequately institutionalized for what the Chinese leadership has called the "socialist market economy." The banking system offers a striking example. Whereas in the early 1990s China began to diversify the banking system beyond the People's Bank of China by building specialized banks for agriculture, construction, and other purposes, the banking system remained a poor link for macroeconomic control. Indeed, the People's Bank often served as cashier for the central government and had no effective control over money supply or interest rates. Until recently, domestic real interest rates were consistently negative as politicians sought to bolster ailing state enterprises and reward those with political connections. Bank lending was generally based on bureaucratic rationing rather than careful assessment of creditworthiness. The banks and their local branches were allowed to set up affiliated investment and trust companies and given easy access to bank credit.

Because the Chinese economic system was characterized by the underdevelopment of institutions for macroeconomic management, the room for policy discretion was especially wide and necessarily so. Each time the economy overheated, the leadership was forced not only to pull the few economic levers available to them, but also to resort to various extra-economic measures such as imposing price controls and tightening political discipline among CCP party members, as was the case in 1989. In other words, while China's leaders were often criticized for interfering too much in the economy, the point being made here is that poor institutionalization necessarily led to politicization of economic policy and vice versa. In such a milieu, the lack of a precommitment to macroeconomic parameters was to be expected.

In the absence of a credible precommitment, elite strife tended to accentuate macroeconomic instability. Moreover, as lack of precommitment was perceived to be part of the system, lower-level officials worked with a shorter time horizon than would have been the case under other circumstances, seeking to exploit windows of opportunity before they were closed. Such opportunistic behavior accentuated the various perverse tendencies of the economic system.

Fiscal Decentralization

As numerous Chinese and Western commentators have pointed out, a key feature of China's post-Mao reforms has been the ongoing realignment of central-local relations, especially in terms of fiscal arrangements. Prior to 1994, a central theme of the reforms was the decentralization of fiscal resources from the center to localities. Government budgetary revenue as a share of GNP declined from 35 percent in 1978 to less than 20 percent in the early 1990s. Moreover, in tandem with the downward shift of fiscal resources, the center transferred to local governments many spending responsibilities (such as basic education, public works, and welfare subsidies).

The transfer of both resources and obligations to lower levels of governments created strong fiscal incentives for these governments to promote local economic growth in order to raise revenue. In contrast to local governments in the former Soviet Union and Eastern Europe, local governments in China have had property rights in economic agents such as state-owned enterprises—by historical tradition, by investment in the fixed capital of the agent, or both (Granick 1990). The fact that about half of all local governments suffered from budgetary deficits as of the late 1980s and early 1990s compounded the revenue imperative, whether through development or sometimes through development-cum-predation. (Local cadres may have mixed motives for pursuing economic growth—not just profit but also promotion or honor—though as local resources expand, local officials have fewer incentives to move to the center.) In the meantime, for most of the 1980s, incomplete reforms virtually ensured that new investments would be profitable and thus encouraged local governments to become direct investor-owners (Oi 1992).

It is an article of faith in principal-agent analysis that, in situations of multiple principals and agents, the divergence of interests among principals and agents means that "agents are likely to make suboptimal decisions from the principal's viewpoint, unless they are effectively constrained" (Eggertsson 1990, 41). In other words, in the case of China, decentralization increased the need for macroeconomic coordination and control. The center argues that the entire economy should be like a chessboard, to be planned and managed or at least guided from the center. However the various agents, including local governments and enterprises, acted like generals on the battlefield—they would pay lip service to central directives but frequently choose to ignore them. They not only took independent initiatives but also possessed the resources to do so.

The implications of fiscal decentralization were compounded by other reform measures, especially the decentralization of the banking system that made it susceptible to local government influence. As a World Bank study put it:

> The decentralized financial network was overly generous (under political prodding) in responding to the demands for credit from enterprises. . . . Unless the intense investment hunger can be blunted and provinces induced to adhere to common development goals, the demand for credit will remain strong, as will the political pressure on banks to grant credit even if it means violating [credit] ceilings. (World Bank 1990, xiv)

The investment hunger phenomenon and the resultant investment fervor were thus both cause and symptom of the tendencies toward macroeconomic imbalance. As a result, the center must from time to time step on the brakes to cool down the economy, thereby creating boom-and-bust cycles.

Local Competition, Central-Local Interaction, and Macroeconomic Instability

The theory of agency predicts that local governments will pursue their own interests when they possess property rights, including part of the fiscal revenue stream. Nevertheless, the center may use other mechanisms, such as a tightly controlled *nomenklatura* system, to moderate localist tendencies (Greenhalgh 1990, White 1990). Wong (1991) argues that in fact fiscal direction from the center was quite substantial in spite of the fiscal decline of the center. Indeed, the severity of the austerity program of 1988–1991 underscored the degree of central discretion that was available. Inadequate institutionalization and fiscal decentralization thus did *not* equal macroeconomic instability and overheating.

In this section, I suggest that a simple model can account for the tendency of local governments to compete and emulate each other in adopting reformist policies and therefore points to the need for macroeconomic control. Theoretically, it is possible that all local units can get together to coordinate their economic activities and strive for macroeconomic stability. In actuality, leaving aside the issue of inadequate information, each local government has strong incentives to pursue reformist policies. This can be illustrated by the following example.

Suppose there is a country composed of two adjacent and similar local governments, A and B. Both have to pay out subsidies to urban consumers who purchase rationed grain at state-set (and lower-than-market) prices. To reduce the fiscal pressure caused by the subsidies, leaders in both adminis-trations consider whether to liberalize grain prices (assuming that the cen-tral government encourages but does not dictate the decision). There are four possible choice combinations in this case.

1. Both decide, whether independently or jointly, to persevere with the status quo and not to liberalize. The fiscal pressure remains.
2. Both choose, whether independently or jointly, to liberalize, for example, by freeing grain prices at the same time. The move effectively removes the fiscal pressure, though at the cost of a rise in discontent by those who benefited from the subsidies.
3./4. In two other choices, however, either A or B liberalizes grain prices before the other does and, assuming that there is a considerable time lag before the other liberalizes, then obviously grain will move from the subsidized area to the liberalized area. As a result, the late liberalizer will face procurement problems and is likely to adopt administrative measures (such as border blockades) to stop the grain from being taken out; other-wise, outflow may precipitate a grain shortage in the subsidized area. The late liberalizer is the sucker in a competitive policy game. (For details of the model, see Yang 1997, 60–61.)

Evidently, where the central government favors reform, and provided that information is relatively free-flowing, then the local governments will compete to reform. This model of competitive liberalization can be extend-ed to a country comprising a multitude of local governments endowed with a certain degree of policy autonomy: It does not pay to liberalize later than the others.

The above discussion applies not just to price liberalization but also to other policy areas such as investment. In the case of investment, the long-term differential impact on early and later liberalizers can be very signifi-cant; because investments tend to be lump-sum, they are relatively difficult to move from one place to another, and they produce agglomeration effects. Theorists of regional change from Hirschman to Krugman have empha-sized that regions that come to dominance in earlier periods tend to retain their preeminent positions for long periods (Myrdal 1957; Hirschman 1958; Richardson and Tonwroe 1986; Krugman 1991, 1993). Given relatively homogeneous spatial units, if one unit or area adopts preferential policies toward investors significantly ahead of other areas of the country, then this area will likely attract a disproportionately large share of the total invest-ment and remain ahead of the others for a long period to come. Because of the dynamics described here, one expects localities to emulate and compete against each other to liberalize, to invest, and to offer more preferential policies to attract investment from outside.

The end result of the spread of such policies, however, may not always be favorable to all. The competition to liberalize will speed up the liberalization process and, if liberalization is deemed desirable, then the equilibrium outcome is welcome even though the process will also generate significant price pressures. The rush to invest, however, will place strains on the budget. With soft budget constraints and political interference in banks, the investment race will also tend toward too much money chasing too few goods. In terms of preferential investment policies, the competition to offer ever more attractive terms may simply make the entire country a giant special economic zone, with no locality being more attractive than the others in policy terms. (Investors will also consider other factors such as labor quality, however.)

In short, given the local government incentives to engage in competitive liberalization and to compete for investment, local governments are likely to generate tendencies for macroeconomic instability. For each local government, macroeconomic order is a public good best provided by others. In consequence, China's transitional economy will tend to overheat and will thus need central direction to achieve macroeconomic balance. The center is cast in the role of coordinator as well as balancer to provide the public good of macroeconomic stability.

Yet, as mentioned earlier, the center faced tough challenges to fulfill its role as supplier of macroeconomic stability. Not only was the Chinese economy poorly institutionalized for market-based regulation, but it was also being transformed from a command economy into a market-oriented economic system. The dynamics of macroeconomic policy was in essence an iterated game between center and localities. Much depended on the credibility of the central leadership in formulating and implementing macroeconomic policies.

Macroeconomic Destabilization: Deng Xiaoping, Local Initiatives, and the Center's Credibility Gap

Before discussing the macroeconomic turmoil of the early 1990s, it is worth referring back to the previous economic cycle. In 1988, when the Chinese economy was already getting overheated, it was the decision of Deng Xiaoping and Zhao Ziyang to launch comprehensive price reforms; these touched off panic buying and skyrocketing inflation that reached 50 percent on an annualized basis in summer 1988. Rising inflation and rampant official corruption were two major sources of widespread social discontent that fueled demonstrations around the country in 1989. While the ensuing military crackdown put a lid on social discontent, Chinese politics remained tense and uncertain, especially after the collapse of communism in the Soviet Union and Eastern Europe.

To cool down the overheated economy, Premier Li Peng's administration carried out a tough austerity program that reduced government spending and restrained credit issue and investment scale. The Chinese leaders apparently miscalculated the impact of the stabilization program, however, and brought the Chinese economy into recession by late 1989 (Naughton 1992b). In early 1990, to restart growth, the leadership began to ease off on its austerity policies by furiously pumping funds into the system, especially to debt-laden state enterprises. As Naughton pointed out, "Total bank credit increased 22 percent in 1990, a remarkably high rate considering that prices increased by only a few percent and the economy hardly grew at all" (1992b, 81). In the meantime, in line with the spirit of the June 1989 party plenum, reforms were resumed in foreign trade, urban housing, and the deregulation of certain consumer prices. The Chinese leadership clearly sought to use economic revitalization to consolidate its political control.

By 1991, the Chinese economy had resumed expansion. Real GNP grew a respectable 7 percent, and industrial output, led by non-state-owned enterprises, rose 14 percent. Exports continued their robust expansion, jumping 16 percent to $71.9 billion and posting a surplus of $8.1 billion for the year. Fundamental structural problems remained, however. State sector growth remained slow as at least a third of state enterprises lost money. The government budget deficit also continued to expand. An attempt to broaden the revenue base stalemated owing to opposition from localities that faced fiscal pressures of their own.

Yet the recovery from the recession of 1989 and the limited reform measures were deemed inadequate by Deng Xiaoping and the more radical reformers among the top elite. To set the agenda for the fall 1992 Fourteenth Party Congress, in the spring Deng Xiaoping went on a highly symbolic tour of southern China and put his prestige behind faster economic growth (see also Saich 1993, CIA 1992, Yuan and Han 1992). In his remarks on the tour, Deng emphasized that economic development was vital to the legitimacy of the Chinese Communist Party and called for bolder experimentation with reforms. For Deng, the economic adjustment of 1988–1991 was necessary but served only the goal of stability and did not adequately promote growth. Deng gave special encouragement to locally based growth:

> Areas with adequate conditions should try to grow faster; as long as they emphasize efficiency, quality, and export orientation, [we] should not worry about them; slow growth [in the context of faster growth rates by China's neighbors] is tantamount to stagnation, even retrogression. [We] must seize the opportunity and the present is a good opportunity. (Quoted in Lu 1992, 207)

In particular, Deng pointed out that Guangdong, Shanghai, and Jiangsu should grow faster than the national average. Indeed, Guangdong "should strive to catch up with the Asian 'four little dragons' in twenty years." Deng reportedly called for 10 percent annual GNP growth in China; in contrast, in his government report presented to the National People's Congress (NPC) in March 1992, Premier Li Peng offered only 6 percent, apparently concerned that a very high growth rate threatened to bring back high inflation (Saich 1993, 22–23). Nevertheless, after an initial attempt to downplay Deng's push for reform, both Jiang and Li quickly turned themselves around and jumped on the Deng bandwagon.

Deng's Southern Tour sparked a new wave of reform euphoria among the localities. A variety of central policies introduced after the Deng tour to speed up reform augmented the freewheeling atmosphere. Specifically, Central Document No. 4 (issued in June 1992) extended the policy of opening up from the coast to the rest of China, thus empowering localities in the interior regions to pursue local interests.

In effect, Deng allied himself with the provinces, as Mao had done on numerous occasions. By praising those provinces that had grown faster than the national average during the 1989–1991 austerity program, Deng made it seem that it was all right for local leaders not to pay careful attention to central policies as long as the locality generated superior economic growth. Thus, when at the end of 1992 the center started to talk about preventing economic overheating, some local leaders argued that they should not repeat the error of suppressing economic expansion as they had done during the 1989–1991 austerity program. Instead, provincial leaders claimed that their provinces were growing far more slowly than provinces such as Guangdong and therefore did not need to be concerned about overheating. In other words, learning from recent experience, provincial leaders concluded that they should concentrate on generating growth rather than follow central directives to the letter.

In short, the flip-flopping around Deng undermined the prestige and credibility of the central leadership centered on Jiang Zemin. On the one hand, provincial authorities could now invoke Deng to justify highly expansionary policies, thereby precipitating a round of intense emulation and competition among the localities in adopting "innovative" policies. On the other hand, as central leaders jumped on the bandwagon of bolder reforms one after another, there was no longer any serious effort to prevent economic overheating from occurring (Yuan and Han 1992, 89–141). Words of caution might easily be interpreted as political disloyalty. Indeed, Deng reportedly stated that whoever obstructed the reform campaign ought to be removed. The balance thus tipped toward the localities. As every locality sought to do better than average, macroeconomic stability became the casualty of uncoordinated local actions. As far as macroeconomic policy was concerned, the central government would have a major credibility gap to close when it again wanted to rein in the provinces to prevent a repeat of high inflation.

Economic Turmoil and Unsustainable Growth

Before analyzing the center's responses to macroeconomic disorder from 1993 on, let us first take a look at the symptoms of the rush to "growth." These symptoms included a race to establish development zones, land and property speculation, a dramatic rise in investment, and a banking crisis.

Zone Rush and Real Estate Speculation

As can be expected from our analysis of the dynamics of local competition, once the center gave the signal that all localities could set up development zones, a so-called zone rush ensued. Whereas at the end of 1991, China had only 111 such zones (including twenty-seven centrally approved), by September 1992 the number of development zones had hit 1,951. In addition, there were some 8,700 rural development zones (*CD* 24 May 1993, 4).

Localities set up such zones by offering preferential policies to attract outside investment. Since the amount of such investment was not infinite, inevitably localities competed against each other to offer more favorable terms in tax reductions and exemptions; moreover, the rush to develop real estate and processing industries also had the effect of diverting much-needed funds from infrastructure and basic industries such as agriculture, mining, raw materials, and energy. Overseas investors setting up shop in the zones were free of income tax for the first two years and enjoyed tax reduction during the next three. Some areas, such as a Guangxi city, in violation of China's Law on Land Management, even eliminated the land-use funds charged investors in other words, investors could use the land for free.

The proliferation of development zones caused a serious drop in farm acreage. In 1992, nearly 2 million acres of farmland were taken out of cultivation, followed by another 1.8 million acres in 1993. In Sichuan province, 1.4 million *mu* (230,640 acres) of land were earmarked for 162 development ment zones (CCTV 1997). Most of the zoned areas remained to be developed, however (*CDBW* 10 May 1993, 8).

While the zones attracted industrial investment, the most noticeable activity was real estate development. The number of real estate companies grew from 3,700 in 1991 to 12,400 in 1992. In 1992, China invested 73.2 billion yuan in real estate development, up 117 percent over a year earlier. Actual foreign investment in real estate business in 1992 reached U.S.$700 million, up more than 200 percent over 1991. Most of the money went into upscale housing beyond the reach of most Chinese (*CDBW* 10 May 1993, 8). The speculative fervor in real estate was particularly acute in Guangdong and Hainan, fueled by investment from both overseas and other provinces. Real estate prices skyrocketed. In Guangzhou, the price in 1992 was 85 percent higher than in 1991 and in Shenzhen, prices doubled (*CD* 15 June 1993, 4).

Local officials set up development zones not just to attract investment but also to create rent-seeking opportunities. With few rules to follow, those in charge of allocating and leasing state land under preferential terms usually received kickbacks and other favors from investors. As one reporter put it, "The deals . . . say less about market economics than about simple corruption" (*NYT* 8 May 1993, 3). While the center had cracked down on the involvement of cadres and their relatives in private businesses in the aftermath of Tiananmen, in 1992 many localities abrogated the ban on such involvement, thereby accentuating the trend toward bureaucratic corruption.

Investment Fervor and Banking Crisis

For the first eleven months of 1992, the cumulative number of basic construction and renovation projects with a minimum investment of 50,000 yuan reached 49,870, up 9,943 from the year-earlier period (a 24.9 percent increase). Of these projects, 46 percent were new ones. According to the State Council Development Research Center, the scale of total construction investment reached 2,640 billion yuan by the end of 1992, an annual increase of 37.4 percent (*Guanli shijie* 1993 no. 2, 15). In 1993, fixed-asset investment increased by 61.8 percent from a year earlier. China had not seen such growth since the calamitous Great Leap. A bubble was in the making.

Because of inflation, the real interest rate on loans was negative (partly to protect money-losing state enterprises), so the demand for credit was virtually insatiable. Moreover, local government officials exerted pressures on bank branches to issue credit to fund the sharp increase in investment. In a go-go atmosphere, banks poured their funds into long-term fixed-asset investments, including real estate, and ignored lending quotas or simple prudence. Substantial bank funds were also funneled into speculative investments, including the nascent stock market.

Normally, if savings deposits keep rising fast enough, banks would have little trouble meeting both long- and short-term demands for funds. However, as economic growth accelerated and inflation increased, depositors withdrew money from fixed-rate bank savings and put them into purchases of goods and other investments, such as stocks and gold. This fueled brisk retail sales, long queues for stock offerings, and a rise in world gold prices. By spring 1993, growth in savings deposits slowed to a standstill. Private savings in state banks dropped by 4.5 billion yuan in March 1993, the first decrease since 1988 (*FEER* 3 June 1993, 59). China faced a financial crisis; the banks were simply running out of cash.

According to the veteran banking analyst Yang Peixin, banks usually set aside as much as 6 yuan in cash reserves for each 100 yuan in deposits, but in May 1993, the average was only about 1 yuan. Many banks had become overextended in capital investment and property speculation and had little cash to pay farmers or lend to factories for operating funds and wage payments. Interbank lending rose briskly to more than 300 billion yuan, with money flowing from the interior to the coast, especially Guangdong, Hainan, and Guangxi's Beihai (*AWSJW* 31 May 1993, 20; *Dow Jones News* 30 June 1993; interviews).

Investment Fervor and Inflationary Pressures

Domestic credit expanded by about 35 percent and bank loans by 20 percent for 1992. Real GNP grew by 13 percent, industrial output by 21 percent, and fixed capital investment by a whopping 38 percent. The actual amount of foreign direct investment was estimated at more than $11 billion. Retail prices overall rose less than 6 percent, but in the thirty-five major cities by 11–12 percent (*The Economist* 6 February 1993, 42; 24 April 1993, 35). In short, judging by these figures, China in 1992 had an outstanding growth record and moderate inflation.

The rising urban inflation rate, partly attributable to the freeing up of agricultural prices in early 1992, nevertheless raised concerns about economic overheating. In August 1992, the government appeared to have heeded the warning signs by issuing a decision to strictly control the number of new projects. However, on 30 January 1993, at a time when the economy was rapidly heating up, Li Guixian, governor of the People's Bank of China and a close associate of Premier Li Peng, publicly stated that nobody should fear a credit squeeze in 1993. Instead, Li Guixian announced that the government would by no means implement a tight monetary policy. Bank loans would grow at about the same rate in 1993 as in 1992 (*The Economist* 6 February 1993, 42). Indeed, the central banks added 50 billion yuan in liquidity in the first half of 1993.

Whether Li Guixian made the statement on his own initiative or not, he clearly sent the wrong signal. However, even if he had mentioned tightening credit, it would not have altered the local spending patterns immediately. In fact, the mere mention of the possibility of tightening would have sent the localities and enterprises to work harder to spend money in anticipation of the slowdown. Thus whatever the center did around the turn of the year, there was no way that it could *talk* the economy into moderation without actually doing something about it. Local expectations about central action virtually guaranteed that the economy would continue to heat up for the moment.

When economic figures for the first quarter of 1993 were released, most observers agreed that the Chinese economy was headed for inflationary trouble. During the quarter, fixed-asset investment by state units reached 9.72 billion yuan, up a whopping 68.9 percent, and industrial production expanded by 25.2 percent (both relative to first quarter 1992). Also worrisome was the retail sales trend. Led by institutional purchases, which reached 11 billion yuan (a 34 percent increase), total retail sales reached 106.8 billion yuan in the first quarter, an increase of 18.5 percent over the year-earlier quarter. Sales of consumer goods increased by 22 percent. The booming sales were partly spurred by buyers' anxiety about inflation as well as the devaluation of the yuan. The pace of inflation picked up substantially. Living costs in the thirty-five major cities rose by 16 percent in the first quarter (*CDBW* 31 May 1993, 8).

In the months that followed, these trends continued and, in some areas such as retail sales, even accelerated, owing to the introduction of new price reforms. For the first half of 1993, the Chinese economy grew by nearly 14 percent, faster than the 12.8 percent for all of 1992. Industrial production increased 25.1 percent (and 30.2 percent for June) compared with the same period of 1992. Measured on a year-to-year basis, inflation accelerated to 21.6 percent in large cities in June after averaging 17.4 percent through the first half (*Dow Jones News* 20 July 1993). Owing to rapid economic growth, widespread speculation, and the continuing construction boom, the rise in raw materials prices was even steeper. Prices of sixteen major industrial raw materials, including steel, timber, rubber, cement, and chemicals, rose an average 44.7 percent compared with the year-earlier period (*Financial Times* 13 August 1993, 24).

During the previous austerity program from 1988 to 1990, the Chinese government devalued its currency and tightened controls over trade in order to rein in a growing trade deficit and avoid a balance-of-payments crisis in a hostile international environment (Yang 1991). These measures—and the dynamism of China's export sectors—helped give China a comfortable trade balance sheet up to 1992. As the domestic economy heated up, soaring imports driven by frenzied consumer and institutional spending began to impinge on the trade balance. During the first half of 1993, China had a trade deficit of $3.54 billion, more than half of which was raked up in the months of May and June. Imports surged a staggering 23.4 percent over the same period in the previous year (to $40.69 billion), while exports grew a scant 4.4 percent, to $37.15 billion (Reuters 5 July 1993, *Dow Jones News* 5 July 1993).

In short, by mid-1993, all indicators suggested that the Chinese economy was headed for trouble. The State Statistical Bureau (SSB) concluded that the Chinese economy had entered the "red light" danger zone by mid-1993 (*Liaowang*, overseas ed., 12 July 1993, 4–5). In an apparent reference to the economic crisis that helped precipitate the Tiananmen debacle, SSB economists warned that if the feverish growth rate continued, "it might trigger an over-expansion of consumer demand, thereby leading to the recurrence of a 'double swelling' of demand for both high investment and high consumption as was seen a few years ago" (*CD* 9 July 1993, 1).

The Politics of Macroeconomic Stabilization

Why did it take the Chinese leadership such a long time to react to economic overheating in 1992–1993? It appears to me that two factors—one epistemic, the other political—largely account for the delayed reaction. It is hard to assess a transitional economy, and harder still when the assessors are jockeying for position during a political succession.

The epistemic factor refers to the divergent economic assessments and forecasts made by Chinese economists, which made it difficult for policymakers to come to a definitive conclusion about the economic situation. By the summer of 1992, Chinese economists were engaged in a running debate about whether the economy was becoming overheated. In light of the rapid increase in investment and output, the Chinese leadership issued a document in August 1992 that, in an apparent attempt to stabilize the macroeconomic situation, called for strict restrictions on new projects.

By the end of 1992, macroeconomic instability had become a recurring refrain among top leaders. Speaking at the National Planning Conference in December, Jiang Zemin warned against the danger of economic overheating. In mid-January 1993, at a national conference of bank directors and insurance company managers, Li Peng and Zhu Rongji further expressed their concern about excessive credit issue and rising prices and cautioned against economic overheating. Zhu Rongji in particular argued that the banking system should strictly control investment scale and currency issue and play its role of macroeconomic management (*Xinhua yuebao* 1993 no. 1, 92–93). In this context, it was ironic and politically irresponsible for Li Guixian, the governor of the People's Bank of China, to go out on a limb at the end of January to say that credit tightening was not in the offing in 1993.

Yet, leaving aside the consideration that Li Guixian's patron—Premier Li Peng—feared a repeat of recession, Li Guixian probably had some basis for his statement at the time. As late as mid-February 1993, a leading economist from the economic research center of the State Planning Commission argued that the August 1992 measures limiting new investments were taking effect. The economist projected that China's GNP growth would slow to the annualized rate of less than 8 percent after June 1993—which was considered "cool." In consequence, he called for macroeconomic measures to maintain the growth rate at 8 percent or above (*Zhongguo caijing bao* 16 February 1993, 3).

As the economy heated up in spring 1993, especially after economic figures for the first quarter were released, the question of overheating became a major issue among policymakers behind closed doors. Those who thought the economy was already overheated, led by Vice-Premier Zhu Rongji, pointed out that, apart from inflation, all the major economic indicators for 1992 surpassed those of 1988 and the inflation rate, at 15.6 percent in the thirty-five major cities in spring 1993, was still on a rising trend. They warned that the 1988–1989 debacle might be repeated. In contrast, optimists argued that the economy was not overheated because, compared to 1988, an abundance of consumer goods would relieve any fear of consumer panic buying. When figures showed a deceleration in savings deposits at banks, they explained that savings were being diverted into other types of investments, such as equities, and again should not be a cause for concern. Furthermore, the worries about economic overheating were concentrated in the center. In fast-growing areas such as Jiangsu, Guangdong, and Shanghai, local officials were unanimous that their economies could and should grow even faster. As to be expected from our general discussion, officials in inland regions did not want to be left behind either, and racked their brains to make their local economies grow faster (ZSZ 20–26 June 1993, 42–44).

Up to a point, economic figures were subject to multiple interpretations and therefore politically ambiguous. However, Deng turned eighty-nine in August 1993, and the dynamics of political succession and Deng's reform push made it difficult for a central leader to come out openly in favor of "cooling down" and not be seen as obstructing reform. As late as early April, the message being sent out from the center was still "Seize the Opportunity, Accelerate Development," as the title of an editorial of the leading party journal *Seek Truth* put it (*Qiushi* 1 April 1993, 2–4). Since both General-Secretary Jiang Zemin and Premier Li Peng had been slow in jumping onto Deng's reform bandwagon in 1992, and since Li Peng had been criticized for making the austerity program too severe in 1988–1991, both Jiang and Li had reasons to be extra cautious in arguing for slowing the economy down. Worries about an overheated economy were thus kept behind a seemingly relaxed political facade.

In April, nature intervened. Premier Li Peng suffered a heart ailment following a confrontation with his executive vice-premier Zhu Rongji over economic policy and the role of Liu Guixian. Zhu, a reformer praised by Deng as someone who truly knew economics, was given overall charge of the economy. Already convinced of the need to fight inflation in January 1993, Zhu immediately set to work. In April the center sought to rectify the monetary chaos by issuing a series of directives that called for limiting the rampant issuance of corporate bonds and stocks, which drained funds from the savings pool. To tame the sharply rising inflation rate, the center raised interest rates on savings deposits in mid-May and would again do so in July.

Zhu's effort was given a strong boost on May 19, when General-Secretary Jiang Zemin wrote a letter to the State Council. Jiang feared time was running out and asked the government to solve the prominent economic problems in a timely manner lest they result in big trouble (personal interview). Jiang's fear was not unfounded because, in late May, a demonstration against inflation and the imposition of fees for previously free medical services in Lhasa, Tibet, escalated into an anti-Chinese riot. The authorities were able to end the four-day riot through heavy troop reinforcements and a promise to address the price issue within forty-eight hours (*FEER* 3 June 1993, 13). Nevertheless, the incident could not fail to revive memories of 1988–1989 and to remind the leadership of China's volatile situation.

In the meantime, the economic situation continued to worsen in terms of increasingly excessive rates of investment and growth. Worried about inflation, residents continued to avoid state treasury bonds and accelerated their purchases of home electronic products and gold jewelry. There was rapid growth in speculative activities, including pyramid schemes that offered interest rates as high as 60 percent per year. When the yuan was allowed to float in swap centers in June, its value plummeted against the dollar. China's foreign exchange reserves dropped as low as $18 billion, raising the specter of major currency instability and threatening China's attractiveness for international investment.

Thus, in the face of mounting evidence on rising inflation and other destabilizing factors, Zhu led a concerted effort to bring order to the economy. The center sent out seven investigative teams to visit fourteen provincial units. On the basis of these investigations, the State Planning Commission, the Ministry of Finance, and the People's Bank of China drafted a list of sixteen suggestions on strengthening macroeconomic control, which were discussed in a series of meetings convened by the State Council from late May to early June. On 24 June 1993, the Central Committee and the State Council issued the suggestions in the form of a secret document (No. 6) on the current economic situation and on measures for strengthening macroeconomic control. Complementing the central policy on macroeconomic control was a circular issued, also in late June, by the CCP's Central Commission for Discipline Inspection and the Ministry of Supervision. The circular pointedly stated that some localities and departments had not taken effective action to implement the various party and government documents and regulations designed to deal with problems in the economy; it also demanded that all localities strictly abide by the principles of discipline outlined by the party and the government (*CD* 23 June 1993, 1).

Reestablishing Financial Discipline

Document No. 6 emphasized the use of economic levers in stabilizing the economy. Nevertheless, the stabilization program was multipronged.

General-Secretary Jiang Zemin used his party portfolio to enhance party discipline, fight against corruption, and tighten ideological control. NPC chairman Qiao Shi repeatedly emphasized that the top priority of the National People's Congress was to speed up economic legislation and establish a sound legal framework for the market economy. While these aspects are worthy of study, the focus in the rest of the chapter will be on financial stabilization and central-local relations.

The first action in the financial stabilization program was political. On 2 July, President Jiang Zemin issued a presidential order to remove Li Guixian from the post of governor of the People's Bank of China, apparently for failing to curb monetary expansion. Even though Vice-Premier Zhu Rongji could have controlled the People's Bank through the recently established State Council Leading Group for Reforming the Fiscal, Tax, and Financial System, as well as through the executive board of the People's Bank, he was nevertheless still appointed governor of the People's Bank.

The abrupt dismissal of Li Guixian was a master political stroke. To officials in the localities, it sent a signal that the center was dead serious about curbing monetary expansion and rampant financial speculation. To the banking system and financial community, it signaled political accountability and warned that the semiautonomous bank branches should follow orders from the center. To international investors, putting reformist Zhu Rongji in charge of stabilizing the economy helped instill confidence that China would stay on the reformist road even though it needed stabilization measures.

Three days after Zhu became central bank governor, a national financial conference was convened in Beijing. At the conference, Zhu called banking officials to task. First, he asked banks immediately to stop and sort out all unauthorized interbanking lending and to recall all unauthorized loans by 15 August 1993. Second, no financial institution was allowed to raise savings and lending interest rates and to use rate hikes to compete for savings. Kickbacks for loans were forbidden. Third, banks were immediately to stop pouring funds into various economic entities set up by the banks themselves, such as trust and investment companies, and to sever relations with these entities.

The banks swung into action after the conference. By the end of October 1993, 81 billion yuan in interbanking loans had been withdrawn. Jiangsu had 24 billion yuan in borrowing from other provinces and 15 billion in loans in May 1993. By 15 August, 4.5 billion yuan had been sorted out, reaching 8.5 billion at year's end. By 1996, 148 of the 186 trust and investment companies affiliated with state commercial banks (Bank of China, Bank of Industry and Commerce, China Agricultural Bank, and Bank of Construction) had been closed. Shares in thirty-three others were transferred to other parties (CCTV 1997). Numerous local branches were also closed or transferred. This was painful medicine—the withdrawal of funds caused many a project to remain half-finished (to this day) and caused the stock market to crash.

The action on banks was but the first in a series of important moves Zhu made to put China's financial house in order. He again raised interest rates in July to attract savings and increase the cost of borrowing. Also in July, Zhu and bankers worked out a plan to stabilize the exchange rate that had seen the Chinese currency plummet from 7.4 to 10.90 to the dollar. On 12 July, for the first time in the history of the People's Bank of China, the bank intervened in the limited foreign exchange swap market. Eventually, the bank spent $1.7 billion, and the exchange rate soon stabilized at around 8.6–8.8 to the dollar. Zhu had won the first battles.

The center also made a strenuous effort to tackle the zone fever. After issuing directives to dam the flood of stock offerings in April, the State Council in May issued a circular that reasserted its power over the establishment of local economic development zones. Noting that local governments competed among themselves to set up development zones with preferential policies to attract outside investment, the circular concluded that the development had resulted in the loss of large tracts of farmland and aggravated the shortage of funds going into basic industries. The circular decreed that only provincial authorities and the central government had the authority to set up development zones. A review of the zones that had been set up without proper authorization was to be conducted; those zones that lacked adequate infrastructure and funding were to be suspended (*CD* 17 May 1993, 1). By August, provincial authorities along the coast had eliminated 1,000 of 1,200 development zones set up by local officials without proper approval. However, in an apparent gesture to interior interests, the center indicated that it would promote development zones in inland and riverside regions, in order to bridge the growing gap between coast and interior (*CD* 18 August 1993, 1).

Reining in the Localities

Whatever policies the center adopted to temper the excesses in the economy, the key to success lay in policy implementation. Given the dynamics of local expansion, emulation, and competition discussed earlier, the center could not succeed without gaining the cooperation of the localities.

Yet the task of gaining local compliance had been made difficult by Deng's encouragement of local initiatives in 1992. Whereas during 1988–1990 the center tightened control and put a premium on provincial compliance with central policies, by 1992 it was precisely the provinces that pursued growth policies *despite* the austerity program (such as Guangdong, Jiangsu, and Shandong) that got praise from Deng and then the center. This flip-flop sent a powerful signal to local leaders that economic performance rather than compliance with central economic policies had become the key criterion for cadre evaluations. As Zhu launched the stabilization program in mid-1993, localities were likely to blunt the punches from the center and protect local initiatives with greater verve than they had in 1988–1990.

As mentioned earlier, the perception of economic overheating was largely confined to the center. Whereas leaders in more developed coastal provinces favored full speed ahead, their counterparts in interior regions were concerned about lagging behind the coast and emphasized the need to catch up. All (including some central leaders) justified their pro-growth attitudes by conveniently invoking the authority of Deng (*ZSZ* 25–31 July 1993, 50–51).

Judging by the interaction between central and local leaders, the central leadership recognized the difficulties of eliciting local compliance with central policies. In spring 1993 President Jiang Zemin personally chaired at least two regional economic conferences: a meeting of leaders from six provinces in East China in April and a meeting of leaders from five provinces in Northwest China in June. At the East China economic work conference, Jiang admitted limitations on the center's ability to control the economy and chastised localism. He stated that it would be dangerous and harmful to the interests of both party and state if local leaders were interested only in local development and local interests. He warned local officials to have a clear sense of the situation and keep in line with the center. The center and the localities were in the same boat, Jiang said. If the whole economy were out of control and the central government were unable to restore control, there would be grave risks, and in the end local interests would not go unscathed. He urged leaders in East China to set an example and support the center's endeavor to exert macroeconomic control (*ZSZ* 4–10 July 1993, 16–17).

Other top leaders similarly drummed on the theme of macroeconomic coordination and control at central meetings as well as during visits to the provinces. In late May, for example, Qiao Shi, a member of the Politburo Standing Committee and NPC chairman, pointed out at the Central Party School that China's most pressing challenge was macroeconomic control. Pointing to the decentralization of authority to lower levels, Qiao called on localities and departments to share common responsibility, strengthen macroeconomic control, overcome departmental selfishness, and have a sense of the big picture (*RMRB* 24 May 1993, 1).

As the point man for tackling the macroeconomic turmoil, Vice-Premier Zhu Rongji worked hard and had intensive interaction with local officials. As he rapidly assumed leadership over the financial system, Zhu reportedly summoned provincial governors to the capital to urge them to act quickly to reduce inflation by putting a stop to property and share speculation, easy credit, and other inflationary factors (*Dow Jones News* 30

June 1993; *NYT* 1 July 1993, C4). Zhu also traveled to the localities—or sent representatives to them—to force through administrative streamlining and supervise credit control at local bank branches; this was done to get the funds to bottleneck industries such as electricity, railways, and other energy projects (*ZSZ* 27 June–3 July 1993, 14–16).

Fortunately for Zhu, he did not have to work through the transitional financial system alone but could still get some assistance from the creaky party-state machine. Document No. 6 was virtually accompanied by a circular from the CCP's Central Commission for Discipline Inspection and the Ministry of Supervision calling for observance of party and government discipline. Considering the context, one of the reasons behind the dramatic dismissal of Li Guixian was probably what Chinese usually call *shaji jinghou*—killing the chicken to frighten the monkey. After all, localities during the reform era had learned the following maxim: "Where there is a policy from above, there is a countermeasure from below" (*shang you zhengce, xia you duice*).

Since the success of the stabilization program depended crucially on how the localities responded to central policy, the dynamics captured by the above maxim made the process more unpredictable. On the one hand, central policies for control might not get implemented because of local resistance and diversionary tactics. On the other hand, a local leader could anticipate that the center would expect local resistance and act tough. Local leaders thus had reason to be reluctant to challenge openly the center's prerogative to reestablish macroeconomic stability.

Nevertheless, provincial grumbling could be heard. At a midyear meeting, local leaders reportedly warned the center to take responsibility for any crisis that might follow the imposition of tightening measures, apparently thinking of the demonstrations that followed the imposition of austerity policies in 1988–1989. They also asked the center to pick up the welfare tab for workers who might be put out of work by the stabilization program (*ZSZ* 27 June–3 July 1993, 14–16). In response, central leaders, especially Zhu Rongji, repeatedly stated that they had no intention of imposing a comprehensive austerity program of 1988–1989 vintage. Instead, what they wanted was a soft landing that would still allow breathing room for sustained economic growth.

There was also evidence that local leaders tried to blunt the impact of central policies, especially because various provincial government departments had invested heavily in projects to be curtailed. In Guangdong, for example, after the center had called for tightening, Governor Xie Fei made no mention of inflation or overheating and still called for a continuation of high-speed development through 2010 at the provincial party congress. Apparently Xie invoked Deng Xiaoping's statement that Guangdong should try to catch up with the four Asian dragons in twenty years (*FEER* 3 June

1993, 21). The central authorities called for cleaning up trading in illegally offered shares, in an attempt to clamp down on rampant fundraising and help the banking sector. The Sichuan provincial government, rather than force the issuing enterprises to buy back shares, simply introduced a system that legalized the trading of unapproved stocks (*AWSJW* 2 August 1993).

The fact that central leaders were willing to make exceptions for some provinces also encouraged other provinces to seek similar treatment. Jiang Zemin and Zhu Rongji decided to give Shanghai—where both Jiang and Zhu had served before moving to the center—generous credit targets and other exceptions in order to keep it growing (*ZSZ* 29 August 1993, 19). Reportedly Zhu also gave his backing to the attempt of the impoverished province of Guizhou to catch up with its prosperous neighbors. Zhu spared Guizhou from the national austerity drive, allowing it to expand its fledgling real estate market and to build more development zones and tourist facilities (*FBIS* 21 July 1993, 15).

In general, however, central-local relations during the economic stabilization conformed to earlier patterns (Huang 1996). When the center united, the locals largely complied with the center's decisions. While not all unauthorized loans were withdrawn, enough were recalled to puncture the bubbles of stock market and real estate speculation. Localities also complied with the center after the center stipulated in September that local governments would no longer be allowed to grant new tax reductions or exemptions.

For Zhu and his colleagues, while it was necessary to cool down the overheated economy, it was crucial that the tightening not have the recessionary impact of the 1988–1989 austerity program. The key was to fine-tune the economy to ensure stable growth, not stifle it. Therefore, Zhu stated that his goal was to "redirect financial resources away from speculative sectors to areas that are more important for the overall economy." Credit-tightening measures targeted only certain sectors of the economy, such as the speculative property market. Loans illegally extended to these projects were called in, and the resources were redirected to support infrastructure, energy, and agricultural projects (*Dow Jones News* 30 July 1993).

To their credit, Zhu and his colleagues stuck to this policy of "appropriate tightening." Broad money supply growth rate was reduced from 37 percent in 1993 to 25 percent in 1996. The growth rate of fixed-asset investment was reduced from 61.8 percent in 1993 to 18 percent in 1996. The deceleration of demand was reflected in the inflation rate. While the annual inflation rate in 1994 galloped to 21.7 percent, the highest in the history of the People's Republic of China, it was brought down to 6.1 percent in 1996, allowing the People's Bank to begin a series of interest rate cuts. In the meantime, economic growth rate remained high, averaging 12 percent from 1992 to 1996. Zhu had indeed achieved a soft landing for the Chinese economy.

Economic Crisis and Institutional Transformation

While the soft landing is a major accomplishment by any measure, the scope of institutional changes that the leadership introduced has been equally important. As mentioned earlier, when Chinese leaders launched the economic stabilization program in 1993 with Document No. 6, they made clear that they preferred control by economic and legislative means instead of control by administrative fiat. As Zhu Rongji put it at a meeting in June 1993, economic and legislative means would be primary, and "necessary administrative means" would be adopted only as a supplement (*CD* 1 July 1993, 1; *RMRB* 1 July 1993, 1).

As China's leaders grappled with the economic turmoil, however, they quickly realized that the Chinese financial system was not conducive to the sort of fine-tuning they had in mind. While the various stabilization efforts—currency intervention, interest rate hikes, the promotion of bond sales—suggest the adoption of market-conforming measures, nearly all of these measures had to be accompanied by strong-arm tactics in order to be made effective. The interest rate changes were backed up by lending quotas. While the People's Bank poured dollars into the swap centers to stabilize the dollar-yuan exchange rate in the summer of 1993, the government also had to increase administrative control in currency transactions. Swap center authorities restricted access to the market, requiring buyers of dollars to submit applications one trading day in advance. They also required proof that buyers actually needed dollars for imports. As a result, the currency exchange rate in swap centers remained a contrived rate, with enterprises unwilling to sell dollars at the intervention rate (wire reports).

The promotion of bond sales was similarly subjected to atavistic practices for the moment. As rising inflation diminished the attractiveness of state treasury bonds, the Finance Ministry twice adjusted bond yields upward in conjunction with interest rate rises on bank deposits, finally pegging bond yields to inflation. In mid-July, the Finance Ministry cheerfully reported that all 30 billion yuan worth of treasury bonds issued in 1993 had been sold off. But the Finance Ministry had to resort to far more than simple yield hikes to attract buyers. In a circular issued by the State Council in June, the central government asked local authorities to adopt all possible measures to improve bond sales. No locality would be allowed to issue stocks and corporate bonds before its allocated quota of state bonds was sold. It was also stipulated that corporate bond yields could not exceed those of state treasury bonds. To add insult to injury, even though the government had two years earlier announced that bond sales would henceforth rely on voluntary subscriptions, millions of workers found their June salaries summarily allocated for bond purchases (*CD* 19 July 1993, 1; *CDBW* 21 June 1993, 3; *NYT* 23 July 1993, A3). (The bond purchase turned out to be highly profitable because of the drop in inflation rate.)

Frustrated by the difficulties of maneuvering a makeshift economic system, and afraid that they might not be able to get the house in order before Deng died, the Chinese leadership began to push for sweeping rationalizing reforms of the economic system. In November 1993, the Third Plenum of the Fourteenth Party Congress issued its *Decision . . . on certain questions regarding the establishment of a socialist market economic system,* which provided the blueprint for transforming the Chinese economy into a market economy. Among its provisions, the decision called for the government to concentrate on macrocontrol and guidance rather than micromanagement of enterprises. The central bank, for example, would shift from allocating credit through administrative means to using indirect methods such as changes in interest rates and reserve ratios as well as open market operations to set monetary policy. All in all, this reform program has touched every aspect of China's economy, including fiscal structure, taxation, finance, foreign trade, foreign exchange management, planning, investment, prices, public housing, and social security. It is to the credit of the Chinese leadership that in nearly all these areas, the trend in the 1990s has been in the direction of the market. For reasons of space, I discuss only briefly the fiscal and taxation reforms and their relationship to macroeconomic stabilization.

As is well known, the adoption of fiscal contracting between center and localities during the reform era caused a steady decline in the central government's control of the revenue stream. In 1993, the central government's intake of the budgetary revenue was only 22 percent of the total. Fiscal deficit reached 29.9 billion yuan. The fiscal enervation of the center made central leaders feel that they were piloting an aircraft carrier using the tools for a small boat. In the words of Finance Minister Liu Zhongli, "When the government does not have money, its words no longer count."

After the first few skirmishes in the stabilization program, the center convened a national fiscal affairs and taxation conference in September. During the conference, the central leadership laid down three rules. First, because local governments had offered numerous tax reductions and exemptions that affected fiscal revenue, the central leadership stipulated that tax reductions and exemptions must be strictly controlled. There would be no new tax reductions and exemptions in the rest of 1993. Various tax reduction and exemption policies that had been adopted by local governments without authorization should immediately be abrogated and sorted out. Zhu warned that anyone offering new tax reductions and exemptions would be severely dealt with. Second, the inflationary practice of both central and local governments simply to borrow from banks must be stopped. In addition to strictly controlling expenditure, the central government would finance its fiscal deficit through the issuance of treasury bonds. Local governments would no longer be allowed to incur fiscal deficits. Third, taxation and revenue departments and their affiliated organizations could not engage in commercial operations without authorization from the People's Bank. Existing finance companies should sever their links with government departments within a specified time period.

The three rules, particularly the second, constituted no less than a program for financial revolution for China. They promised fundamentally to revamp the way the government did its business. By using bonds rather than bank drafts (money creation) to finance its deficit, the center, like Ulysses, decided simply to tie its own hands and credibly bind itself to fighting inflation. Without bringing inflation down, the government would have to compensate bond buyers with higher yields and thus incur higher costs.

Yet the central leadership pushed for more. In September 1993, at the symposium on economic work in ten provinces of the Southwest and Central South, President Jiang Zemin called for introducing major reforms in the fiscal, taxation, planning, and investment systems in 1994. It is not possible to do full justice to the breadth of institutional reforms that have been made. Instead I would like to briefly discuss the reforms of the fiscal and taxation systems.

There was much uncertainty at the time the reforms were first broached, in late 1993. The inflation rate remained in double digits. Rumors of impending reforms caused panic buying of home appliances. Yet Jiang and Zhu pressed on. They invoked alarmist visions and the authority of Deng to drive a bargain with provincial authorities while promising that the provinces would retain what they already had. Afraid that provincial leaders might present a united front in collective bargaining, the central leadership adopted a divide-and-rule strategy (Yang 1994, 85–87). A special working group, made up of more than sixty people, including central leaders such as Zhu Rongji and officials from the Ministry of Finance and other government departments, traveled to seventeen provinces one by one to hammer out the base revenue figures for each province and readjust the fiscal relations between center and provinces.

By the end of 1993, a sweeping reform of the taxation and fiscal systems had been put together for implementation starting in 1994. In contrast to the fiscal contracting system that gave the center only a set amount of revenue, the new and federalist tax assignment system was clearly designed to help the central government benefit from the marginal growth in the economy and in revenue generation, which required the center not to slow down the economy too much (Yang 1994). The fiscal reforms were introduced without much difficulty and had an immediate impact on the division of revenue between the center and provinces. In 1994, the center's share of budgetary revenue rose to 55.7 percent, an increase of 33.7 percentage points from a year earlier. While most of the increased central revenue has been returned to the provinces as rebates, the center's effective control over the revenue stream is expected to grow over the long run. The improvement in the fiscal situation, plus a steady growth in foreign reserves (which reached more than $130 billion in fall 1997), have given the center confidence to tackle other problems, especially reform of state-owned enterprises.

Conclusion

Until the early 1990s, China's transitional economy was characterized by two major features. First, for all the legacies of central planning, it had extremely rudimentary institutions for fine-tuning a market economy. The mixture of market allocations and administrative fiat made such fine-tuning doubly difficult to accomplish. Second, one fundamental feature of the reforms has been the devolution of fiscal resources as well as obligations to lower administrative levels, thereby enhancing the incentives for local agents-cum-principals to pursue their own interests, which do not necessarily coincide with those of the central government. Both of these features tended to accentuate the problems of macroeconomic management. In particular, both Chinese and Western scholars have pinpointed fiscal decentralization as the root cause of the investment fervor that periodically swept through the economy.

Yet it would be misleading to equate fiscal decentralization with the tendency toward overheating (Jin 1994). Such a conclusion obscures the mechanisms by which overheating is produced. For, one might ask, since the localities still possessed the decentralized resources during the austerity period of 1989–1990, why did the economy not overheat during that period? Conversely, economic overheating was a phenomenon long before the era of reform. In this chapter, I have highlighted the dynamics of competitive liberalization that explains the rush for adopting reformist policies in localities. Such competitive dynamics, in the context of under-institutionalization and fiscal decentralization, increase the need for central coordination and guidance. The boom-bust cycles in the Chinese economy can best be characterized as the unintended result of an iterated game between center and localities.

I have argued that the model sheds important light on China's early 1990s macroeconomic difficulties. I suggest that it was Deng's Southern Tour that tipped the balance to the localities and unleashed another round of local emulation and competition centered on the extension of preferential treatment to outside investment in development zones. This zone rush plus the resultant speculative property market and buoyant industrial production thus led to the economic overheating. The center stoked the fire of growth by rapidly increasing liquidity and relaxing financial supervision in a system that was already under-institutionalized. It took much political drama, including the dismissal of the governor of the People's Bank, before the central leadership regained its credibility with the localities and gradually brought the economic situation under control. An economic crash landing would have frayed China's already fragile social fabric and severely complicated the chances for a smooth political succession, with consequences that would have been felt far beyond China. The stakes were unusually high.

Each economic crisis inevitably affects and realigns the distribution of political power. The fact that the team centered on Jiang Zemin and Zhu Rongji did finally succeed in steering the economy to a soft landing strengthened both their political careers and the trend toward liberalizing reforms. Indeed, prompted by the economic crisis and the fear of political vulnerability after Deng's death, the Chinese leadership fought hard to introduce sweeping reforms of economic institutions, including the replacement of feudal central-provincial fiscal contracting with a federalist revenue assignment system, reforms of the banking system, greater supervision of financial institutions and the stock markets, and reforms of price and foreign exchange management. Equally important, the central leadership went beyond boosting revenues and strengthening financial supervision and chose to fundamentally reshape the way the government finances its deficit. The shift from bank draft to treasury bond operations and the curb on local government deficit should make the Chinese government a more prudent and responsible economic player and its actions less inflation-prone. In the meantime, declining profitability in domestic investments arising from intense competition has sharply reduced local government desire to make their own investments, which had been a major demand factor. In essence, Jiang Zemin and Zhu Rongji have managed to change the rules of the game for economic governance in China from a set of rules that tended to cause economic fluctuations to one that has in-built mechanisms for moderating inflationary pressures. These new rules can still be upset by political conflicts, but political leaders will most likely think twice before attempting such changes.

In short, the Chinese leadership has not only survived a major economic crisis in a stronger position, but also has moved the Chinese economy far closer to the market. Major problems continue to plague the Chinese economy, including a virtually insolvent banking system and continuing losses at a high percentage of state enterprises. Nevertheless, the soft landing and the institutional reforms paved the way for the smooth final farewell to Deng in early 1997 and China's relative robustness in weathering the Asian financial meltdown that came later that year.

Notes

An earlier version of this chapter was presented at the annual meeting of the American Political Science Association in Washington, D.C., 2–5 September 1993.

The revised version draws on interviews conducted during several research trips to China in subsequent years. I am grateful to Avery Goldstein, William Parish, anonymous reviewers for the publisher, and especially Edwin Winckler for helpful comments and suggestions. The research was generously supported by the Social Sciences Divisional Research Fund and the Committee on Chinese Studies of the University of Chicago.

1. Formally, $G_{re} < G < G_i$, where G is growth rate, G_{re} is the minimum growth rate needed to sustain employment at a certain level as well as government revenue, and G_i is the growth rate beyond which inflationary pressures will accelerate. It is the government's objective to keep the economic growth rate within a target zone between G_{re} and G_i. This is, of course, an ad hoc formulation; but virtually all macroeconomic models are of this nature (Persson and Tabellini 1990, 12). Chinese economists have used 7–8 percent as the rule-of-thumb figure for acceptable economic growth.

PART 4

Sociocultural
Transition

7

Re-enforcing
State Birth Planning

Edwin A. Winckler

Many observers consider communism virtually dead in China, particularly since the fall of communism in Eastern Europe and the Soviet Union. After all, since the inauguration of Dengist reforms in the late 1970s, China's economy has gradually been slipping from center to provinces, plan to market, and public to private. Surely other policy sectors cannot be far behind? Nevertheless, reports of "death by devolution" of central direction of the world's largest country may be premature, at least for some policy domains. China is the main case of "late communism"—a regime that, although under reform, is still only partly postcommunist, despite the fall of most other communisms. In principle, China remains a communist party-state—a Leninist system committed to social transformation through elite planning and mass compliance. In practice, the party center is refurbishing some policy instruments with which to continue to guide the system, albeit more selectively and less directly.

This chapter focuses on one intrusive and demanding policy—state birth planning—in which the party-state and its transformative intent have displayed remarkable resilience. During the 1980s, despite some relaxation from the nominal "one-child" limit toward a de facto "two-child" quota, state birth planning was largely maintained. Surprisingly, in the 1990s, state birth planning has been both reintensified in the short run and institutionalized for the long run. In 1991 the party Central Committee and government State Council issued a joint decision that drastically increased the pressure on subnational leaders to implement birth planning strictly. Since then the birth planning system has struggled to reduce its reliance on crash campaigns, and to strengthen the legal basis and positive incentives for gaining compliance. These developments certainly did not presage an across-the-board restoration of totalitarian control in China. However, they do illustrate that the Chinese leadership remained determined to demonstrate the "superiority of socialism" in combating the anarchy, not only of economic production, but also of social reproduction. (For the rationale of the 1991

181

decision to re-enforce state birth planning, see JPRS 16 April 1991; for the *People's Daily* editorial signaling the new policy, see *FBIS* 29 April 1991; for an English text of the decision itself, see *FBIS* 20 June 1991; for the Chinese text, see the 1992 *China Birth Planning Yearbook,* hereafter abbreviated as *ZJSN.*)

Not only does China's party leadership insist on continuing state birth planning, the party itself remains heavily involved in implementing it. This is partly for technical reasons—the program's own administrative infrastructure remains inadequate, and mobilization remains necessary to overcome public resistance. Even more important are political reasons. In the short run, limiting births may cost the party some political support in its rural base. In the long run, however, Chinese leaders hope that higher per capita incomes will salvage political support for their regime. Hence the vigorous enforcement of state birth planning in late communist China.

This vigor illustrates some general themes. First, the devolution of Leninist systems contains the possibility of countercurrents, including successful attempts at the restoration and even the elaboration of control. Second, the economic transition from plan toward market, though fundamental, does not fully determine state-society relations in other sectors. Third, state strength and regime stability are sectorally specific—the "governability" of each policy domain depends on particular matchups between policy tasks, policy instruments, and policy environment.

This chapter relates "macro" regime characteristics to "meso" program institutions and their "micro" foundations in information and incentives. The section "Problematique" briefly sketches an organization-theoretic approach to population policy in a late communist regime. The body of the chapter explores the organizational characteristics of China's state birth planning as a policy area, considering in more detail the interplay of institutions, incentives, and information. The concluding section briefly notes some implications for social science, international policy, and postcommunist politics. Throughout, "program" refers to the Chinese state birth planning system, and "program leaders" refers to officials and advisers of its highest organ, the State Birth Planning Commission (SBPC).

Pursuing its "meso" theme, the chapter emphasizes the particular policy characteristics of demographic processes and concepts. The main dependent variables are rates of national population growth and individual fertility. As we shall see, there are some important tensions between national and individual measures. Among independent variables, proximate demographic determinants include age structure, age at marriage, and timing of childbearing. Program inputs include current "services" preventing or terminating pregnancy (primarily IUD insertion, sterilization, and abortion) and long-term investments such as propagandizing birth planning and building facilities. Remote determinants include broad processes of economic, social, and cultural change.

Interactions between these processes can be elusive and difficult to address in policy formulations. In the 1970s, the interactions among proximate determinants were well captured by China's "later, longer, fewer" policy, (later marriage, longer spacing between births, and fewer births—see Chen and Kols 1982). In the 1980s, policy focused on "fewer" to the neglect of "later" and "longer," partly because "fewer" was the ultimate goal and partly because the 1980 Marriage Law and 1980s economic reforms made "later" and "longer" harder to control. In the 1990s, policy seems determined not only to slow population growth, but also to smooth fluctuations in age structure. Such technical complexities are compounded by the "politics of numbers" (Alonso and Starr 1987). The state struggles to impose definitions and collect data on both program and society. Programs struggle to improve the appearance of their performance. Society struggles to resist, conceal, evade, and benefit. All of this is particularly true in China, where the population is huge, the program prominent, and the stakes high.

Problematique

We begin by sketching a path from macro to meso, moving from general features of the policy process, to specific characteristics of particular policy areas, to state birth planning in particular.

Policy Process

Leninist dualism implies three general features of the policy process—multiple delegation, sequential attention, and mixed implementation.

By *multiple delegation* we mean chains of principal-agent relations, connecting party to government and top to bottom. Particularly in the zone between hierarchies and markets, delegation can be more effective than direct control, despite some "agency costs" of deviation from the principal's original intentions. However, the principal must carefully craft the original mandate and adequately monitor agent performance. Much of late-communist reform is an attempt to deploy and perfect such delegation. China's revolutionary elders have increasingly delegated authority down a three-tier system of central guidance, subnational administration, and grassroots implementation. Delegation has worked well in population policy, where both mandate and monitoring are relatively clear. The center does allow provinces some latitude in policy, and the provinces do allow the grassroots some latitude in implementation. Nevertheless, the center has remained amazingly successful in obtaining fertility decline.

By *sequential attention* we mean the periodic shift of attention between competing priorities on the policy agenda. A strength of party-state dualism is that the party can intervene to force progress on matters the government neglects. A weakness is that policy overload shifts from government to party, so the party center must signal its real current priorities emphatically. For example, the one-child policy was launched in 1980 by an unusual "open letter" to all party and youth league members. Sequential party intervention in successive policy areas makes intensity of implementation as important a determinant of policy outcomes as the details of government policy. This seems obvious but can be confusing. For example, Greenhalgh (1990) and Aird (1990) disputed whether, in the 1980s, the birth limitation program gradually relaxed, or cycled between hard and soft lines. Arguably they were both right—policy evolved but implementation cycled. In the 1990s, implementation was re-enforced and policy has continued to evolve quite purposefully.

By *mixed implementation* we mean the combination of mobilization and institutionalization that results from party intervention in government administration. Tyrene White (1990) has noted what she calls "institutionalized mobilization"—the continuing role of the party as cheerleader and watchdog, and periodic campaigns intensifying propaganda and coercion. Here we relate the general *possibility* of mixed implementation to the nature of the Chinese party-state. We relate the particular *proportions* of the mix to the particular situation of state birth planning. We also emphasize *change* in the mix and relate that change to the interaction of leaders' goals and the reform environment. In the 1990s the Chinese program has continued to rely somewhat on periodic crash campaigns to supplement weak routine work conducted by grassroots cadres. However, the program has attempted a "shift of mechanisms" toward greater institutionalization— more personnel and resources, greater professionalism and legality, more benefits and services.

Policy Organization

We continue along the path from macro to micro by previewing organization-theoretic formulations of institutions, incentives, and information.

As regards *institutions and tasks,* the organization of particular policy areas results from interaction between general regime characteristics and specific task requirements. Most broadly, the administration of things and the government of people pose different tasks. Nevertheless, the general objective of socialism is to assimilate politics to administration through scientific planning. The specific objective of state birth planning is to assimilate social reproduction to economic production (Wang and Hull 1991; White 1994a, 1994b). However, where there is a gap between state demands and popular desires, people will resist. Mobilization is necessary to correct deviations and fill the gap. This is true even of economic production where the object of policy is things. It is all the more true of social reproduction where the object of policy is people themselves. In late-communist China, the gap has largely disappeared in economic policy but not in social policy, at least not in population control.

As regards *incentives and compliance,* we demonstrate the continuing relevance of Etzioni's classic analysis to the Chinese case (Etzioni 1961, applied to China by Skinner and Winckler 1969). Compliance theory is particularly apposite to the Chinese birth planning program, about whose coerciveness the international community has been justifiably concerned. Unfortunately Etzioni's analysis suggests a practical affinity between coercion and contraception. In the final analysis, enforcing birth limitation is a negative "order goal" of preventing undesired behavior, something at which coercion is inherently effective, at least in the short run. Of course, as Chinese work style prescribes, coercion can be minimized by proper ideological preparation, including more education for women. Moreover—as Eztioni argues and China has found—for sustaining compliance over a long time, remunerative incentives are most reliable. In 1990s Chinese population policy, this has meant raising the costs and lowering the benefits of children, rewarding families for limiting births, and advertising the higher per capita family incomes that result from having fewer children. Nevertheless, the program remains fundamentally coercive, since birth limits are mandatory and enforced by law. (A sophisticated Chinese discussion of the incipient shift in the 1990s from coercion toward more gentle administrative guidance and more spontaneous self-interested compliance is Gu and Mu 1994.)

As regards *information and technology,* we apply another Eztioni insight, this one concerning shortcut solutions to difficult social problems through a "technological fix" (Etzioni 1975). Both Western-style family planning and Chinese state birth planning are prime examples, exploiting the availability of cheap and effective contraceptive devices. China has shifted from short-term means such as condoms toward longer-term means such as IUDs, increasingly supplemented by permanent sterilization for women who have already had too many children. China's main goal since about 1980 has been preventing third-and-higher births, again made possible by a particular combination of information and technology. By building a new mass organization dedicated to population functions, the Chinese party-state has achieved the surveillance capacity to identify out-of-plan pregnancies. By building a stand-alone paramedical system dedicated to birth planning, China has achieved the gynecological capacity to eliminate current unauthorized pregnancies through abortion and to prevent future unauthorized pregnancies through IUDs and sterilization. (On Chinese contraceptive technology and contraceptives, see *China Today* 1992 162–205, 227–249.)

Population Control

International family planning originated between the two world wars, partly out of concern about China's huge, poor population (Finkle and McIntosh 1994). Political-religious issues and technical inadequacies delayed implementation until the 1960s. As practiced in the West, "family planning" is voluntary, at least in theory. It facilitates contraception only by making knowledge and access readily available, to minimize any gap between potential demand and actual supply. However, as implemented in Third World countries, fertility control programs are sometimes somewhat coercive (e.g., Warwick 1982, 1986).

Communist China at first largely adhered to Soviet-Marxist opposition to birth control, which reflected Russia's labor scarcity. However, the leaders of labor-surplus China quite early began moving toward not just voluntary family birth control but rather systematic state birth planning (Hou 1981, White 1994a). During the 1970s, largely through "administrative measures," China reduced fertility much faster than its then low level of development would naturally have done—from around six children per couple to around three (Coale 1984). This is the single largest accomplishment by a national population policy in history.

In the 1980s, however, Chinese population policy was subject to crosscurrents. On the one hand, in order to achieve still further reductions in fertility, around 1980 China adopted an even more stringent goal of only one child per couple. Some rural economic changes tended to reduce fertility. For example, at least in some areas studied, the household responsibility system and price reform increased the cost of raising children, particularly weddings and housing for sons. On the other hand, in practice most rural couples continued to have at least two children. Other rural economic reforms tended to increase fertility. For example, dissolution of collectives undermined enforcement mechanisms. The 1980 national Marriage Law lowered the de facto marriage age by undercutting more stringent provincial regulations, and rural economic development may have temporarily raised the value of children in some areas (Greenhalgh 1993, 1994).

In 1981–1982 fertility rose, and in 1983 the party-state overcorrected with a nationwide mass sterilization campaign. This produced mass resistance, so in 1984 the center relaxed implementation and moderated policy. However, localities and public overresponded to these adjustments, causing fertility to rise and hard-liners to call for tightening policy and strengthening implementation. Around the turn of the decade, renewed interest in central economic planning reinforced interest in population control. As China formulated new five- and ten-year plans, it faced a "third peak" of women in their reproductive prime. Political and program leaders decided not to tighten existing policy. They decided instead to strengthen implementation of existing limits by raising the program's priority and by holding political leaders at all levels responsible for program success (P. Peng 1990, White 1991, *FBIS* 12 June 1991).

In the 1990s program leaders have been surprisingly responsive to suggestions by outsiders—international agencies, foreign foundations, and nongovernmental organizations. The program has upgraded technology, improved counseling, and launched efforts to raise service quality and improve women's reproductive health. Program leaders have been more reluctant to adopt repeated foreign suggestions that they abandon mandatory local birth quotas, fearing that fertility might rebound and they might be criticized (interviews on 2, 4, 8 July 1993, and later communications). Meanwhile, political leaders have rejected foreign criticism of coercive implementation. They maintain that China's birth planning combines state guidance and mass voluntarism, and they claim that any instances of coercion are deviations by overzealous local leaders or inexperienced local implementors. In the late 1990s program leaders deny foreign media reports that the program is being relaxed, except in the most developed areas (e.g., *FBIS* 23 February 1998). Nevertheless, a main long-run goal of program leaders has been a "shift in mechanisms" from "social restraint" toward a combination of social restraint and voluntary compliance based on economic self-interest (e.g., *FBIS* 12 September 1997). (On foreign contacts, an increasingly important dimension of an originally autarkic program, see *China Today* 1992, 309–334.)

Institutions

Chinese state birth planning is a social adjunct to state economic planning (Wang and Hull 1991). Thus a leading institutional feature is numerical targets, not only for economic production but also for social reproduction. Since around 1980, China's main long-run population goal has been to keep year 2000 population as low as possible to facilitate reaching per capita economic goals. In the early 1980s, the main policy target was 1.2 billion, with annual targets calculated backward from that. In the mid-1980s, the goal was loosened to "around 1.2 billion," and current annual figures were treated more as data than as targets (Tien 1991, 134–135). In the early 1990s, the target was further loosened to "under 1.3 billion," but annual targets are being taken more seriously (*FBIS* 1, 4 October 1991). (On population policy and the population plan, see *China Today* 1992, 61–76, 105–120.)

National Level

Post-Mao national *political leaders* have displayed much agreement and continuity on these goals. Both Deng Xiaoping and Chen Yun were early advocates and implementors of population policy (Wang 1991). They remained the two main backstage economic policy leaders through the early 1990s. Whatever their differences over the pace of economic reform, evidently they both still favored population control. Nevertheless, it is noteworthy that the emphasis on strict birth limitation around 1980 and 1990 coincided with Chen's attempts to consolidate economic gains. Conversely, when Deng gave precedence to rapid economic growth—as in the mid-1980s and mid-1990s—he may inadvertently have subordinated population control along with other stabilization objectives (JPRS 16 August 1993). In the late 1980s, Chen protégé Li Peng became the leading advocate of stronger implementation of birth planning. Deng protégé Li Tieying supervised population matters for the Politburo (as one can see from his leading most relevant meetings). Other top leaders involved were Wang Shoudao, one of the party's original rural revolutionaries, and Song Ping, a regional administrator and central planner. Both helped build the Birth Planning Association into a major new mass organization (e.g., *FBIS* 24 July 1991, 3 February 1993).

At its inception in 1973 as a "leading group," the SBPC was little more than a coordinating body. Even in staff functions, it long remained dependent on the State Planning Commission and the State Statistical Bureau. In line functions, contraceptive distribution and medical operations were long performed by the state pharmaceutical company and the Ministry of Public Health. Even after achieving ministry-rank commission status in 1981, as a consumer rather than producer of economic resources, the SBPC remained inherently weak. Early *program leaders* were associated with rural policy (Hua Guofeng), cybernetic theory (Song Jian), and women's organizations (Chen Muhua, the first SBPC head). Later SBPC heads included Qian Xinzhong (too hard-line), Wang Wei (too soft-line), and, from 1988 to 1998, Peng Peiyun (a clever compromise). With strong party and educational credentials, Mme. Peng advocated both short-run enforcement and long-run professionalization (e.g., *FBIS* 19 January 1990). (For a detailed account of the history and structure of the program, see *China Today* 1992, 1–60.)

During the 1980s and 1990s, in its internal *program development,* the SBPC has gradually tried to construct some "stand-alone" administrative capabilities in its major administrative divisions: general administration, planning and statistics, finance and contraception, and even science and technology (*ZJSN,* various years). It began training its own cadres, conducting its own surveys, formulating its own population targets, building its own sterilization clinics, and even improving on such foreign contraceptive inventions as the U.S. Norplant and French RU-486 (*ZJSN,* various years). Its mass organization, the Birth Planning Association (BPA), has grown enormously (*ZJSN* 1993, 319). After taking over the SBPC in 1988, Mme.

Peng appointed many scholars to head program divisions and strengthened the role of China's academic demographers as program advisers (*ZJSN* 1989, 60–61). Nevertheless, SBPC's organization remains deficient. For example, program workers still lack a stable career path, and frequent transfers disrupt implementation (interview 2 July 1993). SBPC statistical work has improved, but grassroots data collection remains flawed. As Mme. Peng has recently observed, "China was rather late in establishing its contingent" of birth planning cadres, and they still need strengthening (*FBIS* 18 March 1998). (On capital construction and staff development, see *China Today* 1992, 273–308.)

In birth planning as in other policy areas, during the 1990s the regime has strengthened the legal foundations of government policy. Previously the main legal basis for birth planning was provisions in the 1978 constitution and 1980 Marriage Law. In 1989 as in 1979, there was much discussion of promulgating a national birth planning law, but it was shelved in 1990 pending the accumulation of more experience with provincial differences (Feng and Hao 1992). The national program is still based mostly on party instructions and administrative orders. A late 1991 regulation on birth planning for the migrant population was the first specifically birth planning regulation properly approved by the government cabinet and formally promulgated for implementation by the SBPC (*FBIS* 6 January 1992, *ZJSN* 1992, 177–178). Other relevant 1990s legislation includes a 1991 adoption law and 1994 law on maternal and infant health care (*FBIS* 31 December 1991; *ZJSN* 1993, 64–65; *RMRB* 28 October 1994). The SBPC provides only technical guidance to provincial programs, which report to their provincial governments. Authoritative central intervention requires instructions from the government State Council to the provincial government or, better, from the party Politburo to the provincial party first secretary.

Subnational Level

Thus the *provincial* level is the cornerstone of program administration and, so far, of program legislation as well. In the 1980s, subprovincial decrees were continuously revised and, in the 1990s, provincial regulations were gradually formalized (Feng and Hao 1992). In the early 1990s, a key step in strengthening program implementation was making the provincial party secretary and provincial governor personally responsible for provincial program performance, a charge that continues in the late 1990s (*ZJSN* 1992, 6–9; *FBIS* 18 March 1998). On the one hand, direct involvement of the top provincial leadership increases program resources and helps ensure they are used for program purposes. It also mobilizes resources from other systems, including free manpower transferred to program tasks during crash campaigns. On the other hand, direct involvement of political leaders somewhat shifts implementation from professionalism toward mobilization. Moreover, it puts tremendous pressure on subprovincial programs to produce results—sometimes voluntary, sometimes coerced, and sometimes fictional (interview 14 July 1993).

The *prefectural* level is only supervisory, with no budget or functions of its own. Nevertheless, the prefecture is important. First, Chinese provinces contain too much variation and too many counties for the provincial government to deal directly with them. Second, prefectures are a key link in the one-level-at-a-time Chinese administrative system. For example, national birth planning cadres train provincial cadres, who train prefectural cadres, who train county cadres. The main current emphasis is on training prefectural cadres (interview 20 July 1993). Third, the leadership of individual prefectures can make a difference, and prefectures are a conspicuous unit for awarding public commendation (and privately assigning blame). For example, in southern Shaanxi, Hanzhong prefecture has long been a model (interview 14 July 1993).

The *county* is a crucial operational level—the lowest one that is really fully funded, staffed, and trained by the state. It is also, at least formally, the lowest level for disaggregating national population targets. The county also supervises community finances, including new social security and retirement pension schemes. Most crucial to birth limitation, it is the lowest level for difficult medical operations. Most sterilizations are performed either at the county hospital or program clinic, or by mobile medical teams sent out from the county to the townships and villages during crash campaigns. Some provinces still rely mostly on Ministry of Public Health hospitals. Some have constructed many "stand-alone" program clinics, which appear more effective for program purposes.

Grassroots

Theoretically, disaggregation of national targets stops at the county level, because there is too much demographic variation within smaller units to impose national averages on them. In practice, however, the county consults townships (and townships consult villages) to estimate a reasonable number of specific births they can be allowed. Grassroots cadres cannot deal with more sophisticated targets. Townships and villages pay the salaries of their own cadres, so the number and quality of grassroots workers depend on local resources. (On the grassroots level, see *China Today* 1992, 250–272.)

The *township* is still often the lowest level with any full-time paraprofessional program worker. The program is constructing township birth planning clinics, which include suction abortion machines and other simple equipment. Township cadres are sufficiently removed from village networks that, at least during crash campaigns, they can be more loyal to program than to community. Besides, the application of "responsibility systems" to birth planning means that cadres lose salary if they do not meet campaign targets. The township is also the lowest main organizational locus for the BPA, which the township party secretary heads. Villages have branches that report to the township BPA.

The *village* is the main unit of natural community. Here program organization is best conceived as complementary and overlapping administrative and personal networks. These actually perform the crucial program tasks—influencing, servicing, monitoring, and mobilizing individuals. Program workers are only part-time—for example, the main worker is usually the "head" of all village women's activities. They propagandize the program, deliver contraceptives, and try to ensure that couples use them. To supplement cadre efforts, the BPA is increasingly central, a classic example of a communist mass organization for augmenting party-state control. Initially its village branches were composed largely of reliable retirees (the "five olds" of party, government, associations, models, and elders). Recently these older people have been supplemented by more women of childbearing age. Members are assigned a few households, usually ones with which they normally have intimate contact anyway. Association members conduct propaganda, provide emergency services, monitor contraception, and identify pregnancies (Cheng 1990, *FBIS* 3 February 1993). They mobilize women for periodic gynecological inspections and for any required contraceptive operations, particularly during crash campaigns (interview 14, 15 July 1993). (On the BPA, see *China Today* 1992, 335–348.)

The *couple,* and individual *women,* are the lowest units of program administration. The program makes a point of actively delivering its "services" of education and contraception to the household door, not waiting passively for clients to come to program facilities. One northeastern province recently pioneered a system of making one "central household" responsible for liaison with nine other households, which resembles the imperial Chinese *bao-jia* system for maintaining order and collecting taxes. For their part, families respond with myriad strategies for evading birth limits (JPRS 30 May 1991). Women wishing "excess" children often leave their home village to bear the child elsewhere, possibly leaving it outside the village for a few years. If the family wants the child, eventually it can bring it home as the child of a "relative," or pretend to adopt it. If the family does not want the child—usually because it is a girl—the family may adopt it out to another family (Johansson and Nygren 1991). Thus many children, particularly girls, are not reported at birth but may reappear in population statistics a few years later (Zeng et al. 1993). Others are not reported because they are abandoned, killed, or aborted (Johnson, K. 1993, Greenhalgh and Li 1995).

Incentives

Chinese determination to press fertility decline faster than social change creates a gap between state birth limits and popular fertility aspirations. Achieving compliance requires administering appropriate incentives. Chinese program targets are mandatory, but they are also carefully differentiated and carefully focused. (On incentives see White 1987.)

Mandatory targets

For *program incentives,* China has always preferred persuasion, but makes liberal use of any economic incentives it commands and resorts to direct compulsion when necessary. *Normative* appeals include both nationalism and filiality. Evidently the political leadership sincerely believes that the long-run viability of the Chinese race is at stake. Ingeniously, the program also argues that family obligations now involve not the quantity but the quality of descendants. *Remunerative* incentives have included one-shot fines and rewards (Feng and Hao 1992). More significant is discrimination between children in access to land, education, employment, and other resources. Single children are rewarded, second children may be allowed, third children are excluded. As regards *coercion,* the program admonishes cadres against physically dragging women from their houses for "operations," and against committing symbolic acts of violence against property, such as poking a hole in a house wall or roof. (The latter usually happens only when the "client" has fled and the cadre must demonstrate to superiors that he "did something" nevertheless.)

The strength of these program incentives must be evaluated relative to the strength of alternative incentives in the *program environment.* Thus, as regards *normative* power, to be effective, program propaganda must gradually transform community norms, and evidently largely has. Few dispute the general principle of limiting births, though some dispute the application of the principle to their special circumstances, and some simply try to evade the law. As regards *remunerative* power, to be effective, program fines and rewards must seem substantial relative to household income. This may be true in the poorest interior areas but not in rich coastal ones, where many households gladly pay fines for extra children, even on installment plans! Finally, as regards *coercive* power, where law-and-order is poor, the desire for sons to protect the family greatly outweighs any fear of minor coercion from program workers. Resentful citizens have physically attacked program workers (JPRS 30 May 1991). Overt violence, by either cadres or clients, is more likely in villages governed by personalistic bosses than where routine administration is impersonal.

In the 1990s, as noted above, program leaders have tried to achieve *program change,* a "shift in mechanisms" toward institutionalizing incentives appropriate to an economically reformed and politically liberalized China (e.g., Huang 1990, Peng 1990, Song 1991, JPRS 9 June 1993, *FBIS* 12 September 1997). As regards *normative* power, this involves reproductive education for marrying adults and population education for school-children. Moreover, Chinese authorities now stress that birth limits are legitimate because they have been passed by provincial legislative bodies. Crash campaigns now involve mobilizing a range of higher-level executive, legislative, and association officials to demonstrate that legality. As regards *remunerative* power, the program is adding long-term positive rewards for the parents themselves, such as preferential access to collective enterprise jobs and private entrepreneurial opportunities, and to pension programs substituting for support by children in old age, where the community can afford them. As regards *coercion* of recalcitrant clients, the program is trying to eliminate any remaining outright violence against persons or property, substituting the threat of trial and punishment according to law.

Moving Targets

Chinese population policy recognizes three types of areas according to stage of development. These constitute distinctly different environments for birth planning work, particularly as regards incentives (Peng 1993).

A relatively small part of rural China remains *underdeveloped,* with Total Fertility Rates (TFR) of three or more. (The TFR is the total number of children that the average woman is likely to bear, if present age-specific fertility rates continue.) Fertility aspirations here remain high, either because of minority cultures or a "culture of poverty" that regards children as assets. Though exempting minorities in the 1960s and 1970s, in the 1980s the program began urging them to practice contraception, a call reiterated in the 1990s (*ZJSN* 1993, 40–44). By the late 1980s, the program became increasingly concerned with other poor areas, arguing that small families not large ones were the best way to overcome poverty. Around 1990, "integration" of antipoverty and birth planning programs became a theme of national policy—couples with two children must be sterilized to receive antipoverty benefits (*ZJSN* 1990, 28–29). In the late 1990s, poor rural areas are the main remaining quantitative program target.

Most of rural China is *developing.* Program measures hold TFRs to around 2.5, but fertility aspirations are higher, so the achievement is unstable. If the program relaxes, fertility will rise. Here few people are willing to have only one child, and then only if it is a boy. Most people want at least two children, usually a boy and a girl. Couples that have only girls want to keep trying for a boy. Most couples need at least one boy for heavy chores, to provide old-age support, and to continue the family line. Some people could use extra manpower to exploit labor-intensive economic opportunities or protect themselves. During the 1990s, the program has experimented with softening implementation in such areas by providing counseling services and allowing choice of contraceptive method.

Some of China is already quite *developed,* with TFRs well under two. China's three main cities (Shanghai, Beijing, and Tianjin) are most advanced, but this category also includes most other cities, and most of some highly urbanized provinces (Liaoning, Jilin, and Heilongjiang in the northeast, Jiangsu and Zhejiang in the east). Here not only is the transition to below-replacement fertility largely complete, but also it is largely backed by socioeconomic change (interviews 7–10 July 1993). Given the high cost and low benefits of raising children in urbanized areas, most people conclude that they cannot afford more than one child, and most care much less than in the past whether it is a boy or a girl. Consequently birth planning work is relatively easy and is shifting from limiting the quantity to improving the quality of population. These areas confirm political and program leaders in their belief that as the population's economic and cultural "level" rises, all Chinese will not only accept, but actually want, birth limitation. (On improving the health of births and the quality of population, see *China Today* 1992, 206–226.)

Minority Targets

The communist approach to China's rural population long involved explicitly mobilizing a majority against a *targeted minority,* such as poor peasants against rich peasants or loyal socialists against "capitalist roaders." Exactly where to draw the line was always an important tactical issue. Though Dengist China has eschewed such divisive campaigns, population policy does implicitly involve an analogous tactic. In effect, the majority of rural couples who bear at least one boy among their first two children are pitted against the minority, who are so unlucky as to have two girls. Moreover, the unborn cannot complain, while most of the living benefit from their absence. These considerations help answer several questions. How could China's political leaders, concerned to maintain their rural base, attempt to force rural fertility so low? In particular, how could they have done so around 1990 when weakened by economic reform and political challenge? In the future, how can rural leaders maintain unpopular birth limits and still achieve popular election? The answer is that, at any given moment, program targets keenly affect only a small proportion of the total population. The program is a pain for everyone, but it is not as though mobile medical teams were roaming the countryside indiscriminately.

The *reproductive arithmetic* is worth spelling out. Assuming a roughly equal probability of having a boy or a girl, in the first round of reproduction half of all couples produce a boy and half a girl. Some of those who have a boy may be content to stop, but most want a second child, either a boy or a girl. Those who had a girl the first time want to try again for a boy, and most provincial regulations permit this, after a wait of several years (Feng and Hao 1992). In this second round, again half produce a boy and half a girl. Thus roughly a quarter of the rural population ends up with two girls and want to try again for a boy, but this is forbidden by all provincial regulations. The government knows it cannot easily stop rural couples from having at least two children, but it is determined virtually to eliminate third and more births, preferably through sterilization of one member of all couples who already have two children. Evidently the government takes it for granted that couples that already have at least one boy should be willing to be sterilized, so in the early 1990s it particularly targeted couples with two girls. Some demographers argue that allowing couples to continue trying for a boy indefinitely will have little impact on total population, because with successive children such couples decline rapidly as a proportion of the total population (to an eighth, a sixteenth, and so on). So far, political or program leaders have not agreed, presumably lest such "excess" births set a precedent for everyone.

An important modification of the above account is significant skewing of the *sex ratios* at birth for later children, evidently in part through sex-selective abortion. Modern techniques for identifying the sex of an unborn baby are rapidly becoming widely available, albeit illegally (Zeng et al. 1993). Stringent birth limits aggravate the traditional preference for boys and even codify it into program regulations. There is not much sex selection among first children, for whom the sex ratio at birth was 105 in 1989–1990, or roughly the international norm. However, sex selection becomes increasingly intense for successive children. Even official national figures show a sex ratio of 121 for second children and 125–132 for third and higher children (Zeng et al. 1993). Unofficial local figures show much higher ratios (e.g., Greenhalgh and Li 1995). However, it remains unclear how many of these "missing girls" were never born, how many were not yet reported, and how many were never reported and disposed of through abandonment or infanticide.

Information

This section considers first measures of population outcomes and their proximate demographic determinants, then measures of program inputs, then measures of more remote processes. To foreigners, program leaders increasingly emphasize remote determinants, to minimize any appearance of coercion. To national political leaders, program leaders emphasize program impact, to maximize the program's contribution. Vis-à-vis subnational leaders, evidently there has been some shift in evaluation from program outcomes to program inputs and back to program outcomes. In the late 1980s, subnational political leaders tended to substitute the appearance of program effort for the more arduous reality of actual fertility reduction (interview 20 July 1993). In the early 1990s, national political leaders are interested not in program efforts but in demographic results.

Demographic Determinants

Both the quantity and quality of *population statistics* have vastly improved since the Maoist era. The State Statistical Bureau (SSB) has successfully conducted two decennial censuses, and quinquennial and annual surveys. Nevertheless, because citizens try to conceal "excess" children, even the SSB faces underreporting of births, estimated at perhaps 20 percent (interview 2 July 1993). SBPC sample surveys and annual reports involve the further problem of misreporting by program cadres eager to make their work look good. Evidently this reduces reporting of births by at least another 10–15 percent, even more in localities where the program's statistical system remains particularly weak. Attempts to reconcile SSB and SBPC figures have led to arbitrary revisions of SBPC figures (interview 2 July 1993). These data problems may recently have worsened, not improved, for both SSB and SBPC. Agency officials know that making local leaders responsible for program performance has induced systematic misreporting by entire localities. SBPC does not expect to solve this problem until the gap between program birth limits and popular fertility aspirations disappears. (On family planning statistics see *China Today* 1992, 121–160.)

Since 1980, emphasis in *population targets* has gradually shifted from eventual total population to current rates of natural increase (crude birth rate minus crude death rate). Arithmetically, the two should be closely related (external migration aside). Politically, however, the 1980s taught the center not to commit itself to a firm final target figure that it cannot meet. Moreover, for provinces, calculating rates may provide more flexibility than reporting totals, since the total population is buried in the denominator, where it can more easily be fudged. For example, with rising interprovincial mobility, provinces may add in-migrants but not subtract out-migrants, thereby increasing their denominators and reducing their rates. Another problem is competition between provinces to "exceed the national average" on simplistic performance measures, as in the 1990s they have been exhorted to do. This puts undue pressure on backward provinces to achieve the impossible.

Using total population and increase rates as program indicators obscures the interaction of demographic determinants, particularly *age structure*. These measures reflect the number of women currently "at risk" of bearing children, over which the program has little control. They do not identify the total number of children the average woman will eventually bear (the TFR), which is what the one-child policy is supposed to limit.

This vagueness may be partly deliberate. The Chinese program emphasizes adverse effects of current age structure to justify tightening policy or strengthening enforcement. However, program personnel do not appear particularly interested in refined analyses of whether fertility is rising or falling because of program inputs or cohort change. Political leaders are not interested in accommodating state policy to such demographic realities but rather intend to change them. Evidently this includes not only slowing population growth but also smoothing population fluctuations, by forcing the fertility of large cohorts particularly low. By the middle of the next century the population should be not only less large but also more constant—doubly convenient for planning. (On program indicators see Wang 1991 and tables at the back of the annual *China Birth Planning Yearbook.*)

Program Inputs

Program information also involves more specific indicators more directly relevant to the program itself: particular measures of program activity, reproductive outcomes, and reproductive behavior. Program variables can affect reproductive behavior either directly (increasing contraception, requiring abortion) or indirectly (raising the age of marriage, lengthening the time between births).

As regards *program activity,* the most general measures are funding and personnel. In the early 1990s, both grew at about 20 percent a year, as fast as feasible (*China Birth Planning Yearbooks*). A more specific indicator is the proportion of couples who have signed "one-child certificates" promising not to have a second child, a fairly modest 19 percent (*ZJSN* 1993, 339). Another more specific indicator is the proportion of couples who are contracepting—in 1992 an astonishingly high 91 percent (*ZJSN* 1993, 335). However, these numbers are quite unreliable. They include such distortions as couples who pay doctors to certify that they have been sterilized when they have not. State birth planning shares a problem with all central planning, that functionaries maximize the behaviors on which they are measured, neglecting other obviously desirable results. The SBPC has tried to perfect its evaluation system to optimize cadre behavior by identifying and weighting all the desired behaviors, including such desiderata as not driving fertility too low and improving quality of care (interview 20 July 1993). However, SBPC must still negotiate provincial acceptance of such a system. (On evaluation indicators, see under Planning and Statistics in the annual *China Birth Planning Yearbook.*)

As regards *reproductive outcomes,* better measures are harder to calculate and understand. TFRs are now common in national policy dialogue but virtually never appear in media reporting of provincial performance. Another basic indicator is the proportion of out-of-plan births. A third is the proportion of all births that are first children, second children, third children, and so on. This enables the program to identify where "excess children" need eradication. So far, only a few Chinese experts use "parity progression ratios," which show the exact proportion of women who progress from marriage to one child, from one child to two children, and so on (e.g., Feeney and Yu 1987, Gu and Yang 1991). They are slightly more precise but much more difficult to calculate. These are all "period" measures reflecting only a composite of current behaviors. So far, the program does not use "cohort" measures that distinguish the different behaviors of different age groups, which would be useful for anticipating change.

Operationally, the critical information problem for birth planning is not to measure reproductive outcomes after the event, but rather to monitor *reproductive behavior* as it occurs. This is much more difficult—monitoring must be continuous and exhaustive and must penetrate couples' privacy and women's bodies. Surprisingly, however, despite economic reforms, China has succeeded in restoring its capacity for such social surveillance. Evidently the key is the rapid growth of the Birth Planning Association, which ensures that all women report for periodic medical checkups, to ascertain that they are still contracepting and to identify when they become pregnant (interview 15–18 July 1993). In a few test counties, SBPC is attempting to establish computerized databases containing complete records on the reproductive and health status of each woman and her children (interviews 9, 10 July 1993). Ostensibly this is to improve the delivery of health services, but it could also be used for control. Many health objectives could be achieved more cheaply by event-based information systems that leave clients anonymous. In any case, it is doubtful that China can afford to computerize client information for more than a small proportion of counties.

Remote Processes

Program information also involves more remote processes. We briefly discuss coordination with collateral programs, qualitative recognition of collateral processes, and quantitative assessment of these effects. Remote processes can work directly on fertility (changing parents' values, changing the value of children). Or, they can work through proximate variables (employment may delay marriage, migration may separate couples). Or, they can work through intermediate variables (e.g., the program itself is stronger in more developed areas).

As regards *collateral programs,* since around 1990 program leaders have increasingly emphasized that population outcomes involve many inputs besides purely demographic ones. Moreover, with the help of political leaders, program leaders have improved coordination between such collateral programs and fertility decline. Other agencies are now supposed to allocate land, education, jobs, and other resources so as to reward single children and punish excess children (e.g., *ZJSN* 1992, 6–9). They are supposed to tighten marriage registration, establish pension insurance schemes, and raise women's status. They are supposed to integrate birth planning with antipoverty programs, disaster-relief, and community development. Particularly for poor areas, the program has formalized its recognition of collateral objectives by linking family planning to economic development and peasant enrichment, and to more "civilized and happy" peasant households.

Program personnel are certainly aware of *collateral processes* of economic, social, and cultural change. However, they tend to view them simply as making program work more or less difficult, while still regarding program impact as decisive. As regards economic change, everyone now stresses that with returns from agriculture declining, parents are now less interested in raising children for farm work and more interested in transferring themselves to nonfarm work. Thus as regards social change, recently much attention has gone to an upsurge in migration. Program leaders originally thought that population mobility would increase fertility (because migrants escape program control). However, they later concluded that mobility may decrease fertility, because migrants are preoccupied with making money (interview 2 July 1993). The transient population remains a main program target in the late 1990s (e.g., *FBIS* 18 March 1998). Finally, as regards cultural change, program leaders regard rising levels of literacy and education as long-run prerequisites for a completely voluntary program. In the short run, program leaders emphasize the effect of lifestyle changes (for example, many young people are now more interested in having fun after work than in raising children).

There have been some attempts at *quantitative assessment* of influences on China's fertility decline. Clearly the program has an independent impact, or there would not be so much resistance to it, or such a tendency for fertility to rise when enforcement slackens (Greenhalgh most articles, Wang 1988). One study shows the independent impact of urban household registration, which subjects individuals to stricter administration (Li 1995). Most studies indicate that both socioeconomic modernization and program administration have contributed significantly to China's fertility decline, but that available data do not allow one to specify how much of each (e.g., Poston and Gu 1987, Lavely and Freedman 1990). Complicating subnational assessment is the fact that a locality's level of modernization affects not only individual behavior but also program strength—more modern areas have both stronger programs and more modern publics, while less modern localities have less modern publics and "need" stronger programs but cannot afford them. A comparison of the Japanese and Chinese demographic transitions concludes that in China the contributions of social modernization and state program have been about equal (Feeney and Wang 1993).

Conclusion

In the late 1990s, China's birth planning program has declared a preliminary victory in slowing population growth and passing the "third peak" of
fertile women, while affirming the need for continued long-term effort
(retiring Peng Peiyun in *FBIS* 18 March 1998). In 1995 the SBPC issued
four guidelines for future work that reaffirmed past goals and methods but
urged a further shift toward integration with other programs of economic
and social development (*FBIS* 12 September 1997). After the Fifteenth
Party Congress in September 1997, the SBPC outlined "fighting tasks" for
the next fifty years, which the Politburo endorsed (Jiang Zemin in *FBIS* 18
March 1998).

On the negative side, the SBPC designated 15 February 1995 as the
day it calculated that China passed its original 1.2 billion population target
for the year 2000. Program leaders cautioned against any optimism about
China's population problem, and they called for more uniform enforcement, particularly in the countryside, to keep China's population to 1.3 billion in the year 2000 (*FBIS* 15 February 1995). The program has somewhat
downplayed its nominal one-child target but continues its vigilance against
"excess" children (more than two). Reviewing the performance of the birth
planning program during the Eighth Five-Year Plan (1991–1995), Mme.
Peng found the low birth rates that the program had achieved to be "unstable" in most regions (i.e., they would easily rise if not vigorously sup-
pressed). She attributed this instability to continued implementation
through administrative fiat and to weakness of grassroots work in the countryside (*RMRB* 4 January 1996). Consequently she still found it necessary
to urge a shift from "administrative means, remedial measures and shock
tactics." With population growth in urban areas relatively under control, the
SBPC has focused on the countryside, particularly poor areas in populous
provinces (*FBIS* 23 October 1995, 7 November 1995).

On the positive side, the program continues its shift from enforcing
quotas to delivering services, and from "social regulation" to "economic
means" (objectives for the 1996–2000 five-year plan, reported in *FBIS* 23
March 1995). By 1997 the commission's director for policy legislation
claimed that the Chinese government's approach to enforcement had shifted over the previous five years. "You can't simply threaten people any-
more, you have to try to persuade them. Relations between the local government and the people are changing greatly and this is precisely why we
are changing our methods. . . . Only economic development is going to
control population growth. Even if we wanted to make every family have
only one child, it would be impossible" (*NYT* 17 August 1997).

On balance, the Chinese party-state's accomplishment in fertility control has been truly sobering. China reduced the average woman's total fertility from about six children in the early 1970s to roughly two in the early

1990s, and to roughly one in such urban models as Shanghai. Underreporting in later surveys has produced national TFRs as improbably low as 1.5, but Chinese demogaphers suspect that the national average at the end of the 1990s is slightly below two (1998 conversations). At least according to program statistics, 91 percent of all couples of reproductive age regularly practice contraception, in both highly urbanized and largely rural provinces. Since the massive sterilization campaigns of 1983, one member of about half of all couples has been sterilized—roughly 40 percent of women and 12 percent of men (*ZJSN* 1993, 335). To maintain this proportion, China performs 5 to 10 million new sterilizations each year. Overall, by the late 1990s, the program claims to have "averted" over 400 million "excess" births.

The notion of a gap between government birth limits and popular fertility aspirations has been fundamental to this chapter. Clearly such a gap exists, since most rural families still demand at least one son and desire at least one son and one daughter, and since government officials routinely bemoan the fact that popular fertility aspirations exceed state program targets. Beyond that, despite numerous surveys, it appears that Chinese citizens cannot meaningfully respond to hypothetical questions about how many children they might want under other circumstances. On the one hand, institutional setting defines information and incentives. In the mid-1980s, most respondents said they wanted about one more than the number of children they were allowed. This suggests information processing that started from institutional cues but held open the possibility of playing the system for one more than the official limit. On the other hand, by the early 1990s, many urban people said they wanted only one child, and most rural people said they wanted only two, largely because of economic not political constraints (for many, two sons were now too expensive). This suggests that in the 1990s the gap between popular aspirations and program norms may finally be narrowing. Either way, to most people, more children are now simply inconceivable. (On recent trends in preferences about numbers of children see Tian with Hu 1994, Greenhalgh, Zhu, and Li 1994.)

For *international policy*, the difficulty of assessing "true" preferences could mean that the Chinese birth planning program is so coercive that people cannot even figure out what they want. Or it could mean that the program may not be so coercive as it appears. In any case, occasional cadre violence against property is not the problem—it mostly reflects incomplete institutionalization. Rather, if there is a problem, it is the institutionalization already achieved—state birth planning that is, in the final analysis, ineluctably compulsory. Further institutionalization will further routinize the program but make it still more inescapable. China claims that much public compliance results from "nongovernment organizations" such as the Birth Planning Association, which develop the "voluntarism" and "self-reliance" of the masses. However, these mass organizations are nongovernmental only in the sense that the party itself is nongovernmental. They are autonomous, not in the sense of permitting individual choice, but only in the sense of delegating enforcement from government to quasi-governmental organization. China claims that this approach parallels that in Indonesia, where allegedly not the state but local communities enforce contraception (interview 20 July 1993). Actually, the Indonesian state intervenes (Warwick 1986), and the Chinese state intervenes still more strongly. In other words, the Chinese program combines both strong state control and strong community control.

For *comparative politics,* Chinese birth planning shows how "governability" is specific to policy characteristics and institutional design. Unfavorable factors included the conflict between state and society over family size, and the privacy of the behavior to be controlled. Favorable factors included increasing agreement of officials and citizens that limiting population is necessary and the availability of effective but inexpensive contraceptive technology. Program success required the personal commitment of top political leaders to a high priority for restraining population growth, authoritatively communicated through party channels to party members. Program success also required good institutional design. At the top, the national political leadership lodged state birth planning in a ministry-level commission with the political resources to promote interministerial cooperation and the economic resources to improve contraceptive technology. In the middle, the national leadership defined clear goals for subnational policy administrators and made those goals a part of both government performance evaluation and party political disciple. At the bottom, the leadership created a new party-led mass organization to provide contraceptives, monitor reproduction, and enforce compliance.

For *postcommunist politics,* the Chinese birth planning program suggests that late communism may still have some future, if it plays its cards right. Astute social policy may be one of those cards. Late communism does still grant political leaders a longer time horizon than democracy permits its politicians. Communist leaders can choose to incur short-run political costs in the hope of long-run political gains. The center in China remains more robust than its endemic skirmishes with subnational governments are usually taken to imply. National leaders do pay significant "agency costs"—neither subnational leaders nor grassroots cadres do exactly what national leaders would ideally prefer. Nevertheless, on balance, the ultimate principals can remain better off than if they had tried to run everything themselves. Stronger implementation of population control after 1990 presumably benefited from the renewal of the regime's coercive credibility that resulted from 1989 repression. Evidently the regime reinvested its new coercive capital for midterm remunerative returns while continuing its long-run shift from mobilization toward institutionalization. Achieving "a modestly comfortable standard of living" for most Chinese by the year

2000 has become the regime's main political plank and its main hope for long-run viability. Population control contributes strategically to this objective. Hence the vigorous enforcement of state birth planning in late-communist China.

Note

This chapter is based on the following. For about fifteen years I have had the opportunity to discuss Chinese population affairs with my wife, Susan Greenhalgh, a leading specialist in that area. In July 1993, Susan and I participated in a three-week mission from the United Nations Population Fund to evaluate reports about abrupt Chinese fertility decline (Kristof 1993). In preparation for the mission, I reviewed the secondary literature on Chinese population policy, the previous five years of relevant *FBIS* articles, and the previous five years of all Chinese-language demographic journals available to me in New York, including some provincial ones. During the mission, Susan and I interviewed a wide range of leading population officials and academic demographers in Beijing, Shanghai, and Xian. We also visited an advanced county in Jiangsu and a backward county in Anhui, and revisited the "middling" urban district in Shaanxi where Susan had done fieldwork in 1988. During the mission I consulted still more national and provincial Chinese population journals, and I collected much other Chinese-language material. After the mission I read through the previous five years of the official *China Birth Planning Yearbook* that we had obtained in Beijing. Since then I have updated the chapter from new secondary literature, *FBIS* coverage, recent documents hand-carried by friends from China, and a few interviews with Chinese experts traveling in the United States. The most and best English political analysis of the Chinese program appears in the articles by Susan Greenhalgh and Tyrene White listed in the References.

8

Reconstituting
the Arts and Sciences

Richard Kraus and Richard P. Suttmeier

Introduction

The huge enterprise of intellectual activity that contributes to the making of "culture" in China ended the Maoist era in a badly damaged state. The Cultural Revolution story is by now depressingly familiar: Intellectuals were prime targets of mobilized Red Guards, and the institutions for promoting intellectual life—universities, research institutes, professional societies, and the media for scholarly and artistic communication—were severely disrupted. The Cultural Revolution, however, was but a stage (albeit, the most dramatic) in the evolution of political control *and* political sponsorship of the cultural sphere. The various stages of control and patronage proceeded according to different party assumptions about (and views of) science and the arts and their proper roles under (and in transition to) socialism (Kraus 1989, Suttmeier 1974).

The end of the Maoist era and the onset of reform policies saw the broadening of the menu of assumptions and views, but has in the process also created a crisis in what we may call the "constitution of culture," that is, in the norms, rules, and policies by which political control and sponsorship are defined and legitimated. Arguably the crisis has both helped and harmed cultural production, but understanding its causes and history sheds important light on the etiology of the distinctive decay of Leninism in China. Central to the coming of the crisis is of course the institution of the market and the ways it has been embraced in the cause of producing culture. Recognizing that the "transition from Leninism" is a provocative and problematic phrase, we seek to avoid the full-blown teleology of much of the popular and optimistic "transitions to democracy" literature. We are concerned with the relationship of the reconstitution of culture to democratization, but we do not dismiss the possibility of undemocratic, if non-Leninist, outcomes.

The borders of "culture" in contemporary China are poorly defined. In this chapter we examine two of its elite manifestations: the new institutions of science and the older world of humanistic literary intellectuals. These two kinds of culture are not often considered together. They have followed distinct, yet roughly parallel paths through much of the history of the People's Republic. In the most turbulent periods of Chinese politics, many scientists have found a safe harbor in their technical skills, while artists, under continuous pressure to address social issues, have been at higher risk. We ask if two decades of reform have brought their experiences closer together. We mean to be inclusive of all professionals in both arts and sciences, ranging from poets to filmmakers in the former category, and from astrophysicists to physicians and computer engineers in the latter. We do not consider in this essay other professionals who work in culture, such as lawyers, advertising executives, and religious officials.

A central question for Chinese *science* at the end of the Maoist era was whether radical politics should control scientific research and technological innovation. The answer provided by Deng Xiaoping, stated perhaps most strongly at the 1978 science conference, was that radical politics had no role in science. This answer was both a derivation from ideological assumptions and a response to a series of practical problems. In ideological terms, the new political understanding of science and technology was entailed in the Dengist view that the material conditions of communism did not yet obtain in China. A future transition to communism did not require a revolution in the superstructure—the Maoist tenet that inspired the Cultural Revolution—but required instead an enlightened commitment to the development of productive forces. Science and technology should be seen as productive forces, and Deng pledged his support for their promotion with his famous oath to be a loyal foot soldier in the battle to advance science and technology (Suttmeier 1980).

One senses that for a pragmatic Deng Xiaoping, these ideological innovations were ultimately driven by the practical problems that confronted China with Mao's passing. The increasing international exposure of Chinese science and technology during the 1970s made it inescapable that the Cultural Revolution had contributed to the stunting of Chinese research and innovation in most fields of inquiry and application. To compensate for the lost years, new policies were required that would address the age and quality "cohort gaps" in the technical community and reorient the material and organizational foundations of science and technology. From the outset, these initiatives involved the search for science and technology assets in the international community.

In the *arts,* the years immediately following the death of Mao Zedong saw the party attempting to loosen the hold of politics on the cultural sphere. But in comparison with science, the depoliticization of the arts was more complex and less successful.

Reform politics effectively lowered the political temperature in the arts, but did so by offering political patronage for less radical causes than those advocated by the Maoists. Typical was the "scar" movement in fiction, film, and painting. The state encouraged China's arts professionals to create works condemning the excesses of their former patrons, at the same time as campaigns sought to root out radicals. Many artists were encouraged by the regime's public protestations of a new way of doing things, especially after the 1979 National Arts Congress, an obvious analog to the science conference of the preceding year. Yet the cultural vision of Deng Xiaoping's entourage rarely moved beyond restoring a supposedly purified pre–Cultural Revolution system of state patronage and propaganda. There was little official encouragement to challenge the fundamental system by which the arts had been organized since the early 1950s, although this began to change as the economic reforms began to have a broad impact in society. International influences also increased, with a more ambiguous impact than in science.

Processes

In both arts and science, the post-Mao transition came to acquire a dialectical quality—domestic change leading to new patterns of foreign influence, with the latter then stimulating new directions of domestic change. However, the force of this dialectic was considerably stronger in science, as we will show below.

Domestic Developments

The sciences.   Domestic change in science was driven by an evolving set of reform policies (Gu 1994a). In the early post-Mao period, these sought to restore Chinese science and technology to a pre–Cultural Revolution mode of regularized bureaucratic planning and direction of research and innovation. In this mode, policies toward technical intellectuals would accord them status as important national resources while also extending a measure of political control through a loosely coordinated, but party-dominated, network of professional societies.

By the early 1980s, reform policies broke more clearly from the pre–Cultural Revolution model. In part, key players in science policy were frustrated by the Cultural Revolution's legacy of power and prominence for work units. The ability of the work unit to control human and material resources for its own purposes—"unit ownership" instead of "ownership by the whole people"—worked against the full reestablishment of centralized bureaucratic direction that was recalled with fondness by some members of the Dengist elite. Thus an important objective of reform at this stage was to shake loose the resources controlled by the unit in order to facilitate their redirection by the center.

In addition, some in the science policy community came to understand that the pre–Cultural Revolution system was itself defective, especially when contrasted with the dynamism of science and technology found in the capitalist world. While the image of the "golden years" of science and technology from before the Cultural Revolution might still linger in the minds of many who had been active in that period, the system itself seemed inappropriate for China in the 1980s, especially in its incapacity for generating research-based technological innovation needed for economic strength and competitiveness, and also because it had become discredited in its original home, the Soviet Union. Science and technology policy reformers therefore began to summarize reform experiments that had been carried out since 1978, preparing the documentation for what became the science and technology structural reform policies of 1985. These policies sought new mechanisms to get research to serve production through the introduction of "technology markets" and contract research, and through the progressive reduction of the budgets of research institutes (IDRC 1997, Saich 1989, Wang 1993, Conroy 1992).

As with the arts, domestic reforms in science also facilitated the reintroduction of elitist norms, nominally derived from achievement criteria, into cultural production. In 1980, for instance, the Chinese Academy of Sciences reestablished its system of selecting elite scientists as "department members" (*xuebu weiyuan*) and has now conducted five elections to recruit new members into this prestigious role. On the occasion of establishing the separate academy of engineering in 1994, the "department member" designation in both academies was changed to the more honorific "academician" (*yuan shi*), a title enjoyed by only slightly more than 1,000 of China's scientists and engineers (Cao 1997). The institution of achievement-based norms favoring the development of elitist values became further established with new competitive, peer-reviewed funding programs, with the introduction of designated "key" universities and "key" laboratories, and with new regulations for graduate degrees and academic promotions that—in most fields—stress the need for publication in international journals.

The arts. The initial wave of reform in the arts certainly lightened the hand of the state in ways that most citizens and arts professionals welcomed. The condemnation of the Gang of Four permitted the rehabilitation of thousands of veteran artists and arts officials who had run afoul of the intolerance of Cultural Revolution radicalism. Ordinary citizens witnessed an immediate broadening of the range of styles and subjects in the arts, as new ventures were encouraged and old, formerly disgraced works were revived.

Parallel to the new treatment of scientists, the Communist Party ended its generation-long celebration of the amateur artist. Radicals had urged professional artists to learn from amateurs, who were imagined to embody a more reliable political purity, untarnished by the elitism of the conservatory and academy of fine arts. In reality, this cult of the amateur was often superficial (Laing 1984). But as a symbol, it weighed heavily on arts professionals, who began the 1980s with the ideal that they were the real artists and that they should be able to run their own affairs without deferring to worker and peasant amateurs.

Far from being depoliticized, the arts became a weapon to promote a gentler political and administrative style. Writers, filmmakers, and poets struck blows against the propaganda machine, which was perceived as the last remaining base of old Maoists. This was generally successful, though with painful interludes in which artists have been criticized for leading their fellow citizens down the road to bourgeois liberalization. Periodic campaigns have disrupted the careers of individual artists, but throughout the 1980s these campaigns diminished in vitality so that few targeted artists were cowed (Silbergeld 1993).

But the bloody repression of popular protest in Beijing and elsewhere in 1989 strengthened the determination of the party establishment to maintain control. Domination of the streets of Beijing was followed by a revived effort to dominate ideology, and thus the arts. Yet this effort was also unsuccessful, although all artists felt the cold wind on their backs. In practice, relatively few new restrictions were reimposed on the working lives of China's artists; the post-massacre climate of making money wherever possible tended to marginalize many artists, to their profound disappointment.

The party loosened its controls over both arts and sciences in the reform era, yet leaders were far less clear about how to lighten their hold over the arts. In part this stemmed from the distinctive nature of the two cultural products. Scientists were rather quickly treated as active contributors to China's economic growth, but artists, almost always involved in the representation of the actual world and commentary upon it, easily encountered controversy, with few obvious offsetting benefits. The consequence was a sometimes troubled oscillation between relatively open and closed periods for artists, as new limits were pressed against often unwilling state patrons.

International Interactions

The domestic sources of change in both the arts and science cannot be understood without understanding the ways in which foreign influences began to shape Chinese thinking and practices.

The sciences. In science, the Dengist leadership's abandonment of Maoist commitments to self-reliance has certainly been of equal importance to indigenous structural reform in spurring change in the science and technology system. The Cultural Revolution's legacy of backwardness could not be overcome rapidly without tapping into the resources for scientific and technological development found beyond China's borders.

Technology transfer has been one approach. Between 1979 and 1994, China acquired an enormous amount of foreign technology—valued at more than U.S.$40 billion—through commercial relations (*CD* 15 August 1994, 2). These technology transfers not only have had notable advantages for the productivity of the economy, but also have had the effect of exposing Chinese technical personnel to international "best practices" in engineering and management (Sato 1994). A great deal of the technology transferred to China comes via investment by foreign firms. These have provided new career options to Chinese scientists and engineers, and have also spread appreciation of the institutional setting for capitalist technological innovation, including the roles of capital markets, intellectual property rights, and managerial sensitivity to the importance of human capital. The diffusion of knowledge about such institutions and practices, however imperfectly emulated by Chinese organizations, strikes at the ideological foundation of socialist thinking about knowledge and innovation. Thus, in addition to its economic effects, China's technology transfer experience can be seen as an important part of the reconstitution of cultural production.

Educational exchange has served as a second mode of interaction with foreign science and technology and has had profound consequences for transitions within science and technology and for the structure of the Chinese technical community. For instance, as part of the effort to get recently graduated, foreign-trained doctoral students to return to China, the government initiated a number of policies intended to appeal to these scientists, such as special research funding and new research stations for returnees. Presence abroad has, in effect, put the government in the position of a bidder in competition for the talents of its youth (Broaded 1993, *China Information Bulletin* 1994). Although the government has not displayed notable success in this competition, it is important to note that this condition represents a subtle but significant change in the nature of the relationship between state and scientist.

The continuing preference for study abroad among large numbers of recent science and engineering graduates has important impacts on the organization and staffing of laboratories and research groups within China. Graduates from "first-tier" and more cosmopolitan institutions (with their reputations for quality, foreign language training, and a variety of foreign connections) have better opportunities to seize the golden ring of studying abroad. This leaves the research groups of the first-tier institutions with a shortage of new talent among their own students for their own graduate programs and research assistantships. They are thus forced to compete for the leading students of second-tier institutions who have less of a chance to go abroad. While this development might be seen as a force for the leveling down of quality work, it is also a force against inbreeding and for the diffusion of advanced knowledge and practices beyond the first tier.

The contours of the "Chinese scientific community" have been profoundly altered by study abroad and subsequent brain drain, but the losses to China from this increasing diaspora must be seen in context. While one can speak of a "national" technical community of those actually working on the mainland, the brain drain is also strengthening an emerging transnational Chinese scientific community (the "extended community") that is linked by 747s, international conferences, faxes, and e-mail, as well as ethnicity (Suttmeier 1993b). Apart from the manifest losses of talent to the national community, the latter nevertheless also gains from internationalization and from the contacts it maintains with its best and brightest abroad. Many of these, of course, are positioned at the world's premier universities and research centers and often maintain residual sympathies and feelings of identity with institutions in the national community. With the large number of retirements in the national community expected after the turn of the century, the importance of the extended community for the vitality of Chinese science will only increase.

A third mode by which China has interacted with the international community is through government-to-government science and technology cooperation agreements. These have facilitated exchanges of personnel and foreign training, and provided technical and material assistance to China. Very important, they have given China greater understanding of the science and technology policies of countries in the capitalist world. Enhanced understanding of alternative policy models and institutions for science has stimulated further reform and restructuring in China.

The influence of foreign policy models is evident in the adoption of technical standards for regulatory policies (concerning, for instance, the environment, nuclear power, health, and safety), and in the innovation of new institutions for supporting research. The best example of the latter is the establishment of the Natural Science Foundation of China, inspired by the United States National Science Foundation, and the adoption of competitive peer review procedures for evaluating and funding scientific work. Exposure to foreign models has also led to a significant reorientation in Chinese policy thinking concerning the kinds of research that should be funded by government not industry, the relative share of the national expenditures that should come from these two sources, the modalities of funding, and the relative distribution of funding among basic research, applied research, and development.

Finally, the involvement of international organizations, especially the World Bank, has contributed to the transition in science. The Bank's first loan to China was to strengthen science education through the modernization of university laboratories and laboratory equipment. Additional loans of this sort followed throughout the 1980s, involving more academic institutions. More recently, the Bank has supported a project to enhance the research and training capabilities of 133 "key laboratories" chosen by the government for their achievements and promise. With this support, the Bank has provided material reinforcement for the processes of professionalization and internationalization that have characterized much of the science policy reforms in the post-Mao period.

The arts. While China's scientists entered the reform period keenly aware that their work lagged behind international standards in most fields, artists also suffered from the isolation of the Cultural Revolution, but in somewhat different ways. Many artists in China believe that the concept of "progress" can be applied to their work and that China's culture had failed to advance in recent decades. However, artists confronted a more complex issue than scientists, as it is far less obvious what is "advanced" in oil painting or music than in biophysics or computer science. "World standards" in virtuoso piano playing may perhaps be measured by prizes in international contests, but no such reference is available for drama or poetry.

But there was no controversy about the fact that China's artists were simply out of touch with recent international trends in their respective genres. Maoist self-reliance had merely reinforced the Middle Kingdom's serene indifference to the arts of other lands. Whole aesthetic movements have risen and vanished in other parts of the world without many Chinese artists taking note.

A trickle of foreign art in the 1970s reminded China's painters that they were ignorant of abstract art, musicians that their violins were poorly made, and writers that their short stories were rather old-fashioned. In part to appeal to urban intellectuals, Deng Xiaoping quickly abandoned the cultural isolation of the 1960s and 1970s, and artists began to think anew of how their work should be related to aesthetic developments beyond China.

The impact on the arts world was profound. Older artists reestablished youthful foreign connections they had formerly concealed, while younger and middle-aged artists competed fiercely for the privilege of foreign travel. Trips abroad became a fundamental index of social status, assuming an importance nearly comparable to an advanced degree. Often it seemed to matter little where an artist might go, just so he (and less frequently she) traveled: Tasmania, Munich, and Iowa seemed virtually interchangeable as destinations. When one literary critic's trip to the United States was canceled, he was offered a year in Germany instead. No matter that he spoke English rather than German; he went, with pleasure. The critic was not confused; he was merely responding to the vagaries of domestic politics. His U.S. trip had been canceled in the wake of the Beijing massacre, and he was under the scrutiny of the public security forces, who control departures from China.

Foreign travel and foreign influence have intersected with the party's often uncertain efforts to retain control over the arts. When the party decides that artists are going "too far," it intervenes with awkward and ineffectual campaigns. Organizationally, things were much simpler when foreign culture was clearly marked as enemy terrain, as in the late Mao years. In an age when it has become a legitimate source of inspiration, as well as occasional contamination, officials and artists alike are often confused about how to regard foreign culture.

In important respects, state managers continue to view the arts as their handmaiden. Just as science has come to be an important part of relations with Taiwan (Suttmeier 1993a), artists have been assigned a political role in working toward China's reunification. The exchange of writers and painters between Taiwan and the mainland is not innocent but rather part of a protracted and elaborate courtship. Just as the state once penalized artists for having "connections" with Taiwan and demanded that they create propaganda against the Kuomintang, it now urges artists to show the human side of life on the mainland, to bring the two sides closer together.

The Chinese community abroad has an importance that easily transcends these political goals. As with scientists, the artists of "greater China" share so much that Chinese artists in Taiwan, Hong Kong, North America, Australia, and Europe are playing a key role as intermediaries between the mainland and the West. Certainly there is direct importation of Western cultural products and concepts. But Chinese artists outside the mainland can easily draw upon their longer experience to serve as cultural brokers, introducing Freud, Mondrian, Stravinsky, Derrida, and Habermas to their mainland colleagues.

Of the scientists' various modes of interaction with the international community, only two have been important for the arts. Commercial purchase of foreign arts products has introduced into China an unprecedented array of new aesthetic influences, ranging from the high art of Western oil paintings seen in fine arts books to the popular culture of Walt Disney, whose images have been widely adopted—to the great frustration of the Disney corporation, which must alter Chinese attitudes toward intellectual property if it is to gain substantial profit.

Educational exchange has played a role in the arts similar to the sciences. Large-scale emigration of talented young artists has created a broader and more active international Chinese arts community. The impact has varied by genre, with Western-style musicians perhaps emigrating most frequently to countries such as the United States, where the crippling of public school music education has created a demand for string players. Ink painters, in contrast, have fewer opportunities abroad, as well as strong reason to remain in touch with a very "national" art form. Poets and novelists have often had the most difficult time abroad, where it is difficult to write when cut off from one's country.

Government-to-government cooperation agreements for science and technology are echoed in state-to-state visits by writers, artists, and performing artists. These ultimately have a rather shallow impact in China, beyond their role in further legitimizing foreign art. International organizations have thus far undertaken few arts projects and have had no impact comparable to, say, the World Health Organization on Chinese medical science. For instance, UNESCO has recognized several Chinese structures as important monuments of human civilization but has not provided funds for their rehabilitation or maintenance.

Commercialization

The rise of the market has introduced a powerful force that links domestic developments and international influences in both science and the arts.

The sciences. A central thrust of efforts to reform science policies has been to permit market forces to shape research and development. This has had major consequences for both the institutions of science and technology and for the careers of technical personnel.

The absence of an effective linkage between research and production bedeviled the science and technology system from the 1950s (Baark 1987). Though complex, the problem's essential features were the culture and incentive structure of research institutes, which discouraged active ties with enterprises, and the absence of sufficient incentives for enterprises to pursue technological innovations that would lead them to seek close working relations with research centers. Efforts had been made to change these conditions in the past by administrative direction and, at other times, by more radical mechanisms such as "sending down" personnel to the production line; but the problem remained intractable.

The 1980s saw the introduction of a new approach that, by "breaking iron rice bowls," was intended to introduce competition and accountability into the lives of scientists and the practices of research units and enterprises. For the research sector, the state's strategy relied heavily on reducing normal operating budgets in the expectation that the research units would be forced to seek funding from research contracts with enterprises. While contract research has grown since the mid-1980s, the reforms also stimulated a less clearly anticipated change—the movement of research units themselves into the world of commerce, and the emergence of technological entrepreneurship among members of the technical community (Gu 1994b).

This new technological entrepreneurship has come to China via two routes. The first is the active sponsorship of new commercial activities by established state research institutes. This began to happen in the mid-1980s, especially in the Zhongguancun area of the Haidian district of Beijing, with the appearance of new high-tech companies spun off from institutes of the Academy of Sciences (and to a lesser extent, from institutions of higher education). Although many of these startups had innovative ideas and technologies, few had experience in managing commercial enterprises. Fortuitously, however, because salaries and facilities were guaranteed by the parent institutes, they did not have to bear all of the entrepreneurial risks involved in starting new companies.

A somewhat different pattern of technological entrepreneurship began at about the same time. Nominally "independent" entrepreneurs—people who had formally broken with relations of state employment—set out to start new nonstate firms. The most celebrated representative of this model is, of course, Wan Runnan, the founder of the Stone Corporation. Stone represented an institutional breakthrough, although it enjoyed high-level political connections that helped buffer such entrepreneurial risks as finding business partners and financial resources outside the state sector, hiring personnel, and establishing production facilities.

By the mid-1980s, technological entrepreneurship had become increasingly commonplace but had also created challenges for policymakers. Were such entrepreneurial innovations politically correct? Would they be economically viable, and how would such viability be defined? Would they contribute to the transfer of research to production? What would be the legal standing of the new enterprises; who would be responsible for failures and who would appropriate the benefits from success? How would the provision of housing and social services be managed if ties to the parent work unit were severed? Unambiguous answers to all these questions have yet to appear, but they have at least been addressed.

The Party Central Committee endorsed the political correctness of the new entrepreneurship in 1988 after a two-year investigation of the Zhongguancun experiments. Although the involvement of Wan Runnan in the events leading up to the Tiananmen crackdown, and his subsequent flight from China, led to some rethinking about the Stone case, Stone has grown into one of China's largest nonstate enterprises, and the spirit of Zhongguancun is now widely diffused around the country. The Academy of Sciences established a special bureau to deal with the business promotion and legal implications of such entrepreneurship, and the Haidian district government established new offices to help create a favorable business climate. In addition, the State Science and Technology Commission drafted new policies intended to spur technological entrepreneurship for the nation as a whole, through technology transfer incentives, "incubator" schemes for new high-tech firms, and the establishment of special high-technology zones with preferential policies for startup firms.

Although the promotion of commercial science and technology has been a major thrust of reform policies, it has not been the only one. Significant changes have come in the funding of research, with new specially focused programs and institutional mechanisms for financial support. Quality standards have been more completely applied in the selection of institutions and individuals for funding and, as noted above, the entire system has been increasingly internationalized. The net result is that in mid-1990s China, the doing of science and the life of the technical intellectual are notably different than they were fifteen to twenty years ago.

The arts. In the arts, as in science, commercialization brought a real jolt to the existing system. The extensive commodification of culture that accompanied the spread of the market in China influenced not only the organization of artistic work, but also the presumptions under which that work is done. The impact assumed several forms.

First, rising personal incomes, combined with greater laxity in policing the sale of cultural commodities, stimulated the emergence of a thriving market in popular culture. New entertainments such as video games and video parlors (where patrons pay to watch tapes of movies played on a VCR) began to cut into popular cultural traditions such as storytelling. Yet other traditional forms were buoyed by the economy. Peasants in prosperous regions have restored the tradition of private opera performances for weddings and other celebrations. The range of culture available to China's citizens has grown enormously; along with this has come greater complexity in the relationship between "official" state-sponsored culture, "traditional" culture, and "popular" culture.

Second, commercialization led to new state policies to cut subsidies to cultural institutions. China's most elite arts organizations will retain their state subsidies as bearers of national identity, but the state now expects the great majority of opera companies, film studios, literary magazines, and performing arts ensembles to raise more of their own income from sales of tickets, magazines, books, or pieces of art. In contrast to the experience of scientists, who found new sources of funding in the reform era, arts organizations did so less easily, often resulting in shrinking budgets. This is of course not necessarily bad for Chinese culture; many organizations had become bloated with superfluous personnel and had lost any artistic edge to their work (Mackerras 1987).

Third, commercialization challenged the self-identity of the many professional artists who had justified their social role as providing wisdom, insight, and spiritual value to their nation. In practice, the Maoist regime supported arts organizations in large measure for their propaganda value, but the Deng regime sent the message that artists are no more valued than textile workers. This may be an appropriate view in a society that is still at least nominally socialist, but it is not what most artists want to hear. The Maoist regard for artists as propagandists was certainly oppressive to many artists, yet at one level it echoed, even if in distorted form, traditional Confucian notions of the artist as a teacher of the community. The extension to arts organizations of the principles of economic reform has been rancorous. It has had a dispiriting impact upon the morale of artists, few of whom are eager to become entrepreneurs and many of whom regard commercially successful popular art as vulgar.

Government support for the risky jump into commerce has been much more generous for scientists than for artists. For instance, the state encouraged scientists to initiate entrepreneurial communities such as in the capital's Zhongguancun neighborhood. Yet when a group of avant-garde artists tried to band together in Beijing's Yuanmingyuan village to share both ideas and customers, the police harassed them as undesirable bohemians, while cultural officials ignored their plight.

Some larger arts organizations have been able to ride the market economy by developing an entrepreneurial streak. This superficially resembles the experience of science entrepreneurs who started up from a state institutional base. But in fact groups such as the Fujian Writers Association and Fujian Television have turned to such non-arts activities as operating hotels, restaurants, and advertising agencies in order to subsidize their cultural missions—practices not unheard of among institutions of science as well. Many of the big arts institutions have adapted to the commercial economy by setting up subsidiary companies that often make money by manufacturing, or by speculation in real estate.

State policy in science was to link research more clearly to production, a goal that gave policy considerable coherence. It was difficult to formulate an analogous policy for the arts, where "production" is far more ambiguous. Many reformers encouraged arts organizations to tie their activities to production by treating readers, viewers, and audiences as consumers. Yet other officials were loath to abandon the state's ultimate claim on artists to serve its ends, even if in a gentler fashion than before. At the same time, many state leaders regarded commercial culture as a source of ideological confusion and antisocial values; they appealed to professional artists to counter vulgarity with high-minded purity, thereby confusing all who sought a simple formula for the new relationship between art and market.

Assessments

What are the implications of the changes described above for the question of the role of culture in China's movement away from Leninism? In order to bring some coherence to what is a most complicated topic, the discussion will focus on three issues: the broader significance of commercialization, the implications of internationalization, and the current state of the enduring themes of "science and democracy."

Commercialization

The sciences. The invasive presence of market forces in the Chinese technical community has produced a number of problems for science and technology. It has disrupted long-term research agendas and diverted talent—often inappropriately—into commercial activities. The emphasis on commercialization also imperfectly serves the establishment of a modernized basic research tradition linked to quality higher education and advanced training. More seriously, perhaps, it seems to be discouraging talented young people from incurring the costs of elite technical training; when high incomes, mobility, and international lifestyles are available to the young in careers that do not require spending long hours in laboratories, it is understandable that some fraction of China's best and brightest, in contrast to the situation in the still recent past, would choose careers outside of science.

At a deeper philosophical level, there is thus a real possibility that "profit" will greatly overshadow "truth" in the hierarchy of Chinese cultural values. This danger, however, must be seen against a tradition where truth was already overshadowed by another value, that of power. Put somewhat differently, science in Chinese modern history has, on balance, been institutionalized in subordination to the state. Various attempts in the precommunist period to establish institutional autonomy for science either fell victim to the political upheavals so characteristic of twentieth-century Chinese history, or lacked the financial and physical infrastructure to succeed. The modern technical intellectual in China thus did not escape from the problematic relationship with the state that has characterized the role of the intellectual more generally since imperial times, a relationship in which autonomy was severely constrained and dependency—in the absence of other sources of material sustenance—was unavoidable.

When scientific development is viewed in comparative perspective, it is clear that the protection of sufficient autonomy for technical communities to perform their social functions requires a plurality of sources of material support—private industry, private philanthropy, and so on, as well as government. The terms of support from varying sources, and the relative shares from each, are matters that characterize the ways in which societies negotiate the nature of cultural production. Over time, the general rules of the game come to be understood, even as negotiation continues over shifting shares and changing modalities.

In this sense then, the growing commercialization of science and technology in China can be seen as a positive development in opening up new sources of material support for the technical enterprise. Independent of the state, these new sources also introduce possibilities for renegotiating the terms of cultural production. However, the rules for these negotiations in contemporary China remain "immature," and therein lies one cause of constitutional crisis in the cultural realm alluded to at the outset. Emblematic of this immaturity are confusion over the assignment and protection of intellectual property rights, confusion over the responsibilities that might accompany such rights, problems of scientific fraud in reporting research results, and problems in the quality of new products reaching the market-place (Agence France Presse 1994).

The arts. The commercialization of the arts has affected the constitution of culture by exacerbating the gap between the prosperous coastal provinces and the poorer interior, thereby heightening regional opportuni-ties. Just as the coastal provinces are growing more rapidly, so too are they enjoying more varied cultural fare, as their higher standards of living sup-port more new items of popular culture. Their official arts organizations can also better meet the state's demands for self-sufficiency. In Guangdong, Fujian, Zhejiang, and Shanghai, new arts foundations and contributions from entrepreneurs and companies have become an important source of financial support for cultural organizations. By contrast, arts organizations in poorer, interior provinces, including drama companies and public libraries, are less able even to maintain past standards.

Private financial contributions and market-earned profits also become a source of political leverage. As the state makes ever-diminished financial contributions, propaganda officials discover that they have less ability than ever to discipline errant artists.

But artists generally make poor entrepreneurs, in China or in any nation. While many felt smothered by the formerly tight controls of the work unit, many of the same artists are also uncomfortable with the new need to hustle for customers. While the Ministry of Culture identified model cultural units in adapting to the market, most artists have been left to their own devices in adjusting to a new world of commerce. What many Chinese artists prefer is what intellectuals around the world covet but rarely find: maximum public financial support with minimum state intervention in the content of their work.

One of the most difficult aspects of the reforms for many artists is the increasing irrelevance of elite culture, either that supported by the party in the 1950s or the somewhat bolder, reform-minded high art (Kraus 1995). Arts-minded young people are often avoiding the painfully long training necessary for traditional (and ill-paid) careers in the elite arts, although many are trying out new avenues in such commercial realms as acting or popular music. In the 1980s, there was a particularly steep decline in the numbers of young writers in reform-minded Fujian.

To many artists, China is now awash with vulgarity. National commer-cialization has turned everything into a commodity, including the artworks that traditional literati have historically insisted should not be sold. In reali-ty, the proscription against gentlemen selling their art was much stronger in rhetoric than reality (Cahill 1994). But the commodification of culture is constantly expanding its reach, now extending even to calligraphy, perhaps the last sacred refuge for the self-esteem of a traditional intellectual (Kraus 1991).

The disenchantment of some artists has given rise to an avant-garde in most genres. As in the West, China's avant-garde rejects established, increasingly bourgeois values (e.g., some of the paintings in Doran 1993). In China, the rise of experimental, alienated painting (Andrews and Gao 1995) and poetry (Su and Larson 1995) has created a new scene in which self-styled advanced artists speak mostly to each other, with little interest in an audience that cannot understand, and thus will not patronize, their work. Such groups of artists exist for the first time since 1949 outside or on the fringe of the established arts institutions, such as the Writers Association or the fine arts academies in Beijing and Hangzhou.

The new reconstitution of culture thus includes some new experiments with partial autonomy for artists. This autonomy is not so much officially sanctioned as endured, so long as the artists speak mostly to other elite intellectuals and agree not to tempt the wrath of the state by trying to reach out to ordinary citizens. Such autonomy is highly tentative, subject to sudden withdrawal, and perhaps politically irrelevant. Yet it may also prove to be a way of marking out a new space for art, at arm's length at least from state supervision.

Internationalization

The sciences.   Uncertainty about the constitution of culture is also inherent in the local-cosmopolitan tensions that internationalization inevitably generates. In the sciences, whether it be a matter of international technology flows or the increasingly transnational character of the "Chinese technical community," China has both committed itself to interdependence with the rest of the world *and* continued to pursue modern science and technology as the sources of *national* wealth and power. China, of course, is not alone in facing this tension. The globalization of technology, and the international mobility and cosmopolitan culture of technical intellectuals, force many nations into re-examining the meanings of *national* science, *national* technology, and *national* culture. Nevertheless, managing these tensions in China may be especially taxing. The national "wealth and power" symbolism is not easily shed and the forces of transnational expansion are not easily denied, yet legitimate forums for exploring and discussing this contradiction have been slow to appear.

The arts.   Scientists have rushed to create the conditions to work at international standards in their fields. Artists have instead debated what international standards ought to be and how China might best interact with the international artistic community. If the Chinese technical community is increasingly transnational, the Chinese arts community is less clear about the value and nature of interaction with colleagues abroad. The state's interest in using the arts to strengthen a sense of "greater China" identity is clear enough. So is the willingness of most Chinese artists to join this effort for their own reasons. More problematic is how to deal with the very different international community of artists with no connection to China. One way Chinese artists seek validation is from international cultural prizes, which are often given greater credence in China than abroad. This has focused special attention on the question of the Nobel Prize for literature; never won by a Chinese, it is coveted by many nationalistic writers for one of their own. However, others reject the contest as unfair or inappropriate (Larson and Kraus 1989, Owen 1990).

China's science and technology program is certainly motivated partly by nationalism, but nationalist competition in the arts is more complicated. Does national achievement mean celebrating I. M. Pei, a modernist architect of the international style who is ethnically Chinese but whose work could plausibly be that of a Norwegian or Ethiopian? Or does it mean that China should cultivate its native arts to make a distinctively Chinese impact abroad? The recent Western successes of the films of Zhang Yimou and Chen Kaige may suggest a way to the latter. Certainly few governments can resist the political appeal of celebrating their native culture, and perhaps trying to present it abroad as an expression of universal values. Nationalist movements in any nation tend to treat the arts as a political vehicle; as the Communist Party became more explicitly nationalistic in the 1990s, artists could make their peace with power by participating in the celebration of China's glory, a mission many found quite palatable.

The internationalization of culture, simultaneous with its commodification, results in a frequent obsession with using art to obtain hard currency, both for the state and for individual artists with foreign contacts. This has many manifestations, including jealousies among practitioners of various genres. For example, oil painters regard ink painters as privileged because they can work more quickly; ink painters feel that foreign patrons understand only the Western art of oil painting and shun their own wares. Access to foreign patrons, sometimes bitterly contested, has produced such curiosities as a Chinese opera company that performs in English to tourists.

As with science and technology, the arts world is learning to deal with intellectual property rights. There has been a steady Western pressure, especially from the United States, for China to adopt Western concepts of intellectual property. These do not come easily in a culture where, historically, bold artistic innovation has been prized less than the ability to work convincingly in the styles of ancient masters.

Science, Arts, and Democracy

In the twentieth century, China's cultural wars have linked both the sciences and arts not only to national "wealth and power" but to democracy as well. In the post-Mao era, the culture and democracy theme has assumed new importance. Nevertheless, while rhetorically engaging, the relationships between culture and democracy in China remain obscure, both analytically and sociologically.

The sciences. Some phenomena in Dengist China suggest an organic relationship between science and democracy. Symbolized by Fang Lizhi, science and engineering faculties have been well represented among domestic democracy activists, and there is evidence of democratic dissent from individual scientists in China. Within the dispersed network of students and scholars abroad, many scientists have taken as part of their professional responsibility the extra tasks of educating themselves about democratic principles and procedures. Nevertheless, one might argue that for the (national) technical community on the mainland as a whole, there is no especially evident relationship between science and democracy. Scientists seem offended by what undemocratic practices often do to their sense of truth, and by the limits such practices put on the scientists' ability to "speak truth to power." However, they have also enjoyed considerable favor from the Dengist regime, and most would probably subscribe to the notion that China's technical and economic progress requires a well-ordered society (Miller 1996).

How one regards the science and democracy issue, and its relationships to the production of culture and to a transition from Leninism, may depend on one's assumptions about democracy and democratization in the Chinese context. The assumption here is that although science and democracy are not necessarily related to each other, they can be in some historical contexts, and China is such a context. However, the relationship is complex, at three levels.

At the first level, science (and technology) are forces for creating and strengthening civil society in China. During the Dengist era, science and technology have played this role in a variety of ways. Because the regime has placed a premium on its development, the technical community has enjoyed some domestic liberalization and international intercourse that have then partially diffused to other segments of society (Hayhoe 1990, Bonnin and Chevier 1991). Proponents of reform in science and technology have enjoyed a relatively free voice. In the name of science (and the requirements for its development), these reformers also became advocates for economic liberalization, and for new thinking about law and property rights as well. While entrepreneurship and new forms of ownership are often associated with township and village enterprises, concern for the development of science and technology legitimized these early in high-technology industry as well. In viewing science and technology as forces for strengthening civil society, however, the key players have often been less the demonstrable "democracy activists" than liberal-leaning bureaucrats and policymakers who have been the shepherds of the reforms in science. These players have sanctioned policies that have strengthened civil society, including opportunities for more autonomous professional associations for technical personnel. While it is true that an awakened civil society does not a democracy make, it does help create conditions that force new thinking about power sharing. However, in this context, the strong drift toward elitism in science must be considered. As with the arts, elitism may reinforce trends toward more autonomous professional groups, and thus be a step toward pluralism. On the other hand, elite status has become an important resource in the quest for the material support of science. It promises to increase inequalities within the professional community and could perhaps make access to material resources and social privileges more a function of position and reputation than of merit.

A second level at which science and democracy can be related is that of policymaking itself. Reformist critics of past (and present) styles of Chinese policymaking have often noted its personalistic qualities—policy has reflected the personal preferences and aspirations of an aging leadership. The record of such a policymaking style is seen, in turn, as one of countless policy mistakes that have imposed unnecessary costs on Chinese society since 1949. For some critics, the problem has been that policymaking has not been "democratic" (i.e., has not been inclusive in the preferences policy reflects). For others, it has not been "scientific" (i.e., the empirical premises of policy thinking have been woefully uninformed and untested). Other critics, of course, have seen the Chinese policy tradition as being both undemocratic *and* unscientific.

Both problems have been of concern during the Dengist period. The extreme forms of personalism, characteristic of the latter half of the Maoist period, have been the object of the political reform that has ebbed and flowed since the late 1970s. Clearly there have been a number of initiatives to bring science into policymaking. An example is the panoply of new think tanks and policy research institutes, whose functions include soliciting and coordinating the best technical judgments from the scientific community on technical matters of national importance and, increasingly, participating in international epistemic communities on problems of global importance. Interestingly, these research and advisory mechanisms have been defended not only as more "scientific" but also as more "democratic" (by challenging feudalistic personalism). The skeptic, however, might argue that the appearance of change is greater than the reality. Thus, in spite of a greatly expanded role for an internationally engaged technical community in policymaking, the personal wishes of the leadership still often prevail, and technical analysis inevitably gets skewed to support leadership preferences. A prominent example is the Three Gorges project (Economy 1997).

China probably cannot afford to continue in this manner. The increasing complexity of technology, the growing evidence of safety problems, and the worsening degradation of the environment all require greater objectivity in the technical analyses used for national policies. As the experiences of other countries amply demonstrate, achieving that objectivity is not easy. A necessary condition is free and open debate, grounded in truly independent professional organizations. Technical debate of policy issues *has* become more open, and the revitalization of professional societies *has* helped build a sense of collective identity and solidarity in the technical community. Professional life still does not yet enjoy genuine autonomy, but arguably that is only a matter of time.

Then, at a third level, more open debate will reveal to policy elites and the general public alike that experts disagree among themselves. Paradoxically, therefore, the achievement of political autonomy will help demystify technical expertise and, with it, the planning assumptions and technocratic pretensions that are part and parcel of the legitimizing myths of the current regime. In short, effective management of the social costs of Chinese modernization will require new formulas for dealing with the inevitable conflicts entailed in reconciling personal preferences and technical judgments. How well prepared the technical community is for this very basic constitutional issue remains to be seen. However, some of the changes noted above—the emergence of alternatives to the state for material support and the growing internationalization of Chinese science and technology—clearly are resources for meeting this challenge.

The arts.   What is the relationship between the arts and the prospects for democracy in China? There are two ways of answering that question, one in terms of artists as individuals, the other in terms of artists as corporate groups.

As individuals, most professional artists—like their scientist counterparts—support reforms, despite sometimes serious reservations about what they see as the degradation of Chinese culture by commerce. Their living and working conditions have surely been improved by increased personal income and by lightened political control; it is not surprising that relatively few professional artists have been at the forefront of demands for democratic reform. Of course, there are many exceptions, including writer Bai Hua early in the 1980s, the literary critic Liu Xiaobo, or the Central Academy of Fine Arts students who made the "goddess of democracy" statue in Beijing in 1989. Yet even in these instances it should not be surprising that criticism of the existing regime is a different matter from developing a program for democracy.

In fact professional artists retain a profound reservoir of distrust of democracy, much like most Chinese intellectuals (Kelliher 1993). Conscious of their own claims to elite status, they have serious questions about how these claims might be treated under a new regime that encouraged the political participation of hundreds of millions of peasants. Moreover, artists in China are a remarkably diverse group, including individuals from radically different backgrounds and holding very distinct political preferences. It is tempting to view them romantically, as knights-errant in battle against a hostile state for the people's democratic rights. But most artists are not rebels against the state, and some are its firm supporters.

The alternative perspective would look not at individual frustrations but at changing corporate identity. The elitism of China's artists has flourished during the reform period, producing more frequent claims for professional autonomy. Artists have not been able to match the successes of scientists here, for the regime presumes that all art is potential propaganda and that art is less pressing than the creation of an internationally competitive technical infrastructure.

Yet the reform period's combination of ever more impuissant political campaigns and the rise of private funding for the arts has brought about some real changes in the constitution of culture. The professional organizations for writers, filmmakers, fine artists, calligraphers, dramatists, opera workers, and so on were established in the 1950s, primarily as a Soviet-style device for regulating the behavior of arts professionals. But in the 1980s some of these groups became increasingly professional, even representing their members against the state. If one seeks sources of an emerging civil society within China, these and newer, unofficial groupings of arts professionals must be counted along with developments in science and technology. Arts elitism and suspicion of democracy may in fact be harnessed to create a more democratic constitutional regime.

The arts might also offer another potential contribution to democracy: an increased toleration of rival points of view. This does not come easily, and many artists initially supported the reforms by creating works denouncing the radicals who had fallen from power. But a decade and a half later, the need to propagandize against Maoism seems remote, and China's aesthetic palette may be more diverse than ever. Much of this tolerance is still passive, ignoring what one does not much like. Few in China will yet make a positive virtue of defending the rights of adversaries to make speeches, much less paint ugly canvases or compose unappealing symphonies. Yet this is one way in which democracy can be learned, and the work of artists may force them to discover how to become tolerant, as the authority of the state is ever less appealing as a final arbiter of taste. Such a development would be important in two ways. First, increased tolerance among artists themselves would permit more of a competition of ideas, which often remain rather nakedly bound to political supporters. Second, artists might well have a slow but politically helpful demonstration effect on other citizens.

The idealized traditional social roles for Chinese artists, whether as tutors to the people or as remonstrators against tyranny, claim for artists a special status that is simply undemocratic. One perhaps unrecognized contribution of the reform period to the democratic reconstitution of Chinese culture is the slow process of depoliticization through which artists have abandoned state propaganda and turned to the exploration of increasingly personal themes. As long as artists regard themselves as properly above ordinary citizens, their relationship to democratization must be ambiguous.

Conclusion: The Reconstitution of Culture

What does this review of the experiences of arts and sciences suggest for the impact of reform on the transition from Leninism? The sometimes fitful yet continuing movement away from Leninist methods of tight central control has resulted in an uneven devolution of apparent power in several points of the cultural system. Has this reached a point where party control is seriously threatened? We have taken some pains to point out that criticism of the current regime must be distinguished from democratic reform. Similarly, we caution that the reconstitution of culture in China, however gentle the new relationships may seem, does not imply loss of effective party domination. Party leaders have discovered that they no longer need to use unpopular Leninist devices to maintain control. To date, diminished political supervision has worked out well for the party, with only a few individuals taking advantage of the new relaxation to annoy the regime. The displacement of economic costs from Beijing to lower levels has thus far preoccupied many with the need to learn about profits in the new system, a quest that has proven quite in harmony with political self-restraint. This may well change, but that is not preordained.

In the ongoing reconstitution of the rules and expectations by which culture is created, China's scientists and artists have followed parallel but not identical paths.

Chinese *science* and technology thus seem to be moving from Leninism in ways that differ markedly from the near collapse of science that has been noted in transitions from Leninism elsewhere (American Association for the Advancement of Science 1994). The Cultural Revolution's legacy created unique conditions from which the transition began. The timing of economic reform and marketization was, on balance, synchronized with reforms in science and technology in ways that have been mutually reinforcing. The aggressiveness with which China has seized opportunities for improving its science and technology through the use of internationally available resources, and the unique modalities for this strategy afforded by the existence of the extended Chinese technical community, also are characteristic features of the transition.

Optimism about the *arts* is harder to come by, for two rather different reasons. First, art may well nurture the soul, but the cash value of beauty is easily contested in the marketplace. The arts community has been shaken roughly by the shocks of China's new commodity economy. Second, although the arts are freer from political manipulation than perhaps at any time in China's modern history, the social content and implications of art ensure that they will often be controversial in ways that science is not.

For professional artists, among the many rueful aspects of the reconstitution of Chinese culture is the realization that the historical domination of humanist literati has ended. For a while it appeared to many that the relentless harshness of the Cultural Revolution might be replaced by a revival of the Communist Party's putative golden age of the 1950s, with an honored place for literary intellectuals. Yet commercial reform has shown how little demand the market has for the skills of these artists, and the political world may have little need for them as well. China now has engineers as president and prime minister. "Engineers of the human soul" was a slogan borrowed from Stalinist Russia that was taken over with surprising enthusiasm by modern Chinese artists, not because they were Stalinist, but because the phrase echoed their own Confucian social mission. Engineers of the human soul are now giving way to real engineers. China may soon witness its own version of the West's postwar discussion of the "two cultures" of science and humanities, and how they should relate to one another.

PART 5

Conclusion

9

Comparing Asian Transitions from Communism

Edwin A. Winckler

A growing literature compares transitions from communism in Eastern Europe and the former Soviet Union (noted in the editor's Introduction to this volume). The Asian cases of postcommunist transition have received less comparison, even among themselves. Initial comparisons of the Asian and European cases were mostly economic, and these comparisons mostly contrasted a European-Soviet "big bang" of simultaneous political and economic reform with an Asian gradualism in economic reform alone (e.g., Sachs and Woo 1994, Nolan 1995). However, within that contrast, there is great diversity in both regions (Rozman 1992b, Walder 1995c, World Bank 1996). Moreover, there is more diversity in Asia than in Europe, because the Asian cases were more independent of the Soviet Union and more independent of each other. (Early partial comparisons include Womack 1987, 1993; Goodman 1988; Scalapino 1992; Kim and Sigur 1992; Ljunggren 1992, 1993; Rana 1993, 1995; Wurfel 1993; Yoder 1993, 169–203.)

This chapter focuses on the Asian communist cases, emphasizing the *differences* between them and identifying the processes that differentiate them. The chapter treats all Asian communist countries that were not Soviet republics: China, North Korea, and Mongolia in northeast Asia; Vietnam, Laos, and Cambodia in southeast Asia. (I omit Afghanistan, where the would-be communist regime was never fully installed.) The upshot is to shift explanatory emphasis from regional groupings such as European versus Asian to causal processes such as degree of external dependence and nature of internal development. The most basic difference between communist countries was their geopolitical centrality to Russian security, reflected in their political status as former Soviet *republics,* Soviet *satellites,* or largely *independent* countries, and in graduations of dependence within each of those categories. Geopolitics is particularly salient in differentiating Asian communisms because they include the only communisms that fought each other (Yoder 1993). External strategic realignments both interacted with internal reform by individual countries and linked reforms in different countries—for example, in Indochina through changing relationships to Cambodia (Chanda 1993).

In this chapter the main *dependent variable* is degree of reform—political, economic, and sociocultural. In all three sectors, the degree of reform ranges from an initial *personalism,* to administrative *rationalization,* through controlled *liberalization,* to all-out political *democratization,* economic *marketization,* or sociocultural *pluralization.* These gradations provide an analytical halfway house between an undifferentiated notion of "reform" and a detailed inventory of all the policy measures and social processes involved. Throughout, the analysis draws on the three dimensions defined in the editor's Introduction to this volume—functional sectors, structural levels, and temporal dynamics. For example, internal reform usually has external counterparts, such as liberalization of trade and communication and even reorientation of trade and diplomacy.

In non-Soviet communist Asia, reform came in three waves. In the late 1970s the first wave was generated largely internally by the poor economic performance of communist institutions. In China and Indochina, this wave involved a mix of economic rationalization and limited economic liberalization—and in China, limited political rationalization as well. In the mid-1980s the second wave was caused partly internally by the consequences of the first wave of reforms and partly externally by the example of reforms in China and the Soviet Union. This wave involved limited economic rationalization in North Korea and Mongolia, further economic liberalization in China and Indochina, and limited political liberalization in China. The third wave began in 1989–1991, mostly from external causes—the fall of communism in Eastern Europe and the disintegration of the Soviet Union. This wave accelerated economic marketization everywhere except North Korea, but reversed political liberalization everywhere except Cambodia and Mongolia, which began democratization. During the 1990s this third wave has flowed differently in different countries, as a result of differences in both internal institutions and external relationships. (Country sources are cited below.)

In this chapter, the main *independent variable* is the extent and nature of the *environmental "shocks"* impelling reform, particularly from the termination of external dependence (military-political, political-economic, and sociocultural). High dependence made a country vulnerable to abrupt termination of external support, which usually produced rapid and drastic internal change (the "European" model, also true of Mongolia). Low dependence prevented external shock and permitted gradual and controlled reform, mostly economic (the "Asian" model, particularly China). However, shocks could also originate from the internal environment—for example, policy failures, natural disasters, or political disturbances.

Overall, the Asian cases suggest three kinds of *causal chains* connecting these variables. The primary effect occurs *within* sectors—that is, withdrawal of external political support invites internal political challenge, withdrawal of economic support creates economic change, and collapse of internationalism activates nationalism. Secondary effects occur across sectors—for example, withdrawal of external economic support reduces internal political support, directly as a signal of declining external political support, and indirectly through internal economic decline. A third effect is "conjunctural": The exact effect of any particular external or internal shock depends on the combination of circumstances—supranational, national-institutional, and domestic-societal. Consequently the chapter first identifies the separate processes, then indicates how they interact within each country.

These causal chains between degree of shock and extent of reform were mediated by a main *intervening variable* of *national institutions*. This includes the extent and pattern of previous totalitarianization, the relationship between personalism and institutionalization, and the perceptions and preferences of incumbent elites. These differ significantly across the non-Soviet Asian communisms (Tanaka 1992).

The *extent and pattern of previous totalitarianization* was largely time-dependent. Overall, the earlier the system was founded, the more complete the totalitarianization and the greater the difficulty of both initiating and implementing reform. The later-founded systems never fully collectivized their agricultures, did not develop much state industry, and therefore never fully penetrated either rural or urban society and culture. Transition tended to begin in the less totalitarianized sectors: agriculture everywhere except Mongolia, small-scale commerce in Indochina, and even some never-suppressed Buddhist organizations in Indochina.

However, both the effect of totalitarianization and the response to shock were modified by the *relationship between personalism and institutionalization*. All the non-Soviet Asian communist regimes have been relatively personalistic, but in somewhat different ways. At one extreme is the ideological rigidity of early-founded North Korea, where personalism was individual-leaderist but stably institutionalized, thereby inhibiting reform. The other extreme is the pragmatic flexibility of late-founded Laos, where personalism was collective and informal, facilitating reform. In between were the erratic cases of China and Cambodia, where personalism had been individual-leaderist and under-institutionalized, inflicting destructive bouts of extreme totalitarianization that, paradoxically, weakened communism and invited reform. In Mongolia personalism was both created and stabilized by Soviet supervision, which long inhibited reform but eventually promoted it. In Vietnam personalism had always been relatively collective and gradually became increasingly institutionalized, which prevented extreme policies under both communism and transition but has made reform incremental and tortuous.

Finally one should note that policy response has depended on the *per-*

ceptions and preferences of elites. To some extent these too derive from institutions and environment—the recruitment and socialization of personnel, the interests and information of organizations, and national culture and international diffusion. However, they also derive from idiosyncratic individual temperament and experience. Only a Chinese Mao Zedong or a Korean Kim Il-sung would have defined the particular ideologies that they did; only a particular Vietnamese or Laotian elite would have maintained the moderation and pragmatism that they did.

The first part of the chapter sketches the range of both outcomes and causes within each sector and locates the cases along these continua. The second and third parts discuss each of the non-Soviet Asian communisms, proceeding roughly from most to least independent. China was by far the largest and most independent Asian case, and it has been the model for gradual economic reform based on sustained political control. Vietnam was second in size, independence, gradualism, and control. It formed the center of an Indochina subsystem that included Laos, whose communist movement had long depended on Vietnam, and Cambodia, whose 1980s moderate-communist government was installed by Vietnam. North Korea achieved substantial independence from both the Soviet Union and China and pursued its own idiosyncratic path of nonreform. Satellite Mongolia was the most Soviet-oriented, and its reform path was closest to that of the Eastern European satellites.

Variables

The outcome or dependent variable includes four degrees of reform (elaborating O'Donnell and Schmitter 1986, and Hasegawa 1992). The least institutionalized condition is *personalism*—autocratic decisionmaking by a few individuals, accompanied during implementation by clientelism and corruption that is exacerbated by parochial loyalties that undermine the party-state. Many late-communist regimes suffered from personalism, sometimes centered on one individual such as Ceausescu or Kim, sometimes permeating a more collective leadership as under Brezhnev or Deng.

Typically in the early 1980s communist regimes attempted to correct personalism through *rationalization*—strengthening institutions, professionalizing elites, disciplining masses, and imposing an identity such as communist internationalism or official nationalism. Politically, rationalization required constitutionalizing collective leadership and restoring party discipline (e.g., Roeder 1993 on Russia, McCormick 1990 and O'Brien 1990 on China). In politics, only Mongolia has gone much beyond rationalization, and it remains to be seen whether North Korea can achieve even that. Economically, rationalization remained hostile to much use of markets, to the domestic private sector, and to international capitalism—a stance that for early 1980s Vietnam has been called *hard reform* (Fforde and de Vylder 1996). This was the initial approach to economic reform of Andropov and Gorbachev in the Soviet Union, and of Deng and his original economic czar Chen Yun in China.

When rationalization proved insufficient, in the late 1980s some Leninist regimes attempted to save communism by supplementing rationalization with *liberalization*—granting elites and masses greater autonomy and initiative in order to improve information and incentives and to allow some expression of sociocultural diversity. *Political* liberalization typically involved inviting more feedback through investigative reporting and public opinion, and airing minor local issues through some local political competition. Gorbachev's *glasnost* was the classic example. Deng periodically allowed some limited liberalization in the 1980s (Baum 1994). Vietnam has persisted in political "renovation" even in the 1990s (Turley 1993). *Economic* liberalization attempted to preserve a core of state ownership and state industry, while allowing increasing use of markets, the private sector, and international capital—a stance that for late 1980s Vietnam has been called *soft reform* (Fforde and de Vylder 1996). Such "market socialism" was also the trend in late 1980s China under Zhao Ziyang and, after some hesitation around 1990, again in the 1990s under Jiang Zemin (Naughton 1995). (In the economics transition literature, "liberalization" often includes all stages of marketization—e.g., World Bank 1996. Following political science usage, this chapter restricts "liberalization" to the initial stage of relaxation in all three sectors.)

Liberalization often proved unstable and inadvertently slipped toward all-out political *democratization,* economic *marketization,* and sociocultural *pluralization.* This fourth degree or stage of reform involves not just allowing or endorsing these processes, but also actively building the institutions necessary to consolidate their dominance. In Europe, slippage did eventually accelerate into comprehensive transformation, though only after Soviet political withdrawal and only where domestic elites genuinely embraced such transformation (northern as opposed to southern Eastern Europe, e.g., Michta 1994). Among Asian communisms, only Mongolia has successfully democratized. (Cambodia held 1993 elections, but its democratization remained limited and a 1997 coup returned it to authoritarianism.) Vietnam and Laos have gone furthest toward marketization, combining the freeing of prices with stabilization of inflation and much commercialization of state firms. All the Asian communisms have shifted from communism toward nationalism, most based on one dominant nationality.

Among causal or independent variables, this chapter emphasizes the differences between the Asian communisms in the degree and kind of initiating "shock" they experienced. The least shock involved a sequence of moderate problems in only a few functions, as in China. The greatest shock involved simultaneous crises in many areas, as in Mongolia.

Military-Political Variables

The *least political shock* would be experienced by a communist party that had no external political dependence, that had well-institutionalized external defense and internal security, and that faced a society with no tradition of democracy. In the ideal case, the party had made its own revolution, built its own regime, and distanced itself politically from the Soviet Union. The leadership regarded Soviet political liberalization as a mistake and restricted policy choice to bargaining within elites. *China* is the Asian exemplar of maintaining political independence and limiting political reform (Lieberthal 1995). *Vietnam* is another case, its political independence only slightly diminished by eventually accepting Soviet military aid in its struggle with the United States and, later, China (Porter 1993).

The *most political shock* would come from the abrupt termination of high external political dependence by a weak regime, challenged both by a re-emerging subnational civil society and by supranational social networks of exiled dissidents. In a nominally independent country, foreign communist military force was the ultimate guarantee of domestic party political control. When the guarantee was withdrawn, the choice of rulers and policies shifted from elite bargaining to mass elections. Whether the incumbent elite survived then depended on the extent to which it represented popular interests (economic security, cultural nationalism) and its electoral capacity (charismatic national politicians or local electoral machines). In the worst case, democratization would be complicated externally by diplomatic isolation from the West, regional rivalries, or cross-border ethnic tensions.

Among Asian communisms, the closest approximations to this extreme have been *Mongolia* and *Cambodia,* small peripheral countries where withdrawal of external political support and reorientation from East to West did force much initial internal democratization. However, in both cases the former communist parties retained sufficient influence and popularity to remain in power for some time. Mongolia was destabilized by the withdrawal of Soviet political support for satellite regimes, the fall of communism in Eastern Europe, and the cost to China of repressing democratization. An international "donors club" coordinated by Japan supported Mongolia's marketization, democratization, and independence, while essentially defenseless Mongolia has constructed a more distant relationship with Russia and a less distant relationship with China (Ginsburg 1995, Boikova 1997). Cambodia was destabilized by previous external war, continuing internal war, and the withdrawal of Vietnamese political support.

International intervention brokered democratization and initiated marketization (Klintworth 1993).

Other Asian communisms experienced *intermediate political shock.* Despite initial Soviet and Chinese help, *North Korea* gradually achieved enough external political independence and internal political support to define its own political ideology and to refuse political reform. In the 1990s its main remaining supporter has been China, which has not encouraged political reform. Nevertheless, North Korea risks severe external military-political shock by pursuing a confrontational foreign policy that alarms both old allies Russia and China and old enemies Japan and the United States (Foster-Carter 1994, 14–25). *Laos* had moderate political dependence on Vietnam, but Vietnam has continued its political support and Laos has gradually diversified its diplomacy. Consequently Laos has experienced little external political shock and conducted little internal political reform (*Asia Yearbooks,* Economist Intelligence Unit).

Political-Economic Variables

The *least economic shock* would be experienced by a regime with low external economic dependence, little state enterprise or social programs, and low development (a largely subsistence agriculture in which agriculture was exploited). In agriculture the abandonment of socialism quickly produced not pain but gain, and the population soon parlayed those gains into rural industrialization that prolonged the boom. In industry a smaller state-industrial sector both lowered political resistance to industrial reform and made industrial reform less essential. Nonstate enterprise was temporarily able to subsidize inefficient state enterprise, while state enterprise scrambled to become competitive. Supranational social networks from outgoing or incoming diasporas provided channels for trade and investment.

Among Asian communisms, *China* was economically the most independent from the East bloc because of its large size, previous autarky, and incipient opening to the West. In China it was not external shock but internal dissatisfaction that induced the initiation of economic reform in the late 1970s. Economic reform was not part of political collapse but rather part of a strategy for political survival. Economic liberalization was gradual and tortuous, creating periodic macroeconomic instability. Growth has been uneven but rapid, aided by much foreign trade and investment, mostly Chinese (Hamrin 1990, Lardy 1992, Shirk 1993, Naughton 1995).

The *most economic shock* would have come from abrupt termination of high external economic dependence by a conservative regime unsuccessfully defending inefficient state industries and overgenerous social programs. Internal economic breakdown would induce spontaneous liberalization from below. Agriculture would be small, or highly subsidized, or depend on imported inputs. Termination of East bloc trade and aid would create steep declines in domestic production and purchasing power, forcing abrupt and comprehensive economic change. Several years of negative economic growth would produce much political backlash and some slowdown of economic reform. Eventually growth would resume, aided by reorientation to the capitalist West (Therior and Metheson 1979; World Bank 1996, 22–43). However, having opened to global capital flows and Asian-regional economic relations, in the late 1990s the economy would then be sideswiped by Asian economic contraction. The question would then become, which is more economically effective and less politically risky—retrenching or accelerating economic reform?

Among all the Eurasian communist cases, *Mongolia* was the most extreme in degree of external economic dependence—East bloc subsidies had equaled between a third and a half of GDP! Mongolia was also quite extreme in the suddenness of the collapse of external economic supports, the severity of the resulting internal economic recession, and the completeness in shift of dependence from East to West. However, Mongolia's response was uneven—it was early to privatize state firms but slow to decontrol prices and trade. Despite Mongolia's eagerness to diversify its foreign trade, geography dictates that Russia and China remain its main economic partners (Boone 1994; Pomfret 1996, 75–90; Boikova 1997). *North Korea* too had depended significantly on East bloc subsidy of a standard of living that was high for communist Asia. Here the impact has been less abrupt, somewhat cushioned by continuing aid from the Chinese government and from Koreans in Japan and China. However, China is hardening the terms of its aid in order to encourage reform, and expatriate Koreans are becoming impatient with the regime's recalcitrance, unpredictability, and ingratitude. Being a political pariah has prevented North Korea from shifting its economic dependence from East to West (*FEER* 10 October 1996).

The Indochinese communisms experienced *intermediate economic shock*. Overall, they had less industry with less external aid and fewer worker benefits, and more agriculture with greater self-sufficiency, though agriculture too used foreign machinery and fuel (Perkins 1993). In the late 1970s the third Indochina war had contributed to deep economic crises in all three Southeast Asian communisms, which induced them to allow agricultural liberalization. However, the war had also increased Soviet aid, which at first allowed them to expand state enterprise but later encouraged them to try economic reform (Ljunggren 1992, 33–41; Chanda 1993). At the end of the 1980s, the termination of Soviet support accelerated internal liberalization. As regional geopolitics gradually permitted, Japan began supplying economic aid (St. John 1995). For most of the 1990s, a favorable external economic environment was created by improving political relations with capitalist countries, rising Western economic aid, rising intraregional trade, and increasingly formal ties with the Association of Southeast Asian Nations (ASEAN). Nevertheless, at the end of the 1990s, the Indochinese postcommunist economies still remained sufficiently autarkic to moderate the impact of financial crisis elsewhere in Asia.

In *Vietnam* during the 1980s Soviet aid grants and trade subsidies constituted 10–20 percent of GNP and provided most of state investment and state enterprise profits. Termination of Soviet help forced drastic restructuring of state enterprise, while U.S. hostility prevented Western aid. However, Vietnam's economic transition was somewhat softened by rising exports to other countries, particularly of oil (Ljunggren 1992, 124–129; Than 1993). *Laos* too depended significantly on the East bloc in budget and trade, even though not formally a member of the East bloc's Council of Mutual Economic Aid. Termination of East bloc aid induced much liberalization, particularly since Laos shifted its external economic dependence from East to West (Ljunggren 1992, 129–131). In *Cambodia* the Khmer Rouge had so decimated both state and economy that external aid had become indispensable (Curtis 1989). Cambodia too was able to shift its dependence from East to West, which demanded marketization as Cambodia shifted from recovery to reconstruction (Ljunggren 1992, 131–137; EIU).

Sociocultural Variables

The *least sociocultural shock* would be experienced by countries where communism was an expression of nationalism, where state boundaries largely coincided with the home areas of one main nationality, and where the party-state exercised firm control over flows of people and ideas across national borders. Ideally the main nationality would have both a large population at home and a large diaspora abroad. A long continuous cultural history and globally recognized civilization would have created a robust cultural identity. Communist organization would not have incorporated most of the population into state-funded social welfare programs, and communist ideology would not have imposed near absolute control over information, thought, expression, and behavior. Most non-Soviet Asian communisms experienced relatively little sociocultural shock, but none reached the minimal extreme.

Overall, *Mongolia* may come the closest. Communism and nationalism were basically aligned, because Mongols had sought Russian protection from Chinese domination. Mongolia represents only part of a larger nationality, but the Mongols in China and Russia have been politically quiet until recently (Alatalu 1992, Sullivan 1995). Postcommunist Mongolia has downplayed pan-Mongolism, in order to get along with both Russia and China (Haining 1991). Mongolia's geographic isolation facilitates border control, though there are expatriate Russian (and now Chinese) communities that Mongols increasingly resent. In *Vietnam* too, communism represented nationalism, one nationality was dominant, and borders were closed. Nevertheless, Vietnam suffered outflow of southerners and Chinese, and it does have some highland minorities.

The *most sociocultural shock* would occur in countries where nationalism and communism were most opposed, where state and nationalities were worst aligned, and where borders were most porous. In the worst case the main nationality would have a small population with few abroad, a weak or interrupted cultural history, and a correspondingly insecure national identity. Conversely, the country would historically have been penetrated by supranational social networks of incoming foreign-national diasporas that liberalization could reactivate. Communism would have incorporated most of the population into state-funded social welfare programs, and communist ideology would have imposed near absolute control over information, thought, expression, and behavior.

Among Asian communisms, *Laos* is perhaps the most vulnerable in society and culture. Internally, it contains the most ethnic diversity with the least social and spatial integration. To overcome this, the Pathet Lao was deliberately based on communist internationalism. In contrast, in the 1990s a shift toward (lowland) Lao nationalism is exacerbating ethnic tensions (Batson 1991, *FEER* 11 January 1996). Externally too, Laos feels somewhat threatened—the Lao are part of the large family of Tai peoples that includes the Thai, who have already assimilated 80 percent of all Lao into northeast Thailand. Moreover, Laos's porous borders prevent the party-state from controlling entry and exit.

Cambodia is also somewhat problematic in society and culture. Historically the Khmer too have been squeezed between Thai and Vietnamese. Cambodia's boundaries correspond well with the Khmer nationality, but they too are porous (Chandler 1992). There are only 8 million Cambodians in Cambodia and few abroad. Communism has not expressed nationalism—Cambodia's first communist regime inspired domestic revulsion, and its second was imposed by Vietnam (Chandler 1991). There is a Vietnamese minority that many Cambodians consider threatening. The postcommunist party retains strong ties to Vietnam, while the royalist party has strong ties to Thailand. Elections tempted the two main parties to accuse each other of subservience to foreigners (Carney and Choo 1993). Meanwhile, Cambodia's small Chinese minority is reasserting its historic dominance of the economy and even assuming prominence in politics (*FEER* 8 January 1998).

Some Asian communisms experienced *intermediate sociocultural shock*. In *China* communism has expressed Han nationalism, minorities have been firmly subordinated, and borders have been tightly controlled. China has the world's largest population, oldest continuous civilization, and perhaps most robust cultural identity. Nevertheless, China contains some large minority areas, ranging from thoroughly dominated Inner

Mongolia, through somewhat unstable Xinjiang, to quite volatile Tibet. China's claim to Taiwan has become an internal political issue. Regional and local identities potentially fragment even the People's Republic of China (PRC) Han Chinese themselves (Heberer 1989, Dittmer and Kim 1993).

Finally *North Korea* too has mixed sociocultural credentials. It has not yet experienced much sociocultural stress but may be in for a shock. Communism was in part externally imposed but soon became quite nationalistic (Cumings 1981). North Korea has few minorities, closed borders, and a significant overseas diaspora. Nevertheless, North Korea represents only a third of all peninsular Koreans and remains vulnerable to absorption by the other two-thirds in the South. Its population is highly incorporated into state welfare programs and mass ideological rituals, which may have helped sustain the regime until recently but now may be breaking down (McCormack 1993).

Cases: Economic Reform Under Leninist Regimes

We now examine the conjunction of these analytical dimensions in each of the non-Soviet Asian communisms. First we consider the cases in which the incumbent communist regime has conducted much economic reform but refused much political reform. We proceed from very independent China, to quite independent Vietnam, to quasi-independent Laos. Each case starts by noting the degree of economic and political reform, then briefly summarizes the mix of processes involved—both the long-run conditions impeding or speeding reform, and the short-run functional need and political opportunity that actually occasioned reform.

China

In China, reform began in the late 1970s as a mix of rationalization and liberalization. In the late 1980s, attempts to parlay liberalization into marketization and democratization produced conservative backlash that partially reversed liberalization. In the 1990s, economic reform has progressed strongly toward marketization. Political reform has largely regressed toward rationalization, though bottom-level elections could eventually evolve into "creeping democratization" from below. The regime has relaxed many controls over private society and popular culture. However, it continues to insist on the primacy of pan-Chinese solidarity over ethnonationalist pluralization and on the primacy of socialist ideology over cultural pluralization. (Overviews include Hamrin 1990, Dittmer 1994, Baum 1994, Lieberthal 1995, and Naughton 1995. Because the rest of this volume treats China, the summary here is short.)

In China reform has responded largely to internal dynamics but has benefited from external supports: mass initiatives toward economic and political liberalization, elite politics that embraced economic reform but blocked political reform, and supranational connections that have promoted both economic and political liberalization (Hong Kong, Taiwan, and the Chinese diaspora). Compared to the Soviet Union, China enjoyed several background *economic conditions* favorable to economic reform. Agriculture remained the largest sector, collectivization had been relatively brief, and agriculture was exploited to develop other sectors. In industry, the old regime had begun decentralization, the inefficient state sector was smaller than in the Soviet Union, and the efficient nonstate sector expanded rapidly (*CQ*144). (However, compared to the Southeast Asian cases, agricultural collectivization lasted long and state industry became large.) Hong Kong, Taiwan, and the overseas Chinese gave China links to capitalist eastern Asia, for models and advice and for trade and investment. Meanwhile, stagnant productivity growth and living standards produced increasing *economic need* for economic reform. However, the most immediate economic impetus was the conjunction of a rise in technology imports and a decline in oil revenues with which to pay for them (Naughton 1995).

In China, background *political conditions* both impeded and impelled reform. On the one hand, founding father Mao Zedong and his followers had adamantly blocked liberalization; on the other hand, the political and economic instability that they had caused made much of both the party elite and mass population ready for change. Mao's demise created the *political opportunity* for reform, and economic performance became a political issue in the ensuing succession struggle (Lieberthal 1995, 122–144).

In *economic reform,* a balance between rationalizers and liberalizers in the early reformist coalition produced a relatively long period in a hybrid transitional economy (Baum 1994, Naughton 1995). This produced economic growth and marketization, but also inflation and corruption that provoked periodic retrenchments. However, even the consolidation periods inadvertently contributed to marketization—by showing the superior competitiveness of commercialized firms and by eroding the credibility of bureaucratic correctives (Naughton 1995). Because the party's ideology blocked macrosystemic change, reform started with microeconomic reform of agricultural organization and enterprise management (Naughton 1995). Economic reform has followed a political logic in which policies that distributed benefits to localities (such as internal decentralization and external opening) prevailed over policies that attempted to impose disciplines (such as price reform or hard budget constraints) (Shirk 1993). After Tiananmen, a conservative attempt to reimpose bureaucratic controls produced a "hard landing" of the economy that restored support for renewed reform. By the mid-1990s the entire Chinese leadership had accepted marketization and made some progress toward constructing the institutions necessary to regulate it (Naughton 1995, Yang this volume). The leadership's reaction to Asian economic contraction was not to retrench marketization (except of external financial flows) but to bolster domestic demand through government investment (*FEER* 5 March 1998, *NYT* 8 March 1998).

As regards *political reform,* China's high external independence prevented vulnerability to withdrawal of external support, and its strong internal control has withstood growing mass opposition. Originally the Chinese party represented Chinese geopolitical patriotism, economic developmentalism, and cultural nationalism. However, the Chinese party discredited itself by utopian policies, leadership instability, and, eventually, mass repression. In the 1980s, the Dengist leadership favored some rationalization (combating personalism and corruption, separating party and government) and limited liberalization (increasing the role of legislators and intellectuals) (McCormick 1990). In the 1990s, the party has managed leadership succession well—the passing of the personalistic revolutionary elders leaves a generation of younger technocrats in more institutionalized control (Shambaugh 1998). The leadership remerged party and government but renewed its fight against corruption. The leadership has restricted substantive public criticism, but it has allowed national representatives some role in drafting legislation, and it has promoted village elections to air community issues and improve village administration. Personalism and authoritarianism remain problems (Lam 1995). Nevertheless, deliberately or not, China is gradually shrinking the scope of its once-totalitarian party-state and laying both the economic and political foundations for a possible future political transition to mass electoral democracy.

Vietnam

Vietnam's reforms largely parallel China's, but with some differences. Economically, in the late 1970s spontaneous liberalization of agricultural cooperatives started slightly later than in China, and in Vietnam was accompanied by some spontaneous liberalization of state enterprise. In the early 1980s Vietnam went through the same early reform mix of rationalization and liberalization as in China. However, in the late 1980s, when economic liberalization slowed in China, it accelerated in Vietnam. By the early 1990s marketization had proceeded further in Vietnam—planning had ended, prices were freer, and state enterprise was more commercialized. However, in the late 1990s, whereas the response to Asia's economic contraction by China's newer leadership has been mostly to accelerate marketization, the response by Vietnam's older leadership has been to continue to rely heavily on state firms and to proceed only gradually with further private marketization (Turley and Selden 1992, 1993; Marr and White 1988; Turley 1993; Thayer 1992, 1993; Probert and Young 1995; Nordlund, Gates, and Dam 1995; Fforde and de Vylder 1996; World Bank 1996, 21;

Dawkins and Whalley 1996; Morley and Nishihara 1997; *FEER* 12 February 1998).

Politically, as in China, leadership was personalistic but more stably collective. Vietnam began political rationalization earlier, in the form of gradual but orderly generational succession, which has continued (Thayer 1988, Sidel 1998). As in China, during the late 1980s political reform advanced to some liberalization—media feedback, public debate, and associational activity (e.g., Thayer 1993). As in China, during the early 1990s political reform retreated somewhat toward elite rationalization (e.g., rein ing in the legislature and media). However, not having suffered a Tiananmen-type challenge, the Vietnamese leadership was more able to renew efforts to preempt incipient liberalization by improving mass participation under party guidance (Khng 1993; Thayer 1993, 1995). By the late 1990s electoralization has progressed further than in China and may have generated more public debate about national issues (*NYT* 21 July 1997).

As in China, internal processes were primary in initiating *economic reform,* but in Vietnam external shocks later helped accelerate it. As in China, subsequent reorientation to Asian-Pacific capitalism then provided increasing external economic support. Among initial *economic conditions* affecting reform, main differences from China included chronic involvement in Indochina wars, the need to merge the quite different North and South of Vietnam, and much dependence on East bloc aid and trade. Even in the North, Vietnamese "war communism" was more a system for distributing East bloc aid than a system for coordinating internal production. A functioning peacetime socialist economy had not been consolidated in the North before it tried to absorb the capitalist South, which helped precipitate economic transition. Relative to the original Soviet model, Vietnam shared several characteristics with China, but even more so: a still more agricultural economy, a still later communist revolution, a still shorter period of agricultural collectivization, still less socialist industry, and still more decentralized industry. These facilitated a still faster response to economic liberalization, once adopted (Fforde and Paine 1987, de Vylder and Fforde 1988, Petrasovits 1988, Beresford 1989, Than 1993, Naughton 1996, Thalemann 1996, ASEAN 1996).

In the late 1970s, the immediate *economic need* for initiating economic liberalization arose from both internal and external crises. Internally, the incongruity between the official model and economic reality became increasingly unmanageable, particularly when the model was extended from North to South. Southern resistance to agricultural collectivization dangerously reduced food procurement and strained relations between northern and southern leaders. Externally, victory over the South terminated U.S. aid to the South and reduced East bloc aid to the North. Then, war with Cambodia and China terminated aid from China and the West.

Resulting shortages induced farmers and managers to abandon central planning for direct exchange. The leadership acquiesced in this spontaneous liberalization as a temporary expedient (Ljunggren 1992, 60–70, 80–93; Fforde and de Vylder 1996).

In Vietnam, a *political condition* affecting economic reform was the leadership's tradition of collective decisionmaking, which facilitated consideration of reform but compromised and delayed its implementation (Porter 1993, 101–151). In the early 1980s, as in China, a balance of rationalizers and liberalizers produced alternating reform and retrenchment. As in China, the resulting hybrid system did produce growth. However, the system also produced creeping marketization that the then Vietnamese leadership did not want, and it produced inflation and corruption that administrative adjustment of prices and wages could not control. This failure of administrative controls created the need for a more definitive endorsement of economic liberalization.

The *political opportunity* for that economic liberalization was provided by the decline of the founding fathers and by the rise of a younger pro-reform coalition of commercialized state enterprise managers and local party officials. In the late 1980s the party endorsed eventual liberalization (1986), authorized gradual implementation of a compromise version (1987), then provided the legislative basis for private industry and agriculture (1988). Then renewed inflation and rising deficits accelerated actual liberalization (1989). Decline of East bloc aid and then subsidized East bloc trade effectively ended plan transactions, precipitating de facto marketization (Fforde and Goldstone 1995).

To Vietnam's leaders, as to China's, the fall of European communism confirmed the *political need to improve economic performance.* Luckily for the leadership, in the early 1990s Vietnam's marketization quickly achieved both growth and stability (World Bank 1996). Vietnam has become a socialist market economy with growing participation by capitalist countries. Vietnam has begun building the institutions necessary to regulate a market economy. However, a coalition of state enterprises, local officials, and even some foreign investors resists privatizing firms. Moreover, Vietnam's leadership has not responded with much urgency to Asia's economic crisis, evidently in part because of conflicting economic diagnoses of where Vietnam's economic problems lie, in part because of conflicting leadership attitudes toward further economic liberalization (*FEER* 18 December 1997, 12 February 1998).

Like China, Vietnam has remained highly independent of any foreign political support whose withdrawal might require more drastic internal *political reform.* Like the Chinese Communist Party, the Vietnamese Communist Party originally represented patriotism, developmentalism, and cultural nationalism (Jamieson 1993). Unlike its Chinese counterpart, the

Vietnamese party has not discredited itself by open elite conflict or open mass repression. Nevertheless, as in China, inflation and corruption have strained the party's legitimacy (Kamm 1996).

To Vietnam's leaders, as to China's, the fall of European communism implied the *political need to strengthen political control.* In 1991 the Seventh Party Congress endorsed political rationalization but rejected liberalization or democratization. In 1992 a new constitution implemented further intra-elite political rationalization, separating the functions of party and government, shifting from collective leadership toward individual accountability, and centralizing administration (Fforde and Goldstone 1995). The party has adjusted the composition of governing bodies to reflect changing elite opinion and social forces, and increased the number of candidates allowed in elections, including some independents (Thayer 1992). In elite-mass relations, an implicit exchange has emerged of economic prosperity for political conformity, as earlier in South Korea and Taiwan. Some Vietnamese leaders anticipate eventual controlled liberalization, aiming for the kind of post-Leninist survival that the Nationalist Party (KMT) achieved on Taiwan (Goodman, A. 1996). Evidently fears that that bargain might eventually break down impelled the 1996 party congress to promote officials from the security sector, maintain the leading role of state firms in the economy, and reassert authority over society and culture (*FEER* 11 July 1996, Stern 1997). Nevertheless, the 1996 congress, mid-1997 elections, and a late 1997 party plenum produced orderly generational succession within the elite and possible eventual mass democratization (*FEER* 24 July 1997, 25 September 1997; Sidel 1997, 1998). However, ostensibly retired party leaders remain active in policymaking (*FEER* 12 January 1998).

Laos

Laos is to its mentor Vietnam as Vietnam is to China—parallel in transition but faster in tempo and lower in both economic development and state capacity. In Laos too, economic reform began in the late 1970s with agricultural liberalization and progressed in the early 1980s to experiments with industrial liberalization. In the mid-1980s, the party endorsed industrial liberalization at the same time as Vietnam but implemented it more quickly (Rigg 1995). Traditionally organized into small principalities, postwar Laotian elite politics has remained personalistic—collective like Vietnam's, but more pragmatic and less "regularized." As regards mass participation, Laos has revised its constitution, conducted elections, and given its national assembly a legislative role (*AY*, EIU). Nevertheless, since party control remains firm, these political reforms are more rationalization than liberalization, let alone democratization.

As in Vietnam, economic transition was first internally initiated, then externally accelerated. Many of the same *economic conditions* favored economic reform, but even more so. The economy was even more agricultural and the experience of agricultural collectivization still more brief and less successful. Laos had less state capacity to reorganize the countryside and fewer landless peasants to benefit from collectivization. State enterprise was even less developed than in Vietnam, posing little obstacle to policy change (UNDP 1991, Funck 1993, Rigg 1995). Main *political conditions* affecting economic reform have been the surprising pragmatism of the founding leadership and the legitimizing example of Laos's mentor, Vietnam. Also, the United States was less hostile toward Laos than toward Vietnam, allowing Laos greater access to international economic institutions (EIU).

As in Vietnam, the *immediate need* for agricultural reform was not just the poor economic performance of collective agriculture, but also a political crisis in relations with the peasantry, aggravated in Laos by the threat of mass exodus through porous borders (Ljunggren 1992, 70–74). The immediate need for industrial reform was the unmanageability of a hybrid plan-market economy, aggravated by a porous border that allowed Thai imports to enter, making economic closure and controlled planning impossible (Ljunggren 1992, 93–100). The *political opportunity* for economic reform may have been the fact that the new Laotian leadership was not yet committed to highly socialist institutions. (Available accounts indicate no leadership changes accompanying the initiation of reform, only in 1991 after reform was well under way—e.g., Zasloff and Unger 1991, Funck 1993.)

The communist movement in Laos originated in 1930 under Vietnamese auspices and completed its conquest of Laos only in 1975, as part of the wider communist conquest of Indochina. Economic policy then evolved backward from failed attempts, first at Stalinist wartime mobilization and then at agricultural collectivization, through a more liberal-Leninist "New Economic Policy," and finally to the boldly marketizing "New Economic Mechanism" (Funck 1993). Thus in the late 1970s when the Lao People's Revolutionary Party (LPRP) attempted to shift from nominal communes to real cooperatives, the peasants resisted and the LPRP relented (Evans 1990; Ljunggren 1992, 46–52). In the early 1980s, reformers tried granting more autonomy to enterprises and villages, but resulting inflation reinstated planning and cooperatives. By 1985 economic failure and political repression were producing a mass exodus, inducing experiments with more drastic decentralization and marketization, which the 1986 Fourth Party Congress endorsed.

In the late 1980s, the LPRP unleashed a flurry of liberalizing reforms, including aggressive privatization, before both China and Vietnam (Ljunggren 1992, 93–100). In 1991 the Fifth Party Congress responded to the collapse of the Soviet Union with more economic opening and further economic liberalization, receiving additional Western international support and praise. The LPRP added a new economic czar to the Politburo, in charge of a new economic pilot agency similar to a Ministry of International Trade and Industry, and accompanied by a strong minister for infrastructure construction. Foreign trade shifted from the Soviet bloc to Southeast Asia. In 1997 Laos formally joined ASEAN, institutionalizing external pressure for long-run marketization (Johnson 1992, 1993; Funck 1993; Stuart-Fox 1998).

Nevertheless, Laos's vigorous reforms have not produced strong growth, because Laos remains internally undeveloped and externally remote. Laos's economic problems went beyond the liberalization of command economic institutions, which could be done quickly, to the construction of institutional, physical, and social infrastructure, which will take decades. Most of the population remains rural, poor, undereducated, and isolated, even from markets. At first the main immediate problem was inflation, resulting from external economic vulnerability and internal administrative weakness (Funck 1993, Rigg 1995, *FEER* 9 February 1995). By 1996 the Sixth Party Congress reacted to accumulating problems with political backlash. Concerns included macroeconomic instability indicating that reform was out of control, capitalistic practices indicating deviation from revolution, and fears of external economic and cultural subversion. The congress dumped the reformist economic czar and infrastructure minister, and Laos has since attempted to strengthen its remaining state enterprises (Far East *FBIS* 27 and 29 March 1996).

Politically, continuing good relations with Vietnam, and improving relations with China and ASEAN, have spared Laos any external political shock requiring internal political reform. Western aid donors have urged democratization, and Laos has resumed elections (1989), revised its constitution (1991), given the National Assembly an active role in building market institutions, and restaffed it with younger and better-educated representatives. Nevertheless, political change has not gone beyond such institutional rationalization, and the communist LPRP remains firmly in control. Opposition has been weak since 1990, when three ex–government officials who advocated real democratization were jailed (EIU Laos 1995-1, 20). The 1991 Fifth Party Congress formally rejected political liberalization. The 1996 Sixth Party Congress contained a large military representation, and it elected a nine-man politburo consisting of six generals and three ideologues (Far East *FBIS* 27 and 29 March 1996). Internally, there is still little elite liberalization or mass demand for democratization. Simultaneously, the LPRP has attempted to strengthen regime control by staffing the National Assembly with party and military figures, and it has attempted to consolidate popular support by balancing urban-rural and ethnic representation (*FEER* 18 December 1997). Externally, Laos is balancing its "special relationship" with its mentor Vietnam through improved relations with Thailand, China, other Mekong basin countries, and ASEAN (*AY*, EIU).

The rise in military influence within Laos parallels the military domination of the regimes in many of those countries.

Cases: Political Regime More Strongly Affects Economic Reform

Second, we consider the non-Soviet Asian communisms in which economic reform has been more strongly affected by political regime. We start with Cambodia, where an externally dependent Leninist regime began economic reform, but where an externally dependent post-Leninist authoritarianism has distorted both democratization and marketization. We continue with Mongolia, where high external dependence produced high external shock, which precipitated abrupt democratization. This in turn launched marketization, which has continued despite high economic transition costs and some electoral backlash. We conclude with North Korea, which remains stubbornly independent, and whose personalistic political regime has precluded both economic and political reform.

Cambodia

In Cambodia, under Vietnamese tutelage, economic reform followed the Chinese pattern of gradual liberalization but was accelerated in the early 1990s by the end of aid from the Soviet Union and Vietnam. As in the rest of Indochina, reform began with agricultural liberalization—in the late 1970s from Khmer Rouge hypercollectivism to low-level collectives, in the late 1980s from low-level collectives to household production (Ljunggren 1992, 74–79). The Khmer Rouge had destroyed what little industry Cambodia had had, so industrial liberalization was not much of an issue (Ljunggren 1992, 100–105). Cambodian politics, historically royalist, has remained personalistic. After 1970 politics degenerated into a civil war that the Khmer Rouge won. One could regard Vietnam's 1979 replacement of the ultraradical Khmer Rouge with a moderate communist regime as a form of externally imposed rationalizing political reform. In the early 1990s, the international community sponsored a partial cease-fire and fragile democratization, but a July 1997 coup returned the country to authoritarianism. By the late 1990s, external actors are eager to "de-internationalize" Cambodian politics, and certified the July 1998 elections even though they proved largely a sham (Far East *FBIS* 18 February 1998, *FEER* 13 August 1998). Both political activity and economic administration have remained highly personalistic and elitist (Chandler 1991).

Cambodia is a case driven mostly by the interaction of external and internal military-politics. During the Cold War, Cambodia became an arena for foreign rivalries. In the mid-1970s turmoil of the third Indochina war, radical-communists overran the country, backed by China and, indirectly, the United States. In 1979 Vietnam intervened to install a moderate communist dictatorship. This regime was soon challenged by guerrilla insurgents backed by China and Thailand. As the Cold War ended, the "Cambodia problem" became an obstacle to the realignment of regional power relations. Foreign countries reduced their support to domestic factions, and the international community brokered internal democratization and marketization. Postcommunists and royalists formed the core of a coalition government, with the postcommunists dominant because of their control of the security apparatus. It was the military-political disintegration of the Khmer Rouge that precipitated the 1997 coup, as postcommunist co–prime minister Hun Sen and royalist co–prime minister Norodom Ranariddh competed to coopt their support (Klintworth 1993, *FEER* 17 July 1997).

In Cambodia, the main *long-run condition* favoring political and economic reform was extraordinary political and economic crisis. In the late 1970s, the radical-communist Khmer Rouge had almost completely isolated Cambodia from the world and had almost completely destroyed the country. In the early 1980s, Cambodia only partially recovered under the Vietnamese-backed moderate communist regime. The radicals, royalists, and republicans continued their resistance (Curtis 1989; Frings 1994; Findlay 1995, 1–10). Around 1990 the main *immediate need* for reform arose when Vietnam and the Soviet Union removed their support from the moderate communist regime. Maladministration and corruption undermined the communists' popularity, while the regime and resistance remained in military stalemate. Foreign powers increasingly found it in their interest to solve the "Cambodia problem." By the early 1990s, international intervention was both necessary and feasible (Klintworth 1993).

Unfortunately, in the early 1990s, the players who had created Cambodia's problems remained the main candidates for solving them. The incumbent communist regime counted on its dominance of security and administration to maintain its rule as it became the postcommunist Cambodian People's Party (CPP). Former king Sihanouk attempted to restore his prewar practice of manipulating a broad coalition government from above factional or constitutional constraints. A royalist party was based on Sihanouk's popularity but, under Sihanouk's son Ranariddh, gradually assumed some organizational independence from the king. Former communist dictator Pol Pot continued to lead an again insurgent Khmer Rouge, until his fall and death (*FEER* 7 August 1997, *NYT* 17 April 1998). A small republican-Buddhist party, and a still smaller millenarian movement, appealed to nonroyalist noncommunists (Findlay 1995, 11–20).

UN intervention achieved a cease-fire but failed to disarm the Khmer Rouge and persuade them to participate in elections. Despite Khmer Rouge threats, the population participated enthusiastically in 1993 parliamentary elections, awarding the royalist party the most votes and seats (45 percent of the vote to 38 percent for the CPP). Nevertheless, the incumbent post-communists used their control of the state to increase their political leverage, through postelection power plays such as courting Sihanouk and threatening secession. The National Assembly restored Sihanouk as monarch, and he brokered a coalition government dominated by postcommunists and royalists but including the two minor parties. A new constitution later formalized these power-sharing arrangements (Carney and Choo 1993; Findlay 1995, 52–100; Heder and Ledgerwood 1996).

After 1993 declining health reduced Sihanouk's influence. The postcommunist and royalist parties maintained their uneasy "ruling coalition," perpetuating their joint power by disciplining National Assembly members and the media, and by dividing provincial and district leaderships between them. At the same time, all parties were wracked by factional infighting, not least over the terms of their cooperation with each other. Hard-line postcommunists tried an abortive coup. The royalists purged their major economic reformer, Finance Minister Sam Rainsy, who attempted to launch a new party, which the government has tried to prevent. The Buddhists and republicans split. The Khmer Rouge gradually divided into rival factions: One aligned with the postcommunists, then another attempted to ally with the royalists, provoking the postcommunist coup. Evidently Hun Sen feared that the still popular royalists would beat him again in the 1998 parliamentary elections (after which there is to be only one prime minister). So he purged and exiled his main royalist rival Ranariddh, and encouraged the formation of still more minor parties as a token opposition. Meanwhile he denies the opposition access not only to the media but also to the countryside (*FEER* annual, EIU quarterly, Ojendal 1996, Woods 1997, Peou 1998, *FEER* 29 January 1998, Far East *FBIS* 18 February 1997).

Economically, the problem has been not so much reform, or even development, as postwar recovery and reconstruction, including reconstruction of state economic administration itself. As in Laos, porous borders made it impossible to control trade with Thailand, which accelerated marketization (Ljunggren 1992, 100–105). In 1992–1993 the large UN presence itself created a temporary boom that assisted transition from a command economy but also aggravated inflation and inequality. Since then, inflation has fallen but so has growth (Findlay 1995, *AY,* EIU). Cambodia still needs both rationalizing reform of personalistic institutions and long-term reconstruction of institutions and infrastructure. Even before the coup, some viewed Cambodia as an incipient narco-state (*FEER* 23 November 1995).

Mongolia

Reform began in Mongolia only in the late 1980s with some industrial rationalization and liberalization (upgrading technology, enterprise autonomy) but little political liberalization (criticizing previous autocracy, recognizing Mongolian nationalism). Mongolia's main reform occurred in 1990–1991, including both sudden democratization and resulting marketization. During the 1990s Mongolia's democratization has progressed the furthest of any of the Asian communist cases, already including electoral alternation of party control in both the parliament and presidency, with the government and presidency usually controlled by different political groups (Ginsburg 1998). In 1996 parliamentary elections, the noncommunist opposition finally defeated the still incumbent postcommunist party and took control of the government. Conversely, in 1997 the postcommunist candidate for president defeated an incumbent supported by the "opposition" government. However, marketization has been uneven, with continuingly high transition costs (Ginsburg 1995, 1998; Pomfret 1996, 75–90).

As in other Soviet satellites, these dramatic changes were largely driven by external political and economic shock. The withdrawal of Soviet support was as complete as in Eastern Europe and as devastating as in Soviet Central Asia. However it was the response of the communist Mongolian People's Revolutionary Party (MPRP) that dictated rapid political reform but gradual economic reform. Mongolia's specific transition dynamics resulted from a combination of high *actual* levels of political and economic dependence (characteristic of other central Asian areas that were Soviet republics) and long-standing *nominal political* independence (characteristic of Eastern Europe satellites). This combination both required and allowed the ruling Communist Party to adjust, and it permitted the international community to intervene with economic and political support for democratization and marketization.

Long-run conditions in Mongolia had not favored reform. Mongolia's history of Leninism was second in length only to that of the Soviet Union itself. Politically, precommunist Mongolia had remained a Buddhist theocracy with no experience of democracy. The Soviet Union installed a communist regime as a buffer against China. The Soviet presence increased in the 1960s during the Soviet Union's active confrontation with China (Milivojevic 1991a). Economically, precommunist Mongolia remained a pastoral society with no experience of capitalism. Rural collectivization had intensified only in the 1940s and centralized industrialization only in the 1960s. Nevertheless, by the 1980s the Soviet Union was subsidizing an artificially high standard of living, not only for an unnaturally large urban-industrial sector, but also for the remaining rural pastoralists. Mongolia's economic dependence on the Soviet Union was exceptionally high—Soviet subsidies equaled perhaps a half of Mongolia's GDP, compared to at most a quarter in the Eastern European cases (Boone 1994). Socioculturally, communism and nationalism were well aligned—fear of traditional Chinese dominance made Mongolia welcome Soviet protection. However, Soviet resentment of Mongol conquest had required that Mongol nationalism be downplayed (Haining 1991).

Appropriately for a Soviet satellite, developments in Mongolia strongly reflected those in the Soviet Union. Unlike the China-oriented Southeast Asian countries, Mongolia did not receive a pulse of agricultural liberalization in the late 1970s; its pastoral rural economy was benefiting from socialism, not suffering from it (Boone 1994). In 1984 reportedly Andropov engineered the shift from the conservative Tsendenbal to his designated successor Batmonh. However, it was only in the late 1980s that, reportedly at Gorbachev's insistence, Batmonh began implementing the Mongolian version of economic restructuring and political opening—a mix of rationalization and liberalization (Sanders 1991). Socioculturally, increasing celebration of Mongolian history and culture cast the MPRP as the bearer of Mongolian nationalism. (Overviews include Akiner 1991 and Bruun and Odgaard 1996.)

Batmonh's initial reaction to the fall of communism in Eastern Europe was to reaffirm socialism. Nevertheless, at the beginning of 1990 the Mongolian regime faced both rising internal urban political opposition and declining Soviet economic aid, creating an *immediate need* for reform. The *political opportunity* for *political reform* arose from the strength of reformers in the MPRP and the strength of the MPRP in society, particularly the countryside. After some internal debate, the MPRP decided against repressing the opposition, changed its own leadership, and nimbly seized the banner of rapid political reform. The extent of previous repression and the swiftness of events meant that the opposition remained disorganized. The MPRP called a snap parliamentary election for July 1990, which it won handily. Its victory was facilitated by the fact that real economic transition costs had not yet begun, and by gross malapportionment in favor of the rural constituencies that had benefited most from communist rule (Milivojevic 1991b, Ginsburg 1995).

Rapid political reform produced only partial and gradual *economic reform*. On the one hand, despite the new government's genuine enthusiasm for marketization, under conditions of externally imposed economic crisis, in practice the government tried to maintain transitional economic control through managing foreign trade, administering domestic prices, and purchasing and rationing commodities. On the other hand, a coalition of Establishment reformers and the reformist Opposition passed privatization, property, and banking laws that increased enterprise autonomy and created a private sector. The continuing controls over prices and procurement, and the fact that ownership was transferred mostly to those already staffing existing economic organizations, prevented privatization from improving productivity. Meanwhile, rising private microeconomic initiative undermined government macroeconomic controls. The result was a shrinking economy, rising inflation, and falling living standards (Lee 1993, Boone 1994, Denizer and Gelb 1994, Korsun and Murrell 1995, Murrell, Dunn, and Korsun 1996, Spoor 1996).

In 1992 parliamentary elections, the MPRP cleverly attributed these transition costs to a too-rapid pace of economic reform, blamed the Opposition, and promised to slow marketization. The MPRP won again (Ginsburg 1995). The economy eventually resumed growth, but economic transition costs continued to rise, and in 1996 parliamentary elections the public finally held the MPRP responsible. The opposition won a victory that was both unexpected and overwhelming. However, the new government then drastically *accelerated* marketization, causing a new round of economic dislocation, including perhaps 50 percent unemployment and even some risk of starvation for some (*FEER* 27 March 1997). To protest, in 1997 voters supported the MPRP candidate for president. Whether shock therapy will eventually produce prosperity remains to be seen. If the turnaround does not occur before the next national parliamentary elections in 2000, voters may then return the formerly communist MPRP to power.

North Korea

Among the world's remaining communisms, North Korea is distinctive in refusing virtually any economic or political reform, despite now complete geopolitical isolation and acute internal economic crisis. Its leadership has remained highly personalistic, socialistic, nationalistic, and moralistic. Despite the death of founder Kim Il Song, the regime remains dominated by the founder's relatives and their carefully recruited associates, who have a high personal stake in the regime's Stalinist socialism and nationalist isolationism. The leadership has wanted to improve economic performance, but its solution has been more socialist mobilization, not a switch to capitalist marketization. Even the end of Soviet aid did not bring significant liberalizing economic reform, only minor and largely unsuccessful attempts to attract foreign capital into export enclaves while leaving the rest of the economy unchanged. Meanwhile, the economy has shrunk, infrastructure has deteriorated, and agriculture has failed. North Korea has conducted no evident political rationalization, let alone liberalization or democratization. As in the other two cases discussed in this section, political change may be a necessary precondition for economic change (Lee and Yoo 1991; Kang and Lee 1992; Lee 1996; Pomfret 1996, 130–142).

Long-run *economic conditions* largely impede reform. North Korean socialism started early from a low base and gradually achieved a high level of "misdevelopment"—the European communist model of state enterprise and heavy industry, high urbanization, and high welfare benefits. These genuine early achievements confirmed elite convictions and earned popular support. However, from around 1980 growth rates declined, becoming negative in the 1990s. Causes include overreliance on Maoist mobilization, increasing misallocation of resources to military and monuments, cutoff of East bloc aid and trade, and the absence of private-sector supplements on the eastern Asian late-communist model. Nevertheless, North Korea does have assets that would help economic reform succeed, such as natural resources and a disciplined labor force (Kim 1993; Foster-Carter 1994; Eberstadt 1995, 3–50).

North Korea's economic rigidity may largely reflect long-run *political conditions*. In politics too, North Korea has had some striking achievements: It is the oldest remaining communist state, with among the most stable leaderships of any country and the most militarized population in the world (Eberstadt 1993). High external political independence and high internal political control enable the North Korean regime to refuse reform. Externally, North Korea has withstood the United States and South Korea, and it has gradually achieved political independence from its Soviet and Chinese mentors. Nevertheless, North Korea's problematic "stateness" and economic weakness now make it vulnerable to absorption by South Korea. Internally, high mass party membership and high military service incorporate a large proportion of the population into the regime, and a huge security apparatus maintains internal control over the rest. Nevertheless, elite defections and mass uprisings suggest that control is becoming increasingly fragile (Eberstadt 1995, 51–77; *FEER* 26 June 1997; Satterwhite 1998).

The immediate *economic need* for reform has been obvious—GNP has shrunk throughout the 1990s and the country now verges on starvation (*FEER* 10 October 1996, 26 June 1997). Nevertheless, the regime has made only marginal economic adjustments, allowing only some private-plot farming and free border markets, and half-tolerating a growing internal black market (*FEER* 10 July 1995, 23 October 1997). Nevertheless, economic need may not be politically decisive so long as the security apparatus remains well provisioned. Moreover, there may be little *political opportunity* for reform. In choosing between reaction and reform, Kim Jong Il may face such unattractive alternatives and high uncertainty that he is unable to make up his mind. Even if he personally wishes to reform, he may face intra-elite disagreement or declining mass control that make economic reform too risky politically (Foster-Carter 1994, 26–32). Evidently the upshot is that Kim has tilted from technocrats toward officers, replacing older military leaders with younger loyalists, in order to reconsolidate his control of the military, and through it control of party, government, and society (*FEER* 13 March 1997).

Careful assessments of North Korea's prospects vary widely. Some Korean scholars find the regime rational—conducting shrewd geopolitics and stealthy economic reform (Kang 1995, Lee 1992). Most Chinese analysts believe the regime is politically stable now but disagree about its durability; most believe the regime is economically viable but disagree about the extent to which it will liberalize (Garrett and Glaser 1995). In contrast, most Western observers predict eventual collapse, even if the regime attempts gradual reform. Eberstadt even suggests that the North

Korean regime itself may anticipate such a demise and be continuing the development of nuclear weapons to ensure that foreign powers find it necessary to provide North Korea sufficient support to avoid chaos (1993). In the late 1990s, an increasing proportion of analysts have concluded that rising starvation will bring down the Kim regime sooner or later, probably through elite coup not mass uprising (*FEER* 26 June 1997). In any case, since neither South Korea, China, Japan, nor the United States want catastrophic collapse, the possibility emerges of externally orchestrated "controlled collapse" (Foster-Carter 1994). This would create a new mode of transition from communism.

Conclusion

This chapter has treated *Asian* transitions from communism, but in order to show how they differ. Among the cases involving mostly economic change, independent China has provided an important alternative to European transition paths. Some other Asian communisms have paralleled China's course, some not. Vietnam comes closest, though there the need for initial agricultural liberalization arose from a more general crisis, the liberalization of state enterprise occurred more spontaneously, and the end of Soviet subsidies brought a more abrupt end to planning. As a client of Vietnam, Laos has resembled Vietnam but deviated still further from the Chinese experience: still more rapid marketization due to lesser development, porous borders, and greater access to the West. Among the more political cases, North Korea deviates from the Chinese model by refusing even economic reform, because a founding family remains in control and because economic reform risks internal revolt and external absorption. Cambodia deviates still further: International and internal war led to international intervention to assist first political regime change, then marketizing economic reconstruction. Finally, Mongolia followed the Soviet-oriented model: Abrupt political collapse produced drastic political reform but uneven economic reform.

This chapter has analyzed *reform,* but in order to show that it is not entirely a matter of deliberate national policy. Obdurate policy can block reform, as North Korea illustrates. However, where change has occurred, it has involved a declining capacity of the party-state to control events, and it has involved the interaction of national policy with both supranational and subnational constraints and initiatives. In the cases in which transition *began* with gradual economic reform, elites have been as conspicuous in resisting as in promoting it. In China and Vietnam, reform was initiated by spontaneous liberalization from below and was at first condoned by national policymakers largely as a way of salvaging socialism. China and Vietnam are commercializing their state enterprises but still resist privatizing them, so that socialism can continue to control the commanding heights of the economy. All the Asian communisms were slow formally to endorse households and markets as the main basis for agriculture. In Laos, Cambodia, and Mongolia, reform was accelerated by the transfer of economic dependence from East to West. Even in Mongolia, which experienced the most drastic external political and economic shock and achieved the most drastic internal political change, the democratically elected post-communist party resisted economic decontrol. Policy is not the exogenous cause of the process of transformation but is endogenously generated by it (Fforde and de Vylder 1996).

This chapter has distinguished political, economic, and sociocultural *functions,* but in order to examine how they interact. The degree of systemic reform is mediated by its implications for elite survival. At least in non-Soviet communist Asia, great political security—good internal control backed by strong external support—produced little reform (e.g., pre-1990 Mongolia). Moderate security—good political control potentially threatened only by poor economic performance—has produced gradual economic reform (China). Moderate insecurity—good political control threatened by a few internal and external crises—has produced somewhat faster economic reform (e.g., Vietnam, Laos). Great insecurity—fragile political control threatened by many actual or potential crises—has produced either drastic reform (post-1990 Mongolia) or no reform (North Korea). The political survival of communist and former communist parties, electoral or otherwise, depends partly on politics (repressive capacity, institutional engineering), partly on economics (the level of transition costs and who gets blamed for them), and partly on sociocultural processes (alignment with historic nationalism). In the short run economic growth has helped stabilize reforming communisms, but in the long run it may undermine them. In the 1990s, elites have strengthened political control accordingly.

Overall, the different transition paths of different Asian communisms reflect both the particular environmental challenge and the particular institutional composition of each. If transition paths are a series of constrained choices, the structure of the environment constitutes the constraint, while elite institutions, perceptions, and preferences largely determine the choice. The more rational the elite, the more the timing and scope of environmental challenge have shaped the tempo and extent of reform.

Note

This chapter focuses on the period of transition from communism. For reasons of space, the chapter does not attempt to cite the main studies of each country before then. For the transition period, the chapter first cites academic books and articles when available. However, these remain scant, except for China and to some extent Vietnam. Many of the best short overviews are special reports for private organizations such as the Economist Intelligence Unit or Bureau of Asian Research. The chapter cites these second whenever available and relevant. When not, the chapter refers the reader to recent editions of the next most systematic coverage—such serials as the *Far Eastern Economic Review*'s annual *Asia Yearbook,* and the quarterly reports in the relevant country series from the Economist Intelligence Unit. (In EIU citations, 1995-1 indicates first quarter 1995.) Among less regular coverage, the *Far Eastern Economic Review* is invaluable, particularly its occasional country cover stories. The author scanned the last ten years of the Foreign Broadcast Information Service's *Far East Report,* but its coverage of most "minor" Asian communisms has been quite thin. Particularly for the less researched countries, there are other sources of systematic coverage that have informed this chapter but that, for reasons of space, the chapter does not cite systematically. These include the following additional annual reviews: *Asian Development Outlook* (Asian Development Bank), the January and February issues of *Asian Survey,* Asia issues of *Current History,* the *Korea Briefing* (the Asia Society), and *Southeast Asian Affairs* (Institute of Southeast Asian Studies, Singapore).

10

Explaining Leninist Transitions

Edwin A. Winckler

The editor's Introduction to this volume sketched some dimensions for *describing* transitions—temporal dynamics, functional sectors, and structural levels. Here, the editor's Conclusion resumes that discussion, exploring more analytical analogues of those three dimensions for *explaining* transitions—in reverse order, analytical levels, sectoral analysis, and temporal dynamics. As Andrew Walder has insisted, it is not enough to identify big processes that probably affected transition; it is necessary also to model and document exactly how that effect was produced (Walder 1994, 1995c; editor's Introduction this volume). This Conclusion discusses some of the strengths and weaknesses of alternative theoretical approaches to explaining Leninisms and their transitions, noting some implications for further research. (For a guide to discussion of these themes in this volume, see the Index under *Analysis, approaches; Levels, analytical; Sectors, analytical; Dynamics, analytical.*)

Because delegation by principals to agents is a main theme, we begin with a brief sketch of agency theory and its relevance to Leninism and transition. Delegation theory is particularly apposite for analyzing post-Mao China, where contracts became the preferred instrument for delegating responsibility and maintaining control, and where by the mid-1990s agency theory was actually guiding economic-administrative reform (You 1998, 193). We then discuss a "vertical" dimension—the relationship between macro, meso, and micro *levels* of analysis. "Meso" analysis, starting from institutions themselves, is a necessary meeting ground for macro and micro approaches. Institutions provide components for macroprocesses and parameters for microprocesses. We next treat a "horizontal" question—differences between functional *sectors* in how they are organized. Specifying these differences, particularly through delegation theory, is an important front both for analyzing Leninist transitions and for elaborating institutional theory. Different sectors involve different degrees of vertical delegation with different propensities to "slip" inadvertently into transition. Finally we

return to a "longitudinal" question—different approaches to explaining stability and *change*. So far, "hard" microanalysis such as game theory is better at explaining stability than change. This leaves a role for more explicitly
temporal theories such as "soft" macro "historical institutionalism."

Introduction: Transition as Delegation

Much of the theoretical interest of Leninist transitions is the opportunity to
observe the wholesale deconstruction and reconstruction of institutions. A
main area of recent progress in institutional analysis has concerned delegation or agency. This section briefly summarizes some basic elements of
agency analysis, discusses their application to the successive stages of
Leninist transitions, and notes some issues raised by transferring agency
analysis from capitalist systems to communist transitions. (For a guide to
the application and development of agency theory in this volume, see the
Index under *Agency Delegation, Principal-agent,* and cross-references
from there.)

Elements of Agency

Essentially, agency theory analyzes the struggle for control within a contractual relationship in which a principal delegates control over assets to an
agent, whom the principal rewards for managing the assets in the principal's interest (Eggertsson 1990). The basic variables are *incentives and
information*—the various costs and benefits to the principal and agent, and
the various kinds and quality of information available to each (Arrow 1985,
White 1985).

The *practical appeal* of agency relationships is that they are efficient,
flexible, and versatile. Agency can function inside major mechanisms such
as bureaucracies and markets, acting as a building block for them, or bol-
stering or refining them (e.g., under Leninist systems). Alternatively,
agency can function outside the major mechanisms, flourishing in the gray
areas between them, and when the major mechanisms are in decline (e.g.,
during Leninist transitions).

The *political interest* of agency is that it illuminates the extent and limits of control, and the strategies of principal and agent for maximizing control. According to classical agency analysis, the outcome is determined by
how astutely the principal crafts and manages the relationship, and by how
craftily the agent uses the relationship for his own purposes. In China as in
the United States, agency political analysis often reveals that the principal
maintains more residual political control than it usually chooses to exercise.

The *theoretical significance* of agency relationships is that they facilitate precise modeling of important dynamics in larger structures. One can view an agency relationship as an elementary form of a contract in a market, of a superior-subordinate relationship in a hierarchy, or of a patron-client relationship in a sociocultural network (Eggertsson 1990, White 1985, van de Walle 1991, respectively). Even for a single dyadic relationship between one principal and one agent, analysis can become quite subtle as it considers alternative configurations of information and incentives.

Different academic disciplines have elaborated different aspects of agency relationships, which illuminate different aspects of Leninisms and their transitions and even produce quite opposite interpretations. Typically economists have emphasized the *problems* that principals face in maintaining control despite their ostensible authority (starting from Ross 1973). This helps analyze the gradual *decline* of Leninism, both in economic performance and in political control (e.g., Walder 1995c). Thus most economists viewed China's economic decentralization as eroding central economic and political control (Wong 1985, Naughton 1987). Many political scientists agreed (e.g., Jia and Lin 1994, Goodman and Segal 1994). In this view, the misbehavior of provincial agents exceeded what the central principal was willing to tolerate, but the center was unable to curb it.

Political scientists have emphasized the *success* of principals in maintaining control, despite the inactivity of principals and the apparent autonomy of agents (e.g., Kiewiet and McCubbins 1991). This helps analyze the *persistence* of Leninism (e.g., Winckler on the military and birth planning this volume). Thus recently some political scientists have argued that, in China, devolution of economic assets need not mean devolution of political power (Yang 1994). Moreover, the center has actually increased its political control, by tightening its control of appointments and by improving its monitoring of performance (Naughton 1992a, Huang 1996). In this view, provincial misbehavior has fallen within the range that the center would tolerate, or provincial misbehavior has eventually been corrected, as in the center's 1994 fiscal recentralization.

Some political scientists have explored situations of "reciprocal accountability," in which actors are simultaneously principals and agents vis-à-vis each other (Roeder 1993, Shirk 1993). This helps explain the *transformation* of Leninism—for example, the tendency within Leninism toward constitutionalization (Roeder) and decentralization (Shirk). Some recent principal-agent literature has viewed the relationship more from the agent's point of view. A sociologist has called attention to "agency reversal," in which the agent not the principal calls the shots, and may even establish ownership over the assets delegated to him (White 1985). This helps explain the sudden *collapse* of Leninist systems (e.g., Solnick 1996).

One sociological formulation of agency relationships is particularly apt for analyzing Leninist transitions (Hechter and Szelenyi 1994). Michael Hechter analyzes individual compliance in terms of *dependence and control,* the latter disaggregated into *monitoring and sanctioning* (1987). This formulation is helpful because it situates information monitoring and incentive sanctioning into a social context that specifies the overall relationship of power and dependence between the principal and agent. As Walder early described, dependence of individuals on their state-run work units was crucial to both the stability and the dysfunctions of communist China (Walder 1986). At least in Hungary and China, economic reform gradually reduced the dependence of subordinates and the capacity of superiors to monitor and sanction behavior, both in relations between party leaders and party-state cadres and in relations between party-state cadres and the public (Walder 1995c). In this volume, microanalyses of compliance include Tong's chapter on the evolution of central-local fiscal contracts, and Winckler's chapter on the reinforcement of monitoring and sanctioning in Chinese state birth planning.

Agency and Transition

For Leninist *systems,* agency analysis illuminates both the necessity for delegation and the success of the principal in retaining control. In agency terms, a basic dynamic of Leninist systems was their reluctance to delegate. Leninist dictatorships rested on a claimed delegation of political authority from proletarian masses to vanguard party. If they could, to maximize control, communist leaders would have performed all functions at the center themselves or delegated functions only to their immediate agents—personal czars for security, development, and legitimation affairs. However, such total centralization produces dysfunctional results, so Leninist systems delegated functions from the "party center" to professional security managers, central planners, and party ideologues; to national party and state bureaucracies; and to the subnational extensions of those bureaucracies. Communism then wrestled with the consequences: repeated cycles of decentralization and recentralization within the party-state apparatus itself, and repeated attempts at limited reform through mass mobilization or market exchange.

For Leninist *transitions,* agency analysis illuminates both the necessity for further delegation and the difficulty of maintaining control. In agency terms, most Leninist transitions began as attempts to break out of reform cycles through more drastic delegation, and they accelerated through the breakdown or reversal of the relationship between principal and agent. Typically delegation began in ad hoc arrangements for dealing with pressing problems, then cumulated into contending formulas for systemic reform. Debate over reform concerned the size and design of the "cage" that the principal—the party center—should maintain around the activities it delegated. Typically, agents have increasingly escaped that confinement and even assumed de facto ownership of the assets assigned them. In response, the erstwhile principal has shifted from issuing instructions to agents on how to act in the principal's interest, to setting rules for actors who are now independent and pursuing their own interests.

Thus, heuristically, Leninist transitions involve a progressive shift *from operative, through delegative, toward regulatory* state. The "operative" baseline is a maximal system in which the party-state tries to run everything and penetrate everywhere, commanding virtually unchallenged authority. During the delegative stage, the party-state devolves assets and functions to progressively wider circles of actors but succeeds in maintaining ultimate control. Finally, if this control breaks down, or the party-state deliberately privatizes assets and functions, the party-state retreats to regulation—intervention in social activities that is less direct and more selective but, the party hopes, more efficient and more sustainable. In this transition, agency analysis promises to clarify both the actors' ongoing struggle over control and the system's shift from stage to stage.

Students of Leninisms and their transitions are well into exploring the subtleties of relationships between one principal and one agent but remain far from exhausting them (e.g., again Roeder 1993, Shirk 1993). Meanwhile, theorists have begun to address more complex relationships between principals and agents—multiple agents and multiple principals at multiple levels (e.g., Tsebelis 1993, Landa 1994). Comparative postcommunism has begun to employ these more complex models as well. For example, multiple agents are central to Solnick's "bank run" model of the breakdown of hierarchy in the Soviet Union and, potentially, China (1996). Models of multiple principals should illuminate China, where overlapping jurisdictions typically subordinate organizations to "many mothers-in-law" (Wei 1994). Attention to multiple levels should help place leader-bureaucracy and bureaucracy-public relationships into a more general model of leader-bureaucracy-public relationships (e.g., see Manion 1992 for a three-level analysis of the implementability of Deng's cadre retirement policies).

Relationships between principals and agents are embedded in institutional contexts that strongly affect them (Scharpf 1993a). One strategy for analyzing the effect of institutional context on actors' interactions is to consider separately the effects on collective action of different social mechanisms, such as hierarchies, markets, networks, and culture (Lichbach 1995). Here lies much of the challenge of applying "hard" economic models to Leninisms and their transitions. How does one retain the precision of formal modeling while addressing "soft" real world complexities? This Conclusion will encounter this challenge for several hard analytical approaches, not only principal-agent theory but also game theory and transaction cost economics.

Comparative postcommunism will certainly need these more complex theories, because Leninisms and their transitions involved all of these complications. For example, in the Soviet Union the breakdown of hierarchy resulted not only from deterioration within principal-agent relations, but also from open struggle between contending principals—Gorbachev and Yeltsin (Dunlop 1993). In contrast, in China the principals have maintained communist hierarchy by maintaining at least nominal unity, but the effectiveness of their control has varied with the extent of actual policy consensus. Similarly, one should contrast the institutional environments in these and other cases. For example, Huang has argued that in the Soviet Union the center's greater planning and monitoring capacities inclined it to minimize economic delegation, while in China the center's weakness inclined it toward increasing economic decentralization (Huang 1994).

In this volume, the China-sectoral chapters extensively treat agency dynamics, mostly stressing the extent to which the center-principal has retained control. In the security sector, Winckler shows political leaders determined to control military professionals, while Tanner shows police professionals struggling to assert some autonomy from political leaders. In economic policy, Tong uses principal-agent theory to analyze the center's attempts to perfect fiscal delegation, while Yang illuminates the center's successful struggle to control the macroeconomic consequences of economic delegation. In social policy, Winckler argues that the center has retained remarkable control not only of the Chinese state birth planning apparatus but also of mass reproductive behavior. In cultural policy, Kraus and Suttmeier find the state still exercising much control, despite much decentralization, marketization, and internationalization.

Transfer of Agency

Agency theory was originally formulated for relatively placid Western capitalist economic institutions—problems of insurance, accounting, and employment. There agency analysis achieved its precision by examining characteristics internal to the delegation relationship, such as the social and technical characteristics of the transactions and the information and incentives of the actors. (See particularly the second third of this Conclusion.) Such analysis has largely taken for granted the institutional framework of Western capitalist societies, such as well-specified economic property rights and their impersonal enforcement by a centralized legal system. Agency analysis has already been stretched from Western economics to Western politics (e.g., Kiewiet and McCubbins 1991). Even this modest transfer has required significant reformulation. For example, politics often involves multiple principals—for example, in democratic systems, presidents and assemblies (Shugart and Carey 1992). In politics, principals may become legally subject to actions by the agents they appoint (Moe 1990). In democratic politics, property rights are legally enforceable but, unlike economic property rights, they are contingent on winning elections (Moe 1990).

Applying agency theory to Leninist transitions involves "stretching" it still further, to the less institutionalized world of communist politics and to less Western societies. Consequently this volume helps demonstrate the impact on delegation of factors external to the relationship between principal and agent, such as the mix of mechanisms in the immediate institutional setting and the wider technical and social environments. In Leninist systems, the party enforces its own claims to political ownership, which therefore rests exclusively on the credibility of the party's reputation as an enforcer (Solnick 1996). Principals are not just legally subject to some actions by their agents; they rely for their legitimacy *entirely* on selection by officials they appoint, creating "reciprocal accountability" (Roeder 1993, Shirk 1993). The political context of agency relationships is more salient and more variable—from totalitarian coercion and ideological mobilization to socialist legalization and marketization. For example, in this volume, Tong reports the effect of change in political setting on central-provincial fiscal delegation, and Winckler notes the effect of marketization on the enforcement of state birth planning.

One general characteristic of the institutional environment affecting Asian transitions is *personalism*. Even in the more institutionalized communist systems such as the former Soviet Union, concurrent occupation of key party and government posts by the same individuals is essential to avoiding the emergence of multiple principals based on conflicting legitimacies. In less institutionalized communist systems such as China, formal institutions rely even more heavily on informal supports, raising the issue of the relationship between *formal and informal* delegation. Modeling formal institutions is the appropriate "first cut," to see if they account for observed behavior. They may well do so, as in the post-Stalin stabilization of collective leadership in the Soviet Union (Roeder 1993), or the gradual decentralization of the Chinese economy (Shirk 1993). However, if they do not, a "second cut" may reveal that, so to speak, formal institutions are only the agents of informal institutions that are the real principals.

In post-Mao China personalism still has not yet fully died off, and it still frequently intervenes to "correct" the actions of its formal-institutional agents. In the early 1980s Deng sponsored a rejection of "feudal patriarchy" and restoration of "socialist legality," but in the late 1980s himself led an elders' coup against younger officials. In the early 1990s Deng intervened personally to restart reform, arguably the last major personalistic push to institutionalizing marketization (Yang this volume). Meanwhile, on Taiwan, it was the Chiang family's informal autocracy that directed formal political institutions first into authoritarianism and later into democratization (Dickson this volume). In principal-agent terms, in both China and Taiwan, founding leaders still personally "owned" the political system, despite having delegated management to younger protégés. In sum, agency analysis must remain alert to the possibility that formal institutions express the interests of behind-the-scenes principals, whether dictators, oligarchies, institutions, or classes.

Analytical Levels

Recent institutional analysis has progressed through the complementarity and even synthesis of several levels of analysis (Ostrom 1995). Nevertheless, social scientists display surprisingly little agreement about the dimensions and gradations to which terms such as "macro" and "micro" refer (Alexander et al. 1987). This section distinguishes macrohistorical, mesoinstitutional, and microindividual approaches to institutional analysis, noting the strengths and weaknesses of each, particularly as applied to Leninist transitions. Given the "institutional realist" assumptions of most of this volume, this section highlights the contributions of a distinctively "meso" level between macro and micro (Grafstein 1992, White 1992). As the chapters in this volume illustrate, mesoanalysis can improve macronarratives by disaggregating them into mesoprocesses, and it can improve microanalyses by embedding them in their mesoinstitutional context.

Macrohistory

"Macro" analysis is "top-down," studying aggregate properties or overall processes. The unit of analysis has usually been the nation-state, and the actors have usually been large-scale entities such as states and classes. Supranational analysis of global dynamics can usefully be designated "macro-macro"—for example, most recently, Stallings 1995, Risse-Kappen 1995, Keohane and Milner 1996. Macrodiscourse accepts macroentities as given, in order to pursue "soft" historical narrative or "hard" causal comparison. Macroexplanations are often structural, emphasizing the constraints that large-scale processes place on the actors' choices, and even on their preferences (Hechter 1987, Introduction). Most macroanalysts concede that macroprocesses require specification of intervening meso- and microprocesses. Nevertheless, macroapproaches remain indispensable for describing and analyzing large-scale processes, which are usually the outcomes of greatest practical concern (Tilly 1984, Kohli et al. 1995). Moreover, macroanalysis is indispensable for establishing the nature of the conflicts involved, as a step toward more formal modeling (Aggarwal and Allan 1994). However, structural concepts easily become reified and then have difficulty analyzing change, "totalitarianism" being a classic example.

Most macroanalysis of transition starts by distinguishing different types of old regime. Over the past two decades, characterization of regime type has become increasingly specific. The initial distinctions were the broad systemic categories of totalitarian, authoritarian, and democratic (Linz 1975). Analysis then progressed toward systemic subtypes such as "high" versus "post" totalitarianism, "hard" versus "soft" authoritarianism, and adversarial versus consensual democracy (e.g., Lowenthal 1970, Linz 1978, Lijphart 1984). Linz further distinguished nondemocratic regimes by different mixes of institutions, particularly leader, party, army, and government (1975). Perlmutter showed how in nondemocratic regimes different combinations of institutions produce different political dynamics (1981). Analysis continues of institutional subtypes of authoritarianism, such as personalist versus military versus party regimes (e.g., Riggs 1993, Geddes 1995), and of institutional subtypes of democracy, such as parliamentary versus presidential (Lijphart 1992, Linz and Valenzuela 1994). Some recent analysis further disaggregates institutions into their component functions and powers (e.g., for different kinds of democracies, Shugart and Carey 1992).

In their most recent work, Linz and Stepan retain the three basic regime types, but add two more particularly relevant to recent transitions—post-totalitarianism and sultanism (1996). Evidently comparative politics needs a more explicit set of underlying dimensions, probably mesoinstitutional and preferably with clear microfoundations. For example, "sultanism" may be a type of system, but it also implies an important dimension of all regime types—personalism versus institutionalization. This dimension is particularly pertinent to the Leninist cases which, although party-based, often shade into personalism, particularly in East Asia. Recently other authors have recommended bypassing regime type altogether, in order to examine the effects of particular *institutions* such as party systems (e.g., Haggard and Kaufman 1995). However, one can regard an institutional approach not as an alternative to regime analysis but as an elaboration of it. For example, parties probably perform differently in different kinds of regimes, so that specifying the kind of regime in which a party system is embedded remains an important element of their institutional specification. As Dickson shows in this volume, "Leninist" parties behaved quite differently in authoritarian Taiwan and totalitarian China.

Microanalysis

"Micro" analysis is "bottom-up," starting from actors and their interactions and using them to account for stability or change in any patterns that may emerge. The paradigmatic actor is the individual person but can range upward through groups and organizations to states and even alliances. However, for most political topics, the key to microexplanation is not individual actors but the *interaction* between multiple actors (e.g., strategic interaction as in game theory or "social construction" as in cultural theory). Microapproaches can be either "hard" or "soft." The hard side includes the rationalist, political-economic, decision-theoretic, transaction-cost, and game-theoretic. The soft side includes the interpretivist, sociocultural, psychological, cultural, and critical. Both rationalist and interpretivist microinstitutionalisms are indispensable for critiquing and refining macroexplanations, and both have made remarkable progress toward supplementing macroexplanations with micro ones (Johnson 1993, Bates and Weingast 1995).

Broadly speaking, bottom-up approaches are making an increasing contribution to analyzing Leninist transitions in general, and China's transition in particular. However, one should distinguish several microapproaches, often combined in the same analysis. The first type is bottom-up only in the descriptive sense of identifying inputs from society or initiatives by individuals (discussed in the editor's Introduction). The second type is micro, mostly in the economic sense of disaggregating to organizations (really mesoanalysis, but in the economic "theory of the firm" usually with minimal institutional detail). Such approaches are particularly appropriate for China's economic transition, which emphasized "micro" reform of enterprise management because of ideological resistance to "macro" reform of the price system (Naughton 1995). Such an approach reveals similarities of sequence across economic transitions that an approach propounding an "optimal order" of macroeconomic reforms may miss (McMillan and Naughton 1996a). The third type is micro in the stricter sense of starting from individual actors, preferably persons (according to liberal "methodological individualism"). Increasingly, scholars are trying to provide "microfoundations" for their accounts (e.g., on China, Manion 1993, Tsou 1994, Huang 1996, Yang this volume). Full-fledged versions remain relatively rare (e.g., Jin 1994).

In this third sense, much contemporary microanalysis is really "micro-micro," since it disaggregates individuals into still smaller components, either political-economic or sociocultural. The new institutional economics reduces individuals to their transactions (Williamson 1975, 1985). Political-economic "neo-institutionalism" reduces transactions to such primitives as information and incentives. Similarly, sociocultural "new institutionalism" disaggregates individuals into norms and values (March and Olsen 1984, DiMaggio and Powell 1991). Postmodern cultural analysis further deconstructs these into still more fragmentary signs and themes. Thus, despite their stylistic contrast, rationalism and interpretivism converge at the micro-micro level in their intensive analysis of beliefs and preferences (Bates and Weingast 1995).

The abruptness of Leninist collapse in Eastern Europe and the Soviet Union too focused attention on the importance of beliefs (e.g., Kuran 1991, Marks 1992). As both rationalists and interpretivists observed, it was crucial that elites ceased to believe in communist policies and that masses ceased to believe in communist power. This was not just a matter of legitimacy, it was also a matter of feasibility. As successive policies were tried and failed, the options defining the game progressively narrowed and the credibility of the remaining alternatives precipitously declined. For example, in China, attempts to restore central economic planning were gradually discredited (Naughton 1995). Nevertheless, Dengist China was meanwhile busy instilling new beliefs about social objectives such as retirement age and family size (Manion 1993, Winckler this volume). As Kitschelt (1993) notes, it may be possible to endogenize some of these processes—that is, to show how beliefs and preferences arise from within the transition game itself, or were extinguished by it.

The most powerful "hard" microanalysis is *game theory.* So far, it is the only analytical program that promises eventually to integrate our three dimensions of transition. Thus game theory models the *horizontal-functional dimension* as different types of games—cooperative, conflictual, or mixed (Scharpf 1993b). These types may well provide the microfoundations for Etzioni's normative, coercive, and remunerative compliance, respectively. Game theory should improve analysis of compliance by treating it not as unilateral hierarchical administration but as multilateral strategic interaction (for analogous concerns see Levi 1990). As regards regime type, arguably the totalitarian model erred not so much in overstating the state's effort at hegemony as in underestimating the resistance that effort provoked. As regards regime change, evidently one should go beyond decision-theoretic analysis of the trade-offs to rulers between repression and liberalization, to game-theoretic analysis of the interaction between Establishment and Opposition strategies (e.g., Dahl 1971 versus Przeworski 1991).

Game theory also addresses the *vertical-structural dimension,* first by analyzing how interactions between individuals produce institutions, then by pyramiding institutions as nested games (Tsebelis 1990). Moreover, game theory integrates analytical levels by arguing that the basic processes are the same at all of them (Niou and Ordeshook 1994). Finally, on the *longitudinal-temporal dimension,* game theory is the only approach that combines analysis of stability and change. As one of its most fundamental theorems shows, most real-life situations contain many possible equilibria, and actors can be expected to move among them as perceptions, preferences, and other parameters change (Fudenberg and Maskin 1986). Transition becomes a process of falling off one relatively narrow equilibrium path and scrambling either to return to it or to find a new one.

Nevertheless, this same theorem shows that game theory too is explanatorily incomplete. Game theory cannot predict on which of many possible equilibria actors will converge, if any (again, Fudenberg and Maskin 1986). Microrational theorists have only somewhat narrowed the range of possible outcomes by ad hoc restrictions on the nature of the beliefs and the amount of communication that they allow players (Morrow

1994). Behavioralists have proposed alternative supplements, including social norms and even language itself (Johnson, J. 1993). Ostrom has stressed time and history, suggesting that in practice actors can solve these problems because new institutions can arise incrementally, and in the context of old institutions (1990, 1995). The implication for explaining Leninisms and their transitions is that, having used microanalysis to make their questions as precise as possible, mesoinstitutionalists must turn to macronarrative for many of the answers. The last third of this Conclusion elaborates that implication.

Mesoinstitutions

Mesoanalysis is "middle-out," exploring the large gap between macro and micro. "Meso" analysis accepts institutions and their discourses as real, analyzes them as important in themselves, and uses them both to refine macroanalysis and to situate microanalysis (Grafstein 1992, White 1992). Classic examples of mesoanalysis include social-anthropological analysis of small-scale societies, constitutional-legal analysis of political institutions, and multidisciplinary analysis of formal organizations. Early organization theory typically focused within one organization, or on the interaction between one organization and its environment ("meso" proper). Later organization theory expanded the focus from single organizations to relations between a few or many organizations ("meso-meso"). Much of this Conclusion pursues such meso-meso interorganizational analysis, particularly of how institutions interact to constitute functional "sectors" of state or society. By the late 1990s, new institutional organization theory embraced soft approaches such as social constructionism and discourse analysis (March and Olsen 1984, DiMaggio and Powell 1991, *Administrative Science Quarterly* September 1983 and June 1996).

Mesoanalysis plays a strategic role between macro- and microanalysis, as the volume chapters illustrate. Mesoanalysis improves *macro*analysis by disaggregating macronarratives into institutional processes, making the original macroaccount more precise. For example, in this volume, Dickson is most explicit about treating the adaptation of whole Leninist party-states as the interaction between organizations and their environments. Winckler too tracks the effect of "shocks" from the supranational and subnational environments on whole Asian Leninist party-states. The sectoral chapters treat the interaction between sectoral organizations and sectoral environments. (For a guide to this approach in this volume, see the Index headings that begin with *Environment, Organization,* and *Performance.*)

Hard mesoanalysis can also significantly transform the original macroaccount by stripping off formal macrodynamics to show the informal mesodynamics within. As Eastern Europeans themselves argued, communism failed because in "actual socialism" the state pursued its own interests not those of society. In delegation terms, this was a case of "agency failure" and even "agency reversal" between the state and its ostensible principal, society (Verdery 1991). The interaction between formal and informal runs throughout the chapters in this volume. Soft mesoanalysis emphasizes that elite institutions and elite interpretations "mediate" between apparent macrostructural "imperatives" and apparently "inevitable" macrostructural outcomes. Most volume authors emphasize this (Dickson, Tanner, Yang, Kraus and Suttmeier, Winckler on Asian transitions). Tanner in particular highlights ideological struggle—over the interpretation of organizational history and environment, and over the definition of organizational mission and methods—as a key mechanism of sectoral change within Leninist systems. (For a guide to this approach in this volume, see Index headings beginning with *Ideology*.)

Mesoanalysis can also improve *micro*analysis, by situating micromechanisms in the mesoinstitutions on which they depend. Several of the chapters in this volume do just that. For example, on the hard side, Yang argues that for Dengist China devolution of property rights does not by itself explain local developmentalism; it does so only when put in an institutional context of weak central-local macroeconomic control and weak central political institutions. On the soft side, following Douglass North, Tanner argues that for political leaders effectively to oversee a security agency requires ideological congruence between them, and finds such congruence problematic in late Dengist China.

A powerful "meso" approach to institutions, much used in comparative communism, analyzes them as mixes of *mechanisms*—classically markets, hierarchies, bargaining, and elections (Dahl and Lindblom 1953). Other mechanisms that are important for Leninism and transition are networks, culture, and agency. Mechanisms can combine into additional mechanisms—for example, networks and culture combine into professionalization and mobilization, both central to the discussion below. *Professionalization* is coordination through an elite culture of occupational expertise and vocational commitment, reinforced through professional networks. *Mobilization* is coordination through mass social networks and mass culture.

Mechanisms provide a rich institutional formulation of communism and transition, and provide a useful next step in analyzing sectors. In these terms, communism and transition have produced a spectrum of models for organizing sectors, ranging from pure mobilization on the left, through pure bureaucracy in the middle, to pure marketization on the right. In the Soviet Union, early "war" communism (1917–1921) was a hybrid of elite bureaucracy, revolutionary professionalism, and mass mobilization—essentially the application of military-revolutionary methods to economic and socio-cultural development. Mature "Stalinist" communism (1930s–1950s) gradually shifted from mobilizational professionalism to technological professionalism—essentially the application of heavy-industrial methods to all sectors. These are the radical-leftist and moderate-centrist models between which Maoist China later oscillated (Kaple 1994).

Late "Brezhnev" communism became a chronic case of state failure, plagued by bargaining between elites, punctuated by attempts to reform bureaucracy, and accompanied by covert "second" sectors: black markets, private networks, elite dissent, and mass resistance. Utopian Leninism provoked neopatrimonialism, which obstructed rational-legal reform (Jowitt 1992, McCormick 1990). In the absence of clear rules and real prices, policy was subject to protracted bargaining (Lampton 1992). Meanwhile, as periodic attempts to restore the centrist bureaucratic model increasingly failed, Dengist China gradually evolved a new rightist-marketizing socialism. The strength of the Dengist model was rapid market-induced economic growth; its weakness was the commercial corruption of other sectors (in this volume, see Winckler on the military and Kraus and Suttmeier on culture). Marketization increased bargaining and networking, not reduced them (Solinger 1989, Walder 1992, Naughton 1992a, Wank 1995). Thus postcommunism is a struggle to avoid the worst of three worlds—the legacy of a dysfunctional state and the prospect of unregulated markets, both permeated by personal networks.

This spectrum of models has informed much of comparative communism (e.g., Brzezinski 1969; or, on China, Harding 1981; Solinger 1984a, 1984b). It has also informed the work of some of this volume's authors. For example, Suttmeier early showed the changing combinations of bureaucracy, professionalism, and mobilization in the organization of science and technology in Maoist China (1974). Kraus showed the parallel changes in the organization of the arts, specifying the different relationships that the different models imply between artists and audiences (1984). In this volume, Tanner reports continuing debate within the police establishment over these same organizational alternatives: a Maoist mobilization model for struggling against class enemies and reversing marketization, a Leninist bureaucratic model for maintaining order despite marketization, and a liberal model for adapting police work to serve marketization and democratization.

The question here is to what extent identifying such mechanisms in historical processes constitutes explanation. Mechanisms do add some explanatory precision to macronarratives. For example, the mix of mechanisms is itself often a main political issue (e.g., Harding 1981). Moreover, as mesomodels, mechanisms do have some explanatory force—they have both their own inner logic and their own characteristically accompanying outer conditions, concomitants, and consequences (Etzioni 1961, Skinner and Winckler 1969, Whyte 1974). Nevertheless, mesomechanisms themselves require microexplanation. Despite recent microanalytic advances, social science still lacks a comprehensive theory of mechanisms that identifies all possible types and relates them to each other (but see Thompson et al. 1991, and below on the transaction cost approach).

Moreover, a theme that has emerged in even the most "hard" institutional literature is the *particularity* of such mechanisms—no two hierarchies or markets or network are exactly alike (Schanze 1996). The particularity of each manifestation of each mechanism results partly from the particular history of that mechanism, partly from particular admixtures of other mechanisms, and partly from the institutional environment in which that mechanism functions. This particularity affects analysis of Leninisms and their transitions by reinforcing attention to fine details of institutional variation and historical origins. (For example, see Walder's discussion of Nee's provocative "market transition" model, in Nee et al. 1996, and below on historical institutionalism.)

Microexplanation of Mesomechanisms: Williamson

The major approach to the microfoundations of mesomechanisms is transaction-cost economics. It deserves attention because of the power and persuasiveness of its formulation, and because its key concepts have become part of the intellectual infrastructure of comparative politics. Moreover, the associated "organizational failures framework" implies a possible theory of both stability and change, specifying under what circumstances a mechanism will survive or perish (Williamson 1975, 1985; Ouchi 1980). To what extent does such analysis explain Leninisms and their transitions?

Williamson argues that different kinds of transactions require different kinds of governance. His two main variables for distinguishing types of transaction are the frequency of transaction and the specificity of the assets involved (the extent to which they have few or many alternative uses). Ouchi distinguishes transactions according to incentives and information (goal incongruence and performance ambiguity) and extends the analysis from markets and hierarchies to networks. Thus *markets* can exchange standardized assets, regardless of the frequency of transactions, but fail when performance ambiguity or asset specificity raise transaction costs. *Hierarchies* can manage recurrent transactions about idiosyncratic assets but fail when both interest conflict and performance ambiguity raise transaction costs still higher. *Networks* can handle high asset specificity and performance ambiguity but require goal congruence and interpersonal trust (Ouchi 1980; Boisot 1986; on Eastern European transitions, Stark 1990). Some combinations of characteristics preclude any effective governance institution at all (e.g., high asset specificity and performance ambiguity in the absence of hierarchical coordination and interpersonal trust). This produces a fourth kind of organization that is merely *ritual*.

Even these elementary distinctions help characterize the range and change of communist models for sectoral organization. Thus, overall, as *formal* prescription, communism perceived capitalist markets as failing and substituted hierarchy. However, communist hierarchy itself failed, as its formal prescriptions became increasingly ritualistic. Limited reforms, through limited decentralization of bureaucracy and limited marketization of the economy, tried but failed to prevent this ritualization. Drastic reforms, through greatly increasing markets and manipulating rival bureaucracies, undermined hierarchy, producing transition.

In very broad terms, these characterizations do identify basic changes and help explain them. Communist institutions were not, as the theory requires, contractual arrangements in a competitive environment, which helps explain why they were so inefficient. Moreover, communism applied "one-size-fits-all" governance prescriptions that ignored the different requirements of different kinds of transactions. Postcommunism should succeed or fail to the extent that it creates a competitive market and to the extent that actors succeed in correctly matching institutions to transactions. However, the failures framework cannot explain the *details* of communism and early transition. (For example, one would not argue that it was an increase in interest conflict or performance ambiguity that had undermined communist hierarchy, or that it was a decline in performance ambiguity or asset specificity that had facilitated the rise of markets.) Nevertheless, the failures framework gains relevance as marketization gains sway. (For example, building institutions under postcommunism would be difficult if there were too much interest conflict or performance ambiguity for markets or hierarchies and too little trust for all but small-scale networks.)

By extending the typology of governance structures from bureaucracy and markets to networks, the transaction-cost approach also helps explain the *informal* underside of communism and transition (early recognized in Stark 1988, 1990). According to Williamson, occasional transactions about mixed assets (partly standardized, partly idiosyncratic) can be handled privately by the parties themselves with the help of an arbitrator, an arrangement intermediate between market and hierarchy. Frequent transactions about mixed assets justify the cost of building a strong relationship directly between the two parties themselves; such "relational contracting" is intermediate between market and network-culture.

Presumably these formulations help explain the long-standing role of guarantor-mediators in Chinese societies, the role of networks in Soviet-type economies, and the continuing role of personal networks in postreform Soviet and Chinese economic organization. For postreform China, relational contracting helps explain the role of such networks between firms, including how, path-dependently, they derive in part from networks between state and firms in the prereform economy (Solinger 1989).

Networks also help explain why, within firms, Chinese management has resisted both sovietization and westernization (Boisot and Child 1988, Child 1994).

The transaction-cost approach was originally intended to explain the choice of methods for managing transactions only within a capitalist economy. It is a tribute to its power that it also helps explain comparable choices within a socialist economy and during transition (Granick 1990, Solinger 1989). Moreover, in recognizing the basic opportunism of actors, the transaction-cost approach is already more political than conventional economics. Nevertheless, to explain communism and transition, the failures framework requires transposition, not only from capitalism to communism, but also from economics to politics and from statics to dynamics. Though this transposition may well be possible, it has not been fully accomplished. (For a preliminary formulation see North 1990; for similar concerns see Moe 1990; for recent progress see Solnick 1996.)

Thus first, economically, the framework assumes the emergence of "one best" governance structure for each type of transaction. However, the most recent transaction literature itself suggests that, even within capitalist economies, several alternative governance structures may perform equally well and may be used simultaneously, mostly because of the particular initial conditions and historical path through which the institutions were established (Schanze 1996). This introduces a note of indeterminacy into transaction analysis and directs attention to the history and particularity of each institutional formation. Moreover, even as formulated for economic organization in capitalist societies, the failures framework does not specify exactly how governance structures occur—evidently through some combination of deliberate adaptation and competitive elimination. In any case the mechanism would have to be reformulated for communisms and their transitions, where competitive pressures operate differently, if at all. For example, rival communist leaders sponsored rival programs for maximizing economic growth and political control.

Second, politically, the transaction-cost framework has modeled neither political intervention in economic processes nor political organization itself (but see Horn 1995). The highly political nature of economic management in communist countries requires addressing both. Capitalist economic "hierarchy" involves mostly private firms (which still face a market), while communist hierarchy included mostly government bureaucracy (which mostly did not face a market). Moreover, capitalist economic hierarchy involves many independent firms, whereas communist hierarchy involves a monopolistic party-state under dictatorial leadership. The transaction-cost approach may help explain why communist or postcommunist leaders choose particular mechanisms to manage particular transactions. This is particularly so if one assumes that the aim of communist leaders was to minimize transaction costs, not to the economy or the society, but to themselves (Silberman 1993, Horn 1995). Even so, although the transaction-cost approach may help show how the actors may evaluate alternatives, it does not much help analyze the strategic interactions through which the actors chose the outcome they did.

Third, the failures framework assumes the existence of the basic institutions such as political stability, property rights, and social solidarity (Solnick 1996). The failures framework predicts that such institutions will be economically necessary but   at least in its economic version—says little about how actors will go about providing them. Moreover, there are many combinations of economic institutions that might work for postcommunism, and it is not clear that the failures framework—again at least in its economic version—explains which ones are prevailing. At least in the short run, evidently the technical characteristics of economic transactions matter less than the political characteristics of the transition environment. After all, historically in China it has been the absence of the "legal centrism" of modern administration that forced economic actors to rely on "private ordering" by personal networks for *all kinds* of transactions. (For legal centrism versus private ordering on Taiwan see Winn 1994.) Similarly in postcommunist Russia, it is decline in political authority that has increased resort to private networks and shifted private ordering from normative and remunerative incentives toward the coercive sanctions (Handelman 1995).

In sum, the failures framework may help explain the long-run economic failure of communism, but it does not much illuminate its actual collapse, at least in the central case of the Soviet Union. What killed Soviet communism was not its chronic ailments but the medicine it took to try to cure them. The immediate cause of economic collapse was a series of economic reforms and economic policies that devastated the old system without substituting a new one (Ellman and Kontorovich 1992, Introduction). Gorbachev weakened the previously crucial economic coordination roles of the bureaucracy, ideology, and party. He weakened the economy itself through renewed investment in heavy industry that misallocated resources and fueled inflation. Similarly, the immediate cause of political collapse was a series of political reforms that, again, undermined the old system without substituting anything coherent in its place. Gorbachev tried to sidestep party institutions by transferring functions to government institutions, while at the same time maintaining party control over government institutions by staffing them with party personnel. However, the shift in institutional venue created platforms from which rivals could challenge him, particularly when combined with the inauguration of elections and the repudiation of the ideology that had previously legitimized the system. For analyzing such chaotic and strategic events, game theory may prove more helpful than transaction costs.

Sectoral Analysis

Comparative politics has lively literatures that analyze particular policy domains, such as civil-military relations (e.g., Perlmutter 1977), financial organization (e.g., Zysman 1983), and social programs (e.g., Esping-Anderson 1990). However, social science has posited surprisingly little general theory for comparing state sectors (though see Horn 1995, discussed below). This section explores what a theory of sectors might contain and how it might illuminate Leninisms and their transitions. The section begins by noting two major theories of differentiation between states and between sectors, then explores differences between sectors within states. In particular, we explore the degree of delegation and its determinants, and their likely consequences for transition. Are there intrinsic differences between sectors in the technical and social characteristics of the functions they perform that affect delegation? For political systems in general, these are issues that have been much discussed for some institutions within some sectors (e.g., economic and civil-military), less discussed for others (social and cultural), and seldom systematically compared across all sectors. Yet such a framework is needed for comparing Leninisms and their transitions. Did different sectors pose different problems for Leninist systems as they tried to minimize delegation? Did delegations in different sectors have different propensities to "slip," contributing differentially to transition?

This section pursues these issues by noting for each sector some main delegation relationships and some main variables affecting the degree and stability of that delegation. We focus on the relationship between the "party center" and the professional elites within each sector. The party's objective was to craft a delegation that would allow professionals enough latitude to work effectively, but that would limit that latitude through close supervision by bureaucratic administrators who were politically reliable (Walder 1995a). That delegation relationship was inherently problematic, since professionals in principle reject bureaucratic authority over their expertise and identify instead with a professional community, which is not only supra-organizational but also supranational. In different regimes at different times the party center made different trade-offs in its relationship with professionals, ranging from Stalin's promotion to Mao's denigration. Most of the formulations reviewed in this section focus on determinants internal to the relationship between principal and agent. However, we attempt to place those relationships in their social contexts, particularly political institutions, both formal and informal.

Differentiation Between States and Sectors

A major recent theory of differentiation between *states* is Bernard Silberman's explanation of why the modern states that emerged in the late nineteenth century took the different forms that they did (1993). His analysis should apply to postcommunist societies attempting to rebuild their partially collapsed states in the late twentieth century. The two main dimensions of the *outcome* concern whether administrators are *professionals or bureaucrats,* and whether administrators are coordinated through *networks or parties.* In Britain, administrators were professionals coordinated through elite networks, while in the United States they were professionals subject to appointment by competing mass parties. In Japan following the Meiji revolution, administrators were bureaucrats coordinated through elite networks, while in post-revolutionary France and the post-revolutionary Soviet Union they were bureaucrats appointed by a single party.

Silberman *explains* these differences as responses to different levels of uncertainty about the rules for elite succession (*regular elections versus revolutionary transformation*), in the context of the different availability of alternative mechanisms for making administrators accountable to political leaders (*social networks versus party organization*). High uncertainty about succession rules encouraged emphasis on bureaucratic hierarchy, while low uncertainty allowed delegation to technocratic professionals. This suggests that during Leninist transitions *resolving succession problems may be a prerequisite for professionalization* of state administration. In the 1990s, China still faces much uncertainty about succession, and the leadership has reacted not merely by maintaining hierarchy, but even by installing many of its own children to guarantee that successors will be revolutionary (Lam 1995).

When political leaders and government administrators emerged from a common social network or social stratum, political leaders were more willing to grant autonomy to bureaucratic hierarchies. When politicians and bureaucrats did *not* have a common social background, politicians resorted to strong oversight through a political party, as in the original design of the Leninist cases. In other words, in managing delegation, some substitution may be possible between hard political-economic methods of explicit external oversight and soft sociocultural methods of internalization and implicit trust (Putnam 1995, Landa 1994). This suggests that, in Leninist transformations, *informal network solidarity within the elite may be a prerequisite for formal separation of party and government.* Such solidarity could have resulted from long common experience during revolutionary struggle to install communism. It might emerge under communism itself in the form of a "new class" ruling elite. Or it might emerge during the transition from communism as an amalgam of old party and new business elites. Perhaps on the basis of such solidarities, in the 1980s China moved toward some separation of party and government. However, after the Tiananmen challenge from counterelites, China reverted toward direct party control.

Until recently the main proposal for a theory of differentiation between *sectors* came from sociology and referred as much to society as to state

(Scott and Meyer 1991). It analyzed the effect on organizations of the demands placed on them by their social and technical environments—in particular, for the postwar United States, national government regulation and local task requirements. Here "sector" means simply a category of analytically similar organizations. *High technical demands* require production efficiency, as in manufacturing. *High social demands* require organizational conformity, as in the professions. Both *high social and technical demands*—as in finance and infrastructure—produce strong organizations with large administrative components and much internal conflict. Conversely, *low social and technical demands*—as in personal services— produce simple, weak, and evanescent organizations. In the United States, growing postwar national social programs produced growing national administrative regulation and growing local organizational complexity. On this model, Leninist systems should have very high national administrative regulation and very high complexity within each local organization, while Leninist transitions should reduce both.

Evidently Leninist party-states did implicitly recognize such distinctions, since they usually did monopolize most activities whose high technical or social demands require strong organization. Conversely, initial reforms usually privatize first activities whose low technical and social demands require only weak organizations (e.g., retail marketing and personal services). Hence the organizational "dualism" that often figures in transitions—the strong, large-scale, formal, public, and statist versus the weak, small-scale, informal, private, and popular. (On China see Davis et al. 1996, White, Howell, and Shang 1996.) Moreover, it *may* be that during some Leninist transitions national intervention declines, allowing local organization to become less standardized by national social regulations and more differentiated according to local technical requirements. However, in Russia, much of communist organization persists, particularly at the local level (Friedgut and Hahn 1994). In China, economic decentralization has been accompanied by political recentralization and *increased* political standardization (Huang 1996). Economic decentralization has substantially *increased* the complexity of local government, whether centrally standardized or locally differentiated remains to be seen (Shue 1995). Pursuing such issues requires distinguishing functions.

Political-Economic Delegation in the Development Sector

Within the development sector, the main delegation relationship is between the political leadership and economic managers—under communism from the "party center" to ministry officials, local governments, and enterprise managers; during transition also to collective firms and private businesses. Economic delegation has always been central to analysis of communism, as in interwar debates over the feasibility of "market socialism" and postwar critiques of Soviet overcentralization (e.g., as summarized in Nove 1983). As regards managers, the delegation problem involves both internal and external components—both organizational incentives for managers to perform well and environmental marketization to enable them to do so. A further question is whether delegation from the party center is only administrative (to local party-states) or genuinely economic (to business firms). Analysis of Europe stresses that either way, so long as state socialism persisted, managers remained subject to its distinctive economic logics, particularly chronic shortage and perpetual bailouts (Kornai 1992).

In China, as in other communist systems, economic planning was too subject to elite political intervention and too autonomous from social demands. Nevertheless, China raises the possibility of a happier hybrid of state and market. Administratively, analysis of postwar China has traced its distinctive propensity for decentralization of economic activities from central to local governments, and the resulting competition for development between localities (e.g., Jia and Lin 1994, Yang 1997 and this volume). At all levels of administration, government retains a large role as owner, manager, and entrepreneur. Although sometimes economically inefficient, government intervention promotes local welfare and prevents political unrest (Oi 1992, 1999). Economically, in China marketization penetrated the state sector faster than anticipated, and even state firms responded (Byrd 1991, Hay et al. 1994). Privatization of ownership is not the only way to improve information and incentives; recrafting delegation between owners and managers is an alternative (Milor 1993, Wang 1998). Local governments become holding companies, supervising local conglomerates in the pursuit of economic competitiveness (Child 1994).

As noted above, principal-agent theory originated in the analysis of contracts in capitalist economies (Eatwell, Milgate, and Newman 1989, chapters by Stiglitz, and others). Despite its economic origins, agency theory does not suggest any easy formulas for what type or degree of economic delegation to expect, even in private firms, let alone in government economic organization. (On this problem for economic regulation, see Noll 1985, and discussion of Horn 1995 below.) Instead, the literature on economic agency usually assumes some type of delegation, then analyzes what incentive and information arrangements will maximize the principal's interests. The analogous political science literature too mostly presupposes some type of delegation and then analyzes what makes it work (e.g., McCubbins and Schwartz 1984, Lupia and McCubbins 1994, on centralized versus decentralized monitoring).

Margaret Levi's analysis of historical tax systems suggests that *economic delegation should vary with rulers' bargaining power, transaction costs and discount rates* (1988). Applying Levi's analysis to Leninist systems underlines the crudeness of the tax systems on which communism relied—mostly confiscating the profits of state-owned enterprises. Levi's analysis should also suggest how, during transition, changes in rulers' leverage, legitimacy, and likely political longevity may influence changes in state economic administration. The challenge during transition is to create the more sophisticated and voluntary tax systems necessary for long-run development, while avoiding the predation and corruption that shortening time horizons make attractive to politicians. Certainly these have been problems in China. Historically the central government allowed a large rake-off by local agents because it lacked the capacity to collect taxes directly. Chinese communism compounded this problem by delegating most industry to provincial management. Post-1949 history has been a ceaseless search for a stable delegation of fiscal responsibility between center and localities, punctuated by periodic recentralizations at moments of economic crisis and fiscal uncertainty (Oksenberg and Tong 1991, Tong this volume). Meanwhile corruption is rising.

Murray Horn's recent analysis of modern state economic administration suggests that the form of economic delegation should differ according to the transaction costs to the enacting legislature. These include not only the cost of legislating and monitoring, but also the cost of preventing future legislatures from changing policy (1995). This suggests that under Leninism and transition, *delegation may differ according to the degree of polarization within the ruling elite and the security of tenure of the dominant coalition.* A temporary majority that fears it may lose power to another faction may delegate functions so that a rival future majority will be unable to retrieve them and change policy. This may be one reason why both Mao and Deng delegated economic functions to subnational governments. One can also regard internationalization as a form of upward delegation that can have the same effect, even if unintentionally (my reading of Shirk 1996).

Silberman's argument that networks facilitate delegation suggests another hypothesis for future comparison of Leninist economic transitions. Under Leninism, the less that economic elites were inherited from the pre-communist period and the more that they have been recruited during the communist period, the easier it should have been for the party to maintain economic control and the more willing the party should have been to delegate authority to economic bureaus and professionals. Moreover, *in the short run, professionalization may impede transition*—for example, by instilling a commitment to planning or by attaching professionals to the regime. Technocratization may be the most change that a compromise between orthodoxy and pragmatism can produce (Dong 1994). However, *in the long run, professionalization may promote transition*—through commitment to professionalism over personalism, to development over defense, and to consensus over coercion as a basis for political stability. Moreover, during marketization, technocrats fare much better economically than politicians (see the comments by several discussants in Nee et al. 1996).

Analysis of economic delegation in Leninist systems has become increasingly precise, inspired by neo-institutional analysis of capitalist economies and propelled by the accelerating devolution of communist economies. A main theme is agency reversal—de facto transfer of property rights from erstwhile principal to former agent (e.g., on China, Granick 1990; Montinola, Qian, and Weingast 1995). In this volume, Tong argues that in China under Mao high levels of ideology and coercion in the institutional environment helped hold inadvertent economic devolution in check, while under Deng growing economism required perfecting principal-agent contracts themselves. For the reform period, Shirk has emphasized the political logic of economic delegation, attributing China's incremental economic decentralization to the growing influence of subnational leaders within the party Central Committee (1993). Montinola, Qian, and Weingast have praised the resulting de facto federalization of property rights as a main cause of China's increasing efficiency and prosperity (1995). Others emphasize the continuing uncertainty surrounding those property rights that results from capricious intervention by central leaders (Shirk 1993, Yang this volume).

Overall, in the development sector, slippage toward inadvertent delegation appears quite likely. Certainly in China it is in the economy that decentralization from central to local government has proceeded the furthest. Economic goals require motivating and coordinating a wide range of desired behaviors, which requires granting agents much autonomy. Auditing may prevent misuse of resources, but agents command resources with which to suborn auditors. Nevertheless, in the economy too during the 1990s, China's central party-state has maintained the capacity to reassert its prerogatives as economic principal in industry and finance, in the extraction and distribution of revenue, and in foreign economic relations (Huang 1996, Tong and Yang this volume). In any case, to be effective economically, delegation during transition should enable the party center to retain the autonomy from business that it needs for effective policymaking, while achieving the "embeddedness" in policy networks that it needs for informed decisions (Evans 1995). To be effective politically, transitional delegation should give old political elites new economic opportunities without provoking mass discontent at elite corruption, while retaining ultimate control over potential political uses of economic resources.

Military-Political Delegation in the Security Sector

Within the security sector, the main delegation relationship is between the civilian political leadership and the military. In Leninist systems, the party center represents the civilians in this relationship, and security institutions may include a strong police. Most countries keep military affairs highly centralized under the chief executive, as Winckler describes in Chapter 3 for China. During transition, the independence of the police, courts, and legislature also become an issue, as Tanner discusses for the police in this volume.

Leninist security delegation too may provide some support for Silberman's hypothesis that *networks facilitate delegation.* The closer the origins and the longer the fusion of party and army, the more likely that the military will continue to support the party against mass challenge, because they share a communist definition of nationalism and because their institutional interests overlap (Perlmutter and LeoGrande 1982). This contrast exists even between the indigenous revolutions—the party and army were less fused in the USSR than in the PRC. However, it is even sharper between the independent and satellite cases (Eastern European communist parties relied on the Russian military and their own political police, not on their domestic militaries, which were too nationalistic).

As regards the impact of professionalization on transitions, the more *professionalized* the military, the *less* likely that it will support the party against mass challenge, because a professionalized military places loyalty to nation above loyalty to party (Taylor 1995). As the effects of any common historical origins decline, and the effects of professionalization rise, one might expect a decline in the effectiveness of party efforts to maintain control of the military through politicization, in the sense of inculcating loyalty to the ruling party. Evidently professionalization had this effect in the former Soviet Union and may have this effect in China in the future.

Recently Peter Feaver has transferred delegation theory from civilian to military affairs (1996b). As he notes, the main difference from civilian applications of delegation theory concerns incentives—the stakes are much higher in military affairs, given the danger of foreign defeat or domestic coup. Another difference is greater information uncertainty and therefore less information asymmetry—neither the civilian principal nor the military agent can predict military outcomes, justifying some role for both in military decisions. A simplified summary of Feaver's analysis is that four clusters of variables affect the extent of delegation of particular military tasks from civilians to military. Two clusters of *technical variables* are the intrinsic difficulty of the task (including intra-elite communication and doctrinal change) and the incompleteness of information surrounding it (including state secrecy and media role). *The more difficult the task and the less complete the information, the greater the delegation.* Two clusters of *social variables* are the importance of the issue (to both civilians and military) and the degree of disagreement (not only between civilians and military but also between civilians themselves). *The more important the issue and the greater the disagreement, the less the delegation.*

These variables can be applied retrospectively to communist civil-military relations and prospectively to postcommunist ones. During transition, the likely changes may be offsetting. On the technical side, the difficulty of task should increase—assertion of civilian control should complicate intra-elite communication and may involve doctrinal change. However, information should become more complete, to the extent that state secrecy declines and the media become more active. On the social side, as newly independent post-Soviet and post-satellite states assume responsibility for their own security, the importance of security to both civilians and military should increase, possibly increasing the degree of dissensus. For example, in many postcommunist states it may be unclear what level of defense, or degree of association with the West, optimizes the balance between deterring Russia and provoking it. (Of course, these variables must be specified for particular security tasks and organizational missions.)

Overall, in the security sector, inadvertent "slippage" toward unintended delegation appears least likely. Order goals require only preventing a narrow range of unwanted behavior. Security concerns imply a vigilance that facilitates monitoring not only mass misbehavior but also the potential misuse of security assets by security sector elites. The need of states to monopolize force militates against privatizing the means of destruction. The prospect that once major security slippage occurs it is likely to be irreversible provides an additional incentive for vigilance (Winckler on military in Chapter 3 this volume). Here, in China, the center has never intentionally decentralized and recently somewhat recentralized. Nevertheless, in China one can detect at least some minor slippage. At the national level the military is, if not out of civil control, at least achieving a new political equilibrium with civilians, particularly over security policy. At the subnational level, social order has clearly deteriorated, and the state may be returning toward a historic equilibrium that concedes some coercive control to local elites, except when they egregiously abuse it.

Sociocultural Delegation in the Legitimation Sector

Within the legitimation sector, the main delegation relationship is between the party center and the intelligentsia, including the professionals providing social and cultural services. Few communist countries had social or cultural institutions that retained much independence of the Communist Party (the best-known partial exception being the Catholic Church in Poland). Nevertheless, social and cultural elites did retain some professional autonomy over their specialized domains, and even some general role as critical intellectuals (Verdery 1991). In this volume, Kraus and Suttmeier compare the adaptations of artistic and technical elites during transition in China, finding them proponents of modernization but not necessarily of democratization.

Historically, in most countries that later became communist, the training and employment of social and cultural professionals had been largely public not private (Jones 1991). This probably facilitated later party-state control. In addition, the more that, under communism, the party-state was able to produce its own professionals, the easier control should have been and the more willing the party should have been to delegate social and cultural functions. Nevertheless, Leninist regimes have been only ambiguously successful in maintaining a "velvet cage" around professionals to whom they delegated the autonomy to enliven culture (on China see Pickowitz 1995). On the one hand, the regimes did largely control cultural content. On the other hand, intellectuals' critiques did contribute to the regimes' delegitimation, even in China (Ding 1994). During transition, new elites within the old regime may adopt technocracy as an ideology with which to relegitimize themselves (on China see Dong 1994).

So far, delegation theory has not been much applied to social and cultural domains, so does not yet explain these outcomes. Some of Feaver's variables should require only minor respecification (e.g., importance of issue and degree of disagreement). However, others may require some rethinking in light of the distinctive characteristics of social and cultural tasks (e.g., difficulty of task and completeness of information). Social and cultural policies often involve matters about which information is inherently incomplete, such as social values or cultural worth, which complicates communication and consensus. Consequently, social and cultural goals are less amenable than order goals to bureaucracy and less amenable than economic goals to markets, requiring more professionalism.

To elaborate these points, we focus on cultural policy, since it is most different from economic and security policies, and most directly relevant to legitimation. The distinctive problem that culture poses for crafting delegation is that cultural materials are inherently *polysemous*—the more interesting they are the more possible meanings they contain, and therefore the more politically subversive they can be (Frye 1957, Clark 1981, Winckler 1993). This ambiguity invites disagreement among policymakers, who cannot find objective criteria for either political correctness or cultural merit. It creates a steep trade-off between political orthodoxy and cultural creativity in the management of cultural professionals, who tend to be diverse and free-thinking. In addition, the further that reform proceeds, the more autonomy cultural professionals require to do their jobs, the more the state depends on cultural professionals to advance development, and the less the state can afford to discriminate between technical experts and nonscientific intellectuals (Goldman 1996). Finally, the ambiguity of cultural materials creates a steep trade-off between propaganda and popularity with the mass public, who interpret cultural products in ways that are not only diverse, but also increasingly diverge from the official interpretation as transition proceeds (on China see Wasserstrom and Perry 1992, Lull 1991).

These distinctive problems of managing culture particularly threaten communist systems, whose rationale rests on their ideological correctness. Consequently, communist leaders attempt to minimize delegation of authority over culture, particularly ideology. During personalistic periods, official culture may narrow to the leader's pronouncements, but these cannot meet all cultural needs. During periods of more institutionalized rule, at the elite level, the leadership may attempt "question-and-answer" formulations prescribing both the allowable questions and the permitted answers (Schoenhals 1993). At the mass level, the party-state attempts to dominate cultural space, fielding official versions of popular culture intended to preempt unofficial ones—for example, state-popularized music versus independent rock music in China (Jones 1992). Such expedients do not prevent all elite critical thinking or all mass symbolic resistance, but they do inhibit their dissemination and diffusion. Stated more theoretically, given the crucial role that communication plays in achieving the cooperation and coordination necessary for institutional change, the party center's control of public discourse is a crucial political asset (extrapolating from Calvert 1995). Part of the explanation may be incentives—people believe in official ideology and are motivated by it. However, much of the explanation is information—official ideology blocks alternative communications.

Overall, in the legitimation sector, slippage toward inadvertent delegation appears only somewhat likely. Intellectual agents have few assets with which to influence their political principals. Moreover, during transition, intellectuals are likely to be upstaged by politicians and businesspeople (Kraus and Suttmeier this volume). The autonomy of an elite cultural institution, having facilitated initiating transition, may complicate consolidating it (e.g., the Catholic Church in Poland). In China, commercialization of elite and popular culture certainly has opened up cultural space that is somewhat independent of the party-state (Zha 1995; Pei 1994, chapters on Chinese and Soviet media). Nevertheless, in post-Mao China the center has repeatedly reined in cultural liberalization, most dramatically after the 1989 Tiananmen incident (Baum 1994, Goldman 1996). Moreover, continuing control of politically sensitive areas of culture remains a basic party policy, as reflected during the 1990s in Jiang Zemin's renewed emphasis on constructing a "socialist spiritual civilization," and in renewed restrictions on media ownership and information flow, particularly from abroad (Zhao 1998, 175–180). In theory, ideological goals still require positively motivating and coordinating a broad range of prescribed behaviors. In practice, preempting cultural space and preventing proscribed communications may suffice for regime survival.

Temporal Dynamics

The upshot of my discussion of analytical levels was that the more theoretically precise that explanations of Leninisms and their transitions become, the more historical specificity they require. This directs attention to temporal change. Recently both hard and soft approaches have turned toward more explicit analysis along the temporal dimension (e.g., hard extended game theory and nonlinear dynamics or "chaos theory"; soft historical institutionalism and historically situated critical theory). Studies of Leninist transitions too have taken a temporal turn—for example, seeking the origins of distinctive transitions in distinctive earlier crises (e.g., Ekiert 1996, Yang 1996). Turning to history need not mean abandoning generalization, since it is general processes whose conjunctions define particular historical situations. However, turning to history does involve some redefinition of what constitutes an explanation of particular outcomes.

First we note the strengths and weaknesses of hard microapproaches, in which institutional change remains largely exogenous. Second we look further into path dependence, a more explicitly temporal hard approach that combines macro- and microelements. Third we consider historical institutionalism, an emphatically temporal soft macroapproach. Throughout, the basic issues are the relationship between stability and change, and the relationship between gradual and abrupt change.

Microanalysis of Stability and Change

Recent microanalytic formulations have contradictory implications for stability and change.

On the one hand, microanalysis suggests that, if institutions can be established at all, they are likely to *persist*. In part institutions persist because, once established, they involve sunk costs and vested interests that make them hard to discard (North 1990, discussed below). In part institutions persist because it is hard to coordinate action to achieve change, even within elites, let alone masses (Olson 1965). Most generally, institutions may persist because they are equilibria—sets of behaviors that mutually reinforce each other (Calvert 1994, 1995).

Overcoming collective action dilemmas is particularly difficult under Leninism, where major institutions are devoted to aggravating them for potential dissidents (controlling information, deploying incentives). Leninism may also have involved a series of partial equilibria. After crises such as leader reforms or mass revolts, at least some Leninisms did either return to a previous equilibrium (e.g., after Khrushchev's attempted reforms) or broke down (e.g., during Gorbachev's attempted reforms). Nevertheless, an institutions-as-equilibria explanation for the persistence of Leninism would ignore the tremendous input of propaganda and coercion that Leninist leaders found necessary to maintain their systems. One could as easily argue that these systems were in perpetual *disequilibrium,* with strong tendencies to stray from their erstwhile communist paths (Kornai 1980, 1992; Davis and Charmeza 1989).

Thus, on the other hand, microtheories show the *fragility* of order. Coordination to achieve and maintain stability too is difficult, again because of collective action dilemmas and transaction costs, this time within the Establishment. Hard microanalysis reveals the vertical dilemmas faced by managers of hierarchies (Miller 1992), while soft microanalysis shows how domination produces resistance (Scott 1990). Again game theory is most general, showing the impossibility of stable social choice and indeterminacy between multiple equilibria (McKelvey 1976, Fudenberg and Maskin 1986). Applying game theory to democratizing transitions, Gary Marks has distinguished between situations that lack strategic interaction between Establishment and Opposition and those that display it (1992). Without interaction, the outcome of stability or change depends on unilateral assessments by each side that are relatively objective but still unpredictable. With strategic interaction, the outcome depends heavily on evolving subjective assessments of each side by the other that are still more unpredictable.

These theoretical results *may* help explain the breakdown of Leninist hierarchy. Overall, it was difficult for top leaders to contain the tensions within ongoing Leninist institutions (Verdery 1991); it proved impossible to do so while conducting drastic reform (Solnick 1996). More specifically, to the extent that they refused to tolerate opposition, early post-totalitarian regimes have lacked strategic interaction and therefore have either remained brittlely stable or unexpectedly entered "transition through collapse." To the extent that they have allowed opposition (e.g., Poland), late post-totalitarian regimes have displayed strategic interaction and entered a gradual but unpredictable "transition through transaction." Other microanalyses of Leninist transitions address specific institutions (e.g., Hellman 1993 on the Soviet central bank; Solnick 1993, 1998 on the Soviet youth organization).

Recently game theory has shifted from one-shot conflict games to iterated coordination games, which are more typical of human interaction. This implies concern with actors' time horizons, discount rates, and risk preferences. It implies concern also with the *credibility* of actors' present commitments to future acts and therefore concern with reputation and trust (Yang this volume). A temporal turn also implies concern about the *reversibility* of current policy commitments and with strategies for making policies irreversible in the future (Horn 1995).

Nevertheless, game theory still has little to say about the actual process of change. Most work theorizes stability not change. Indeed some argue that the most that social science can do is to explain stability and should not pretend to have a theory of change, particularly during crises (e.g., Fiorina and Shepsle 1982). Particularly where there is strategic interaction between the ruling elite and political opposition, outcomes are unpredictable, not because of the complexity of the situation, the weakness of theory, or the incompleteness of data, but because they depend on small changes in subtle variables involving the actors' expectations about each other (Marks 1992).

In game theory, disequilibrium results within the game from actor error or changes in actors' beliefs and preferences, or outside the game from changes in the payoffs to the actors caused by changes in the environment. (The latter resemble the "change in relative prices" in North 1990 or the "change in the distribution of resources" in Levi 1990.) This helps identify causes of change but does not explain them. Thus applications of game theory to transitions confirm that such soft variables as beliefs and preferences, communication and trust, history and circumstance are indeed central to large-scale political disintegration and reconstruction (Kitschelt 1993 on Przeworski 1991). However, game theory seems unlikely to explain actor error or environmental change, and the extent to which it can explain changes in actors' beliefs and preferences remains to be seen. Ultimately these depend on the particular macrohistorical parameters, mesoinstitutional practices, and microindividual preferences that define the particular "game" being played. Thus even game theory must turn to history for its parameters.

Path Dependence

We now turn toward a more explicitly temporal approach, *path dependence*. The most elaborate statement for whole societies is by Douglass North (1990). His formulation of how societies persist despite being dysfunctional helps explain the *stability* of Leninism. North argues that societies are neither "best" cases of perfectly efficient equilibria, nor even "second best" equilibria that are merely somewhat imperfect because of current transaction costs. Instead, societies are typically only "third best" arrangements, because of how they evolved. Initial historical conditions and small chance events set societies onto idiosyncratic paths. Self-reinforcing mechanisms create *increasing returns* within this path, while *imperfect markets* perpetuate them through high transaction costs and poor information. Thus the dysfunctionality of Leninism was not unusual, and to understand it requires historical studies, including differences between countries.

North's characterization of how *change* occurs helps explain transition from Leninism. North acknowledges the possibility of abrupt change but argues that most change is gradual. Incremental changes in prices and ideas produce continuous renegotiation of contracts and rules. For Leninist transitions, this underlines the strong component of gradual evolution that preceded what otherwise appears to be abrupt revolution. Moreover, North argues, apparently discontinuous change is seldom as discontinuous as it appears: Formal rules change more rapidly than informal constraints, which limit the amount of change. He mentions backsliding during the transition *to* socialism as an example, but his point applies to the transition *from* socialism as well. In many postcommunist transformations, initial superficial revolution has given way to protracted and even regressive evolution (Lewis 1995).

Nevertheless, Leninisms and their transitions suggest the need for more analysis of sudden change—of crises themselves, of postcrisis reconstruction, and of the enduring consequences of both. Thus for the European Leninisms, George Ekiert argues that it was the major crises of 1956, 1968, and 1981 that defined and differentiated the communisms in Hungary, Czechoslovakia, and Poland and eventually set them onto different transition paths (1996). For the European transitions themselves, "hard" analysts have resorted to "tipping phenomena" and "information cascades" to explain the suddenness and rapidity of change (Kuran 1991, Lohmann 1994). For China, Dali Yang has shown how it was the calamity of Great Leap famine that prepared the ground for agricultural reform when the political system allowed it. Addressing North's formulation, Yang argues that "the very notion of path dependence calls for the opposite idea of path rupture" and requires review of the sequences of changes that established the path (1996, 249).

Moreover, North's formulations of change are quite general—for example, it is hard to use them to pinpoint the *differences* between communisms and their transitions. Nevertheless, path dependence is easier to identify than underlying equilibria and points to researchable practical questions: What does it take to make leaders look for a new path (Dickson this volume)? What costs do leaders encounter when trying to switch paths (Naughton 1995)? Does the country in fact change paths? Such questions could provide an orderly formulation of the extent to which the past determines the present during Leninist transitions. For example, is China precluded from having democracy because it never experienced decentralized feudalism, as a deterministic reading of Downing (1992) would suggest? Or is democracy now available to any country, as Friedman (1995) voluntaristically claims? A serious exploration of this issue would identify main branching points in countries with contrasting outcomes and estimate the likely costs of changing paths.

That path dependence is fundamental to historical processes points to the significance of the temporal dimension in analytical typologies. Neither social systems nor cultural discourses can move cleanly from one type to another. Rather they bear the impress of the type from which they have just moved, and typological categories themselves should reflect that. Thus it is no accident that "post" appears in so many analytical labels, not least the Linz and Stepan ideal type of "post-totalitarian" regime (1996).

Historical Institutionalism

Finally, we note the main tenets of a still more explicitly temporal approach, historical institutionalism (Steinmo, Thelen, and Longstreth 1992, Orren and Skowroneck 1995).

First, historical institutionalists emphasize that real institutions are not just neutral mechanisms but rather *embody purposes and exert control.* (Similarly, Knight 1992 stresses that institutions are not attempts to maximize collective benefits but rather by-products of distributive conflicts.) Emphasizing purposiveness and control may provide a needed corrective to mainstream Western accounts of Western institutions, which portray market equilibria or constitutional democracy as impartial. This corrective is less needed for mainstream Western accounts of communism, which always regarded totalitarianism as highly purposive and controlling. However, during transition, the caution about assuming the impartiality of Western institutions becomes relevant again in analyzing the choice and functioning of new institutions (e.g., Lijphart 1992). For China, this suggests going beyond the obvious formal communist purposes and formal Leninist controls to a more circumstantial reappraisal of the actually operative ideologies and organizations—for example, in control over farmers, women, and minorities, (e.g., Gilmartin et al. 1994, Zito and Barlow 1994, Gladney 1991, Harrell 1995).

Second, historical institutionalists emphasize that new institutions emerge not from an organizationally blank state of nature, but *from old institutions.* This remains largely true even for revolutionary situations, in which new regimes are constructed at least in part from the debris of old regimes. For European transitions, Stark early remarked that postcommunism has been built not *on* the ruins but *from* the ruins of state socialism (1992). A prime example is that some former communist parties have survived in opposition and even returned to power by performing democratic functions (Ishayama 1995, Mahr and Nagle 1995).

In Asia there has been even more continuity—so far, not ruins but reconstruction. Under evolutionary transformation, it becomes even more elusive whether a particular institution is perpetuating Leninism or accomplishing transition. For example, as regards ruling parties, on Taiwan the KMT democratized the rules and itself without ever leaving power. Or, Chinese state birth planning itself remains "totalitarian" in its intrusiveness and campaign implementation (Winckler Chapter 7 this volume). At the same time, Chinese social policy as a whole has become merely "authoritarian," to the extent that it has become more selective (birth planning is the main remaining state intervention in private social life) and more institutionalized (economic incentives and legal procedures are replacing crash campaigns).

Third, real regimes include *overlapping cohorts of institutions,* introduced at different times, pursuing different purposes, and operating on conflicting logics. Functional harmony might explain a static stability if either existed, but it is dissonant diversity that explains both systemic robustness and systemic change (Orren and Skowronek 1995). If dissonance is present in stable regimes, it should be more characteristic of fluctuations within regimes and even more prevalent in transitions between regimes.

In fact the historical-institutionalist credo has long been practiced by comparative communism, which has often identified recurring tensions within mixes of mechanisms, particularly in China. Maoist communism abjured markets but tried different combinations of bureaucracy and mobilization (Skinner and Winckler 1969; Harding 1981; Solinger 1984a, 1984b). Dengist transition involved the gradual evolution of new mixes of mechanisms—mostly professionalized bureaucracy and marketized networks (e.g., Solinger 1989, Baum 1994, Naughton 1995). In this volume, Tanner reports the overlap and conflict between competing visions of the history and future of police work, and Kraus and Suttmeier describe crisis and reconstitution in the rules governing the production of culture.

An analytical-historical approach to sectoral organization—stylized characterization of particular mixes and sequences of mechanisms in particular sectors in particular countries—should remain a useful grid for comparing regime type and regime change within and across regions. Of course, returning to history should not become an excuse for abandoning analysis. The challenge is to use historical complexity and analytical complexity to illuminate each other—to confront overlapping cohorts of purposive institutions with complex models of multiple games and interacting mechanisms. Just as analysis situated in historical context is no longer mere generalized abstraction, so history informed by analytical questions is no longer mere chronological narrative.

Conclusion: Institutionalism and Beyond

This Conclusion has compared theoretical approaches to explaining Leninist transitions—macro and micro, political-economic and sociocultural, static and dynamic. This volume has attempted to chart a mesoinstitutional, multisectoral, and intertemporal path between them. The purpose has not been to advance one approach to discredit another, but rather to use all approaches to improve explanation. As both the existing literature and these volume chapters illustrate, these rival approaches are complementary not opposing.

As an antidote to this ecumenical approach, we conclude with three caveats. The first concerns the particular mix of processes most central to transitions from Leninism. The editor's Introduction and Conclusion to this volume have favored starting from the heuristic assumption that all functional sectors, structural levels, and temporal dynamics are involved. Nevertheless, an explanation of any particular event or transition must, after empirical examination, commit to some particular mix of these processes. For example, for Leninist transitions in general, arguably the nature of old-regime Leninist institutions made a coercive party-state enduringly central (Dickson this volume). Even China's early and gradual economic transformation has remained constrained by powerful party, military, and police institutions (Dickson, Winckler, and Tanner this volume, respectively). Departure from communist central planning gradually undermines Leninist party rule, but politics still does not reduce entirely to economics (Huang 1996). The coercive military-police and party-organizational foundations of Leninist rule are harder to research than the economic transformation of communism because, paradoxically for self-proclaimed Marxists, Leninist rulers consider them more fundamental.

The second caveat results from the diversity of institutional approaches. To preserve the integrity of each, one should avoid "stretching" labels from one to the other. For example, an explanation may be solidly institutional simply because it focuses on institutions (e.g., Linz and Stepan 1996, 328–333). It may be *neo*-institutional in spirit if it analyzes such hard variables as incentives and information or strategies in a game (e.g., Winckler and Yang this volume). Or it may be *new*-institutional in spirit if it analyzes such soft elements as organizational ideology or sectoral "constitution" (e.g., Tanner, and Kraus and Suttmeier this volume). However, strictly speaking an account is not really a neo-institutional *explanation* unless it draws on some testable hypothesis—for example, a hard proposition derived from principal-agent theory. Similarly, an account is not really a new institutional *explanation* unless it draws on some specific soft insight—for example, from historical institutionalism. In comparing transitions, examples of such explicit hypothesis testing remain rare (e.g., on China, Huang 1996, Tong this volume).

The third caveat concerns the limits of institutional approaches. The benefits from clarifying the role of institutions should not be exaggerated into an expectation that institutions will explain everything, or that all explanations should be institutional. This is particularly true for regime change. As the China case illustrates, communist institutions themselves could create crises that precipitated transition to alternative institutions. To a significant extent even the process of transition itself has consisted of the endogenous evolution of institutions—national, subnational, and even supranational. Nevertheless, major historical crises unleash major historical forces that destroy and recast institutions. For such episodes, explanation must reach beyond institutions to the maelstrom of extra-institutional processes and interests involved.

References

Abrahamsson, Bengt 1972. *Military professionalization and political power.* Beverly Hills: Sage.

Adelman, Jonathan R. 1980. *The revolutionary armies: The historical development of the Soviet and Chinese People's Liberation Armies.* Westport, Conn.: Greenwood.

Agarwala, Ramgopal 1992. *China: Reforming intergovernmental fiscal relations.* Washington, D.C.: The World Bank.

Agence France Presse, English Wire 1994. "Government to crack down on scientific fraud." *China News Digest* (28–29 November) 40.

Aggarwal, Vinod K. and Pierre Allan 1994. "The origins of games: A theory of the formation of ordinal preferences and games." In *Cooperative models in international relations research,* edited by Michael D. Intriligator and Urs Luterbacher. Boston: Kluwer, 299–325.

Aguero, Felipe 1997. "Toward civilian supremacy in South America." In Diamond et al. eds. 177–206.

Aird, John S. 1990. *Slaughter of the innocents: Coercive birth control in China.* Washington, D.C.: American Enterprise Institute.

Akiner, Shirin ed. 1991. *Mongolia today.* London: Kegan Paul International.

Alatalu, Toomas 1992. "Tuva—a state reawakens." *Soviet Studies* 44,5 (September) 881–895.

Alexander, Jeffrey C., Bernard Giesen, Richard Munch, and Neil Smelser eds. 1987. *The macro-micro link.* Berkeley: University of California Press.

Almond, Gabriel and Sidney Verba 1965. *The civic culture.* Boston: Little, Brown.

Alonso, William and Paul Starr eds. 1987. *The politics of numbers.* New York: Russell Sage.

American Association for the Advancement of Science 1994. "Storm clouds over Russian science." *Science* 264 (27 May) 1259–1282.

Amnesty International 1984. *China: Violations of human rights, prisoners of conscience and the death penalty in the People's Republic of China.* London: AI.

Amnesty International 1989. *People's Republic of China: Preliminary findings on killings of unarmed civilians, arbitrary arrests and summary executions since June 3, 1989.* London: AI.

Amsden, Alice, Jacek Kochanowcz, and Lance Taylor 1994. *The market meets its match: Restructuring the economies of Eastern Europe.* Cambridge: Harvard University Press.

Andrews, Julia and Gao Minglu 1995. "The avant-garde's challenge to official art." In Davis et al. eds. 221–278.

APSA = American Political Science Association. Unpublished paper written for the annual meeting.

Arrow, Kenneth 1985. "The economics of agency." In Pratt and Zeckhauser eds. 37–51.

Arthur, W. Brian 1994. *Increasing returns and path-dependence in the economy.* Ann Arbor: University of Michigan Press.

ASEAN 1996. *Vietnam in ASEAN.* Special issue of the *ASEAN Economic Bulletin* 13,2 (November).

Asia Watch 1990. *Punishment season: Human rights in China after martial law.* New York: AW.

Avant, Deborah 1994. *Political institutions and military change: Lessons from peripheral wars.* Ithaca: Cornell University Press.

AWSJW = Asian Wall Street Journal Weekly.

Axelrod, Robert 1984. *Evolution of cooperation.* New York: Basic Books.

AY = Asia Yearbook, published by *Far Eastern Economic Review.*

Baark, Eric 1987. "Commercial technology transfer in China 1981–86: The impacts of science and technology policy reforms." *China Quarterly* 111 (September) 390–406.

Bachman, David 1989. "The Ministry of Finance and Chinese politics." *Pacific Affairs* 62,2 (Summer) 167–187.

Bahl, Roy and Christine Wallich 1992. *Intergovernmental fiscal relations in China.* Washington, D.C.: World Bank. (Policy Research Working Papers, Public Economics, WPS 863)

Barany, Zoltan D. 1991. "Civil-military relations in communist systems: Western models revisited." *Journal of Political and Military Sociology* 19,1 (Summer) 75–99.

Barany, Zoltan 1995. "The military and political transitions in Eastern Europe." American Political Science Association paper.

Bartlett, David and Wendy Hunter 1993. "Comparing transitions from authoritarian rule in Latin America and Eastern Europe: What have we learned and where are we going?" American Political Science Association paper.

Bates, Robert H. and Barry R. Weingast 1995. "A new comparative politics: Integrating rational choice and interpretivist perspectives." Center for International Affairs, Harvard University. (Working Papers, 95–3)

Batson, Wendy 1991. "After the revolution: Ethnic minorities and the new Lao state." In Zasloff and Unger eds. 133–158.

Batt, Judy 1992. "East-Central Europe: From reform to transformation." In Rozman ed. 245–276.

Baum, Richard 1991a. "Epilogue: Communism, convergence and China's political convulsion." In Baum ed. 183–199.

Baum, Richard ed. 1991b. *Reform and reaction in post-Mao China: The road to Tiananmen.* New York and London: Routledge, Chapman and Hall.

Baum, Richard 1994. *Burying Mao: Chinese politics in the age of Deng Xiaoping.* Princeton: Princeton University Press.

Beresford, Melanie 1989. *National unification and economic development in Vietnam.* London: Macmillan.

Berger, Peter L. and Thomas Luckman 1966. *The social construction of reality.* New York: Doubleday.

Bermeo, Nancy ed. 1991. *Liberalization and democratization: Change in the Soviet Union and Eastern Europe.* Baltimore: Johns Hopkins University Press.

Bernstein, Richard and Ross H. Munro 1997. *The coming conflict with China.* New York: Random House.

Binder, Leonard ed. 1971. *Crises and sequences in political development.* Princeton: Princeton University Press.

Bird, Richard 1978. *Intergovernmental fiscal relations in developing countries.* Washington, D.C.: World Bank. (Staff Working Papers, 304)

Bird, Richard and Christine Wallich 1993. "Fiscal decentralization and intergovernmental relations in transition economies: Towards a systematic framework of analysis." Washington, D.C.: Policy Research Department, World Bank. (Working Papers, WPS 1122)

Blecher, Marc 1991. "Developmental state, entrepreneurial state: The political economy of socialist reform in Xinji municipality and Guanghan county." In White ed. 265–291.

Blondel, Jean 1982. *The organization of governments: A comparative analysis of governmental structures.* Newbury Park, Calif.: Sage.

Boikova, E. 1997. "The problem of Mongolia's national security and its guarantees." In *Security politics in the Commonwealth of Independent States: The southern belt,* edited by Mehdi Mozaffari. London: MacMillan, 53–65.

Boisot, M. H. 1986. "Markets and hierarchies in a cultural perspective." *Organization Studies* 7, 135–158.

Boisot, M. H. and J. Child 1988. "The iron law of fiefs: Bureaucratic failure and the problem of governance in the Chinese economic reforms." *Administrative Science Quarterly* 33,4 (December) 507–527.

Bonnin, Michel and Yves Chevier 1991. "The intellectual and the state: Social dynamics of intellectual autonomy during the post-Mao era." *China Quarterly* 127 (September) 569–593.

Boone, Peter 1994. "Grassroots economic reform in Mongolia." *Journal of Comparative Economics* 18,3 (June) 329–356.

Bova, Russell 1991. "Political dynamics of post-communist transition: A comparative perspective." In Bermeo ed. 113–138.

Braverman, Avishay and Joseph Stiglitz 1986. "Cost-sharing arrangements under sharecropping: Moral hazard, incentive flexibility, and risk." *American Journal of Agricultural Economics* (August) 642–652.

Broaded, C. Montgomery 1993. "China's response to the brain drain." *Comparative Education Review* 37,3 (August) 277–303.

Brommelhorster, Jorn and John Frankenstein 1997. *Mixed motives, uncertain outcomes: Defense conversion in China.* Boulder: Lynne Rienner.

Brook, Timothy 1992. *Quelling the people: The military suppression of the Beijing Democracy movement.* Oxford: Oxford University Press.

Bruckner, Scott 1995. "Beyond Soviet studies: The new institutional alternative." In Orlovsky ed. 198–221.

Bruun, Ole and Ole Odgaard eds. 1996. *Mongolia in transition: Old patterns, new challenges.* Richmond, Surrey: Curzon.

Brzezinski, Zbigniev 1969. *Dilemmas of change in Soviet politics.* New York: Columbia University Press.

Brzezinski, Zbigniew 1988. *The grand failure: The birth and death of communism in the twenieth century.* New York: Scribners.

Bunce, Valerie 1981. *Do new leaders make a difference? Executive succession and public policy under capitalism and socialism.* Princeton: Princeton University Press.

Bunce, Valerie 1985. "The empire strikes back: The transformation of the Eastern

Bloc from a Soviet asset to a Soviet liability." *International Organization* 39,1 (Winter 1984/85) 1–46.

Bunce, Valerie 1992. "Two-tiered Stalinism: A case of self-destruction." In Poznanski ed. 25–45.

Bunce, Valerie 1994. "Should transitologists be grounded?" *Slavic Review* 54,1 (Spring) 111–127.

Bunce, Valerie 1995. "Comparing East and South." *Journal of Democracy* 6,3 (July) 87–100.

Burns, John 1989. "Chinese civil service reform: The 13th Party Congress proposals." *China Quarterly* 120 (December) 739–770.

Byrd, William A. 1991. *The market mechanism and economic reform in China.* Armonk, N.Y.: Sharpe.

Cahill, James 1994. *The painter's practice: How artists lived and worked in traditional China.* New York: Columbia University Press.

Calvert, Randall L. 1994. "Rational actors, equilibrium and social institutions." In *Explaining social institutions,* edited by Jack Knight and Itai Sened. Ann Arbor: University of Michigan Press, 57–93.

Calvert, Randall L. 1995. "The rational choice theory of social institutions: Cooperation, coordination and communication." In *Modern political economy: Old topics, new directions,* edited by Jeffrey S. Banks and Eric A. Hanushek. New York: Cambridge University Press, 216–267.

Cao, Cong 1997. *Chinese scientific elite: A test of the universalism of scientific elite formation.* Unpublished Ph.D. dissertation, Department of Sociology, Columbia University.

Carney, Timothy and Tan Lian Choo 1993. *Whither Cambodia? Beyond the election.* Singapore: Indochina Unit, Institute of Southeast Asian Studies.

CCTV 1997. Special television series on soft landing. Chinese Central Television, December.

CD = China Daily.

CDBW = China Daily Business Weekly.

Ch'i, Hsi-sheng 1991. *Politics of disillusionment: The Chinese Communist Party under Deng Xiaoping, 1978–1989.* Armonk, N.Y.: Sharpe.

Chanda, Nayan 1993. "Indochina beyond the Cold War: The chill from Eastern Europe." In Ljunggren ed. 19–38.

Chandler, David P. 1991. *The tragedy of Cambodian history: Politics, war and revolution since 1945.* New Haven: Yale University Press.

Chandler, David P. 1992. *A history of Cambodia.* Boulder: Westview.

Chang, Parris 1978. *Power and policy in China.* University Park: Pennsylvania State University Press.

Chen, Pi-chao and Adrienne Kols 1982. "Population and birth planning in the People's Republic of China." *Population Reports,* Series J, no. 25, J577-J618.

Chen, Xitong 1989. "Report to the National People's Congress on quelling the counter-revolutionary rebellion." Beijing Xinhua English (16 July). In *FBIS* (6 July) 20–36. [Also available in *Beijing Review* (17–23 July) and in Oksenberg, Sullivan, and Lambert 1990, 55–88.]

Chen, Yangde 1987. *Zhuanbian zhongde Taiwan difang zhengzhi* (Taiwan's local politics in transition). Taipei: Dongcha Book Co.

Chen, Yitian 1984. "The provincial party bureau and local autonomy." *Shibao zazhi* (Times magazine) (12 September). [In Chinese]

Cheng, Gang 1990. "CFPA's contribution to population control." *Beijing Review* (19–25 November) 24–26.

Cheng, Hsiao-shih 1990. *Party-military relations in the PRC and Taiwan: Paradoxes of control.* Boulder: Westview.

Cheng, Tun-jen 1989. "Democratizing the quasi-Leninist regime in Taiwan." *World Politics* 41,4 (July) 471–499.

Cheng, Zihua 1981. "Summary report on the work of the nationwide county-level direct elections." *RMRB* (12 September). Translated in *Chinese Law and Government* 15,3/4 (Fall/Winter 1982/83) 172–190.

Cheung, Tai Ming 1994. "Profits over professionalism: The People's Liberation Army's economic activities and their impact on military unity." In Yang et al. eds. 85–110.

Cheung, Tai Ming 1996a. "China's entrepreneurial army: The structure, activities and economic returns of the military business complex." In Lane et al. eds. 168–197.

Cheung, Tai Ming 1996b. "The People's Armed Police: First line of defence." *China Quarterly* 146 (June) 525–547.

Cheung, Tai Ming 1997. "The Chinese army's new marching order: Winning on the economic battlefield." In Brommelhorster and Frankenstein eds. 181–204.

Child, John 1994. *Management in China during the age of reform.* New York: Cambridge University Press.

Chilton, Patricia 1995. "Mechanics of change: Social movements, transnational coalitions, and the transformation processes in Eastern Europe." In Risse-Kappen ed. 189–226.

China Information Bulletin 1994. "China moves to curb brain drain" (March) 4. [Portland, Ore., Northwest China Council]

China Journal 1995. Special issue, *The nature of Chinese politics* 34 (July).

China Today 1992. (Dangdai zhongguo) *The family planning cause.* Beijing: China Today Press. [In Chinese]

Chirot, Daniel 1995. "National liberations and nationalist nightmares: The consequences of the end of empires in Eastern Europe in the 20th century." In Crawford ed. 43–68.

Chung, Jae Ho 1993. *The politics of policy implementation in post-Mao China: Central control and provincial autonomy under decentralization.* Ph.D. dissertation, University of Michigan.

Chung, Jae Ho 1995. "Studies of central-provincial relations in the People's Republic of China: A mid-term appraisal." *China Quarterly* 142 (June) 487–508.

Ci, Jiwei 1994. *Dialectic of the Chinese revolution: From utopianism to hedonism.* Stanford: Stanford University Press.

CIA, Directorate of Intelligence 1992. *The Chinese economy in 1991 and 1992: Pressure to revisit reform mounts.* Paper submitted to the Subcommittee on Technology and National Security of the Joint Economic Committee, Congress of the United States, August.

Clark, Katerina 1981. *The Soviet novel: History as ritual.* Chicago: University of Chicago Press.

CNA = *China News Analysis.*

CNA 1993. "The PLA after the Fourteenth Party Congress," 1478 (1 February).

Coale, Ansley J. 1984. *Rapid population change in China, 1952–1982.* Washington, D.C.: National Academy Press.

Cohen, Youssef 1994. *Radicals, reformers and reactionaries: The prisoner's dilemma and the collapse of democracy in Latin America.* Chicago: University of Chicago Press.

Colton, Timothy 1978. "The party-military connection: A participatory model." In Herspring and Volgyes eds. 53–75.

Conroy, Richard 1992. *Technological change in China.* Paris: Organization for Economic Cooperation and Development.

CQ = *China Quarterly.*

CQ 141. *China's legal reforms.* Special issue of *China Quarterly* (March 1995).

CQ 144. *China's transitional economy.* Special issue of *China Quarterly* (December 1995).

CQ 146. *China's military in transition.* Special issue of *China Quarterly* (June 1996).

Crawford, Beverly ed. 1995. *Markets, states and democracies: The political economy of post-communist transformation.* Boulder: Westview.

Crawford, Beverly and Arend Lijphart eds. 1995. *Post-communist transformation in Eastern Europe.* Special issue of *Comparative Political Studies* 28,2 (July).

Crouch, Harold 1997. "Civil military relations in Southeast Asia." In Diamond et al. eds. 207–235.

Cumings, Bruce 1981. *The origins of the Korean War, vol. 1, Liberation and the emergence of separate regimes, 1945–1947.* Princeton: Princeton University Press.

Curtis, Grant 1989. *Cambodia: A country profile.* Stockholm: Swedish International Development Authority.

CZ = *Caizheng* (Finance). Beijing: Zhongguo caizheng zazhishe. [Began October 1956, ceased December 1996, continued by *Zhongguo caizheng*]

CZSL = *Caizheng shiliao* 1982 (Financial materials), vol. 2. Beijing: Zhongguo caizheng jingji chubanshe.

Dahl, Robert 1971. *Polyarchy: Participation and opposition.* New Haven: Yale University Press.

Dahl, Robert and Charles Lindblom 1953. *Politics, economics and welfare: Planning and politico-economic systems resolved into basic social processes.* New York: Harper.

Dai, Genqu 1990. "An important responsibility in public security theoretical work is clarifying right and wrong things in theory which have been confused by liberalism." *Gongan yanjiu* 3 (nd) 1–4. [In Chinese]

Dai, Wendian 1988. "Research on the initial stage of socialism and crime." *Gongan yanjiu* 2 (nd) 2–3. [In Chinese]

Danopoulos, Constantine P. and Daniel Zirker eds. 1996. *Civil-military relations in the Soviet and Yugoslav successor states.* Boulder: Westview.

Davenport, Brian A. 1995. "Civil-military relations in the post-Soviet state: 'Loose coupling' uncoupled?" *Armed Forces and Society* 21,2 (Winter) 175–194.

Davey, Kenneth 1983. *Financing regional government: International practices and their relevance to the Third World.* Chichester, Eng.: Wiley.

Davis, Christopher and Wojciech W. Charmeza eds. 1989. *Models of disequilibrium and shortage in centrally planned economies.* New York: Chapman and Hall.

Davis, Deborah S. and Stevan Harrell eds. 1993. *Chinese families in the post-Mao era.* Berkeley: University of California Press.

Davis, Deborah S., Richard Kraus, Barry Naughton, and Elizabeth J. Perry eds. 1995. *Urban spaces in contemporary China: The potential for autonomy and community in post-Mao China.* New York: Cambridge University Press.

Dawkins, Chris and John Whalley 1996. "Economic reform and performance in Vietnam." In McMillan and Naughton eds. 297–316.

Deng, X. L. 1994. "Institutional amphibiousness and the transition from communism: The case of China." *British Journal of Political Science* 24 (July) 293–318.

Deng, Xiaoping 1978. "Speech at opening ceremony of the national conference on science." In *Selected works of Deng Xiaoping* (1975–1982). Beijing: Foreign Languages Press, 1984, 101–116.

Deng, Xiaoping 1979. "Uphold the Four Cardinal Principles." In *Selected works of Deng Xiaoping* (1975–1982). Beijing: Foreign Languages Press, 1984, 166–191.

Deng, Xiaoping 1980a. "On the reform of party and state leadership." In *Selected works of Deng Xiaoping* (1975–1982). Beijing: Foreign Languages Press, 1984, 302–325.

Deng, Xiaoping 1980b. "Implement the policy of readjustment, ensure stability and unity." In *Selected works of Deng Xiaoping* (1975–1982). Beijing: Foreign Languages Press, 1984, 335–355.

Deng, Xiaoping 1987. "Main points of Deng Xiaoping's speech on the current problem of student disturbance." *Zhongfa* 1 (16 January 1987). Translated in *Chinese Law and Government* 21,1 (Spring 1988) 18–21.

Denizer, Cevdet and Alan Gelb 1994. "Privatization in Mongolia." In *Changing political economies,* edited by Vedat Milor. Boulder: Lynne Rienner.

Desch, Michael C. 1996. "Threat environments and military missions." In Diamond and Plattner eds. 12–29.

de Vylder, Stephan and Adam Fforde 1988. *Vietnam: An economy in transition.* Stockholm: Swedish International Development Authority.

Diamond, Larry, Juan Linz, and Seymour Martin Lipset eds. 1995. *Democracy in developing countries.* Boulder: Lynne Rienner.

Diamond, Larry and Mark F. Plattner 1996a. "Introduction." In Diamond and Plattner eds. ix–xxxiv.

Diamond, Larry and Marc F. Plattner eds. 1996b. *Civil-military relations and democracy.* Baltimore: Johns Hopkins University Press.

Diamond, Larry, Marc F. Plattner, Yun-han Chu, and Hung-mao Tien eds. 1997. *Consolidating the third wave democracies.* Baltimore: Johns Hopkins University Press.

Dickson, Bruce J. 1990. "Conflict and non-compliance in Chinese politics: Party rectification, 1983–87." *Pacific Affairs* 63,2 (Summer) 170–190.

Dickson, Bruce J. 1997. *Democratization in China and Taiwan: The adaptability of Leninist parties.* Oxford: Clarendon.

DiMaggio, Paul J. and Walter W. Powell eds. 1991. *The new institutionalism in organizational analysis.* Chicago: University of Chicago Press.

Ding, Arthur S. 1996. "Economic reform and defence industries in China." In Segal and Yang eds. 78–92.

Ding, X. L. 1994. *The decline of communism in China: Legitimacy crisis, 1977–1989.* New York: Cambridge University Press.

Dittmer, Lowell 1992. "Patterns of leadership in reform China." In Rosenbaum ed. 31–54.

Dittmer, Lowell 1994. *China under reform.* Boulder: Westview.

Dittmer, Lowell and Samuel S. Kim eds. 1993. *China's quest for national identity.* Ithaca: Cornell University Press.

Dittmer, Lowell and Yu-shan Wu 1995. "The modernization of factionalism in Chinese politics." *World Politics* 47,4 (July) 467–494.

Dong, Lishen ed. 1994. *Administrative reform in the People's Republic of China.* Leiden: International Institute for Asian Studies.

Donnithorne, Audrey, 1967. *China's economic system.* London: Allen and Unwin.

Donnithorne, Audrey 1981. *Centre-provincial economic relations in China.* Canberra: Contemporary China Center, Research School of Pacific Studies, Australian National University.

Doran, Valerie C. ed. 1993. *China's new art, post-1989.* Hong Kong: Hanart TZ Gallery.

Downing, Brian M. 1992. *The military revolution and political change: Origins of democracy and autocracy in early modern Europe.* Princeton: Princeton University Press.

Dreyer, Edward 1995. *China at war, 1901–1949.* London: Longman.

Dreyer, June 1976. *China's forty millions: Minority nationalities and national integration in the People's Republic of China.* Cambridge: Harvard University Press.

Dunlop, John B. 1993. *The rise of Russia and the fall of the Soviet empire.* Princeton: Princeton University Press.

Dutton, Michael R. 1992a. "A mass line without politics: Community policing and economic reform." In Watson, A. ed. 200–227.

Dutton, Michael R. 1992b. *Policing and punishment in China: From patriarchy to "the People."* New York: Cambridge University Press.

Eatwell, John, Murray Milgate, and Peter Newman eds. 1989. *Allocation, information and markets.* New York: Norton.

Eberstadt, Nicholas 1993. *North Korea: Reform, muddling through, or collapse?* Seattle: National Bureau of Asian Research. [*Analysis* 4,3 (September)]

Eberstadt, Nicholas 1995. *Korea approaches reunification.* Armonk, N.Y.: Sharpe.

Eckstein, Alexander 1966. *Communist China's economic growth and foreign trade.* New York: McGraw-Hill.

Economy, Elizabeth 1997. "Chinese policy-making and global climate change: Two front diplomacy and the international community." In *The internationalization of environmental protection,* edited by Miranda A. Schreuers and Elizabeth C. Economy. New York: Cambridge University Press, 19–41.

Eggertsson, Thrain 1990. *Economic behavior and institutions.* New York: Cambridge University Press.

EIU = Economist Intelligence Unit, quarterly country reports.

Ekiert, Grzegorz 1991. "Democratization processes in East Central Europe: A theoretical reconsideration." *British Journal of Political Science* (July) 285–313.

Ekiert, Grzegorz 1996. *The state against society: Political crises and their aftermath in East Central Europe.* Princeton: Princeton University Press.

Ellman, Michael and Vladimir Kontorovich eds. 1992. *The disintegration of the Soviet economic system.* London: Routledge.

Elvin, Mark 1973. *The pattern of the Chinese past.* London: Methuen.

Esherick, Joseph W. and Elizabeth J. Perry 1983. "Leadership succession in the PRC: 'Crisis' or opportunity?" *Studies in Comparative Communism* 16,3 (Autumn) 171–177.

Esping-Anderson, Gosta 1990. *The three worlds of welfare capitalism.* Princeton: Princeton University Press.

Etzioni, Amatai 1961. *A comparative analysis of complex organizations.* New York: Free Press of Glencoe.

Etzioni, Amitai 1975. *Genetic fix: The next technological revolution.* New York: Harper and Row.

Evangelista, Matthew 1996. "Stalin's revenge: Institutional barriers to internationalization in the Soviet Union." In Keohane and Milner eds. 159–185.

Evans, Grant 1990. *Lao peasants under socialism.* New Haven: Yale University Press, 1990.

Evans, Peter 1995. *Embedded autonomy.* Princeton: Princeton University Press.

Falkenheim, Victor 1972. "Continuing central predominance." *Problems of Communism* 21,4 (July/August) 75–83.

Fama, Eugene 1980. "Agency problems and the theory of the firm." *Journal of Political Economy* 88 (April) 288–307.

FBIS = Foreign Broadcast Information Service, China daily report.

Feaver, Peter 1996a. "The civil-military problematique: Huntington, Janowitz and the question of civilian control." *Armed Forces and Society* 23,2 (Winter) 149–178.

Feaver, Peter 1996b. "Delegation, monitoring and civilian control of the military: Agency theory and American civil-military relations." Cambridge: Olin Institute, Harvard University. (Working papers on U.S. post–Cold War civil-military relations, 4)

Feeney, Griffith and Feng Wang 1993. "Parity progression and birth intervals in China: The influence of policy in hastening fertility decline." *Population and Development Review* 19,1 (March) 61–101.

Feeney, Griffith and Jingyuan Yu 1987. "Period parity progression measures of fertility in China." *Population Studies* 41,1 (March) 77–102.

FEER = Far Eastern Economic Review.

Fendler, Karoly 1996. "Economic assistance from socialist countries to North Korea in the postwar years: 1953–1963." In Park ed. 161–174.

Feng, Guoping and Linna Hao 1992. "A summary of the birth planning regulations for 28 regions in China." *Renkou yanjiu* (Population research) 4, 28–33.

Fewsmith, Joseph 1994. *Dilemmas of reform in China: Political conflict and economic debate.* Armonk, N.Y.: Sharpe, 1994.

Fforde, Adam 1994. *The institutions of transition from central planning: The case of Vietnam.* Sydney: Research School of Pacific and Asian Studies, Australian National University.

Fforde, Adam and Stevan de Vylder 1996. *From plan to market: The economic transition in Vietnam.* Boulder: Westview.

Fforde, Adam and Anthony Goldstone 1995. *Vietnam to 2005: Advancing on all fronts.* London: The Economist Intelligence Unit.

Fforde, Adam and Suzy H. Paine 1987. *The limits of national liberation—Problems of economic management in the Democratic Republic of Vietnam.* London: Croon-Helm.

Findlay, Trevor 1995. *Cambodia: The legacy and lessons of UNTAC.* New York: Oxford University Press.

Finkle, Jason L. and C. Alison McIntosh, eds. 1994. *The new politics of population: Conflict and consensus in family planning.* Supplement to *Population and Development Review,* vol. 20.

Fiorina, Morris P. and Kenneth A. Shepsle 1982. "The general possibility of a science of politics." In *Political equilibrium,* edited by Peter C. Ordeshook and Kenneth A. Shepsle. Boston: Kluwer, 49–64.

FJRB = Fujian ribao (Fujian daily).

Foster-Carter, Aidan 1994. *North Korea after Kim Il-sung.* London: The Economist Intelligence Unit.

Frank, Andre Gunder and Barry K. Gills eds. 1993. *The world system: Five hundred years or five thousand?* London: Routledge.

Friedgut, Theodore H. and Jeffrey W. Hahn eds. 1994. *Local power and post-Soviet politics.* Armonk, N.Y.: Sharpe.

Friedman, Edward 1991. "Permanent technological revolution and China's tortuous path to democratizing Leninism." In Baum ed. 162–182.

Friedman, Edward ed. 1994. *The politics of democratization: Generalizing East Asian experiences.* Boulder: Westview.

Friedman, Edward 1995. *National identity and democratic prospects in socialist China.* Armonk, N.Y.: Sharpe.

Frings, Viviane 1994. "Cambodia after decollectivization (1989–1992)." *Journal of Contemporary Asia* 24,2 (nd) 49–66.

Frye, Northrop 1957. *The anatomy of criticism.* Princeton: Princeton University Press.

Fu, Zhengyuan 1993. *Autocratic tradition and Chinese politics.* New York: Cambridge University Press.

Fudenberg, Drew and Eric Maskin 1986. "The folk theorem in repeated games with discounting and with incomplete information." *Econometrica* 54,3 (May) 533–554.

Funck, Bernard 1993. "Laos: Decentralization and economic control." In Ljunggren ed. 123–148.

Gao, Xin 1996. *Zhonggong jutou Qiao Shi* (Chinese communist major leader Qiao Shi) Taibei, Taiwan: Shijie Shuju

Garcia, Edmundo and Evelyn Lucero Gutierrez eds. 1992. *Back to the barracks: The military in democratic transition.* Quezon City, Philippines: National Institute for Policy Studies.

Garrett, Banning and Bonnie Glaser 1995. "Looking across the Yalu: Chinese assessments of North Korea." *Asian Survey* 35,6 (June) 528–545.

Garver, John 1996. "The PLA as an interest group in Chinese foreign policy." In Lane, Weissenbloom, and Liu 246–281.

Geddes, Barbara 1995. "Games of intra-regime conflict and the breakdown of authoritarianism." American Political Science Association paper.

Gilmartin, Christina K., Gail Hershatter, Lisa Rofel, and Tyrene White eds. 1994. *Engendering China: Women, culture and the state.* Cambridge: Harvard University Press.

Ginsburg, Tom 1995. "Political reform in Mongolia: Between Russia and China." *Asian Survey* 35,5 (May) 459–471.

Ginsburg, Tom 1998. "Mongolia in 1997: Deepening democracy." *Asian Survey* 38,1 (January) 64–68.

Gittings, John 1967. *The role of the Chinese army.* London: Oxford University Press.

Gladney, Dru C. 1991. *Muslim Chinese: Ethnic nationalism in the People's Republic.* Cambridge: Council on East Asian Studies, Harvard University.

Gladney, Dru C. 1994. "Ethnic identity in China: The new politics of difference." In *China briefing, 1994,* edited by William Joseph. Boulder: Westview, 171–192.

Godwin, Paul H. B. 1978. "Professionalism and politics in the Chinese armed forces: A reconceptualization." In Herspring and Volgyes eds. 219–240.

Godwin, Paul H. B. 1996. "From continent to periphery: PLA doctrine, strategy and capabilities toward 2000." *China Quarterly* 146 (June) 464–487.

Goldfarb, Jeffrey C. 1989. *Beyond glasnost: The post-totalitarian mind.* Chicago: University of Chicago Press.

Goldman, Merle 1994. *Sowing the seeds of democracy in China.* Cambridge: Harvard University Press.

Goldman, Merle 1996. "Politically engaged intellectuals in the Deng-Jiang era: A changing relationship with the party state." *China Quarterly* 145 (March) 35–52.

Goldman, Merle with Timothy Cheek and Carol Hamrin eds. 1987. *China's intellectuals and the state: In search of a new relationship.* Cambridge: Council on East Asian Studies, Harvard University.

Goldstein, Steven M. 1995. "China in transition: The political foundations of incremental reform." *China Quarterly* 144 (December) 1105–1131.

Goodman, Allen E. 1996. "Vietnam in 1995: It was a very good year." *Washington Quarterly* 19,2 (1996) 137–150.

Goodman, David S. G. 1986. *Centre and province in the People's Republic of*

China: Sichuan and Guizhou, 1955–1965. Cambridge: Cambridge University Press.

Goodman, David S. G. ed. 1988. *Communism and reform in East Asia*. London: Cass.

Goodman, David S. G. and Gerald Segal eds. 1994. *China deconstructs*. London: Routledge, 1994.

Goodman, Louis W. 1996. "Military roles past and present." In Diamond and Plattner eds. 30–43.

Gow, James and Carole Birch 1997. *Security and democracy: Civil military relations in Central and Eastern Europe*. London: Center for Defense Studies.

Grafstein, Robert 1992. *Institutional realism: The social and political constraints on rational actors*. New Haven: Yale University Press.

Granick, David 1990. *Chinese state enterprises: A regional property rights analysis*. Chicago: University of Chicago Press.

Greenhalgh, Susan 1990. "The evolution of the one-child policy in Shaanxi, 1979–88." *China Quarterly* 122 (June) 191–229.

Greenhalgh, Susan 1993. "The peasantization of the one-child policy in Shaanxi." In Davis and Harrell eds. 219–250.

Greenhalgh, Susan 1994. "Controlling births and bodies in village China." *American Ethnologist* 21,1 (February) 3–30.

Greenhalgh, Susan and Jiali Li. 1995. "Engendering reproductive policy and practice in peasant China: For a feminist demography of reproduction." *Signs* 20,3 (Spring) 601–641.

Greenhalgh, Susan, Chuzhu Zhu, and Li Nan 1994. "Restraining population growth in three Chinese villages." *Population and Development Review* 20,2 (June) 365–395.

Grindle, Merilee S. ed. 1980. *Politics and policy implementation in the Third World*. Princeton: Princeton University Press.

Grossman, Sanford and Oliver Hart 1983. "An analysis of the principal-agent problem." *Econometrica* (January) 7–46.

Gu, Baochang and Mu Guangzong 1994. "A new understanding of China's population problem." *Renkou yanjiu* (Population research) 5 (September) 2–10. [Translated in *FBIS* 1995–032 (16 February) 28–36]

Gu, Baochang and Yang Shuzhang. 1991. "Fertility trends in rural China in the 1980s: Cohort effect versus period effect." *Asia-Pacific Population Journal* 6,4 (November) 3–34.

Gu, Linfang 1989. "From the turmoil and the riot looking at class struggle in the initial stage of socialism." *Renmin gongan* 11 (5 October) 3–9, and *Renmin gongan* (nd) 12–18. [Speech at a situation report joint meeting of five departments including the Central Propaganda Department; approximate date late September 1989]

Gu, Shulin 1994a. "A review of reform policy for the S&T system in China: From paid transactions for technology to organizational restructuring." Unpublished paper presented to the UNU/INTECH workshop "Restructuring of industrial R&D institutions in China," Maastricht, 29 June–1 July.

Gu, Shulin 1994b. "Spin-off enterprises in China: Channelling the components of R&D institutions into innovative businesses." Unpublished paper. Maastricht, UNU/INTECH (August).

Haggard, Stephan and Robert Kaufman 1992a. "Economic adjustment and the prospects for democracy." In Haggard and Kaufman eds. 319–350.

Haggard, Stephan and Robert Kaufman eds. 1992b. *The politics of economic adjustment*. Princeton: Princeton University Press.

Haggard, Stephan and Robert Kaufman 1995. *The political economy of democratic transitions.* Princeton: Princeton University Press.

Haggard, Stephan, Chung H. Lee, and Sylvia Maxfield eds. 1993. *The politics of finance in developing countries.* Ithaca: Cornell University Press.

Haining, T. N. 1991. "Between the Kremlin and the forbidden city." In Akiner ed. 32–56.

Hall, Peter and Rosemary Taylor 1994. "Political science and the four institutionalisms." Paper for annual meeting of the American Political Science Association.

Hallagan, William 1978. "Self-selection by contractual choice and the theory of sharecropping." *The Bell Journal of Economics* 9 (Autumn) 344–354.

Hamrin, Carol Lee 1990. *China and the challenge of the future: Changing political patterns.* Boulder: Westview.

Hamrin, Carol Lee 1992. "The party leadership system." In Lieberthal and Lampton eds. 95–124.

Hamrin, Carol Lee and Timothy Cheek eds. 1986. *China's establishment intellectuals.* Armonk, N.Y.: Sharpe.

Hamrin, Carol Lee and Suisheng Zhao eds. 1995a. *Decision-making in Deng's China: Perspectives from insiders.* Armonk, N.Y.: Sharpe.

Hamrin, Carol Lee and Suisheng Zhao 1995b. "Introduction: Core issues in understanding the decision process." In Hamrin and Zhao eds. xxi–xlviii.

Handelman, Stephen 1995. *Comrade criminal: Russia's new mafia.* New Haven: Yale University Press.

Hankiss, Elemer 1990. *East European alternatives.* Oxford: Clarendon Press.

Hannan, Michael T. and John Freeman 1989. *Organizational ecology.* Cambridge: Harvard University Press.

Harding, Harry 1981. *Organizing China: The problem of bureaucracy 1949–1976.* Stanford: Stanford University Press.

Harding, Harry 1986. "Political development in post-Mao China." In *Modernizing China: Post-Mao reform and development,* edited by A. Doak Barnett and Ralph Clough. Boulder: Westview, 13–27.

Harding, Harry 1987a. *China's second revolution: Reform after Mao.* Washington, D.C.: Brookings.

Harding, Harry 1987b. "The role of the military in Chinese politics." In *Citizens and groups in contemporary China,* edited by Victor C. Falkenheim. Ann Arbor: Center for Chinese Studies, University of Michigan, 213–256.

Harding, Harry 1994. "Comments." In Shirk 1994, 91–110.

Harrell, Stevan ed. 1995. *Cultural encounters on China's ethnic frontiers.* Seattle: University of Washington Press.

Hart, Oliver 1983. "Optimal labor contracts under asymmetric information: An introduction." *Review of Economic Studies* 50 (January) 3–36.

Hart, Oliver and Bengt Holmstrom 1978. "The theory of contracts." Unpublished mimeo, 71–155.

Hartford, Kathleen 1985. "Socialist agriculture is dead; long live socialist agriculture! Organizational transformations in rural China." In *The political economy of reform in post-Mao China,* edited by Elizabeth J. Perry and Christine Wong. Cambridge: Harvard University Press, 31–61.

Hasegawa, Tsuyoshi 1992. "The connection between political and economic reform in communist regimes." In Rozman ed. 59–117.

Hay, Donald, Derek Morris, Guy Liu, and Shuje Yao 1994. *Economic reform and state-owned enterprises in China, 1979–1987.* Oxford: Clarendon.

Hayhoe, Ruth 1990. "China's returned scholars and the Democracy Movement." *China Quarterly* 122 (June) 293–302.

Heberer, Thomas 1989. *China and its national minorities: Autonomy or assimilation?* Armonk, N.Y.: Sharpe.

Hechter, Michael 1987. *Principles of group solidarity.* New York: Russell Sage.

Hechter, Michael and Ivan Szelenyi eds. 1994. *The theoretical implications of the demise of state socialism.* Special issue of *Theory and Society* 23,2 (April).

Heder, Steve and Judy Ledgerwood eds. 1996. *Propaganda, politics and violence in Cambodia: Democratic transition under United Nations peace-keeping.* Armonk, N.Y.: Sharpe.

Hellman, Joel 1993. *Breaking the bank: Building market institutions in the former Soviet Union.* Ph.D. dissertation, Columbia University.

Hernandez, Carolina G. 1996. "Controlling Asia's armed forces." In Diamond and Plattner eds. 66–80.

Herspring, Dale R. and Ivan Volgyes eds. 1978. *Civil-military relations in communist systems.* Boulder: Westview.

Hicks, Ursula 1977. *Intergovernmental fiscal relations in less developed countries.* Metropolitan Studies Program, Syracuse University. (Occasional Papers, 32)

Hirschman, Albert 1958. *The strategy of economic development.* New Haven: Yale University Press.

Hirschman, Albert 1970. *Exit, voice, and loyalty: Responses to decline in firms, organizations, and states.* Cambridge: Harvard University Press.

Ho, Samuel S. P. 1994. *Rural China in transition: Non-agricultural development in rural Jiangsu, 1978–1990.* Oxford: Clarendon.

Holmes, Leslie 1993. *The end of communist power: Anti-corruption campaigns and legitimation crisis.* New York: Oxford University Press.

Hong, Peilin 1988. "An initial discussion of the question of the object of the people's democratic dictatorship." *Gongan yanjiu* 3 (nd) 2–6. [In Chinese]

Horn, Murray J. 1995. *The political economy of public administration: Institutional choice in the public sector.* New York: Cambridge University Press.

Horowitz, Donald L. 1993. "Democracy in divided societies." *Journal of Democracy* 4,4 (October) 18–38.

Hoston, Germaine, A. 1994. *The state, identity and the national question in China and Japan.* Princeton: Princeton University Press.

Hou, Wenruo. 1981. "Population policy." In *China's population: Problems and prospects,* edited by Liu Zheng, Song Jian, et al. Beijing: New World Press, 55–76.

Howell, Jude, 1993. *China opens its doors: The politics of economic transition.* Boulder: Westview.

Hsiung, James C. 1986. "Taiwan in 1985: Scandals and setbacks." *Asian Survey* 26,1 (January) 93–101.

Hu, Fu and Yun-han Chu 1992. "Electoral competition and political democratization." In *Political change in Taiwan,* edited by Tun-jen Cheng and Stephan Haggard. Boulder: Lynne Rienner, 177–203.

Hu, Qiaomu 1978. "Act in accordance with economic laws, speed up the Four Modernizations." Xinhua News Agency, 5 October 1978. In *FBIS* 11 October 1978, E1–22.

Huang, Mab 1976. *Intellectual ferment for political reforms in Taiwan, 1971–1973.* Ann Arbor: Center for Chinese Studies, University of Michigan. (Papers in Chinese Studies, 28)

Huang, Maochen. 1990. "Study the new situation, explore the new road, continuously strengthen control mechanisms for birth control." *Renkou yu jingji* (Population and economy) 1 (25 February) 15–19. [In Chinese]

Huang, Philip C. C. ed. 1993. *Symposium: "Public sphere"/"civil society" in*

China? Paradigmatic issues in Chinese studies, III. Special issue of *Modern China* 192 (April).

Huang, Yasheng 1994. "Information, bureaucracy and economic reforms in China and the Soviet Union." *World Politics* 47 (October) 102–134.

Huang, Yasheng 1995. "Why China will not collapse." *Foreign Policy* 99 (Summer) 54–69.

Huang, Yasheng 1996. *Inflation and investment controls in China: The political economy of central-local relations during the reform era.* New York: Cambridge University Press.

Human Rights Watch/Asia, and Human Rights in China 1994. *China: Use of criminal charges against political dissidents.* New York: HRW.

Humphrey, Caroline 1994. "Remembering an 'enemy': The Bogd Khaan in twentieth-century Mongolia." In *Memory, history and opposition under state socialism,* edited by Ruby Watson. Santa Fe, N.M.: School of American Research Press, 21–44.

Huntington, Samuel P. 1957. *The soldier and the state: The theory and politics of civil-military relations.* Cambridge: Harvard University Press, 1957.

Huntington, Samuel P. 1968. *Political order in changing societies.* New Haven: Yale University Press.

Huntington, Samuel P. 1984. "Will more countries become democratic?" *Political Science Quarterly* 99,2 (Summer) 191–218.

Huntington, Samuel P. 1991. *The third wave: Democratization in the late twentieth century.* Norman: University of Oklahoma Press.

Huskey, Eugene 1995. "The state-legal administration and the politics of redundancy." *Post-Soviet Affairs* 11,2 (April–June) 115–143.

IDRC 1997. *A decade of reform: Science and technology policy in China.* Ottawa: International Development Research Centre.

Ilkenberry, G. John, David A. Lake, and Michael Mastanduno eds. 1988. *The state and American foreign economic policy.* Ithaca: Cornell Univesity Press.

Ishayama, John T. 1995. "Communist parties in transition: Structures, leaders and processes of democratization in Eastern Europe." *Comparative Politics* 27,2 (January) 147–166.

Jamieson, Neil L. 1993. *Understanding Vietnam.* Berkeley: University of California Press.

Jamison, Dean T. et al. 1984. *China: The health sector.* Washington, D.C.: World Bank.

Janos, Andrew 1991. "Social science, communism and the dynamics of political change." *World Politics* 44,1 (October) 81–112.

Jencks, Harlan W. 1982. *From muskets to missiles: Politics and professionalism in the Chinese army, 1945–1981.* Boulder: Westview.

Jia, Hao and Zhimin Lin eds. 1994. *Changing central-local relations in China: Reform and state capacity.* Boulder: Westview.

Jiang, Zemin 1997. "Hold high the great banner of Deng Xiaoping Theory for an all-round advancement of the cause of building socialism with Chinese characteristics to the 21st century." *Xinhua* (21 September). In *FBIS* 97–266 (23 September); also in *Beijing Review* (6–12 October) 10–33.

Jin, Leroy 1994. *Monetary policy and the design of financial institutions in China, 1978–90.* New York: St. Martin's.

Joffe, Ellis 1965. *Party and army: Professionalism and political control in the Chinese officer corps, 1949–1964.* Cambridge: East Asian Research Center, Harvard University.

Joffe, Ellis 1987. *The Chinese army after Mao.* Cambridge: Harvard University Press.

Joffe, Ellis 1996a. "Party-army relations in China: Retrospect and prospect" *China Quarterly* 146 (June) 299–314.

Joffe, Ellis 1996b. "The PLA and the economy: The effects of involvement." In Segal and Yang eds. 11–34.

Johansson, Sten and Ola Nygren 1991. "The missing girls of China: A new demographic account." *Population and Development Review* 17,1 (March) 35–51.

Johnson, James 1993. "Is talk really cheap? Prompting conversation between critical theory and rational choice." *American Political Science Review* 87,1 (March) 74–86.

Johnson, Kay. 1993. "Chinese orphanages: Saving China's abandoned girls." *Australian Journal of Chinese Affairs* 30 (July) 61–87.

Johnson, Stephen T. 1992. "Laos in 1991: Year of the constitution." *Asian Survey* 32,1 (January) 82–87.

Johnson, Stephen T. 1993. "Laos in 1992: Succession and consolidation." *Asian Survey* 33,1 (January) 75–92.

Johnston, Alastair I. 1995. *Cultural realism: Strategic culture and grand strategy in Ming China.* Princeton: Princeton University Press.

Johnston, Alastair I. 1996. "Cultural realism and strategy in Mao's China." In *The cultures of national security,* edited by Peter J. Katzenstein. New York: Columbia University Press, 216–268.

Jones, Andrew 1992. *Like a knife: Ideology and genre in contemporary Chinese popular music.* Ithaca: East Asia Program, Cornell University.

Jones, Anthony ed. 1991. *Professions and the state: Expertise and autonomy in the Soviet Union and Eastern Europe.* Philadelphia: Temple University Press.

Jowitt, Ken 1992. *New world disorder: The Leninist extinction.* Berkeley: University of California Press.

JPRS = Joint Publications Research Service, China (JPRS-CAR).

JPRS 1991–030. "Article describes birth control practices." *Chiushih nientai* (The nineties 1 March), 30 May, 78–86.

JPRS 1993–038. "New opportunity for improving family planning program." *Zhongguo renkou bao* (China population report 12 April), 9 June, 43–45.

JPRS 1993–059. "Evolution of 'Three Unchangings' family planning policy." *Zhongguo renkou bao* (China population report 28 June), 16 August, 43–44.

Kahneman, D., P. Slovik, and A. Tversky 1982. *Judgment under uncertainty: Heuristics and biases.* Cambridge: Cambridge University Press.

Kamm, Henry 1996. *Dragon ascending: Vietnam and the Vietnamese.* New York: Arcade.

Kang, David C. 1995. "Rethinking North Korea." *Asian Survey* 35,3 (March) 253–267.

Kang, Myung-Kyu and Keun Lee 1992. "Industrial systems and reform in North Korea: A comparison with China." *World Development* 20,7.

Kaple, Deborah 1994. *Dream of a red factory: The legacy of high Stalinism in China.* New York: Oxford University Press.

Karl, Terry and Philippe Schmitter 1991. "Modes of transition and types of democracy in Latin American, Southern Europe and Eastern Europe." *International Social Science Journal* 128 (May) 269–284.

Kaufman, Stuart J. 1994. "Organizational politics and change in Soviet military policy." *World Politics* 46,3 (April) 355–382.

Kelliher, Daniel 1992. *Peasant power in China: The era of rural reform, 1979–1989.* New Haven: Yale University Press.

Kelliher, Daniel 1993. "Keeping democracy safe from the masses: Intellectuals and elitism in the Chinese protest movement." *Comparative Politics* 25,4 (July) 379–396.

Kelliher, Daniel 1997. "The Chinese debate over self-government." *China Journal* 37 (January) 63–86.

Keohane, Robert O. and Helen V. Milner eds. 1996. *Internationalization and domestic politics.* New York: Cambridge University Press.

Kerkvliet, Benedict J. Tria and Doug J. Porter eds. 1995. *Vietnam's rural transformation.* Boulder: Westview.

Khng, Russell Heng Hiang 1993. "Leadership in Vietnam: Pressures for reform and their limits." *Contemporary Southeast Asia* 15,1 (June) 98–110.

Kiewiet, D. Roderick and Mathew D. McCubbins 1991. *The logic of delegation: Congressional parties and the appropriations process.* Chicago: University of Chicago Press.

Kim, Sungwoo 1993. "Recent economic policies of North Korea: Analysis and recommendations." *Asian Survey* 33,9 (September) 864–878.

Kim, Young C. and Gaston Sigur eds. 1992. *Asia and the decline of communism.* New York: Transaction.

Kitschelt, Herbert 1992. "Political regime change: Structure and process-driven explanations." *American Political Science Review* 86,4 (December) 1028–1034.

Kitschelt, Herbert 1993. "Comparative historical research and rational choice theory: The case of transitions to democracy." *Theory and Society* 22,3 (June) 413–426.

Klintworth, Gary 1993. *Cambodia's past, present and future.* Canberra: Strategic and Defence Studies Centre, Australian National University. (Working Papers, 268)

Kluver, Alan R. 1996. *Legitimating the Chinese economic reforms: A rhetoric of myth and orthodoxy.* Albany: State University of New York Press.

Knight, Amy 1996. *Spies without cloaks: The KGB's successors.* Princeton: Princeton University Press.

Knight, Jack 1992. *Institutions and social conflict.* New York: Cambridge University Press.

Koelble, Thomas A. 1995. "The new institutionalism in political science and sociology." *Comparative Politics* 27,2 (January) 231–243.

Kohli, Atul et al. eds. 1995. "The role of theory in comparative politics: A symposium." *World Politics* 48,1 (October) 1–49.

Kornai, Janos 1980. *Economics of shortage.* Amsterdam: North Holland.

Kornai, Janos 1992. *The socialist system: The political economy of communism.* Princeton: Princeton University Press.

Korsun, Georges and Peter Murrell 1995. "Politics and economics of Mongolia's privatization program." *Asian Survey* 35,5 (May) 472–486.

Koves, Andras 1992. *Central and East European economies in transition: The international dimension.* Boulder: Westview.

Kraus, Richard Curt 1984. "Culture: Cultural politics and the political construction of audiences in China." In Solinger ed. 47–72.

Kraus, Richard Curt 1989. *Pianos and politics in China: Middle-class ambitions and the struggle over Western music.* New York: Oxford University Press.

Kraus, Richard Curt 1991. *Brushes with power: Modern politics and the Chinese art of calligraphy.* Berkeley: University of California Press.

Kraus, Richard Curt 1995. "China's artists between plan and market." In Davis et al. eds. 173–192.

Krieg, Renate and Monika Schadler eds. 1994. *Social security in the People's Republic of China.* Hamburg: Institut für Asienkunde.

Kristof, Nicholas D. 1993. "China's crackdown on births: A stunning and harsh success." *New York Times* (25 April) 1.

Krugman, Paul 1991. "Increasing returns and economic geography." *Journal of Political Economy* 99,3 (June) 183–199.

Krugman, Paul 1993. "On the number and location of cities." *European Economic Review* 37,2–3 (April) 293–298.

Kuran, Tim 1991. "Now out of never: The element of surprise in the East European revolution of 1989." *World Politics* 44,1 (October) 7–48.

Laing, Ellen Johnston 1984. "Chinese peasant painting, 1958–1976: Amateur and professional." *Art International* 27,1 (January–March) 2–11, 40–48, 64.

Lam, Willy Wo-lap 1989a. "Political bureau reportedly endorses purge." *South China Morning Post* (29 August). In *FBIS* (29 August) 6.

Lam, Willy Wo-lap 1989b. "Beijing roots out 'unorthodox' party members." *South China Morning Post* (27 November). In *FBIS* (29 November) 44.

Lam, Willy Wo-Lap 1995. *China after Deng Xiaoping: The power struggle in Beijing since Tiananmen*. New York: Wiley.

Lampton, David M. ed. 1987. *Policy implementation in post-Mao China*. Berkeley: University of California Press.

Lampton, David M. 1992. "A plum for a peach: Bargaining, interest and bureaucratic politics in China." In Lieberthal and Lampton eds. 33–58.

Lampton, David M. 1994. "America's China policy in the age of the finance minister: Clinton ends linkage." *China Quarterly* 139 (September) 597–621.

Landa, Janet 1994. *Trust, ethnicity and identity*. Ann Arbor: University of Michigan Press.

Lane, C. Dennison, Mark Weissenbloom, and Dimon Liu eds. 1996. *Chinese military modernization*. London: Kegan Paul International.

Lardy, Nicholas 1978. *Economic growth and distribution in China*. New York: Cambridge University Press.

Lardy, Nicholas 1992. *Foreign trade and economic reform in China, 1978–1990*. New York: Cambridge University Press.

Larson, Wendy and Richard Kraus 1989. "China's writers, the Nobel Prize, and the international politics of literature." *Australian Journal of Chinese Affairs* 21 (January) 143–160.

Latham, Richard J. 1991. "China's party-army relations after June 1989: A case for Miles' law?" In *China's military: The PLA in 1990/1991*, edited by Richard H. Yang. Boulder: Westview, 103–123.

Lavely, William and Ronald Freedman 1990. "The origins of the Chinese fertility decline." *Demography* 27,3 (August) 357–367.

Lee, Chong-Sik and Se-Hee Yoo eds. 1991. *North Korea in transition*. Berkeley: Institute of East Asian Studies, University of California.

Lee, Doowon 1996. "North Korean economic reform: Past efforts and future prospects." In McMillan and Naughton eds. 317–336.

Lee, Eddy 1993. "Initiating transition in a low-income dualistic economy: The case of Mongolia." *International Labour Review* 132,5/6 (nd) 623–638.

Lee, Hong Yung 1991. *From revolutionary cadres to party technocrats in socialist China*. Berkeley: University of California Press.

Lee, Hy Sang 1992. "The economic reforms of North Korea; The strategy of hidden and assimilable reforms." *Korea Observer* 23,1 (Spring) 45–78.

Lee, Mabel and A. D. Syrokomla-Steganowska eds. 1993. *Modernization of the Chinese past*. Sydney: Wild Peony Press.

Leng, Shao-chuan and Hungdah Chiu 1985. *Criminal justice in post-Mao China*. Albany: SUNY Press.

Levi, Margaret 1988. *Of rule and revenue*. Berkeley: University of California Press.

Levi, Margaret 1990. "A logic of institutional change." In *The limits of rationality,* edited by Karen Schweers Cook and Margaret Levi. Chicago: University of Chicago Press, 402–418.

Lewis, Paul G. 1995. "Contours of the shadowlands: The trials of transition in Eastern Europe." *Journal of Communist Studies and Transition Politics* 11,2 (June) 198–212.

Li, Cheng and Lynn T. White III 1990. "Elite transformation and modern change in Mainland China and Taiwan: Empirical data and the theory of technocracy." *China Quarterly* 121 (March) 1–35.

Li, Cheng and Lynn T. White III 1993. "The army in the succession to Deng Xiaoping: Familiar fealties and technocratic trends." *Asian Survey* (August) 757–786.

Li, Jiali 1995. "China's one child policy: How and how well has it worked? A study of Hebei province, 1979–88." *Population and Development Review* 21,3 (September) 503–538.

Li, Nan 1996. "The PLA's evolving warfighting doctrine, strategy and tactics, 1985–95: A Chinese perspective." *China Quarterly* 146 (June) 443–463.

Lichbach, Mark 1995. *The rebel's dilemma.* Ann Arbor: University of Michigan Press.

Lieberthal, Kenneth 1984. "Domestic politics and China's foreign policy." In *China's foreign policy in the 1980s,* edited by Harry Harding. New Haven: Yale University Press, 43–70.

Lieberthal, Kenneth G. 1992. "Introduction: The 'fragmented authoritarianism' model and its limitations." In Lieberthal and Lampton eds. 1–30.

Lieberthal, Kenneth 1995. *Governing China: From revolution through reform.* New York: Norton.

Lieberthal, Kenneth and Michael Lampton eds. 1992. *Bureaucracy, politics and decision-making in post-Mao China.* Berkeley: University of California Press.

Lieberthal, Kenneth and Michel Oksenberg 1988. *Policy making in China: Leaders, structures, and processes.* Princeton: Princeton University Press.

Lieberthal, Kenneth, Joyce Kallgren, Roderick MacFarquhar, and Frederic Wakeman, Jr. eds. 1991. *Perspectives on modern China: Four anniversaries.* Armonk, N.Y.: Sharpe.

Lijphart, Arend 1984. *Democracies: Patterns of majoritarian and consensus government in twenty-one countries.* New Haven: Yale University Press, 1984.

Lijphart, Arend 1992. "Democratization and constitutional choices in Czecho-Slovakia, Hungary and Poland, 1989–1991." *Journal of Theoretical Politics* 4,2 (April) 207–224.

Lijphart, Arend ed. 1992. *Parliamentary versus presidential government.* Oxford: Oxford University Press.

Ling, Ts'ai and Ramon H. Myers 1992. "Surviving the rough and tumble of presidential politics in an emerging democracy: The 1990 elections in the Republic of China on Taiwan." *China Quarterly* 129 (March) 123–148.

Link, Perry 1989. *Evening chats in Beijing: Probing China's predicament.* New York: W. W. Norton 1992.

Linz, Juan 1975. "Totalitarian and authoritarian regimes." In *Handbook of political science,* vol. 3, edited by Fred I. Greenstein and Nelson W. Polsby. Reading, Mass.: Addison-Wesley, 175–411.

Linz, Juan 1978. "Non-competitive elections in Europe." In *Elections without choice,* edited by Guy Hermet, Richard Rose, and Alain Rouquie. New York: Wiley, 36–65.

Linz, Juan J. and Alfred Stepan 1996. *Democratic transitions and consolidation:*

Eastern Europe, Southern Europe, and Latin America. Baltimore: Johns Hopkins University Press.

Linz, Juan and Arturo Valenzuela eds. 1994. *The failure of presidential democracy: Comparative perspectives.* Baltimore: Johns Hopkins University Press.

Lipset, Seymour Martin 1960. *Political man: The social bases of politics.* New York: Doubleday.

Lipset, Seymour Martin 1993. "The social requisites of democracy revisisted." *American Sociological Review* 59 (February) 1–22.

Liu, Enqi 1989. "On the question of the nature of serious criminal activities as contradictions." *Gongan yanjiu* 3 (nd) 2–7. [In Chinese]

Liu, Wenqi 1990. "Confusion in the theory of the people's democratic dictatorship must be clarified." *Gongan yanjiu* 2 (nd) 20–24. [In Chinese]

Liu, Zaiping 1989. "A preliminary discussion of the democratic functions of public security organs—A discussion of the object of the people's democratic dictatorship." *Gongan yanjiu* 3 (nd) 7–12. [In Chinese]

Ljunggren, Carl Borje 1992. *Market economies under communist regimes: Reform in Vietnam, Laos and Cambodia.* Department of Political Science, University of Southern Illinois at Carbondale.

Ljunggren, Carl Borge ed. 1993. *The challenge of reform in Indochina.* Cambridge: Harvard Institute for International Development.

Lohmann, Suzanne 1994. "Dynamics of informational cascades: The Monday demonstrations in Leipzig, East Germany, 1989–91." *World Politics* 47,1 (October) 42–101.

Lowenthal, Richard 1970. "Development and utopia in communist policy." In *Change in communist systems,* edited by Chalmers Johnson. Stanford: Stanford University Press, 33–116.

Lowenthal, Richard 1983. "Post-revolutionary phase in China and Russia." *Studies in Comparative Communism* 16,3 (Autumn) 191–201.

Lu, Keng 1992. *Deng Xiaoping zuihou de jihui* (Deng Xiaoping's last chance). Hong Kong: Pai Shing Cultural Enterprise, 201–215.

Lull, James 1991. *China turned on: Television, reform and resistance.* London: Routledge.

Lupia, Arthur and Mathew D. McCubbins 1994. "Learning from oversight: Fire alarms and police patrols reconstructed." *Journal of Law, Economics and Organization* 10,1 (April) 96–125.

Ma, Jun 1997. *Intergovernmental relations and economic management in China.* New York: St. Martin's.

Mackerras, Colin 1987. "Modernization and contemporary Chinese theatre: Commercialization and professionalization." In *Drama in the People's Republic of China,* edited by Constantine Tung and Colin Mackerras. Albany: State University of New York Press, 181–212.

Mahr, Alison and John Nagle 1995. "Resurrection of the successor parties and democratization in East-Central Europe." *Communist and Post-Communist Studies* 28,4 (December) 393–409.

Manion, Melanie 1985. "The cadre management system, post-Mao: The appointment, promotion, transfer and removal of party and state leaders." *China Quarterly* 102 (June) 203–233.

Manion, Melanie 1990. "Introduction: Reluctant duelists—The logic of the 1989 demonstrations and massacre." In *Beijing Spring 1989: Confrontation and conflict,* edited by Michel Oksenberg, Marc Lambert, and Lawrence Sullivan. Armonk, N.Y.: Sharpe, xiii-xlii.

Manion, Melanie 1992. "The behavior of middlemen in the cadre retirement policy process." In Lieberthal and Lampton eds. 216–244.

Manion, Melanie 1993. *Retirement of revolutionaries in China: Public policies, social norms, private interests.* Princeton: Princeton University Press.

Mao, Tse-tung 1965. *Selected works of Mao Tse-tung.* Peking: Foreign Languages Press.

March, James G. and Johan P. Olsen 1984. "The new institutionalism: Organizational factors in political life." *American Political Science Review* 78,3 (September) 734–739.

Marks, Gary 1992. "Rational sources of chaos in democratic transition." In *Reexamining democracy,* edited by Gary Marks and Larry Diamond. Newbury Park, Calif.: Sage, 47–69.

Marr, David G. and Christine P. White eds. 1988. *Postwar Vietnam: Dilemmas in socialist development.* Ithaca: Southeast Asia Program, Cornell University.

Marshall, A. H. 1969. *Local government finance.* The Hague: International Union of Local Authorities.

Marwah, Onkar and Jonathan Pollack eds. 1980. *Military power and policy in Asian states: China, India and Japan.* Boulder: Westview.

Matthews, R. L. 1980. *Revenue-sharing in federal systems.* Canberra: Australian National University. (Research Monographs, 31)

McCormack, Gavan 1993 "Kim country: Hard times in North Korea." *New Left Review* 198 (March/April) 21–48.

McCormick, Barrett L. 1990. *Political reform in post-Mao China: Democracy and bureaucracy in a Leninist state.* Berkeley: University of California Press.

McCormick, Barrett L. and Jonathan Unger eds. 1996. *China after socialism: In the footsteps of Eastern Europe or East Asia?* Armonk, N.Y.: Sharpe.

McCubbins, Mathew D. and Thomas Schwartz 1984. "Congressional oversight overlooked: Police patrols versus fire alarms." *American Journal of Political Science* 28,1 (February) 165–179.

McKelvey, R. D. 1976. "Intransitivities in multidimensional voting bodies and some implications for agenda control." *Journal of Economic Theory* 12,3 (June) 472–482.

McKinnon, Ronald I. 1993. *The order of economic liberalization: Financial control in the transition to a market economy,* 2d ed. Baltimore: Johns Hopkins University Press.

McMillan, John and Barry Naughton 1996a. "Elements of economic transition." In McMillan and Naughton eds. 2–16.

McMillan, John and Barry Naughton eds. 1996b. *Reforming Asian socialism: The growth of market institutions.* Ann Arbor: University of Michigan Press.

Meaney, Constance Squires 1995. "Foreign experts, capitalists and competing agendas: Privalization in Poland, the Czech Republic and Hungary." In Crawford and Lijphart eds. 275–305.

Meisner, Maurice 1996. *The Deng Xiaoping era: An inquiry into the fate of Chinese socialism, 1978–1994.* New York: Hill and Wang.

Michels, Robert 1962. *Political parties.* New York: Free Press.

Michta, Andrew A. 1994. *The government and politics of postcommunist Europe.* Westport, Conn.: Praeger.

Migdal, Joel S., Atul Kohli, and Vivienne Shue eds. 1994. *State power and social forces: Domination and transformation in the Third World.* New York: Cambridge University Press.

Milivojevic, Marko 1991a. "The Mongolian People's Army: Military auxiliary and political guardian." In Akiner ed. 136–154.

Milivojevic, Marko 1991b. *The Mongolia revolution of 1990: Stability or conflict in Inner Asia.* London: Research Institute for the Study of Conflict and Terrorism.

Miller, Gary 1992. *Managerial dilemmas: The political economy of hierarchy.* New York: Cambridge University Press.

Miller, H. Lyman 1996. *Science and dissent in post-Mao China: The politics of knowledge.* Seattle: University of Washington Press.

Millet, Richard L. and Michael Gold-Biss eds. 1996. *Beyond praetorianism: The Latin American military in transition.* Miami: North-South Center Press, University of Miami.

Milor, Vedat ed. 1993. *Changing political economies: Privatization in post-communist and reforming communist states.* Boulder: Lynne Rienner.

Moe, Terry 1990. "Political institutions: The neglected side of the story." *Journal of Law, Economics and Organization* 6-S, 213–253. Special issue on the organization of political institutions.

Montinola, Gabriella, Yingqi Qian, and Barry R. Weingast 1995. "Federalism, Chinese style: The political basis for economic success in China." *World Politics* 48,1 (October) 50–81.

Moore, Barrington 1966. *Social origins of dictatorship and democracy.* Boston: Beacon.

Morley, James W. and Masashi Nishihara eds. 1997. *Vietnam joins the world.* Armonk, N.Y.: Sharpe.

Morrow, James D. 1994. *Game theory for political scientists.* Princeton: Princeton University Press.

Mou, Xinsheng 1988. "An initial discussion of the functions of the people's public security organs during the initial stage of socialism." *Gongan yanjiu* 1 (nd) 7–9. [In Chinese]

Mu, Fengyun 1991. "The experience of the history is worth summing up." *Gongan yanjiu* 2 (nd) 1–4. [In Chinese]

Mu, Fengyun 1992. "Use Marxist philosophy to guide the struggle with the enemy." *Gongan yanjiu* 2 (nd) 4–7. [In Chinese]

Murrell, Peter, Karen Turner Dunn, and Georges Korsun 1996. "The culture of policy-making in the transition from socialism: Price policy in Mongolia." *Economic Development and Cultural Change* 45,1 (October) 175–194.

Myrdal, Gunnar 1957. *Rich lands and poor.* New York: Harper and Row.

Nathan, Andrew J. 1973. "A factional model for CCP politics." *China Quarterly* 53 (January–March 1973) 34–66.

Nathan, Andrew J. 1985. *Chinese democracy.* New York: Knopf.

Nathan, Andrew J. 1990. "Is China ready for democracy?" *Journal of Democracy* 1,2 (Spring) 50–61.

Nathan, Andrew J. 1992. "Totalitarianism, authoritarianism, democracy: The case of China." In *East Asia: Case studies in the social sciences: A guide for teaching,* edited by Myron Cohen. Armonk, N.Y.: Sharpe, 235–256.

Nathan, Andrew J. 1993. "China's path from communism." *Journal of Democracy* 4,2 (April) 30–42.

Nathan, Andrew J. 1996. "China's constitutionalist option." *Journal of Democracy* 7,4 (October) 43–57.

Nathan, Andrew J. and Robert S. Ross 1997. *The great wall and the empty fortress: China's search for security.* New York: Norton.

Nathan, Andrew J. and Tianjian Shi 1993. "Cultural requisites for democracy in China: Some findings from a survey." *Daedalus* 122 (Spring).

Nathan, Andrew J. and Tianjian Shi 1996. "Left and right with Chinese characteristics: Issues and alignments in Deng Xiaoping's China." *World Politics* 48,4 (July) 522–550.

National Interest 1993. *The strange death of Soviet communism: An autopsy.* Special issue of *National Interest* 31 (Spring).

Naughton, Barry 1987. "The decline of central control over investment in post-Mao China." In Lampton ed. 51–80.

Naughton, Barry 1992a. "Hierarchy and the bargaining economy: Government and enterprise in the reform process." In Lieberthal and Lampton eds. 245–279.

Naughton, Barry 1992b. "The Chinese economy: On the road to recovery?" In *China Briefing, 1991,* edited by William A. Joseph. Boulder: Westview, 77–95.

Naughton, Barry 1995. *Growing out of the plan: Chinese economic reform 1978–1993.* New York: Cambridge University Press.

Naughton, Barry 1996. "Distinctive features of economic reform in China and Vietnam." In McMillan and Naughton eds. 273–296.

Nee, Victor and Peng Lian 1994. "Sleeping with the enemy: A dynamic model of declining politicial commitment in state socialism." In Hechter and Szelenyi eds. 253–296.

Nee, Victor and David Stark eds. 1989. *Remaking the economic institutions of socialism: China and Eastern Europe.* Stanford: Stanford University Press.

Nee, Victor et al. eds. 1996. *Symposium on market transition. American Journal of Sociology* 101,4 (January) 908–949.

Nelsen, Harvey W. 1972. "Military forces in the Cultural Revolution." *China Quarterly* 51 (July–September) 444–474.

Nelsen, Harvey W. 1977/1981. *The Chinese military system: An organizational study of the Chinese People's Liberation Army.* Boulder: Westview.

NFRB = Nanfang ribao (Nanfang daily)

Niou, Emerson M. S. and Peter C. Ordeshook 1994. "Less filling, tastes great: The realist-neoliberal debate." *World Politics* 46,2 (January) 209–234.

Nolan, Peter 1995. *China's rise, Russia's fall.* New York: St. Martin's.

Noll, Roger G. 1985. "Government regulatory behavior: A multidisciplinary survey and synthesis." In *Regulatory policy and the social sciences,* edited by Roger G. Noll. Berkeley: University of California Press, 9–63.

Nordlund, Irene, Carolyn L. Gates, and Vu Cao Dam eds. 1995. *Vietnam in a changing world.* Richmond, Surrey: Curzon Press.

North, Douglas C. 1981. *Structure and change in economic history.* New York: Norton.

North, Douglas C. 1990. *Institutions, institutional change and economic performance.* New York: Cambridge University Press.

Nove, Alex 1983. *The economics of feasible socialism.* London: Allen and Unwin.

NYT = New York Times

O'Brien, Kevin J. 1990. *Reform without liberalization: China's National People's Congress and the politics of institutional change.* New York: Cambridge University Press.

O'Brien, Kevin J. 1994. "Implementing political reform in China's villages." *Australian Journal of Chinese Affairs* 32 (July) 33–59.

O'Donnell, Guillermo and Philippe C. Schmitter 1986. *Transitions from authoritarian rule: Tentative conclusions about uncertain democracies.* Baltimore: Johns Hopkins University Press.

O'Donnell, Guillermo, Philippe C. Schmitter and Laurence Whitehead eds. 1986. *Transitions from authoritarian rule: Comparative perspectives.* Baltimore: Johns Hopkins University Press.

Offe, Claus 1991. "Capitalism by design? Democratic theory facing the triple transition in East Central Europe." *Social Research* 58,4 (Winter).

Oi, Jean C. 1992. "Fiscal reform and the economic foundations of local state corporatism in China." *World Politics* 45,1 (October) 99–126.

Oi, Jean C. 1999. *Rural China takes off: Incentives for industrialization.* Berkeley: University of California Press.

Ojendal, Joakim 1996. "Democracy lost? The fate of the U.N.-implanted democracy in Cambodia." *Contemporary Southeast Asia* 18,2 (September) 193–218.

Oksenberg, Michel and Bruce J. Dickson 1991. "The origins, processes, and outcomes of great political reforms: A framework of analysis." In *Comparative political dynamics: Global research perspectives*, edited by Dankwart Rustow and Kenneth Paul Erickson. New York: Harper-Collins, 235–261.

Oksenberg, Michel and James Tong 1991. "The evolution of central-provincial fiscal relations in China, 1971–1984: The formal system." *China Quarterly* 125 (March) 1–32.

Oksenberg, Michel, Larry Sullivan, and Marc Lambert eds. 1990. *Beijing Spring 1989, confrontation and conflict: The basic documents.* Armonk, N.Y.: Sharpe.

Olson, Mancur 1965. *The logic of collective action.* Cambridge: Harvard University Press.

Orlovsky, Daniel ed. 1995. *Beyond Soviet studies.* Washington, D.C.: Wilson Center Press.

Orren, Karen and Stephen Skowronek 1995. "Order and time in institutional study: A brief for the historical approach." In *Political science in history,* edited by James Farr, John S. Druzek, and Stephen T. Leonard. New York: Cambridge University Press, 296–317.

Ostrom, Elinor 1990. *Governing the commons: The evolution of institutions for collective action.* New York: Cambridge University Press.

Ostrom, Elinor 1995. "New horizons in institutional analysis." *American Political Science Review* 9,1 (March) 174–178.

Ouchi, William G. 1980. "Markets, bureaucracies and clans." *Administrative Science Quarterly* 25,1 (March) 129–141.

Owen, Stephen 1990. "What is world poetry?" *New Republic,* 203,21 (November 14) 28–32.

Paine, Lynn 1992. "The educational policy process: A case study of bureaucratic action in China." In Lieberthal and Lampton eds. 181–215.

Paltiel, Jeremy T. 1995. "PLA allegiance on parade: Civil-military relations in transition." *China Quarterly* 143 (September) 784–800.

Pei, Minxin 1992. "Societal takeover in China and the USSR." *Journal of Democracy* (January) 108–118.

Pei, Minxin 1994. *From reform to revolution: The demise of communism in China and the Soviet Union.* Cambridge: Harvard University Press.

Pei, Minxin 1996. "Microfoundations of state-socialism and patterns of economic transformation." *Communist and Post-Communist Studies* 29,2 (June) 131–145.

Peng, Huaien 1990a. *Taiwan fazhan de zhengzhi jingji fenxi* (The political economy of Taiwan's development). Taipei: Fengyun luntan chubanshe.

Peng Huaien 1990b. *Taiwan zhengzhi bianqian 40 nian* (Forty years of political change on Taiwan). Taipei: Independent Evening News Publishing.

Peng, Peiyun 1990. "A speech at the Fifth National Population Science Symposium." *Chinese Journal of Population Science* 2,4 (nd) 307–316.

Peng, Peiyun 1993. "Accomplishments of China's family planning program: A statement by a Chinese offical." *Population and Development Review* 19,2 (June) 399–402.

Peng, Zhen 1989. "Speech at an expanded meeting of the Politburo." In *Lun Xin Zhongguo de zhengfa gongzuo* (On the New China's political-legal work), by Peng. Beijing: Zhongyang wenxian chubanshe, 1992, 436–443. [In Chinese; speech given 21 June 1989]

Peng, Zhen 1990. "Key points of a speech to the National Political-Legal Work Conference." In *Lun Xin Zhongguo de zhengfa gongzuo* (On the New China's political-legal work), by Peng. Beijing: Zhongyang wenxian chubanshe, 1992, 444–448. [In Chinese]

Peou, Sorpong 1998. "Cambodia in 1997: Back to square one?" *Asian Survey* 38,1 (January) 69–74.

Perkins, Dwight 1980. "The central features of China's economic development." In *China's development experience in comparative perspective,* edited by Robert Dernberger. Cambridge: Harvard University Press, 120–150.

Perkins, Dwight 1993. "Reforming the economic systems of Vietnam and Laos." In Ljunggren ed. 1–18.

Perlmutter, Amos 1977. *The military and politics in modern times.* New Haven: Yale University Press

Perlmutter, Amos 1981. *Modern authoritarianism: A comparative institutional analysis.* New Haven: Yale University Press.

Perlmutter, Amos and William M. LeoGrande 1982. "The party in uniform: Toward a theory of civil-military relations in communist political systems." *American Political Science Review* 76,4 (December) 778–789.

Perry, Elizabeth J. 1991. "Intellectuals and Tiananmen: Historical persepective on an aborted revolution." In *The crisis of Leninism and the decline of the Left: The revolution of 1989,* edited by Daniel Chirot. Seattle: University of Washington Press.

Perry, Elizabeth J. 1994. "Trends in the study of Chinese politics: State-society relations." *China Quarterly* 139 (September) 704–713.

Persson, Torsten and Guido Tabellini. 1990. *Macroeconomic policy, credibility and politics.* Chur, Switzerland: Harwood Academic Publishers.

Petrasovits, Anna 1988. "Results and limits in CMEA-Vietnamese trade relations 1975–1985." In Marr and White eds. 213–223.

Pfeffer, Jeffrey and Gerald B. Salancik 1978. *External control of organizations: A resource dependence perspective.* New York: Harper and Row.

Pickowitz, Paul 1995. "Velvet prisons and the political economy of Chinese film-making." In Davis et al. eds. 193–220.

Pillsbury, Michael 1980. *Environment and power: Warlord strategic behavior in Szechwan, Manchuria and the Yangtze delta.* Ph.D. dissertation, Columbia University.

Pillsbury, Michael ed. 1997. *Chinese views of future warfare.* Washington, D.C.: National Defense University Press.

Pollack, Jonathan D. 1992. "Structure and process in the Chinese military system." In Lieberthal and Lampton eds. 151–180.

Pomfret, Richard 1996. *Asian economies in transition: Reforming centrally planned economies.* Cheltenham: Edward Elgar.

Porter, Gareth 1993. *Vietnam: The politics of bureaucratic socialism.* Ithaca: Cornell University Press.

Poston, Dudley L. Jr. and Gu Baochang 1987. "Socioeconomic development, family planning and fertility in China: A subregional analysis." *Demography* 24,4 (November) 531–551.

Potter, Pitman ed. 1994. *Domestic law reforms in post-Mao China.* Armonk, N.Y.: Sharpe.

Poznanski, Kazimierz Z. 1992. *Constructing capitalism: The reemergence of civil society and liberal economy in the post-communist world.* Boulder: Westview.

Pratt, John and Richard Zeckhauser eds. 1985. *Principals and agents: The structure of business.* Boston: Harvard Business School Press.

Probert, Jocelyn and S. David Young 1995. "The Vietnamese road to capitalism: Decentralization, de facto privatization and the limits to piecemeal reform."

Communist Economies and Economic Transformation 7,4 (December) 499–525.

Prybyla, Jan 1981. *The Chinese economy: Problems and policies,* rev. 2d ed. Columbia: University of South Carolina Press.

Przeworski, Adam 1991. *Democracy and the market: Political and economic reforms in Eastern Europe and Latin America.* New York: Cambridge University Press.

Putnam, Robert D. 1995. "Tuning in, tuning out: The strange disappearance of social capital in America." *PS* 28,4 (December) 664–683.

Qian, Si 1986. "Questions on classifying revenues in the central and local government budgets in 1986." *Caizheng* 4 (April) 10–11. [In Chinese]

Qian, Y. and C. Xu 1993. "Why China's economic reforms differ: The M-form hierarchy and entry/expansion of the non-state sector." *Economics of Transition* 1,2 (June) 135–170.

Qiao, Shi 1989a. "Excerpts of Comrade Qiao Shi's speech at the closing of the National Symposium on Political-Legal Work." In *Shehui zhian zonghe zhili zhengce fagui huibian* (Selected laws and regulations on the comprehensive management of social order), edited by the CCP Fujian Provincial Political-Legal Committee and CCP Fujian Provincial Party Committee Policy Research Office. Beijing: Qunzhong chubanshe, 60–61. [In Chinese]

Qiao, Shi 1989b. "Qiao Shi's 22 May internal speech." In *Xuewo Zhongguo: Bajiunian Beijing xuechao ziliaoji* (Blood-nurtured China: Collection of material on the 1989 Beijing student movement), edited by Zhizhou He. Hong Kong: New Generation Cultural Association, 1989. Translated in *Chinese law and government* (Spring 1990). Armonk, N.Y.: Sharpe, 76–77.

Qiao, Shi 1990. "Excerpts of Comrade Qiao Shi's speech at the opening of the National Political-Legal Work Conference." In *Shehui zhi'an zonghe zhili zhengce fagui huibian* (Selected laws and regulations on the comprehensive management of social order), edited by the CCP Fujian Provincial Political-Legal Committee and CCP Fujian Provincial Party Committee Policy Research Office. Beijing: Qunzhong chubanshe, 62–64. [In Chinese]

Qiao, Shi 1991. "Qiao Shi inspects Hainan, stresses public order." Beijing Xinhua Domestic Service (16 October 1991). In *FBIS* (18 October) 26–27.

Ragin, Charles C. 1987. *The comparative method: Moving beyond qualitative and quantitative strategies.* Berkeley: University of California Press.

Rahr, Alexander 1993. "The revival of a strong KGB." *Radio Free Europe/Radio Liberty Research Report* 2,20 (14 May) 74–79.

Rana, Pradumna B. 1993. *Reforms in the transitional economies of Asia.* Manila: Asian Development Bank.

Rana, Pradumna B. 1995. "Reform strategies in transitional economies: Lessons from Asia." *World Development* 23,7 (July) 1157–1169.

Remnick, David 1993. *Lenin's tomb: The last days of the Soviet empire.* New York: Random House.

Richardson, Harry and Peter Tonwroe 1986. "Regional policies in developing countries." In *Handbook of regional and urban economics,* edited by P. Nijkamp. Amsterdam: Elsevier Science Publishers, 647–678.

Rigg, Jonathan 1995. "Managing dependency in a reforming economy: The Lao PDR." *Contemporary Southeast Asia* 17,2 (September) 147–172.

Riggs, Fred W. 1993. "The fragility of Third World regimes." *International Social Science Journal* 45,2 (May) 199–243.

Risse-Kappen, Thomas ed. 1995. *Bringing transnational relations back in: Non-state actors, domestic structures and international institutions.* New York: Cambridge University Press.

RMRB = *Renmin ribao* (People's daily) [In Chinese]

RMRB 1981 (8 February). "Democratic reform of the state must be realized step by step under conditions of unity and stability." In *FBIS* (9 February) L5–8.

RMRB 1984 (8 December). "Theory and practice." In *FBIS* (7 December) K1; and correction, in *FBIS* (10 December) K21.

Rodkey, Gretchen R. 1993. "Financial system reform in transitional economies: The role of political institutions." American Political Science Association paper.

Roeder, Philip G. 1991. "Soviet federalism and ethnic mobilization." *World Politics* 23,2 (January) 196–232.

Roeder, Philip G. 1993. *Red sunset: The failure of Soviet politics.* Princeton: Princeton University Press

Rosenbaum, Arthur Lewis ed. 1992. *State and society in China: The consequences of reform.* Boulder: Westview.

Ross, George 1992. "Party declines and changing party systems: France and the French Communist Party." *Comparative Politics* 25,1 (October) 43–61.

Ross, Stephen 1973. "The economic theory of agency: The principal's problem." *American Economic Review* 63,2 (May) 134–139.

Rouquie, Alain 1982/1987. *The military and the state in Latin America.* Berkeley: University of California Press.

Rowe, William 1985. "Approaches to modern Chinese social history." In *Reliving the past: The world of social history,* edited by Olivier Zunz. Chapel Hill: University of North Carolina Press, 236–296.

Rowe, William 1990. "Modern Chinese social history in comparative perspective." In *The heritage of China: Contemporary perspectives on Chinese civilization,* edited by Paul S. Ropp. Berkeley: University of California Press, 242–262.

Rozman, Gilbert 1992a. "Stages in the reform and dismantling of communism in China and the Soviet Union." In Rozman ed. 15–58.

Rozman, Gilbert, ed. 1992b. *Dismantling communism: Common causes and regional variations.* Baltimore: Johns Hopkins University Press.

Rutland, Peter 1985. *The myth of the plan.* La Salle, Ill.: Open Court.

Sachs, Jeffrey D. and Wing Thye Woo 1994. "Structural factors in the economic reforms of China, Eastern Europe and the former Soviet Union." *Economic Policy* 18,1 (April) 102–145.

Saich, Tony 1989. *China's science policy in the 1980's.* Manchester: Manchester University Press.

Saich, Tony 1993. "Peaceful evolution with Chinese characteristics." In *China briefing, 1992,* edited by William A. Joseph. Boulder: Westview, 9–34.

Sanders, Alan 1991. "'Restructuring' and 'openness.'" In Akiner ed. 57–78.

Sato, Ryuji 1994. "China's high-tech spree pays dividends." *The Nikkei Weekly* (7 November) 24.

Satterwhite, David H. 1998. "North Korea in 1997: New opportunities in a time of crisis." *Asian Survey* 38,1 (January) 11–23.

Scalapino, Robert A. 1992. *The last Leninists: The uncertain future of Asia's communist states.* Washington, D.C.: Center for Strategic and International Studies.

Schanze, Erich ed. 1996. *Symposium on new institutional economics.* Special issue of the *Journal of Institutional and Theoretical Economics* 152,1 (March).

Scharpf, Fritz W. 1993a. "Coordination in hierarchies and networks." In Scharpf ed. 125–167.

Scharpf, Fritz W. ed. 1993b. *Games in hierarchies and networks: Analytical and empirical approaches to the study of governance institutions.* Frankfurt: Campus Verlag; Boulder: Westview.

Schmitter, Philippe 1993. "The international context for contemporary democratization." *Stanford Journal of International Affairs* 2,1 (Fall/Winter) 1–34.

Schmitter, Phillippe C. and Terry Lynn Karl 1991. "What democracy is . . . and is not." *Journal of Democracy* 2,3 (Summer) 75–88.

Schmitter, Philippe C. with Terry Lynn Karl 1993. "The conceptual travels of transitologists and consolidologists: How far to the East should they attempt to go?" *Slavic Review* 53,1 (Spring 1993) 173–185.

Schoenhals, Michael 1992. *Doing things with words in Chinese politics: Five studies.* Berkeley: Center for Chinese Studies, Institute of East Asian Studies, University of California, Berkeley. (China research monographs, 41)

Schoenhals, Michael 1993. "Censorship and the social sciences in China: Domestic traditions and Soviet influence." Paper for the annual meeting of the Association of Asian Studies.

Schrodeder, Paul E. 1992. "Territorial actors as competitors for power: The case of Hubei and Wuhan." In Lieberthal and Lampton eds. 283–307.

Schurmann, Franz 1971. *Ideology and organization in Communist China,* 2d ed. Berkeley: University of California Press.

Scobell, Andrew 1995. "Military coups in the People's Republic of China: Failure, fabrication or fancy?" *Journal of Northeast Asian Studies* 14,1 (Spring) 25–46.

Scott, James 1990. *Domination and the arts of resistance: Hidden transcripts.* New Haven: Yale University Press.

Scott, W. Richard and John W. Meyer 1991. "The organization of societal sectors: Propositions and early evidence." In DiMaggio and Powell eds. 204–231. [Original version 1983]

Segal, Gerald and Richard H. Yang eds. 1996. *Chinese economic reform: The impact on security.* London: Routledge.

Shambaugh, David 1991. "The soldier and the state in China: The political work system in the People's Liberation Army." *China Quarterly* 127 (September) 527–568.

Shambaugh, David 1996a. "China's military in transition: Politics, professionalism, procurement and power projection." *China Quarterly* 146 (June) 265–298.

Shambaugh, David 1996b. "China's commander-in-chief: Jiang Zemin and the PLA." In Lane, Weissenbloom, and Liu eds. 209–245.

Shambaugh, David 1996c. "The building of the civil-military state in China, 1949–1965: Bringing the soldier back in." In *The construction of state socialism in China, 1949–1965,* edited by Timothy Cheek and Tony Saich. Armonk, N.Y.: Sharpe, 125–150.

Shambaugh, David 1998. "The CCP's Fifteenth Congress: Technocrats in command." *Issues and Studies* 34,1 (January) 1–37.

Share, Donald 1987. "Transitions to democracy and transition through transaction." *Comparative Political Studies* 19,4 (January) 525–548.

Shen, Weisi 1986. "The division and union of party factions since the retreat to Taiwan." In *Toushi dangnei paixi* (Investigating inner-party factions). Taipei: Fengyun shuxi, no. 3. [In Chinese]

Shi, Shaofa and Xu Yongfa 1986. "On categories of revenues and expenditures in the 1986 state budget." *Caizheng* 1 (January) 15–16. [In Chinese]

Shih, Chih-yu 1995. *State and society in China's political economy: The cultural dynamics of socialist reform.* Boulder: Lynne Rienner.

Shirk, Susan L. 1993. *The political logic of economic reform in China.* Berkeley: University of California Press.

Shirk, Susan L. 1994. *How China opened its door: The political success of the PRC's foreign trade and investment reforms.* Washington, D.C.: Brookings Institution.

Shirk, Susan L. 1996. "Internationalization and China's economic reforms." In Keohane and Milner eds. 186–206.

Shue, Vivienne 1988. *The reach of the state: Sketches of the Chinese body politic.* Stanford: Stanford University Press.

Shue, Vivienne 1995. "State sprawl: The regulatory state and social life in a small Chinese city." In Davis et al. eds. 90–112.

Shugart, Mathew Soberg and John Carey 1992. *Presidents and assemblies.* Cambridge: Cambridge University Press.

Sidel, Mark 1997. "Generational and institutional transition in the Vietnamese Communist Party: The 1996 Congress and beyond." *Asian Survey* 37,5 (May) 481–495.

Sidel, Mark 1998. "Vietnam in 1997: A year of challenges." *Asian Survey* 38,1 (January) 80–90.

Silbergeld, Jerome 1993. *Contradictions: Artistic life, the socialist state, and the Chinese painter Li Huasheng.* Seattle: University of Washington Press.

Silberman, Bernard S. 1993. *Cages of reason: The rise of the rational state in France, Japan, the United States and Great Britain.* Chicago: University of Chicago Press.

Simon, Denis Fred and Merle Goldman eds. 1989. *Science and technology in post-Mao China.* Cambridge: Council on East Asian Studies, Harvard University.

Siu, Helen 1987. *Agents and victims.* New Haven: Yale University Press.

Skinner, G. William and Edwin A. Winckler 1969. "Compliance succession in rural Communist China: A cyclical theory." In *A sociological reader on complex organizations,* 2d ed., edited by Amitai Etzioni. New York: Holt, Rinehart and Winston, 410–438.

Solinger, Dorothy J. 1977. *Regional government and political integration in Southwest China, 1949–1954: A case study.* Berkeley: University of California Press.

Solinger, Dorothy J. 1984a. *Chinese business under socialism.* Berkeley: University of California Press.

Solinger, Dorothy J. ed. 1984b. *Three visions of Chinese socialism.* Boulder: Westview.

Solinger, Dorothy J. 1989. "Urban reform and relational contracting in post-Mao China: An interpretation of the transition from plan to market." *Studies in Comparative Communism* 22,2/3 (Summer/Autumn) 171–185. [Reprinted in Solinger 1993b, 107–125]

Solinger, Dorothy J. 1992. "Urban entrepreneurs and the state: The merger of state and society." In Rosenbaum ed. 121–141. [Reprinted in Solinger 1993b, 256–274.]

Solinger, Dorothy J. 1993a. "China's transients and the state: A form of civil society?" *Politics and Society* 21,1 (March) 91–122.

Solinger, Dorothy J. 1993b. *China's transition from socialism: Statist legacies and market reforms 1980–1990.* Armonk, N.Y.: Sharpe.

Solinger, Dorothy J. 1996. "Despite decentralization: Disadvantages, dependence and ongoing central power in the inland—The case of Wuhan." *China Quarterly* 145 (March) 1–34.

Solnick, Steven L. 1993. *Growing pains: Youth policies and institutional change in the former Soviet Union.* Ph.D. dissertation, Harvard University.

Solnick, Steven L. 1996. "The breakdown of hierarchies in the Soviet Union and China: A neo-institutional perspective." *World Politics* 48,2 (January) 209–238.

Solnick, Steven L. 1998. *Stealing the state: Control and collapse in Soviet institutions.* Cambridge: Harvard University Press.

Somit, Albert and Steven A. Peterson eds. 1992. *The dynamics of evolution: The punctuated equilibrium debate in the natural and social sciences.* Ithaca: Cornell University Press.

Song, Pingshun 1989. "From this political chaos, this counter-revolutionary riot, look at current class struggle." *Gongan yanjiu* 4 (nd) 3–5. [In Chinese]

Song, Ruilai 1991. "On the creation of population control mechanisms that coordinate macro and microlevels." *Renkou yu jingji* (Population and economy) 2 (25 April) 47–50. [In Chinese]

Spoor, Max 1996. "Mongolia: Agrarian crisis in the transition to a market economy." *Europe-Asia Studies* 48,4 (June) 615–628.

Stallings, Barbara ed. 1995. *Global change, regional response: The new international context of development.* Cambridge: Cambridge University Press.

Stark, David 1990. "Privatization in Hungary: From plan to market or from plan to clan?" *East European Politics and Societies* 4,3 (Fall) 351–392.

Stark, David 1992. "Path dependence and privatization strategies in East Central Europe." *East European Politics and Societies* 6,1 (Winter) 17–54.

Steinmo, Sven, Kathleen Thelen, and Frank Longstreth eds. 1992. "Historical institutionalism in comparative politics." In *Structuring politics: Historical institutionalism in comparative analysis,* edited by Steinmo, Thelen, and Longstreth. New York: Cambridge University Press, 1–33.

Stepan, Alfred 1986. "Paths toward redemocratization: Theoretical and comparative considerations." In O'Donnell, Schmitter, and Whitehead eds. *Comparative perspectives,* 64–83.

Stern, Lewis M. 1997. "Vietnam's Eighth Party Congress: Renovated organizations, revised statutes, evolving processes." *Asian Survey* 37,5 (May) 470–495.

Stinchcombe, Arthur 1965. "The social structure of organizations." In *Handbook of organizations,* edited by James G. March. Chicago: Rand-McNally, 142–193.

St. John, Ronald Bruce 1995. "Japan's moment in Indochina." *Asian Survey* 35,7 (July) 668–681.

St. John, Ronald Bruce 1997 "The end of the beginning: Cambodia, Laos and Vietnam." *Contemporary Southeast Asia* 19,2 (September) 172–190.

Stuart-Fox, Martin 1998. "Laos in 1997: Into ASEAN." *Asian Survey* 38,1 (January) 75–79.

Su, Wei and Wendy Larson 1995. "The disintegration of the poetic 'Berlin Wall.'" In Davis et al. eds. 279–293.

Su, Xiaokang and Luxiang Wang 1991. *Death song of the river: A reader's guide to the Chinese TV series Heshang.* Ithaca: East Asia Program, Cornell University. (Papers, 54)

Sullivan, Stefan 1995. "Interethnic relations in post-Soviet Tuva." *Ethnic and Racial Studies* 18,1 (January).

Suttmeier, Richard P. 1974. *Research and revolution: Science policy and societal change in China.* New York: Lexington.

Suttmeier, Richard P. 1980. *Science, technology and China's drive for modernization.* Stanford: Hoover Institution.

Suttmeier, Richard P. 1993a. "Greater China and the development of Chinese science and technology." In *The Chinese and their future,* edited by Zhiling Lin and Thomas W. Robinson. Washington, D.C.: American Enterprise Institute.

Suttmeier, Richard P. 1993b. "The changing international context for Sino-American relations in science and technology." *In Depth,* 3,3 (Fall) 91–111.

Swaine, Michael D. 1992. *The military and political succession in China: Leadership, institutions, beliefs.* Santa Monica: Rand Corporation.

Swaine, Michael D. 1994. "Chinese regional forces as political actors." In Yang et al. eds. 59–84.

Swaine, Michael D. 1996. "The PLA in China's national security policy: Leaderships, structures, processes." *China Quarterly* 146 (June) 360–393.

SWB = *Survey of World Broadcasts,* British Broadcasting Corporation.

Szemerkenyi, Reka 1996. *Central European civil-military reforms at risk.* Oxford: Oxford University Press. (Adelphi papers, 306)

Tan, Songqiu 1990. "Several viewpoints on questions concerning our country's class struggle and people's democratic dictatorship in the current era." *Gongan yanjiu* 2 (nd) 1–5. [In Chinese]

Tanaka, Akihito 1992. "Socialism in East Asia: Vietnam, Mongolia and North Korea" In Rozman ed. 225–242.

Tang, Peter S. H. and Joan M. Maloney 1967 *Communist China: The domestic scene, 1949–1967.* South Orange, N.J.: Seton Hall University Press.

Tanner, Murray Scot 1994. "Reform and coercion: The Gongan Yanjiu debates over public security reform in post-Mao China." Paper presented at the annual meeting of the Association for Asian Studies, Boston, 23–27 March 1994. [Copies available from the author on request]

Tanner, Murray Scot 1997. "Chinese bureaucratic and leadership battles over public security, 1989–1990: Dissecting an organizational disaster." Paper presented to the annual meeting of the Association of Asian Studies, Chicago, March 1997.

Taylor, Brian D. 1995. "Professionalism and politicization in the Soviet and Russian armed forces." American Political Science Association paper.

Teiwes, Frederick C. 1966. "The purge of provincial leaders, 1957–1958." *China Quarterly* 27 (July–September) 14–32.

Teiwes, Frederick C. 1970. "A review article: The evolution of leadership purges in communist China." *China Quarterly* 41 (January–March) 122–135.

Teiwes, Frederick C. 1971. "Provincial politics in China: Themes and variations." In *China: Management of a revolutionary society,* edited by John Lindbeck. Seattle: University of Washington Press, 116–192.

Teiwes, Frederick C. 1974. *Provincial leadership in China: The Cultural Revolution and its aftermath.* Ithaca: China-Japan Program, Cornell University. (East Asia Papers, 4)

Teiwes, Frederick C. 1987. "Establishment and consolidation of the new regime." In *The Cambridge history of China,* vol. 14, edited by Roderick MacFarquhar and John K. Fairbank. Cambridge: Cambridge University Press, 51–143.

Terry, Sarah Meiklejohn 1993. "Thinking about post-communist transitions: How different are they?" *Slavic Review* 52, 2 (Summer) 333–337.

Thalemann, Andrea 1996. "Vietnam: Marketing the economy." *Journal of Contemporary Asia* 26,3 (August) 322–351.

Than, Mya 1993. "Vietnam's external trade, 1975–91: A survey in the Southeast Asian context." In *Vietnam's dilemmas and options: The challenge of economic transition in the 1990s,* edited by Mya Than and Joseph L. H. Tan. Singapore: Institute of Southeast Asian Studies, 207–236.

Thayer, Carlyle A. 1988. "The regularization of politics: Continuity and change in the party's central committee, 1951–1986." In Marr and White eds. 177–193

Thayer, Carlyle A. 1992. "Political reform in Vietnam: Doi Moi and the emergence of civil society." In *The development of civil society in communist systems,* edited by Robert F. Miller. Sydney: Allen and Unwin.

Thayer, Carlyle A. 1993. "Recent political developments: Constitutional change and the 1992 elections." In *Vietnam and the rule of law,* edited by Carlyle A. Thayer and David G. Marr. Canberra: Research School of Pacific Studies, Australian National University, 50–80.

Thayer, Carlyle A. 1995. "Mono-organizational socialism and the state." In Kerkvliet and Porter eds. 39–64.

Therior, L. H. and J. N. Metheson 1979. "Soviet economic relations with the non-European CMEA: Cuba, Vietnam, Mongolia." In *The Soviet economy in a time of change,* vol. 1, edited by the Joint Economic Commission. Washington, D.C.: U.S. Government Printing Office.

Thompson, Grahame, Jennifer Frances, Rosalind Levacic, and Jeremy Mitchell eds. 1991. *Markets, hierarchies and networks: The coordination of social life.* Newbury Park, Calif.: Sage, 1991.

Tian, Xueyuan with Hu Weilue eds. 1994. *Household economy and fertility studies.* Beijing: China Machine Press.

Tien, H. Yuan 1991. *China's strategic demographic initiative.* New York: Praeger.

Tien, Hung-mao and Yun-han Chu 1996. "Building democratization in Taiwan." *China Quarterly* 148 (December) 1141–1170.

Tilly, Charles 1984. *Big structures, large processes, huge comparisons.* New York: Russell Sage.

Tong, James 1989a. "The imperial enterprise: State-building in the Ming dynasty, 1368–1644." Paper presented at the Midwest Political Science Association meeting, Chicago, 13–15 April.

Tong, James 1989b. "Fiscal reform, elite turnover and central-provincial relations in post-Mao China." *Australian Journal of Chinese Affairs* 22 (July) 1–28.

Tong, James 1990. "Effects of fiscal reform on inter-provincial variations in medical services in China, 1979–1984." In *Political implications of economic reform in communist systems: Communist dialectic,* edited by Donna Bahry and Joel Moses. New York: New York University Press, 109–130.

Transitions 1995. *Media: How free?* Special issue of *Transitions* 1,18 (6 October).

Tsebelis, George 1990. *Nested games: Rational choice in comparative politics.* Berkeley: University of California Press.

Tsebelis, George 1993. "Monitoring in networks and hierarchies: Congress and organizations." In Scharpf ed. 351–385.

Tsou, Tang 1983. "Back from the brink of revolutionary-'feudal' totalitarianism." In *State and society in contemporary China,* edited by Victor Nee and David Mozingo. Ithaca: Cornell University Press, 53–88.

Tsou, Tang 1994. *Chinese politics in the twentieth century.* Hong Kong: Oxford University Press. [In Chinese]

Turley, William S. 1993. "Political renovation in Vietnam: Renewal and adaptation." In Ljunggren ed. 327–347.

Turley, William S. and Mark Selden eds. 1980. *Vietnamese communism in comparative perspective.* Boulder: Westview.

Turley, William S. and Mark Selden eds. 1993. *Reinventing Vietnamese socialism: Doi Moi in comparative perspective.* Boulder: Westview.

UNDP (United Nations Development Program) 1991. "The economy of Laos: An overview." In Zasloff and Unger eds. 67–83.

Unger, Jonathan ed. 1993. *Using the past to serve the present: Historiography and politics in contemporary China.* Armonk, N.Y.: Sharpe.

Van de Walle, Nicholas 1991. "The patron's problem: Agency and clientelism in comparative perspective." American Political Science Association paper.

Verdery, Katherine 1991. "Theorizing socialism: A prologue to the 'transition.'" *American Ethnologist* 18,3 (August) 419–439.

Verdery, Katherine 1995. "What was socialism, and why did it fall?" In Orlovsky ed. 27–46.

Vogel, Ezra 1980. *Canton under communism: Programs and politics in a provincial capital, 1949–1968.* Cambridge: Harvard University Press.

Wakeman, Frederic Jr. 1991. "Models of historical change: Chinese state and society, 1839–1989." In Lieberthal et al. 1991, 68–102.

Wakeman, Frederic Jr. 1995. *Policing Shanghai 1927–1937.* Berkelely: University of California Press.

Walder, Andrew G. 1986. *Communist neotraditionalism: Work and authority in Chinese industry.* Berkeley: University of California Press.

Walder, Andrew G. 1992. "Local bargaining relationships and urban industrial finance." In Lieberthal and Lampton eds. 308–333.

Walder, Andrew G. 1994. "The decline of communist power: Elements of a theory of institutional change." In Hechter and Szelenyi eds. 297–323.

Walder, Andrew G. 1995a. "Career mobility and the communist political order." *American Sociological Review* 60,3 (June) 309–328.

Walder, Andrew G. 1995b. "China's transitional economy: Interpreting its significance." *China Quarterly* 144 (December) 963–979.

Walder, Andrew G. ed. 1995c. *The waning of the communist state: Economic origins of political decline in China and Hungary.* Berkeley: University of California Press.

Waller, J. Michael 1994. *Secret empire: The KGB in Russia today.* Boulder: Westview.

Wang, Dingfeng 1989. "Thoroughly root out the evil, leave behind no future trouble. Public security organs must decisively pacify the counter-revolutionary riot." *Gongan yanjiu* 3 (nd), np. [In Chinese]

Wang, Fang 1989a. "Comrade Wang Fang's speech at a meeting of some cadres from Ministry of Public Security organs above the bureau level." *Renmin gongan* 7 (5 June) 10,9. [In Chinese; speech given 22 May]

Wang, Fang 1989b. "Speech at the National Public Security Front's commendation rally for ending the social turbulence and pacifying the counterrevolutionary riot." *Renmin gongan bao* (25 July) 1. [In Chinese; speech given 21 July]

Wang, Fang 1989c. "Minister Wang Fang on role of public security." *Renmin gongan bao* (12 September) 1. In *FBIS* (4 October 1989) 15–20.

Wang, Feng 1988. "The role of individuals' socioeconomic characteristics and the government family planning program on China's fertility decline." *Population Reseach and Policy Review* 7,3 (nd) 255–276.

Wang, Hong 1991. "The Population Policy of China." In Wang and Hull, eds. 42–67.

Wang, Jiye and Terence H. Hull eds. 1991. *Population and development planning in China.* Sydney: Allen and Unwin.

Wang, Shaoguang 1995. "The rise of the regions: Fiscal reform and the decline of central state capacity in China." In Walder ed. 87–113.

Wang, Yeu-Farn 1993. *China's science and technology policy: 1949–1989.* Avebury, Eng.: Aldershot.

Wank, David 1995. "Bureaucratic patronage and private business: Changing networks of power in urban China." In Walder ed. 153–183.

Warwick, Donald P. 1982. *Bitter pills: Population policies and their implementation in eight developing countries.* New York: Cambridge University Press.

Warwick, Donald P. 1986. "The Indonesian family planning program: Government influence and client choice." *Population and Development Review* 12,3 (September) 453–490.

Wasserstrom, Jeffrey and Elizabeth Perry eds. 1992. *Popular protest and political culture in modern China.* Boulder: Westview.

Watson, Andrew ed. 1992. *Economic reform and social change in China.* New York: Routledge.

Watson, Rubie S. ed. 1994. *Memory, history and opposition under state socialism.* Santa Fe, N.M.: School of American Research Press.

Wedeman, Andrew 1995. *Bamboo walls and brick ramparts: Rent-seeking, interregional economic conflict and local protectionism in China.* Ph.D. dissertation, University of California, Los Angeles.

Wei, Li 1994. *The Chinese staff system: A mechanism for bureaucratic control and integration.* Berkeley: Institute of East Asian Studies, University of California, Berkeley.

Wei, Zhimin 1991. *Guanyu woguo jieji douzheng de qianshi* (A few superficial views on class struggle in our country). *Gongan yanjiu* 6 (nd) 6–7, 49.

Weller, Robert 1994. *Resistance, chaos and control in China: Taiping rebels, Taiwanese ghosts and Tiananmen.* Seattle: University of Washington Press.

White, Gordon, ed. 1991. *The road to crisis: The Chinese state in the era of economic reform.* London: Macmillan.

White, Gordon 1993. "Prospects for civil society in China: A case study of Xiaoshan City." *Australian Journal of Chinese Affairs* 29 (January) 63–87.

White, Gordon, Jude Howell, and Shang Xiaoyuan 1996. *In search of civil society: Market reform and social change in contemporary China.* Oxford: Clarendon.

White, Harrison 1985. "Agency as control." In Pratt and Zeckhauser eds. 187–212.

White, Harrison 1992. *Identity and control.* Princeton: Princeton University Press.

White, Tyrene 1987. "Implementing the 'one-child-per-couple' population program in rural China: National goals and local politics." In Lampton ed. 284–317.

White, Tyrene 1990. "Postrevolutionary mobilization in China: The one-child policy reconsidered." *World Politics* 43,1 (October) 53–76.

White, Tyrene 1991. "Birth planning between plan and market: The impact of reform on China's one-child policy." In *China's economic dilemmas in the 1990s: The problems of reforms, modernization, and interdependence,* vol. 1, *Study papers submitted to the Joint Economic Committee, Congress of the United States.* Washington, D.C.: U.S. Government Printing Office, 252–269.

White, Tyrene 1994a. "The origins of China's birth planning policy." In *Engendering China: Women, culture, and the state,* edited by Christina K. Gilmartin, Gail Hershatter, Lisa Rofel, and Tyrene White. Cambridge: Harvard University Press, 250–278.

White, Tyrene 1994b. "Two kinds of production: The evolution of China's family plannning policy in the 1980s." In Finkle and McIntosh eds. 137–158.

Whitehead, Lawrence 1986. "International aspects of democratization." In O'Donnell, Schmitter, and Whitehead eds. *Comparative perspectives,* 3–46.

Whitson, William ed. 1972. *The military and political power in China in the 1970s.* New York: Praeger.

Whitson, William W. and Chen-Hsia Huang 1973. *The Chinese high command: A history of communist military politics, 1927–1971.* New York: Praeger.

Whyte, Martin K. 1974. *Small groups and political rituals in China.* Berkeley: University of California Press.

Whyte, Martin K. 1992. "Urban China: A civil society in the making?" In Rosenbaum ed. 77–101.

Whyte, Martin K. and Gu S. Z. 1987. "Popular response to China's fertility transition." *Population and Development Review* 13,3 471–493.

Williamson, Oliver 1975. *Markets and hierarchies.* New York: Free Press.

Williamson, Oliver 1985. *The economic institutions of capitalism: Firms, markets and relational contracting.* New York: Free Press.

Winckler, Edwin A. 1984. "Institutionalization and participation on Taiwan: From hard to soft authoritarianism?" *China Quarterly* 99 (December) 481–499.

Winckler, Edwin A. 1988. "Elite political struggle, 1945–1985." In Winckler and Greenhalgh eds. 151–171.

Winckler, Edwin A. 1993. "Cultural policy in postwar Taiwan." In *Cultural change in postwar Taiwan,* edited by Stevan Harrell. Boulder: Westview.

Winckler, Edwin A. and Susan Greenhalgh eds. 1988. *Contending approaches to the political economy of Taiwan.* Armonk, N.Y.: Sharpe.

Winn, Jane Kaufman 1994. "Not by rule of law: Mediating state-society relations in Taiwan through the underground economy." In *The other Taiwan,* edited by Murray Rubinstein. Armonk, N.Y.: Sharpe, 183–214.

Womack, Brantly 1982. "1980 county-level elections in China: Experiment in democratic modernization." *Asian Studies* 22,3 (March) 261–277.

Womack, Brantly 1987. "The party and the people: Revolutionary and postrevolutionary politics in China and Vietnam." *World Politics* 34,4 (July) 479–507.

Womack, Brantly 1991. *Contemporary Chinese politics in historical perspective.* New York: Cambridge University Press.

Womack, Brantly 1993. "Political reform and political change in communist countries: Implications for Vietnam." In Turley and Selden eds. 277–305.

Wong, Christine 1985. "Material allocation and decentralization: Impact of the local sector on industrial reform." In *The political economy of reform in post-Mao China,* edited by Elizabeth J. Perry and Christine Wong. Cambridge: Council on East Asian Studies, Harvard University, 253–278.

Wong, Christine 1991. "Central-local relations in an era of fiscal decline." *China Quarterly* 128 (December) 691–715.

Wong, Christine, Christopher Heady, and Wing Woo 1995. *Fiscal management and economic reform in the People's Republic of China.* Hong Kong: Oxford University Press.

Wong, Kam C. 1994. "Public security reform in China in the 1990s." In *China review, 1994,* edited by Maurice Brosseau and Lo Chin Kin. Hong Kong: Chinese University Press, 5.1–5.39.

Woods, L. Shelton 1997. "The myth of Cambodia's recovery." *Contemporary Southeast Asia* 18,4 (March) 417–429.

World Bank 1989a. *World development report, 1989.* New York: Oxford University Press.

World Bank 1989b. *China: Finance and investments, a World Bank country study.* Washington, D.C.: World Bank.

World Bank 1990. *China: Revenue mobilization and tax policy.* Washington D.C.: World Bank.

World Bank 1994. *China: Internal market development and regulation.* Washington, D.C.: World Bank.

World Bank 1996. *World development report, 1996 (From plan to market).* New York: Oxford University Press.

Wu, Hongda Harry 1993. *Laogai—The Chinese gulag.* Boulder: Westview.

Wu, Shihuan 1988. "On the nature and object of the people's democratic dictatorship during the current period—A discussion with Comrade Hong Peilin." *Gongan yanjiu* 4 (nd) 59–65. [In Chinese]

Wu, Yu-shan 1993. "Nationalism, democratization and economic reform: Political transition in the Soviet Union, Hungary and Taiwan." American Political Science Association paper.

Wu, Yu-shan 1996. "Away from socialism: The Asian way." *Pacific Review* 9,3 (nd) 410–425.

Wurfel, David 1993. "Doi Moi in comparative perspective." In Turley and Selden eds. 19–52.

Xiao, Jian 1992. "Three questions about the State Political Security Bureau." *Gongan yanjiu* 1 (nd) 56–59. [In Chinese]

Xu, Yongfa 1985. "Questions on classifying revenues in the central and local government budgets in 1985." *Caizheng* 4 (April) 23–25. [In Chinese]

Yan, Jiaqi 1992. *A conception for a federal China.* Hong Kong: Mingbao Press. [In Chinese]

Yan, Sun 1995. *The Chinese reassessment of socialism, 1976–1992.* Princeton: Princeton University Press.

Yang, Dali L. 1989. "What's next for China?" *Sunday Oregonian* (4 June) D1, D4.

Yang, Dali L. 1991. "China adjusts to the world economy: The political economy of China's coastal development strategy." *Pacific Affairs* 64,1 (March) 42–64.

Yang, Dali L. 1994. "Reform and the restructuring of central-local relations." In *China deconstructs,* edited by David Goodman and Gerald Segal. London: Routledge, 59–98.

Yang, Dali L. 1996. *Calamity and reform in China: State, rural society and institutional change since the Great Leap Famine.* Stanford: Stanford University Press.

Yang, Dali L. 1997. *Beyond Beijing: Liberalization and the regions in China.* London: Routledge.

Yang, Richard H., Jason C. Hu, Peter K. H. Yu, and Andrew N. D. Yang eds. 1994. *Chinese regionalism: The security dimension.* Boulder: Westview.

Yang, Zhaomin and Gongfan Wang 1990. "From the chaos and the riot see clearly the problems of the current class struggle." *Gongan yanjiu* 1 (nd) 8–11. [In Chinese]

Yoder, Amos 1993. *Communism in transition: The end of the Soviet empires.* London: Taylor and Francis.

You, Ji. 1994. Review of Swaine 1992. *Australian Journal of Chinese Studies* 32 (July) 175–178.

You, Ji 1998. *China's enterprise reform: Changing state/society relations afer Mao.* London: Routledge.

Young, Susan 1995. *Private business and economic reform in China.* Armonk, N.Y.: Sharpe.

Yuan, Shang and Han Zhu 1992. *Deng Xiaoping nanxun hou de Zhongguo* (China after Deng Xiaoping's Southern Tour). Beijing: Gaige chubanshe.

Yun, Shiying 1990. "Rely on the leadership of the party committee, give full play to the function of one's organizational capabilities, and strive to do a good job of public security discipline inspection work." In *Zenyang gaohao dangfeng dangji he lianzheng jianshe* (How to do a good job of building party spirit, party discipline and clean government), edited by CCP Central Discipline Inspection Committee General Office. Beijing: Zhongguo fazhi chubanshe, 266–275. [In Chinese]

Zasloff, Joseph L. and Leonard Unger eds. 1991. *Laos: Beyond the revolution.* New York: St. Martin's.

ZCN = *Zhongguo caizheng nianjian* (China financial yearbook). Beijing: Zhongguo caizheng zazhishe, from 1992.

ZCT = *Zhongguo caizheng tongji, 1950–1991* (China financial statistics, 1950–1991). Beijing: Kexue chubanshe, 1992.

ZCTN = *Zhongguo chengshi tongji nianjian, 1992* (China city statistics yearbook, 1992). Beijing: Zhongguo tongji nianjian chubanshe.

Zeng, Yi et al. 1993. "Causes and implications of the recent increase in the reported sex ratio at birth in China." *Population and Development Review* 19,2 (June) 283–302.

ZGCZ = Zhongguo caizheng (Chinese finance). [Began January 1997, preceded by *Caizheng*]

ZGQ = Zhongguo gaige quanshu 1992 (Encyclopedia of China's reforms, 1978–1991). Dalian: Dalian chubanshe. (Monographs on fiscal management reform, 5)

ZGSZ = Zhongguo shuizhi (China's taxation system). Beijing: Zhongguo caizheng jingji chubanshe, 1988, 278–284. [Edited by Zhongguo shuizhi jiaocai bianxiezu]

Zha, Jianying 1995. *China pop: How soap operas, tabloids and bestsellers are transforming a culture.* New York: New Press.

Zhang, Baohui 1997. "Learning and institutional building in China's fiscal reform." American Political Science Association presentation.

Zhao, Suisheng 1995. "The structure of authority and decision-making: A theoretical framework." In Hamrin and Zhao eds. 233–245.

Zhao, Yuezhi 1998. *Media, market and democracy in China: Between the party line and the bottom line.* Urbana: University of Illinois Press.

Zhao, Ziyang 1987. "Advance along the road of socialism with Chinese characteristics." *Beijing Review* (9–15 November) 37–43.

Zheng, Yong-nian 1995. *Institutional change, local developmentalism, and economic growth: The making of semi-federalism in China.* Ph.D. dissertation, Princeton University.

Zhong, Yang 1991. "Civil-military relations in changing communist societies: A comparative study of China and the Soviet Union." *Studies in Comparative Communism* 24,1 (March) 77–102.

Zhou, Kate Xiao 1996. *How the farmers changed China: Power of the people.* Boulder: Westview.

Zito, Angela and Tani E. Barlow eds. 1994. *Body, subject and power in China.* Chicago: University of Chicago Press.

ZJN = Zhongguo jingji nianjian 1986 (China economic yearbook 1986). Beijing: Jingji guanli chubanshe, IV–11–13.

ZJSN = Zhongguo jihua shengyu nianjian (China birth planning yearbook).

Zong, Hesi 1986. "Reforms in the fiscal management structure during the Sixth Five Year Plan." *Caizheng* 11 (November) 19–21. [In Chinese]

ZSZ = Zhongguo shibao zhoukan (China times weekly).

ZTN = Zhongguo tongji nianjian (China statistical yearbook). Beijing: Zhongguo tongji chubanshe.

Zweig, David 1992a. "Internationalizing China's countryside: The political economy of exports from rural industry." *China Quarterly* 128 (December) 716–741.

Zweig, David 1992b. "Urbanizing rural China: Bureaucratic authority and local autonomy." In Lieberthal and Lampton eds. 334–363.

Zysman, John 1983. *Governments, markets and growth: Financial institutions and the politics of industrial change.* Ithaca: Cornell University Press.

Index

Because the main purpose of this book is analytical, the Index concentrates on providing a conceptual guide to help the reader trace themes across chapters.

Most entries are ordinary terms appearing in ordinary type. However a few terms used by the editor to systematize volume themes appear in bolded small caps—e.g., **DIMENSIONS**. Terms common to several chapters or very central to individual chapters appear in ordinary bold—e.g., **Organization** or **Police**. Terms frequently used in relevant literatures appear in small caps without bolding—e.g., TRANSITION. For many analytical headings, the sub-headings are sets of related terms, which therefore appear in logical order, not alphabetical order. The heading **Hypotheses** indexes relatively explicit causal propositions and causal analyses (dependent variable first).

As regards "transition," the Index distinguishes between "systemic" transitions of whole countries and "sectoral" transitions within the functional areas treated by volume chapters. Indexing of "systemic" transition is divided into headings beginning with "TRANSITION, SYSTEMIC" (singular), which treats national transition as a generic process, and headings beginning with "TRANSITIONS, SYSTEMIC" (plural), which compares national transitions across regions or countries. Particular components of each national transition appear under individual country listings—Cambodia, China, Laos, Mongolia, North Korea, Taiwan, and Vietnam.

To facilitate comparison, transitions within each functional sector are grouped under headings beginning with "TRANSITION, SECTORAL." The policy areas treated in this volume are: *party* (Dickson), *military* (Winckler), *police* (Tanner), *fiscal* system (Tong), *economy* (Yang), *birth planning* (Winckler), and *arts* and *sciences* (Kraus and Suttmeier, also *culture*). The Index also groups elements of these policy areas—and to some extent also of countries—under analytical headings beginning with **Ideology**, **Organization**, **Environment**, **Policy**, **Performance**, and **Reform**. The Index reflects the different extent to which different chapters treat these topics.

The only authors indexed are those mentioned in the text. Key works by joint authors are indexed under their joint names (e.g., Linz and Stepan). Indexing of volume authors mostly shows where their chapters are mentioned in the Introduction and Conclusion.

The Contributors

Bruce J. Dickson teaches in the Department of Political Science of the George Washington University in Washington, D.C. He is the coeditor (with Kenneth Liebenthal) of *A Research Guide to Central Party and Government Meetings in China, 1949-1986* and the author of *Democratization in China and Taiwan: The Adaptability of Leninist Parties* from the Clarendon Press and Oxford University Press in 1997.

Richard Kraus teaches in the Department of Political Science of the University of Oregon in Eugene. His books include *Class Conflict in Chinese Socialism* from Columbia University Press in 1981, *Pianos and Politics* from Oxford University Press in 1989, and *Brushes with Power* from the University of California Press in 1991.

Richard P. Suttmeier teaches in the Department of Political Science of the University of Oregon in Eugene. He wrote *Research and Revolution: Science Policy and Societal Change in China* from Lexington Books in 1974 and has published many articles on Chinese science and technology.

Murray Scot Tanner teaches in the Department of Political Science of Western Michigan University in Kalamazoo, Michigan. His *The Politics of Lawmaking in Post-Mao China: Institutions, Processes, and Democratic Prospects* appeared from Oxford University Press in 1998. He is currently researching the Chinese public security system.

James Tong teaches in the Department of Political Science at the University of California, Los Angeles. He has published several articles on fiscal reform in China, several analyses of the 1989 democracy movement, and a book titled *Disorder Under Heaven: Collective Violence in the Ming Dynasty* from Stanford University Press in 1981.

Edwin A. Winckler is a research associate of the East Asian Insitute of Columbia Univesity in New York City. He is the coeditor (with Susan Greenhalgh) of *Contending Approaches to the Political Economy of Taiwan* from M. E. Sharpe in 1988 and the coeditor (with Bernard Grofman and others) of *Elections in Japan, Korea and Taiwan Using the Non-Transferable Vote* forthcoming from the University of Michigan Press in 1999.

Dali L. Yang teaches in the Department of Political Science at the University of Chicago. His books include *Calamity and Reform in China* from Stanford University Press in 1996 and *Beyond Beijing* from Routledge in 1997.

About the Book

This volume deepens analysis of China's transition from communism and places the Chinese case in comparative and theoretical perspective. Six chapters probe the transition process in the three main sectors of the Chinese party-state—military and police, taxation and investment, and social and cultural policies. Introductory and concluding sections address post-Leninist transitions more generally and compare China's experiences to those of Taiwan, Mongolia, North Korea, Vietnam, Laos, and Cambodia.

The authors stress differences between communist countries, between institutional sectors, and between different kinds of institutional analysis. Their analytical approaches range from classic organization theory (particularly of power and compliance) to recent institutional analysis (particularly of delegation and agency).

Edwin A. Winckler is a research associate of the East Asian Institute, Columbia University. His publications include *Contending Approaches to the Political Economy of Taiwan* (coedited with Susan Greenhalgh), and *Elections in Japan, Korea, and Taiwan Using the Single Non-Transferable Vote* (coedited with Bernard Grofman and others).